Branding Hoover's FBI

How the Boss's PR Men Sold the Bureau to America

Matthew Cecil

University Press of Kansas

Published by the University Press of Kansas (Lawrence, Kansas 66045), which
was organized by the Kansas Board of Regents and is operated and funded by
Emporia State University, Fort Hays State University, Kansas State University,
Pittsburg State University, the University of Kansas, and Wichita State University

Library of Congress Cataloging-in-Publication Data

Names: Cecil, Matthew, author.
Title: Branding Hoover's FBI : how the boss's PR men sold the bureau to America /
Matthew Cecil.
Description: Lawrence : University Press of Kansas, 2016.
Includes bibliographical references and index.
Identifiers: LCCN 2016023587
ISBN 9780700623051 (hardback)
ISBN 9780700623068 (ebook)
Subjects: LCSH: Hoover, J. Edgar (John Edgar), 1895–1972. | United States. Federal
Bureau of Investigation—History. | Criminal investigation—United States—History. |
Public relations—United States—History. | BISAC: HISTORY / United States / 20th
Century. | POLITICAL SCIENCE / Political Freedom & Security / Law Enforcement. |
BUSINESS & ECONOMICS / Public Relations.
Classification: LCC HV8144.F43 C423 2016 | DDC 363.250973/0904—dc23
LC record available at https://lccn.loc.gov/2016023587.

British Library Cataloguing-in-Publication Data is available.

Printed in the United States of America

10 9 8 7 6 5 4 3 2 1

The paper used in this publication is recycled and contains 30 percent
postconsumer waste. It is acid free and meets the minimum requirements of the
American National Standard for Permanence of Paper for Printed Library
Materials Z39.48-1992.

CONTENTS

PREFACE

Although the process of writing history is a solitary task, I had a great deal of help and support in gathering the information for this volume. First, the FBI's Records Management Division and its Record/Information Dissemination Section were, as always, unfailingly helpful. Considering the volume of requests that the Bureau's Freedom of Information Act (FOIA) staff deals with, it is remarkable that files are processed and released as quickly as they are. None of my research would be possible without their help, and I am grateful. Special thanks go to Rebecca Bronson from the FBI's Records Management Division, who helped me focus and limit my requests in order to speed up the process.

Many others in far-flung locations helped to create this book. Thanks to Joe P. Harris, who operates a National Archives research business in Maryland. Harris obtained most of the photographs in this book from the National Archives Records Administration (NARA) Still Picture Branch in College Park. The staff in the document section of the NARA assisted me during my visit there to review the Louis B. Nichols FBI file and other related documents. Retired journalist Walter Rugaber consented to an interview that added much to my understanding of FBI official Deke DeLoach. Muriel Jones Cashdollar provided insight into her father, Milton A. Jones, and contributed a photograph of her family with J. Edgar Hoover. Sally Stukenbroeker Pellegrom likewise spoke to me about her father, Fern C. Stukenbroeker.

I am grateful also for the work of authors and historians Douglas M. Charles of Pennsylvania State University and Athan Theoharis of Marquette University, who reviewed the proposal for this book and offered useful feedback and suggestions. Denver-based wordsmith Carrie Jordan edited the first draft of this manuscript, demonstrating great skill and patience and dramatically improving the end product. I appreciate the forbearance of my

Wichita State University (WSU) colleague Jeffrey Jarman, who allowed me to interrupt him frequently to talk through the analysis in these pages. WSU colleagues Jessica Freeman, Kevin Keplar, Bill Molash, Sandy Sipes, and Amy Solano provided endless good humor that lightened my writing hours in the office. My wonderful wife, Jennifer Tiernan, is always supportive and also helped me test and focus the theories and analysis for this and many other research projects. Numerous other WSU colleagues supplied support and good humor as well. Thanks to Ron Matson, dean of the Fairmount College of Liberal Arts and Sciences at WSU, who provided research support and personal encouragement. Thank you to Editor-in-Chief Michael Briggs, Director Charles T. Myers, and the staff at the University Press of Kansas for showing confidence in this project; they are talented and patient, and I am thrilled with the result of their work that you are holding in your hands right now.

I want to thank my parents, Charles and Mary Cecil, who have always given rock-solid support to me and my siblings. Thanks to my son, Owen, for inspiring me with his goofy sense of humor and his remarkable writing talent. Finally, I must offer a special thank you to J. Edgar Hoover for creating the meticulous record-keeping system at the FBI that makes possible the detailed study of the agency he built.

Introduction:

Defining a "Hoover Era"

Historians and politicians like to brand time periods with evocative labels. Eras are declared. Historical epochs are christened. Sometimes, the principal characters of an age attempt to declare an era themselves, with varying levels of success. President Franklin Delano Roosevelt (FDR) offered a New Deal, and it stuck. President Lyndon B. Johnson (LBJ) argued for a Great Society. President Harry S. Truman did not have quite the same success declaring the era of a Square Deal, and few remember the Gerald Ford administration as the WIN years (Whip Inflation Now). At times, eras are named by historians. Senator Joseph McCarthy's four-year tirade of alcohol-fueled fearmongering and self-promotion turned his name into a pejorative, McCarthyism. Events themselves may define an era. The first world war, the Great War in its time, became World War I after a second global conflict arose and was slotted in as World War II. Sometimes, the media name an era, and the name sticks. President Ronald Reagan's eight years of trickle-down policies— Reaganomics or "voodoo" economics, depending on your politics—have become accepted as defining a Reagan era. President Bill Clinton's tenure in the Oval Office gave us what is becoming known as the Clinton years. It seems possible that the Obama era will be defined in the future by his signature legislative accomplishment, the Affordable Care Act, but under a title conferred derisively by some but adopted by Barack Obama himself— Obamacare.

One might imagine, then, that a towering figure like FBI director J. Edgar Hoover, a man who loomed over American society as a singular individual of power and authority for decades, might warrant an era of his own. No influential figure in American history held power longer than the FBI director who served for nearly fifty years, from his late twenties into his late seventies. When Hoover became director, many Americans had yet to have their homes connected to an electrical grid. By the time he died, Americans had tired of routine voyages to the moon. Hoover's reign overlays most of the named eras of the so-called American century, from the Roaring Twenties to the Great Depression, World War II, and McCarthyism and into the Cold War. Eight presidents, from Calvin Coolidge to Richard Nixon, oversaw Hoover's work, at least in theory. Seventeen attorneys general served as his immediate supervisor, at least nominally. None of those attorneys general, save perhaps Robert F. Kennedy (RFK), remotely approached the FBI director's notoriety, and none achieved anywhere near the kind of power he accrued and wielded. Hoover led a seemingly omnipotent agency, capable of tracking outlaws, unmasking spies and communists, and performing miracles of science in its laboratory. Historians generally agree that Hoover's specter loomed over elected and appointed politicians throughout nearly all of his forty-eight years in office as one of the most powerful figures in American society. For decades, the bulldog visage of the FBI director instilled fear in the hearts of criminals, dissidents, and public officials alike. Historians have not generally acknowledged the middle fifty years of the twentieth century as a "J. Edgar Hoover era," yet Hoover's astonishing power and influence over events is frequently acknowledged in studies of other prominent American characters and eras. Though Hoover was viewed by a majority of Americans as a strong and generally effective figure during his lifetime, understandings of the actual extent of his authority over his nominal superiors and of his narrow-minded character have only grown in the decades since he died.

In 1974, two years after the director's death and following intensive investigations of the nation's intelligence agencies, Congress overrode President Gerald Ford's veto of changes to the Freedom of Information Act (FOIA) and thereby helped open Hoover's detailed files to historians.[1] The books and articles that followed in the ensuing decades have laid out the framework of Hoover's secretive agency for the first time. Slowly but surely, the FBI's role in events of those decades, including often excessive and sometimes illegal investigations, has become known.

Americans have learned that the circumstances under which public enemies were shot by Bureau agents in the 1930s were not always as they were portrayed by the FBI and the news media at the time.[2] Americans have discovered that what contemporary critics in the 1940s and 1950s claimed—that the FBI deployed thousands of wiretaps even after they were declared illegal by the Supreme Court in the mid-1930s—was true.[3] In fact, FBI files confirmed that, for decades, the Bureau used so-called black bag jobs (illegal

FBI director J. Edgar Hoover at the height of his power in 1961. (Library of Congress, U.S. News & World Report Magazine Photograph Collection, Call Number LC-U9-6738B-16.)

break-ins) to plant bugs and rifle through files in clear violation of the law, acting under an expansive interpretation of an FDR era executive order as authorization.[4] The files show that FBI agents infiltrated and undermined social movements that were advocating for change in the 1960s. The Bureau's intrusive and disruptive Counterintelligence Program (COINTELPRO) frequently skirted the law, and its existence stood in conflict with multiple First Amendment rights. Hoover's COINTELPRO files confirmed what social reform groups at the time had claimed—that the federal government was the enemy of social change, monitoring and undermining their legal dissent despite clear-cut constitutional protections.[5] Although it is important to acknowledge the FBI's often innovative traditional law enforcement work, the specter of its domestic, political intelligence efforts, mostly hidden throughout the Hoover years, throws a dark shadow on the Bureau's record, as acknowledged, to some extent at least, by several post-Hoover directors. (In the mid-1970s, for example, FBI director Clarence Kelley referred to the excesses of the Hoover era as "foibles and idiosyncrasies.")[6] The reality of the Hoover years was a Bureau that loomed over US society, cheering mainstream Americans with its triumphs and chilling dissenters through its intrusive domestic surveillance and oppressive counterintelligence programs.

As depicted in historical studies, Hoover remains an enigma, a divisive figure who has been reduced in stature even as revelations of his power continue to emerge. Jokes about his sexuality, based on apocryphal tales rather than factual observations, have turned him into a cartoon character, in some ways blunting the harsh reality of his Bureau's actions. Can the mainstream public take seriously concerns about excesses of the J. Edgar Hoover era when the most often encountered traces of him are "Hoover in drag" jokes from late-night talk show hosts?[7] How can we take seriously any claim that Hoover, so often presented as a one-dimensional object of ridicule, was actually a mastermind of secrecy and power who stoked fear to affect the course of events during his tenure? After all, it is difficult to document, quantify, or clearly express the influence that fear of his control of information generated, from the halls of Congress to the hearts of activists. Thus, Hoover has become a historical figure defined by certain moments when his influence became evident or his ability to affect events was acknowledged publicly by others, rather than the overseer of his own, named era. The moments when he stepped into public view include the Bureau's triumphant shootings and captures of public enemies in the 1930s, its World War II–era pursuit of spies and saboteurs on the home front, and the director's seemingly endless crusade against communism during the Cold War. Every few years between 1940 and 1972, off-message portrayals of the Bureau as an American "gestapo" or Soviet-style secret police trickled out. But they were quickly swept away in a deluge of heroic portrayals in the news and entertainment media, never gaining traction among a mainstream audience that wanted to believe the construction of Hoover as a uniquely effective and consistent American hero.[8]

This book suggests a different set of historical moments from the Hoover era to consider, moments that did not necessarily involve any shots fired, spies captured, or communist cells unmasked. Instead, this study focuses on a series of moments that define an essential element of Hoover's long-term success, an underlying source of his power that has scarcely been explored—public relations (PR). As defined by the founders of the practice in the 1920s, public relations involved the crafting of persuasive messages based on an understanding of the audiences for those messages. It was defined by Edward Bernays and his wife, Doris Fleischman, as more than simply P. T. Barnumesque caterwauling aimed at gaining media attention, positive or negative. Public relations, they said, required the gathering of information about an audience and the production of strategically crafted messages that would engage those readers or listeners in a sort of relationship with an organization. Successful PR, as the definition of success came to be understood in the first half of the twentieth century, would result in an audience of people who essentially chose to incorporate the organization's preferred understandings of itself as an element of their own identities.[9] An attack on Hoover's FBI, then, would be an attack on the mainstream Americans who supported him and who, presumably, would at least ignore those messages and might even speak out and counter them.

In the context of the understandings of early public relations, the FBI's shooting of famed outlaw John Dillinger in 1934 becomes important not because it introduced the Bureau to many Americans as a heroic defender of order but because of the public relations messaging failure that ensued whereby FBI agent Melvin Purvis—and not Hoover—was briefly viewed as the nation's top cop.[10] One apparent result of that failure, the 1935 creation of the Bureau's public relations office, the Crime Records Section, represents a little-known but enormously significant moment in the FBI's ascension to iconic status in American society. Prior to the establishment of the Crime Records Section, Hoover and his chief assistants managed the Bureau's public image through happenstance, responding to events of the day rather than shaping any systematic and coherent message about the agency. The establishment of Crime Records led to more than thirty years of highly disciplined control over the Bureau's preferred public image and the development of a reliable cadre of defenders in the news and entertainment media, in Congress, in statehouses and city halls, and in living rooms across the country.

Bureaucratic personnel changes rarely emerge as epic historical moments of note. Hoover's ascension to the directorship of the Bureau is the exception that proves the rule. Historians have indeed noted the importance of that moment in 1924 when an attorney general who was critical of the Bureau's role in the repressive Palmer Raids of 1919 and 1920 oddly chose to name the coordinator of those raids, Hoover, to somehow "clean up" the Bureau.[11] Another pivotal moment, though, the 1935 hiring of a man who might be viewed as the second or third most important person in FBI history, Louis B. Nichols, has at least been noted by historians.[12] An experienced public relations practitioner and natural networker, Nichols oversaw the Crime Records operation for more than twenty years. During that time, the Bureau's enduring public image, centered on scientific law enforcement and a thoughtful reluctance to wield its power with the director as its trustworthy overseer, was created, cemented, and zealously protected. This book explores Nichols's tenure through his management of several public relations crises in those two decades. A consummate networker, Nichols skillfully worked with the opinion shapers of the news media and in Congress to identify and counter challenges to the FBI's preferred public image.

A frequently cited but lesser-known FBI official, Crime Records chief Milton A. Jones, the Bureau's editor-in-chief, served from the early 1940s until he retired after Hoover's death. A quiet Kentuckian and Harvard graduate, Jones was frequently censured by Hoover and Associate Director Clyde Tolson, typically for minor errors in one or two of the thousands of pieces of correspondence and news media material that emerged from his office every week. Yet he was trusted by Nichols as the FBI's top analyst of critical publications, digesting them and formulating counternarratives for the Bureau. Jones and his staff translated the Hoover message and personality into print, and the results speak for themselves. Jones's memoranda and reports are among the most frequently cited by FBI historians. For that reason alone, his tenure marks a moment worthy of consideration.

Other headquarters agents were also responsible for outsized contributions to the Bureau's public image. Jones's close friend, Crime Records agent Fern Stukenbroeker, became a reliable surrogate speaker for Hoover. Stukenbroeker, a professorial figure who held a PhD in history, was a talented and engaging public speaker, ghostwriter for the director's many law journal articles, and one of the contributors who created Hoover's book *Masters of Deceit*. Stukenbroeker performed the remarkable trick of managing to stand out while somehow never eclipsing the director. Two other key advisers who would later become giants in shaping Bureau policies and messages, Cartha "Deke" DeLoach and William C. Sullivan, joined the FBI during the 1940s but would not emerge for their moments in the spotlight until the 1960s.

There were outsiders as well whose moments in Hoover's favor allowed them significant influence on Bureau public relations. Press agent, journalist, and sometime literary figure Courtney Ryley Cooper helped Hoover and Nichols create an FBI public relations template emphasizing scientific law enforcement and establishing the Bureau's legitimacy in the 1930s. That basic story structure, termed the "FBI myth" by historian Richard Gid Powers, was employed for decades, finishing its run in the public eye in 1974 when the Bureau's prime-time television show, *The F.B.I.*, starring Efrem Zimbalist, Jr., was finally canceled.[13] Cooper's influence with Hoover waned after he became a source of embarrassment; he departed the scene via suicide in 1939, but his narrative structure lived on. More enduring and timely was the influence of Hoover's liberal mole, American Civil Liberties Union (ACLU) counsel Morris Ernst. United by their ardent anticommunism, Ernst and Hoover (their relationship facilitated and managed primarily by Nichols) collaborated to develop messages that appealed to liberals concerned about the Bureau's power and potential to undermine civil liberties. A reliable FBI confidential informant on ACLU policies and staff, Ernst also provided Hoover with cover on civil liberties issues through his frequent written and spoken defenses of the Bureau. Hoover, through Nichols, relied on Ernst as their embedded liberal to speak up on civil liberties, publicly and privately countering criticism from the political Left. Ernst's most important contribution was an article developed with Nichols and another FBI friend, *Reader's Digest* editor Fulton Oursler. Ernst's "Why I No Longer Fear the F.B.I." appeared in Oursler's publication, the nation's most widely read magazine, in 1950.[14] A full-throated defense of Hoover and his agency, the article became an oft-cited prop in the Bureau's PR campaign of the 1950s and 1960s, dusted off whenever a critical voice from the left popped up to attack the FBI. How could those critiques of Hoover be plausible when there was a liberal icon—an ACLU pioneer and counsel, no less—who had done his own investigation vouching for the Bureau as a protector of civil liberties? Ernst's moment of influence ended abruptly in the late 1950s when his public statements and actions became embarrassing to the FBI. His *Reader's Digest* article, however, lived on and is sometimes still cited by Hoover apologists and in the memoirs of former Bureau officials as proof that the judgments of historians are wrong and that the director was a great protector of civil liberties.[15]

With Nichols's departure in 1957, less talented public relations contact men, among them Gordon A. Nease, emerged for their moments but never achieved the kind of control over the Bureau's public image that their predecessor had established. Thanks in part to his inability to staunch the criticism of a 1958 "smear campaign," Nease did not last long in that vital position, which attracted more than its share of attention from Hoover and Tolson. Nease's failure led the director to turn to the smooth, charming, but iron-willed DeLoach as his top public relations adviser. DeLoach's moment came in 1959 when he was appointed assistant director supervising a renamed and reorganized Crime Research Division, which included the former Crime Records Section responsible for FBI public relations. A sonorous, slow-talking Georgia native, the affable DeLoach had a remarkable talent for cultivating support for the Bureau in Congress; in other agencies; and, as Hoover's liaison to President Lyndon Johnson, in the White House. Whereas Nichols had been a relentless networker, building relationships with journalists by demonstrating that he was one of them, DeLoach fostered goodwill by managing upward, focusing most of his attention on his relationships with high-level opinion leaders in the federal government. He never pretended to understand or identify with the journalists he frequently worked with, as Nichols did, but instead created an aura of authority for himself, ingratiating himself with more powerful men while parroting Hoover's disdain for the news media.

Even as DeLoach worked his way up to become the third-highest official in the FBI, another assistant director, William Sullivan, emerged to challenge him as a key adviser to Hoover on communism, on civil rights, on the antiwar movement, and—because those issues were so dominant in the 1950s and 1960s—on public relations as well. The two rivals were frequently mentioned as potential replacements for Hoover, speculation that ultimately helped lead to Sullivan's firing one year after DeLoach departed in 1970. During his years of influence, though, Sullivan, as well as anyone else in FBI history, channeled Hoover's voice on communism and subversion, using an upward-management, ingratiating style within the Bureau similar to that employed by DeLoach. It was Sullivan who oversaw the Bureau's COINTEL-PRO program, an effort to infiltrate and undermine left-wing activist groups that began in the 1960s. Sullivan's monographs on communist issues became educational materials inside the Bureau and influenced PR messages on the outside. The persistent rumors of his aspirations to replace Hoover helped lead to his departure from the FBI in 1971. When Sullivan became too close to Richard Nixon's White House and too critical of Hoover, he was shown the door.[16]

The late 1960s and early 1970s marked another notable moment for Hoover's FBI—the decline of the director's creaking empire, which, mirroring his physical decline, had fallen completely out of step with American society. DeLoach departed under uncertain circumstances in 1970, leaving the Bureau less able to exert influence among key constituencies in Congress and the White House. His replacement, Thomas E. Bishop, lacked the kinds of relationships with powerful people that his predecessor had developed and nurtured. It is doubtful, though, that even a powerful figure like DeLoach or Nichols could have slowed the accelerating decline of FBI prestige in the early 1970s. As Bishop struggled to enforce a message in that moment, Hoover's failing health and the cultural shifts begun in the 1960s made the job more difficult and made the FBI seem increasingly like an anachronism. The Bureau's public face—Hoover—had aged markedly, and his continued vituperative anticommunist statements and frequent references to the glory days of the Bureau in the 1930s and 1940s did not resonate with audiences during the Vietnam War and civil rights eras. By the time of the director's death from a heart attack on May 2, 1972, the FBI was no longer immune from criticism. Its public relations message was maintained on television by *The F.B.I.* series until 1974, but the unraveling of Hoover's secrets and the related decline of his prestige and the image of the agency itself had inexorably begun.

The one person who was a constant during most of the pivotal moments of Hoover's tenure was his closest companion, Associate Director Clyde Tolson. Tolson was chair of the Bureau's Executive Conference, a group of top executives in the FBI who made public relations and other policy recommendations to the director. Tolson essentially served as Hoover's chief of staff, acting as a gatekeeper within the FBI, controlling access to Hoover, and recommending harsh punishment for Bureau agents who did not toe the company PR line. For more than three decades, until a series of strokes and other health problems left him unable to work regularly, nearly every memorandum that reached the director passed first through Tolson's hands. Many of the people who wished to meet with Hoover had to be recommended to him by Tolson.

In an agency where Hoover's handwritten notes on memoranda defined policy, Tolson's own handwritten recommendations often served as direct advice to the director or confirmed his orders. The two men rarely disagreed; when they did, it was generally Hoover who offered the more moderate solution to a problem. Tolson was an early public relations adviser to Hoover and continued to participate in decisions on PR matters throughout his tenure. Ultimately, though, he was the director's resident protector and defender, serving in a quality control position, enforcing Hoover's worldview, and protecting the FBI and the director against criticism or potential embarrassment. In an FBI that became, over the decades, a nearly mirror-perfect reflection of the personality and worldview of "the Boss," Tolson provided a bulwark against potential dissonance, be it external or internal to the organization. No other adviser during Hoover's tenure understood better than Tolson when to agree and when to disagree with the director. The two men were close confidants, spending an enormous amount of time together, eating lunch or dinner together almost every day, and even vacationing together. Their unusual closeness sparked speculation about the nature of their relationship, speculation that can never be answered definitely.[17]

What is important is that Hoover relied on Tolson as an enforcer, driving out any messages that failed to match the Bureau's preferred internal and external public image and worldview. The hiring of Clyde Tolson in the early 1930s and his meteoric rise to the associate directorship of the Bureau are therefore worthy of note, as was Tolson's declining health in the mid-1960s. By the early 1970s, when the FBI's public image had begun to unravel, a diminished Tolson lacked the physical capacity to act as Hoover's most ardent defender.

This is a book about Hoover's PR men, the people who operationalized the FBI's public relations–defined image from 1935 until 1973 when, about a year after Hoover's death, Milton Jones retired and the Crime Research/Records Section was disbanded by Acting Director L. Patrick Gray III, who was probably concerned about the section's outsized influence within the organization. If public relations is the building and maintenance of communities of meaning with the potential for action writ large, then the FBI was a remarkably successful public relations pioneer. Defenders who were convinced that their personal identities were commingled with the fate of Hoover stepped up to amplify and promote the Bureau's public image whenever needed. At the height of the director's power, from the late 1930s to the early 1960s, most all Americans could provide a coherent explanation of the Bureau's importance and of Hoover's sturdy, admirable character. Thanks to a never-ending deluge of positive portrayals of the FBI in news and entertainment media, serious questions about the Bureau's actions were routinely chalked up to the ravings of radicals and extremists. There can be no doubt about the impact of the FBI's efforts to define itself from 1935 to 1973.

Beginning just fifteen years after theatrical promoter Edward L. Bernays and his wife, Doris Fleischman, coined the term *public relations* as describing an activity in which the understanding of the audience members helps shape the messages they are sent, the FBI began practicing sophisticated public relations. From Nichols to Jones to DeLoach to Tolson, Hoover's PR men internalized the Bureau's preferred public image to the point where it became integrated into their own identities. They then sold that image to journalists, to entertainment executives, and to an overwhelming majority of Americans. Dissent was not tolerated within the Bureau, so over time, the FBI became a monolithic organization of thousands of agents who lived and breathed the agency's public relations message, image, and worldview. Hoover's PR men in Washington became the enforcers and amplifiers of the director's views. Their individual talents—Nichols's bend-your-ear networking, Jones's meticulous analysis, Stukenbroeker's eloquence, DeLoach's ambition and charm, and Tolson's protective, mother-hen instincts—created and maintained the FBI's remarkable public relations successes. Those talents become clear only through an examination of who Hoover's PR men were and how they worked through public relations challenges. By studying moments when they influenced public perceptions of the Bureau, we can understand more about how public relations trumpeted the law enforcement high points and obscured the domestic surveillance low points of the J. Edgar Hoover era.

Chapter One

From Corrupt to Indispensable

On January 2, 1951, Caroline P. Chambers of St. Cloud, Florida, wrote to Director J. Edgar Hoover at FBI headquarters in Washington. "In case of any injury to me—look up [name redacted] in the vicinity of [city redacted], Florida. This is urgent."[1] When the letter arrived at headquarters, it was routed to the Bureau's Crime Records Section, responsible for the agency's public relations, and landed on the desk of Milton Jones.

By 1951, Jones was seven years into a twenty-eight-year stint as chief of the Crime Records Section. A Kentucky native and Harvard Law graduate, he was once described by his boss, Assistant Director Louis Nichols, as the best researcher and writer in the history of the FBI.[2] Jones's relationships with top-level FBI officials such as Hoover and Associate Director Clyde Tolson, however, were much more contentious. After reviewing Chambers's letter, Jones ordered a name check of FBI files and, finding nothing on the writer, turned the letter over to his Correspondence Unit, a team of about a dozen special agents and more than a hundred stenographers responsible for producing the tens of thousands of routine letters mailed from Bureau headquarters each year. "From the information you have furnished," Special Agent Eugene F. O'Keefe wrote to Chambers over Hoover's automated signature, "... there is no indication that a matter within the investigative jurisdiction of the FBI is involved. It is suggested that you rely upon your local law enforcement agency."[3]

A second letter from Chambers, also dated January 2, 1951, was addressed to the Department of Justice (DOJ) and was forwarded to the FBI a few days later: "Immediate investigation Needed [*sic*]. Life in danger."[4] This time, O'Keefe referred that letter to a special file maintained by Crime Records for keeping track of correspondents who were likely suffering from mental illnesses. He marked the letter "Mental—No ack."[5] The "Mental" file, Jones later reported to Nichols, included more than 5,000 correspondents in 1951.[6]

Chambers's pleas for help were forgotten, swallowed up in a never-ending blizzard of PR matters handled by the five units, dozens of agents, and more than 1,500 stenographers and clerks that comprised the Bureau's Crime Records Section. Two months later, however, Miami police chief Clio Hancock contacted the FBI's Washington headquarters and spoke to Nichols. Hancock reported that Chambers had been brutally murdered on March 15, 1951, tied up, soaked in gasoline, and burned alive in her bed.[7] Moreover, Hancock noted, Miami police were told by Chambers's sister that Caroline had been corresponding with the FBI, her letters pleading with Hoover for protection.[8] A flurry of memoranda and meetings in the Washington headquarters, referred to as the Seat of Government within the FBI, followed the revelation of Chambers's violent death. Nichols requested memoranda of explanation from Jones, O'Keefe, and an unknown stenographer unlucky enough to have typed O'Keefe's dictated letter to Chambers. Nichols then reported his findings to Tolson, the director's closest confidant and the one person, other than Hoover, who was part of the Bureau public relations decision-making team from its beginnings in the mid-1930s right up until Hoover's death in 1972.

There is no record in the half dozen FBI documents related to the matter that anyone suggested in hindsight that officials should have responded to Chambers's pleas by intervening in some way. At no point did anyone suggest that O'Keefe might have followed up his letter to Chambers, in which he suggested that she call her local authorities, with his own phone call to St. Cloud police. Instead, as Jones noted in his explanation to Nichols, the sole focus of concern was public relations and the potential for the Bureau to be embarrassed should Chambers's urgent letters and the agency's boilerplate response become public. "From your memorandum of April 9 and from your conversation this morning," Jones wrote to Nichols, " . . . I received the distinct impression that you felt I showed a lack of interest in protecting the Bureau." Jones continued, "As soon as I saw the incoming letter, as indicated, I realized the possibility of embarrassment to the Bureau. . . . I want to emphasize that I do not think there is ample justification to accuse me of being oblivious to the possibility of embarrassment to the Bureau."[9]

In fact, the "Don't embarrass the Bureau" principle was ingrained in all FBI special agents' psyches during the Hoover era. The mantra, often attributed to the director himself, was part of the informal indoctrination of special agents, absorbed as if via osmosis through daily immersion in field office politics. The phrase was even immortalized as the title of a novel by former FBI agent Bernard F. Conners that was published the year Hoover died.

For failing to protect the Bureau from embarrassment (rather than for failing to intervene to protect Chambers), Jones and O'Keefe were censured and placed on administrative probation.[10] Censure notices remained in agents' personnel files, and probation meant they could not receive raises or commendations for the duration of the punishment. Though the FBI detected no media coverage that mentioned Chambers's correspondence, the incident had embarrassed the Bureau by exposing the oversight to an outsider, Sheriff Hancock, a local law enforcement official and thus a member of a key audience for Crime Records PR messages. In the aftermath of the tragedy, there was no change in Crime Records Section correspondence policy. Instead, the incident was viewed as an error caused by the huge volume of correspondence that passed through the section. Rather than treating the woman's plea for protection and her subsequent murder as a law enforcement failure worth investigating further, FBI officials considered the incident only in terms of public relations and protecting the Bureau from embarrassment.

To avoid such embarrassments and promote a particular image of the Bureau, Hoover began building a public relations agency within the FBI in 1935. For nearly forty years under his leadership, hundreds of agents and thousands of clerks in the FBI's Crime Records Section labored to promote the Bureau and avoid PR embarrassments.[11] Crime Records encompassed several distinct units. The Correspondence Unit handled a massive volume of correspondence during an era when much business, routine and otherwise, was handled via mail. The Publications Unit produced the FBI's magazines, including the *FBI Law Enforcement Bulletin*, which was distributed to local police organizations and other law enforcement officials throughout the United States, and the Bureau's internal newsletter, the *Investigator*. The Research Unit produced lengthy monographs on special topics for internal and sometimes external consumption, eventually becoming the ideological and "academic" center of the FBI's anticommunist crusade. The Library Unit was the institutional memory of FBI public relations, storing clippings and other information that officials used to assess the value or utility of relationships built by the work of the Crime Records Section. And the Special

Projects Unit managed Bureau media relations, a particularly important aspect of FBI public relations. Over the course of its nearly forty-year history, which corresponded with Hoover's tenure as director, the Crime Records Section produced an astonishing volume and variety of PR materials, ranging from television and radio scripts to books and magazines, press releases, letters to correspondents, and even comic books.

In essence, the agents and officials of the Crime Records Section managed a decades-long public relations campaign, producing targeted messages and evaluating feedback provided by special agents in charge (SACs) and others around the country, then adjusting the message if need be and starting again. The FBI's preferred image of itself was built and maintained through stories in the news and entertainment media and through special agents in charge who painstakingly developed and managed relationships with local opinion shapers—individual members of key Bureau stakeholders in the media, government, the clergy, local law enforcement, and business. The FBI's adoption of sophisticated image-making and myth-enforcing machinery occurred early in the modern history of public relations, beginning just a few years after Edward Bernays coined the term and helped professionalize the practice in the early 1920s. It is significant that Hoover, director of the FBI for forty-eight years, had no training in PR, yet his Bureau practiced, at an early stage in the development of the field, sophisticated public relations techniques on a nationwide scale to build and maintain a myth that sustained public support for the organization for decades.

Public relations, perhaps merely coincidentally, became the answer to an ongoing crisis faced by Hoover's FBI from his earliest days as director. Hoover was tapped as director in 1924 following a series of overreaches and scandals that had shaken public and, more important, congressional confidence in the agency. Congress had opposed the formation of a bureau of investigation when it was initially proposed in 1908, fearing that a centralization of investigatory power within a federal agency would create the potential for abuse of that great power for political or other purposes. Once the Bureau was created by executive action, critics predicted that the federal investigative agency would succumb to corruption and political manipulation. They were right. By 1924, the Bureau of Investigation's reputation was badly tarnished by its involvement in the Teapot Dome political scandal and by public perceptions of cronyism. Most of all, though, the Bureau's reputation had been damaged by the nationwide Palmer Raids of 1919 and 1920, when thousands of alleged radicals and anarchists were summarily arrested and imprisoned. Most of those individuals rounded up would ultimately be released, but the public was left with the perception that federal agents knocked down doors and hauled people off in the night, acting as an American secret police. Hoover and his boss, Attorney General A. Mitchell Palmer, appeared before Congress and grilled for days. News coverage decried the Bureau's actions, and some called for Palmer's resignation and the dismantling of the Bureau of Investigation. Oddly, the man selected to clean up the Bureau by the new attorney general, outspoken Palmer Raids critic Harlan Fiske Stone, was the same man who had coordinated those very raids, J. Edgar Hoover.

During Hoover's first ten years as director, he maintained a low profile, an approach that is not surprising considering the battering the Bureau took in the early 1920s. From time to time, a news reporter would wander into the agency to write a story, and in 1929, the Bureau began issuing crime statistics annually. But there was no public relations section within the agency, and Hoover (and Tolson when he arrived as a top administrator in Washington in 1930) managed media relations on an ad hoc basis.

For example, on February 14, 1934, *Brooklyn Eagle* reporter Henry Suydam inquired about writing an article on the Bureau (then called, briefly, the Division of Investigation) for *Forum* magazine. Tolson met with Suydam and referred him to the technical laboratory and to Hoover for a short interview.[12] The resulting article was effusive in its praise for the agency and for Hoover. "What is it that enables the federal authorities to succeed where state and municipal authorities so often fail?" Suydam asked. "To what is the phenomenal record of the Department of Justice in the apprehension of kidnapers to be ascribed?"[13] Suydam credited Hoover's "reorganization" of the Bureau in 1924 for its performance in the high-profile kidnapping cases of the early 1930s, and he attributed the agency's success to its cooperation with local police, its training regimen, and its use of scientific law enforcement methods. "There is no magic in it," Suydam wrote, "but rather the two qualities which are demanded of its men—imagination and common sense."[14] His staid prose and statistical analysis were hardly the stuff of later, highly dramatized stories on Bureau exploits, but they foretold the FBI's public relations message of the mid- and late 1930s. Hoover ordered a copy of the article forwarded to the attorney general.[15] In addition to foreshadowing the Bureau's PR template, Suydam's article had another bit of prescience. Six months after its publication, the reporter was named the Department of

Justice publicity officer, ostensibly responsible for supervising public relations for the department and overseeing FBI public relations as well.

Hoover himself oversaw the Bureau's limited media relations efforts from 1924 to 1930. During that time, the agency rarely appeared in the news. That low profile was in keeping with Hoover's marching orders from Attorney General Stone in 1924. Stone told Hoover to remove corrupt agents and professionalize the Bureau. A low profile in the news media fit with that charge and also fit Hoover's tentative approach when it came to media relations and his general preference for secrecy. During his first six years as director, he focused on reforming the Bureau, firing political appointees, establishing the emerging field of fingerprint science as a law enforcement tool, implementing a complex filing and indexing system, and creating a formal training regimen for special agents.[16]

In 1930, the newly appointed assistant director, Clyde Tolson, took on a larger role in all areas of the administration of the Bureau, including public relations. After joining the Bureau in 1928, Tolson had risen quickly through the ranks. In just his first year, he served as a clerk in the Washington, D.C., field office; was briefly transferred to Boston; and was then transferred to FBI headquarters as chief clerk. In mid-1929, he was transferred back to Boston, this time as special agent in charge of the office there, for one week before returning to Washington headquarters and being promoted to the rank of inspector. Then, on August 30, 1930, just twenty-seven months after being appointed a clerk, Tolson was named assistant director of the Bureau, in charge of personnel and administration. In 1936, he was named assistant to the director, making him the second-highest official in the FBI. Tolson would be responsible for the day-to-day management of the agency for thirty-six years. He and Hoover became close companions. Tolson's title was changed to associate director in 1947, and he served in that position until Hoover's death on May 2, 1972. During the last years of Hoover's tenure, Tolson's health declined dramatically, particularly after he suffered debilitating strokes in 1966 and 1967 that made it difficult for him to read—a significant problem in the paper-driven bureaucracy of the FBI. After Hoover's death, Tolson assumed the acting directorship of the Bureau for about twenty-four hours before being replaced by L. Patrick Gray III. Tolson retired from the Bureau on May 16, 1972.[17]

During his long tenure, he proved himself a skilled manager and administrator. As assistant director in charge of personnel and administration, much of his work involved creating or honing Bureau policies, procedures,

FBI associate director Clyde A. Tolson, ca. 1940. (National Archives at College Park, Md., Record Group 65, Series F, Box 1, Folder 9, #3.)

and hierarchies. Tolson's personnel file, spanning forty-four years of service in the Bureau, includes numerous memoranda in which he spelled out policy changes or additions.

More than merely a manager, though, Tolson was also a gatekeeper, disciplinarian, and sometime public enforcer in defense of Hoover and the Bureau. For more than three decades, he was the director's most combative defender inside and outside the FBI. Judging from his approach to managing the Bureau, it is clear that to Tolson, Hoover and the FBI were one and the same, and both were internalized as part of his own identity. He viewed criticism, even mild criticism, as a personal affront, and more than any of Hoover's other top administrators and public relations defenders, he was an uncompromising defender, often recommending rash actions in response to critics. Their close relationship and Tolson's fast ascent up the FBI organizational chart led to rumors that Hoover and Tolson were lovers. When such rumors became known to the Bureau, they were sure to elicit a stern and often angry response from Tolson.

Many scholars have attempted to deal with the reality of Hoover and Tolson's relationship. Some have accepted dubious tales from wronged parties as "evidence" of Hoover's homosexuality. Others have relied on the superficial and visible facts of the two men's close affiliation. They rode to work together most days. They ate lunches together and dinners together many nights. They took vacations together. In his book *Hoover's War on Gays: Exposing the FBI's "Sex Deviates" Program,* historian Douglas Charles began by answering the key questions about Hoover and Tolson in the first chapter, titled "Was J. Edgar Hoover Gay? Does It Matter?" with a clear-cut and apt analysis: "To address the questions posed in this chapter's title simply and directly: we do not, and cannot know; and no [it does not matter]."[18] Whatever their relationship, it is undeniable that Tolson played a central role, usually behind the scenes, in the success of Hoover's FBI as an investigative agency and as an organization that practiced sophisticated public relations. In every instance where PR questions were raised, from the Dillinger case to *The F.B.I.* television series of the 1960s and 1970s, Tolson's opinion, usually written by hand on memoranda, informed Hoover's decision-making processes. One can imagine that those handwritten comments were supplemented by debate and discussion between the two men who, after all, spent an enormous amount of time together. Tolson's ubiquity in all aspects of Bureau management was never acknowledged publicly, though it was manifested concretely in the advice and comments he wrote on innumerable FBI memoranda, all of which flowed across his desk before reaching Hoover.

Hoover and Tolson's public relations efforts prior to the establishment of the Crime Records Section and the arrival of Louis B. Nichols were perfunctory at best and reflected the agency's minimal public profile during Hoover's first ten years as director. Before the passage of New Deal crime laws in 1934 that gave agents the right to carry guns and the ability to make arrests, FBI exploits were confined to investigating violations of a handful of federal laws; among them were the 1910 Mann Act, which made it a federal crime to transport women across state lines for prostitution, and the Dyer Act, a 1919 law making transportation of stolen cars across state lines a federal crime.[19] The World War I era Espionage, Sedition, and Immigration Acts expanded FBI jurisdiction somewhat, but until 1934 and the onset of the glamorous outlaw era, the Bureau was only infrequently the subject of news stories. In 1930, Bureau agents, under Tolson's supervision, began compiling national crime statistics and publishing them annually in report form.[20] When the first Uniform Crime Report, issued in 1930, included two minor errors, Hoover feared the mistakes would become an embarrassment.[21] Tolson, in charge of the administration of the Bureau, wrote a memorandum that instituted policies to double-check the statistics every month.[22] That seemingly innocuous memorandum demonstrates how Tolson acted as fact-checker-in-chief, detail-oriented administrator, and uncompromising defender against public embarrassment. Between 1930 and 1935 and the establishment of the Crime Records Section, Tolson labored to create a more efficient bureaucracy, which included creating a system for answering the ever-increasing correspondence that flowed into the Bureau.

The arrival on the scene of President Franklin Delano Roosevelt and his New Deal in 1933 kicked off an era with a dramatically expanded federal government role in the economy. Less well known is the New Deal's dramatic expansion of the Bureau of Investigation as part of a "war on crime" that may be seen as a response to Americans' loss of faith in the ability of the federal government to have an impact on their lives. Historian Kenneth O'Reilly described an expansion of the Bureau that included two elements: a war on crime and, later in the decade, a domestic intelligence function. "On one hand, the administration consciously built up the FBI to lead a crusade against crime, and in the process encouraged bureau officials to launch a media campaign intended to influence the public's supposedly romanticized view of the depression-era's flamboyant criminals (whose deeds were sensationalized by tabloid publicity)," O'Reilly wrote. "On the other hand, by the time the Roosevelt administration's perception of the seriousness of the threat that criminal activity posed to internal stability broadened to encompass 'subversive' activities, the FBI had the resources to manage this mission as well."[23]

FDR and his attorney general, Homer S. Cummings, understood the power of publicity and used a war on crime rhetoric as a lever to get Congress to pass a series of bills that expanded the FBI's jurisdiction and power.

The leadership of Attorney General Homer S. Cummings (center) was the initial focus of President Franklin Delano Roosevelt's "war on crime." Hoover eclipsed Cummings as the person most identified with the crime war in the mid-1930s. (Library of Congress, Harris & Ewing Collection, Call Number LC-H2-B-10258.)

From this point of view, high-profile outlaws—such as George "Machine Gun" Kelly, Bonnie Parker and Clyde Barrow, Charles "Pretty Boy" Floyd, Alvin "Creepy" Karpis, Kate "Ma" Barker, and John Dillinger—became useful props in a publicity campaign FDR and Cummings envisioned as a powerful prompt for congressional action. The exploits of Dillinger, including ten bank robberies, several jail breaks, shoot-outs, narrow escapes, and even Robin Hood elements, captured the public imagination. At first, Cummings and not Hoover became the focus of the war on crime effort. In an NBC Radio broadcast six months after FDR's inauguration, Cummings pointed to crimes like the kidnapping of Charles Lindbergh's son as examples of the kinds of acts that required a strong federal response. "It is a real war which confronts us all—a war that must be successfully fought if life and property are to be secure in our country," Cummings said.[24]

A series of legislative actions followed the high-profile declaration of war on crime. In May and June 1934, Congress approved nine bills expanding the power and jurisdiction of what was then, briefly, called the Division of Investigation (it became the FBI in 1935). As a result, Hoover's agents could, for the first time, carry weapons and make arrests, becoming a true law enforcement agency rather than merely an investigative entity. The Fugitive Felon Act gave federal agents jurisdiction when criminals crossed state lines. FBI jurisdiction over automobile thefts was expanded. Robberies of federally insured banks were placed under the jurisdiction of the Bureau. And an antiracketeering law made extortion over the telephone or through the mails a federal crime.[25] In addition to expanding the Bureau's jurisdiction and power, FDR sought to raise the agency's public profile. One of his friends in the media, *Liberty* magazine editor Fulton Oursler, recommended to the president's aide Stephen Early that the administration use a publicity campaign to make heroes of the G-men. Suydam, Cummings's publicity chief, was put in charge of the campaign.[26]

Even as the Department of Justice and the Roosevelt administration were gearing up to direct a PR campaign to promote the FBI and as Congress was considering the president's crime bills, events brought the Bureau's work further into public view—and in an unflattering way. On the evening of April 23, 1934, FBI agents, led by Melvin Purvis and Hugh Clegg, surrounded the Little Bohemia vacation lodge on the shore of Little Star Lake near Manitowosh, Wisconsin. In Washington, Hoover announced to the press that Dillinger was surrounded and could not escape.[27] The agents, however, badly botched their approach to the lodge, spooking the Dillinger gang inside by opening fire on three innocent civilians, one of whom was killed. The raid was doomed not only by the agents' announcing their presence but also by a failure to cover the back of the lodge, which allowed Dillinger, Baby Face Nelson, Homer Van Meter, Tommy Carroll, and John "Red" Hamilton to escape after a brief gunfight. A few minutes after the shoot-out, Baby Face Nelson confronted a group of agents and local officers; he killed Special Agent Carter Baum and wounded one other agent and a local police officer. Media coverage of the failed raid was a major embarrassment to the Bureau. A wire service report noted that residents near Manitowosh were "laughing out loud, long and bitterly at what they call 'the bungle of the revenooers.'"[28] Historian Richard Gid Powers summarized the public relations and human tragedy of that evening. "Despite advantages of surprise and numbers, the FBI had surrounded most of the nation's top fugitives in one place, had announced their capture in advance, and had come away empty handed," Powers wrote. "In Washington there was talk of demoting Hoover; a petition from Wisconsin called for Purvis' dismissal 'at least until Dillinger is caught or killed.'"[29] As Powers concluded, the Little Bohemia disaster had "turned the Dillinger case into comedy."[30]

For Purvis and the FBI, redemption was just weeks away. On July 21, 1934, two officers of the East Chicago, Indiana, police department contacted Special Agent in Charge Melvin Purvis in Chicago. The officers had an informant, a woman named Anna Sage, who they claimed was in touch with Dillinger. Purvis, Special Agent Samuel Cowley (whom Hoover had assigned to assist in the Dillinger hunt), and the two officers met with Sage. Facing deportation, she was keen to assist the agents in hopes that her expulsion could be forestalled. Purvis promised to try to help her remain in the United States in exchange for her cooperation. The next evening, Sage called Purvis and said that she, Dillinger, and another woman, Polly Hamilton Keele, would attend a movie that night in one of two theaters. Cowley and a team of agents staked out the Marbro Theater, and Purvis led a team at the Biograph Theater at 2433 N. Lincoln Avenue. At about 8:30 p.m., Dillinger, Sage, and Keele entered the latter theater, and Purvis consolidated the two teams of agents at that location; they covered the rear exits and hatched a plan to capture the outlaw on the street after the movie ended. At about 10:40 p.m., Dillinger and his companions exited the theater and turned left, walking southeast on Lincoln Avenue. Purvis gave the signal, lighting his cigar, and the agents converged. Dillinger was shot three times, and one bystander was injured as well. Dillinger was pronounced dead ten minutes later, with gunshot wounds to the chest and head.[31]

The shooting led headlines the next day and for weeks afterward. In the immediate aftermath, Purvis and Attorney General Cummings took center stage. Hoover was noticeably a secondary figure in the media coverage of the incident. Purvis was the first man quoted in the *New York Times* story. "He saw me give a signal to my men to close in," Purvis said. "He became alarmed and reached into a belt and was drawing the .38-calibre pistol he carried concealed when two of the agents let him have it. Dillinger was lying prone before he was able to get the gun out and I took it from him."[32] Cummings was reported by the Associated Press to be "smiling in elation," and he issued a statement: "The news of tonight is exceedingly gratifying as well as reassuring."[33] Hoover was relegated to second-fiddle status and was quoted as saying, "This does not mean the end of the Dillinger case."[34] Powers noted that news stories made it appear Purvis and Cummings had orchestrated the Dillinger shooting without any help from Hoover. The day after the incident, Cummings was traveling by train across the United States to promote the war on crime. It was arranged for him to stop in Chicago to congratulate Bureau agents for getting Dillinger. The man who met Cummings at the train station was the most famous law officer in the country at the time—Melvin Purvis.[35] According to Powers, Hoover "sounded like an outsider trying to grab credit from the country's newest hero, Melvin Purvis, ace G-Man."[36]

Second-day coverage in the *New York Times*, on July 24, featured Purvis and Hoover with equal billing on page 1 and even included a photo of the Chicago SAC on page 3, where Purvis was quoted parroting Hoover's comments on the front page. "There is plenty to be done today, tomorrow and the next day," Purvis said. "There are others to be captured —Dillinger's pals and those who helped him remain at large for three months."[37] Ensuing days' coverage placed Hoover and Purvis essentially on equal ground, as exemplified in a July 26 story of a meeting between the two men in Washington that included a bit of public relations theater: "Mr. Purvis arrived unexpectedly at the capital late today. He was met by Mr. Hoover, who walked eagerly toward him, grasped him by the hand and congratulated him on his success in bringing the long Dillinger hunt to a successful conclusion."[38] Another story, on July 29, touted the "agents of justice who got Dillinger" in a fawning introduction to the Bureau of Investigation. Again, Hoover and Purvis received equal billing, although Hoover's mug shot appeared with the story.[39]

Hoover responded by working with friends in the news media in what was perhaps the Bureau's first comprehensive effort to that point to convey its preferred public image, with science, responsibility, and Hoover center stage and field agents such as Purvis as mere bit players—nameless, faceless members of the team. The erasure of Purvis from FBI history had begun. Neil "Rex" Collier's six-part series published from July 26 to July 31, 1934, in the *Washington Star* posited that "Hoover himself had directed the nationwide search by long distance telephone from his office at the Department of Justice."[40] On August 19, 1934, a hagiographic article by Collier, "Why Uncle Sam's Agents Get Their Men," appeared in the *New York Times Magazine* and very clearly—and fawningly—placed Hoover rather than his boss, Cummings, or his most famous agent, Purvis, at the head of the war on crime. "Mr. Hoover had been asked to explain the secret of his organization's success in corralling one after another of America's outstanding public enemies," Collier wrote. "His black eyes sparkled as he laughed off the suggestion that there is anything uncanny or mysterious about the achievements of the 'G' men—those close-mouthed Federal detectives designated as special agents of the Department of Justice."[41] The Collier pieces "made any details that detracted from the FBI's performance—the fiasco at Little Bohemia, the murky details surrounding Anna Sage's past, the bargain struck between her and Purvis, and the bystanders wounded at the Biograph—irrelevant," Powers observed. "The real meaning of the case was that Hoover always got his man."[42]

Thus, the shooting of Dillinger marked both the beginning of a higher-profile war on outlaws by the Bureau and the debut of a new public image and expanded focus on public relations for the agency and its director. Prior to that time, PR matters were handled by the Bureau's Research Division, centered almost entirely on producing material distributed to law enforcement agencies. A 1935 reorganization created the Crime Records Section that, under the leadership of several of the most prominent figures in FBI history, shaped public perceptions of the Bureau for nearly four decades. From 1935 until the late 1960s, the Crime Records Section's PR template of scientific law enforcement, the FBI's largely mythical deference to local law enforcement, and the tough but benevolent protector J. Edgar Hoover combined to drown out critical characterizations of the Bureau. By the 1970s, the departure of key PR men such as Louis Nichols and Deke DeLoach, along with the fading health and authority of Hoover and top deputy Clyde Tolson, allowed for an explosion of criticism of the FBI. The failure of Hoover's health, his willingness to discard powerful allies including Nichols and DeLoach, and the resulting failure of the agency's public relations campaign in the early 1970s demonstrate the importance of the earlier, more capable PR men who created and maintained the Bureau's legitimacy and power from the 1930s until the late 1960s.

The impetus that led Hoover to create an alternative reality through public relations was a basic question of the legitimacy of federal law enforcement. He had personally witnessed the results of the early Bureau of Investigation's failure to steer clear of politics, scandal, and corruption. A brilliant bureaucrat, Hoover clearly understood that his own future as director and any dreams he had to expand his Bureau depended on public and congressional support. He also understood that bureaucratic leadership in Washington was fleeting, ever dependent on political connections. Whether through a brilliantly executed strategy or by a fortuitous combination of happenstance and public relations, he managed both to position the FBI as an indispensable agency and to make himself indispensable as the leader of the Bureau.

It is difficult to say whether Hoover clearly saw a dramatic expansion of Bureau public relations efforts as a means to legitimize the work of the FBI over the long term or whether he was merely taking advantage of a flood of interest in the agency in the early 1930s. Was the establishment of the Crime Records Section a proactive move to promote the FBI? Or was it simply that, given mounting public interest in special agents' exploits, managing Bureau PR had become an overwhelming task for the Washington administrative team? The answer seems to be a bit of both. There is little doubt that Hoover understood there was some social capital to be raised through laudatory media coverage and the maintenance of pen-pal relationships with key stakeholders. Yet the Crime Records Section was not created until late 1934, nearly two years after the Roosevelt administration's declaration of a war on crime began a ratcheting up of public interest in Hoover and the Bureau. FBI personnel files for prominent administrators prior to the creation of the Crime Records Section include significant caches of documents indicating that media relations in particular had become extremely time-consuming beginning in the late 1920s. By the early 1930s, managing relationships with opinion shapers and policy makers had obviously become an all-consuming task, but Hoover did not move to establish a public relations section until after the shooting of John Dillinger in 1934.

Chapter Two

The Networker

CBS Radio listeners who tuned in at 8:30 p.m. on Saturday, November 25, 1944, were treated to the dramatic retelling of a 1934 FBI success story, the St. Paul, Minnesota, killing by Bureau agents of Eddie "the Wise" Green, a member of John Dillinger's outlaw gang. At FBI headquarters, Crime Records Division chief Louis Nichols monitored the inaugural broadcast of *The FBI in Peace and War*, a program sponsored by Lava Soap and based on Bureau cases as retold in Frederick L. Collins's Bureau-authorized, best-selling book of the same title.[1]

A native of Decatur, Illinois, and graduate of Kalamazoo College in Michigan, Nichols earned his law degree from J. Edgar Hoover's alma mater, George Washington University, in 1934. As a law student, he worked for the Young Men's Christian Association (YMCA) as a clerk and then as a public relations officer. Nichols joined the FBI in 1934, and after a brief stint in the Birmingham, Alabama, field office, he was assigned to the Research Section at Bureau headquarters in Washington, D.C. In November 1935, he was named chief of the section, which was renamed the Crime Records Section shortly thereafter. Nichols was not the typical straitlaced, athletic FBI agent of the Hoover era. He was a burly man with the countenance of an unmade bed. He had a boisterous and outgoing personality that fueled the development of his network of PR contacts. His desk was untidy and layered with newspapers, the floor around it strewn with cigarette butts.[2] Memoranda often sat on his desk, unread, for days, a cardinal sin in Hoover and Associate Director Clyde Tolson's clockwork bureaucracy.[3] His early scores on FBI procedural exams were startlingly low and only came up after his supervisor at the time, Robert E. Joseph, was chastised by Hoover for the poor performance of his agents.[4] On a memorandum listing the scores of agents under Joseph (Nichols's score was among the lowest, at 56 out of 100), the director wrote: "This is a very bad showing & cannot be tolerated. Certainly we

FBI assistant director Louis B. Nichols, ca. 1950. (National Archives at College Park, Md., Record Group 65, Series F, Box 1, Folder 9, #7a.)

should be able to expect from supervisors an elementary knowledge of the work."[5]

Unlike later Crime Records stalwarts—such as the Bureau's longtime "editor," the meticulous but overextended Milton A. Jones—Nichols tended to be a sloppy writer and editor at times. On a 1951 memorandum the agent wrote to explain an error, Tolson noted, "Nichols *will* not check memos for accuracy." Hoover responded, "Sometime Nick thru such carelessness will really get us in a jam."[6] Yet Nichols was among the very few top FBI officials whose nicknames were used by Hoover in his correspondence and, presumably, in conversation—in his case, "Nick the Greek." Typically, the director simply addressed his agents by their last names.

In addition to a background as a public relations official at the Washington YMCA, Nichols had some radio broadcasting experience, and he was an experienced public speaker. In fact, it was that speaking and broadcasting experience that led his Birmingham supervisor to suggest him for administrative work in the Bureau's D.C. office.[7]

Why would Nichols, a former football player and PR counselor with a law degree, choose to join Hoover's FBI? Like many of the Bureau's 1930s recruits, he was convinced to apply because of the thrilling stories he had heard of FBI exploits and because of the stature inherent in working for the mythical and iconic Hoover. He later cited dramatic, action-packed FBI radio programs as having influenced his decision to join the Bureau.[8] Most FBI historians rank Nichols as one of the three most important individuals in FBI history, along with Hoover and Tolson.

An inveterate networker, Nichols and two outside collaborators, author Courtney Ryley Cooper and journalist Rex Collier, created the Bureau's public relations template, emphasizing science, responsibility, and Hoover's steady leadership.[9] Nichols's strong relationships with FBI friends in a variety of opinion-shaping positions, from the news media to the clergy to Congress, were essential to the establishment and maintenance of the famous FBI brand of the 1930s, 1940s, and 1950s. He personally established the Bureau's preferred image of itself through Crime Records PR policies and procedures. Nichols's ability to develop and sustain relationships, even with enemies of the FBI, often blunted or obscured critical voices. His genius in this regard extended to relationships inside the agency, where he was among the few who were able to moderate Hoover's and particularly Tolson's tendencies to overreact to critical news stories and real or imagined PR embarrassments. The value of Nichols's talents would later be demonstrated by the unraveling, over the course of a dozen years, of the FBI's public relations message after he left the Bureau in 1957. Early in his career, though, his advice and the public relations machine he developed in the Crime Records Section were central to the development of the iconic FBI.

In his 1944 review of the Eddie "the Wise" Green story in *The FBI in Peace and War* program, Nichols noted that the antagonist's name had been changed from Eddie to Johnny for the broadcast and that the narrator had credited the FBI with cleaning up the entire Dillinger gang "J. Edgar Hoover style."[10] Listeners, influenced by the authoritative nature of the program and the invocation of Hoover's name, were likely convinced that the show was authorized and sponsored by the Bureau. That was not the case, and Nichols objected to the failure of Collins and his sponsor to include a specific disclaimer to make that clear. "There was no tag line to the effect that the show has no official connection with the Federal Bureau of Investigation as we had specifically stipulated with Collins previously," he wrote in a memorandum to Tolson. "The impression was very obvious by the use of the Director's name and the statement relative to FBI files that this was an FBI show."[11] As the Bureau's conflict with Collins played out, Nichols's diplomatic and networking skills, along with his understanding of public relations and broadcasting, served Hoover well.

For weeks before the initial broadcast of *The FBI in Peace and War*, Nichols had urged Collins to drop his plans for the program. Given his prior work with the Bureau on an authorized book of the same title, Collins had developed the radio concept and sold it, through the Biow advertising agency of New York, to Procter & Gamble without informing Nichols or Hoover. Collins was to be paid $1,000 per episode by the sponsors, with his primary contribution being access to Bureau PR materials.[12] Nichols expressed the prevailing attitude among top FBI administrators when his review compared *The FBI in Peace and War* to another popular radio program Hoover despised. "All in all," he stated, "the program is very much in the Gang Busters style, and, in fact, Gang Busters might even be considered more dignified."[13]

Nichols's concerns about radio representations of the FBI dated back to the 1936 premiere of the *Gang Busters* program, which quickly became a perennial ratings hit. Developed by producer Phillips H. Lord, *Gang Busters* offered weekly dramatizations of police cases, including an FBI case thrown into the mix from time to time. Known for its cacophonous opener of sirens and gunshots (the show's introduction sparked the saying "coming on like *Gang Busters*") and for its similarly raucous and often violent action, *Gang Busters* and the success it enjoyed led to other law enforcement dramas, including *The FBI in Peace and War*.

Those kinds of action-packed crime radio dramas, with millions of listeners each week, represented a significant challenge to the carefully crafted and meticulously maintained FBI public image that Nichols was charged with protecting. The FBI that was represented in Bureau-authorized articles, books, radio dramas, and motion pictures was a responsible and careful law enforcement agency, frequently shown as being reluctant to intervene in local investigations. The Bureau's constructed public image, created and maintained through Nichols's Crime Records Section, emphasized clinical, scientific law enforcement as an antidote to concerns that such a powerful, nationwide law enforcement agency might abuse its authority. Hoover himself was portrayed in FBI-authorized news and entertainment stories as a tough but fair, avuncular American protector, a thoughtful leader as concerned about preserving civil liberties as he was about catching criminals. In its authorized retellings, any inkling of an out-of-control FBI was scrubbed from the historical record, replaced with themes of science, responsibility, and Hoover's cautious and protective leadership. That restrained image was, according to many FBI scholars, a central element in the physical and jurisdictional growth of the Bureau that began in the early 1930s.[14] By 1936, the FBI, which employed just 100 agents in 1930, had grown to 900 agents in 52 field offices.[15]

The themes of science, responsibility, and Hoover's careful leadership were chosen specifically to counter concerns about the power and potential political corruption of a federal law enforcement agency that predated the director's tenure.[16] Beginning with *Gang Busters*, though, radio dramatizations of FBI exploits often emphasized sensational themes of violence, intrigue, and the potent power of the nation's federal law enforcement agency. With regard to radio representations of the FBI's work, the period from 1936 to 1945 was a largely defensive time during which Nichols and his public relations team battled off-message portrayals of the Bureau behind the scenes.

In 1945, with Nichols's inspiration, the Bureau created its own authorized radio program on the ABC network, *This Is Your FBI*. For the remainder of the era when radio dominated the media, the Bureau continued to battle sensational programs such as *The FBI in Peace and War* through its maneuvering behind the scenes while simultaneously promoting its own program as something objectively and qualitatively different. The details of those efforts offer a cautionary tale on how a government agency, particularly a law enforcement agency, has an outsized ability to influence news and entertainment portrayals of its work; in effect, it can create a mythical version of itself that has the potential to obscure from public view abuses of civil liberties. That is especially true of an agency like the FBI, which had, through its heroic exploits in the outlaw cases of the 1930s, achieved iconic status in American society.

Hoover had first learned of the planned *Gang Busters* radio program through correspondence with producer Phillips Lord in early 1936. A former high school principal, Lord had moved to New York in 1927 and begun writing radio dramas. His first big success on NBC Radio, *Sunday Evening at Seth Parker's*, with a lead character based on his grandfather Hosea Parker, debuted in 1929.[17] Ten years later, Lord produced the thirteen-episode, Bureau-authorized radio program *G-Men*. Hoover personally negotiated the *G-Men* deal with Lord. When the initial drafts did not match Hoover's vision, he brought in two trusted public relations advisers, Cooper and Collier, to work with Nichols on the scripts.[18] The Bureau did not hide its affiliation with *G-Men*, and it actively participated in production of the program, providing story ideas and conducting final script reviews. As a result, the portrayals in *G-Men* were closely aligned with Hoover's science and responsibility narrative.

In proposing that the FBI assist with *Gang Busters*, Lord noted that, thanks to his previous experience working with the Bureau, he could be entrusted with the task of portraying FBI agents in an acceptable fashion. In fact, Lord had resented Hoover's insistence upon a formulaic approach to *G-Men*, and *Gang Busters* was an effort to eliminate direct FBI control over the content, something Nichols and Hoover insisted upon.[19] The new show would focus largely on local police cases, only infrequently involving federal agents. "In some of these cases there will be references made to the Federal Men and in every case where Special Agents are called on the telephone or mentioned, I shall certainly see that every bit of credit is given to your men," Lord stated. "Naturally, after my 'schooling' and the new friends I hope I made in the Federal Bureau of Investigation my loyalty is there."[20]

Even as Lord and his sponsor tried to free themselves from Hoover's control, they simultaneously sought to capitalize on the FBI's elevated status in society. A few days after Lord wrote to Hoover introducing the show's concept, a representative of the Benton & Bowles advertising agency contacted the director to ask if he would contribute to promotional materials for the program, including authoring an introduction for a promotional booklet featuring information about wanted fugitives.[21] Based on policies established by Nichols, similar requests to involve Hoover in the promotion of entertainment or other products received an immediate and terse rejection in the 1940s through the end of Hoover's tenure in 1972.[22] In 1936, though, Hoover and the FBI were required to forward any such requests to Department of Justice publicity chief Henry Suydam for his approval or disapproval. Suydam was a former *Brooklyn Eagle* reporter and had been hired by Attorney General Homer Cummings to lead the department's PR efforts.[23]

When Suydam did not respond prior to the first *Gang Busters* broadcast on January 1, 1936, Hoover made a second request for an opinion.[24] On January 23, Suydam called him and mentioned he had listened to the first *Gang Busters* broadcast. Hoover reported the contents of the conversation in a memorandum to Tolson:

> Mr. Suydam stated that the entire program had a false atmosphere and he did not believe that I should write an introduction to a pamphlet to be used for advertising purposes. . . . Mr. Suydam stated that we would probably have to furnish them with any information they might request concerning closed cases. I stated that any information which was generally available would be made available to them but I did not think we should participate in the program.[25]

The question of the extent of the Bureau's participation in the program was never clearly answered, a mistake Nichols would not repeat. From then on, he insisted upon FBI review of scripts as a prerequisite to Bureau involvement in motion pictures and in radio and eventually television programs. Lord immediately tested the limits of that vague understanding. "I am going to pan the parole system like nobody's business," he wrote four days later, citing a topic—lenient parole boards—that he knew would appeal to Hoover. He asked, "Could you send me unofficially some statistics on parole?"[26] A week later, he requested information from the Bureau's special agent in charge in New York about "innocent persons killed each year by criminals."[27] Those two requests were only the first of hundreds of requests for information contained in the FBI's file on *Gang Busters*.

After Suydam's lukewarm review cited the "false atmosphere" of the program, Hoover ordered Nichols and his Crime Records staff to monitor and review *Gang Busters* each week. Noting that the show opened with "the staccato of machine gun fire, the cry of sirens and a radio voice calling all police and all G-Men," the Crime Records Section agent assigned to listen to the show recounted the plot. He also highlighted the narrator's request for listeners to send information on fugitive Alvin Karpis and "any information on crimes . . . to the 'Gang Busters, New York City,' with an assurance that "the information would absolutely be kept confidential." Tolson, perhaps indicating the Bureau's increasing discomfort with the program's sensational story lines and self-serving promotion, underscored those words on his copy of the memorandum.[28]

Lord, through his staff, continued to request information from the FBI, specifically and repeatedly asking for Phillips Lord, Inc., to be added to a mailing list so the company would receive Identification Orders (IOs) that described fugitives sought by the Bureau as well as narrative descriptions of resolved cases called Interesting Case memoranda. Suydam asked Hoover to provide the information, but the director made one final plea in an effort to avoid complying with the request:

> Before forwarding the collection which you requested for Mr. Lord, I wanted to suggest consideration as to whether it is desirable to make these available to him for his use on the program entitled "Gang Busters." I have listened to this program several times and it is a very unsatisfactory and rather cheap presentation. I, personally, would not like to see any reference made to the Federal Bureau of Investigation on this program, as I do not believe it would enhance the prestige of the Bureau.[29]

Even as he went over Hoover's head to request Bureau information, a tactic certain to anger the director, Lord further alienated the FBI when he asked permission to collect fingerprints as a promotional stunt for the program. In the mid-1930s, Hoover had embarked on a campaign urging all Americans to be fingerprinted for the Bureau's Identification Division fingerprint files. The campaign was part of his sincere and ultimately effective effort to make fingerprint science, which was slow to catch on in the United States, an essential law enforcement tool. Lord's plan was to obtain actual FBI fingerprint cards, distribute them by mail, and forward the prints to the agency. Hoover refused to participate and became angry when Lord then attempted to purchase FBI fingerprint cards from the paper company in Connecticut that supplied them to the Bureau.[30] "This action impressed me as being a rather circuitous method of approach on a matter which had already been turned down," he wrote to Suydam.[31] Attorney General Cummings ultimately sided with the director on the issue of fingerprints but agreed with Suydam that Hoover had little choice but to provide public relations material to Lord.[32]

FBI officials continued monitoring the program, with one of Nichols's Crime Records agents producing a three-page review each week for Tolson and Hoover. None of the broadcasts between February and July featured FBI cases, and on July 3, 1936, Hoover ordered the monitoring of the program to cease. But Lord's requests for information continued, pushing the boundaries of his agreement with the Department of Justice. On August 6, 1936, for example, Lord asked to paraphrase Hoover in a script about Kate "Ma" Barker. He clearly sensed that his relationship with the FBI had soured, and in a rambling plea, he tried to repair it:

> I would also like very, very much, Mr. Hoover, to have you for my guest at lunch or dinner in New York for I feel that there must have been some misunderstanding between us down in Washington which I have never been able to comprehend and I admire you so highly for your outstanding accomplishments that I would like to talk with you across the table and see if such a misunderstanding existed. If so, let us untangle it because I want you to know that if I unintentionally actually did or said something which I should not have, I certainly will apologize for I sincerely tried to please you to the very best of my ability.[33]

Hoover responded in a letter authored for him by Tolson, who handled much of his correspondence until that task was taken over by a correspondence team in Nichols's Crime Records Section in the late 1930s. The response was an edited version of the remarks that would be attributed to him on the program; he offered no specific date for a meeting and coolly thanked Lord: "The kind sentiments expressed in your letter concerning our personal associations are indeed appreciated."[34] Lord responded by forwarding a copy of the Barker script for Bureau review. "I shall not state over the air or in any other way that I have submitted this script to you," he wrote. "The only reason I am doing so is because I am a loyal rooter for the Federal Bureau of Investigation, and I don't want to make any statement that you would prefer I didn't. On the other hand, if there is a little propaganda I can incorporate, I shall be very glad to do so."[35]

After the script was reviewed by Nichols, Hoover, again in a letter written by Tolson, offered a tepid response, merely making several factual changes and expressing kind regards.[36] Already concerned about the status of his relationship with the director, Lord included fewer and fewer FBI cases on *Gang Busters*. At one point, he asked Hoover whether he should eliminate all references to the Bureau from the program. "As long as I do not quote you in any way or place on these references your stamp of approval, would you like to have me bring in the Federal Agents when they do enter the case, or would you prefer to have me omit their work?" Lord asked. "I stand ready to do whatever you advise, but naturally I would like to give the Bureau credit."[37] Hoover's response, again penned by Tolson, was businesslike, approving the inclusion of FBI agents where the story warranted. "Of course," he stated, "I do not feel that you should indicate any authentication of the material used inasmuch as this Bureau is not in a position to enter into any arrangement whereby a review may be made of the material which you do use."[38] That sort of aloof, noncommittal tone became part of the Bureau's public relations tool kit. Repeatedly through the years, FBI correspondence urged news and entertainment media officials to make their own judgments about the propriety of an action. Such nonresponses were actually intended to dissuade requests from individuals who might wisely think twice about proceeding on FBI-related projects without FBI assistance. Essentially, "make your own decision" meant "mention us at your own risk; we will be watching."

Lord further angered Hoover with the way *Gang Busters* characterized the demise of the so-called Brady Gang in October 1937. The gang, led by Alfred Brady and Clarence Lee Schaffer, Jr., allegedly committed approximately 150 robberies and at least 1 murder. When members of the gang traveled to Bangor, Maine, and tried to purchase guns, the Maine State Police notified the FBI. And when the gang returned for their guns on October 12, 1937, local police arrested one gang member and shot gang leader Schaffer. At the same time and just down the street, FBI agents shot and killed Brady.[39] *Gang Busters* announced the killings and capture on its October 13, 1937, broadcast, with a narrator congratulating the FBI and the local police on their conclusion of the case; the following week, the "full facts" were presented on the show. Hoover was not pleased with the results, and when Lord's staff contacted the FBI for more public relations materials, the director ordered them cut off from Bureau information. "No," Hoover wrote on the memorandum. "Just file letter. Their utter lack of credit to us in Bangor case cannot be overlooked."[40] For Hoover, mention of local police involvement tainted the broadcast and turned what was a positive report into an attack.

As ratings for *Gang Busters* grew, complaints about the nature and content of the program began arriving at FBI headquarters. In a letter to Hoover, one Tulsa, Oklahoma, listener described the program as "blood curdling. . . . From the beginning it has been my firm conviction that this program could serve as a course of instruction for the mind which might have criminal tendencies. . . . I ask you Mr. Hoover, do give this some thought—some boy may learn how it is done by listening to the Gang Buster's [*sic*] program."[41] A Pittsburgh man similarly complained that programs like *Gang Busters* encouraged copycat crimes. "If you would always listen to those storys [sic] you would want to try it."[42] An Ohio woman wrote that "the 'Gang Buster' program on the radio is most inspiring to young people to go in the stick up business."[43] Another Tulsa resident wrote that even though *Gang Busters* producers claimed the program prevented crime, "in reality the program is a school of the air for future criminals. It brings out one thing in particular, that is, if you kill your victim you have more of a chance to last at the game, and the more you show your cruelty, the more people will be scared of you."[44] On September 7, 1938, a representative of the Federal Communications Commission (FCC) contacted the FBI about the program, noting that the commission had received "many complaints from civic groups, churches, and homes and others against the program."[45]

Each of those complaints was carefully reviewed by Nichols's Crime Records agents as a challenge to the Bureau's preferred image of restraint. Hoover, in correspondence authored by Nichols, responded to every complaint with a similar refrain, noting the Bureau had no official connection to the program. To make his point crystal clear to regulators, he forwarded to the FCC copies of the complaints the FBI had received as well as his responses. Enclosing the Tulsa man's letter, Hoover told FCC chairman Frank R. McNinch, "I have informed Mr. Bath that this Bureau has no connection whatsoever with the program which he mentions and that his letter is being referred to your office."[46]

For years, the patterns of Lord's requests and Hoover's grudging provision of public source information through Nichols continued, paralleled by a steady stream of public complaints. In 1943, for instance, Hoover decided to withhold PR releases from the *Gang Busters* writers and producers, pleading a wartime paper shortage.[47] *Gang Busters* program supervisor Leonard L. Bass wrote to the Bureau that same day, noting that the show reached 8 million listeners each week.[48] Three days later, Hoover, apparently after a discussion with Nichols, changed his mind, and Lord's producers were placed back on the FBI mailing list.[49] Nichols's unique ability to moderate Hoover's and Tolson's reactionary tendencies, rather than endorsing them and adopting the same views, was one of his most valuable contributions to the success of FBI public relations. Unlike many of Hoover's closest advisers, Nichols was not a yes-man.

That same year, *Gang Busters* inaugurated a new segment, "Gang Busters Clues," on the program. Each week, descriptions of several wanted fugitives were broadcast at the end of the show, with instructions that anyone with information about them should contact police or forward information to the *Gang Busters* producers. Following an internal debate among FBI administrators about whether to start a new file to track the thousands of "clues" that would appear, it was decided that they would be cataloged in the existing file.[50] Every week, one of Nichols's Crime Records agents transcribed information about the fugitives who were described, supplementing that with information from Bureau files when possible. From the vast number of reports of the weekly clues in the *Gang Busters* file, it was no small task, but it was a necessary one. Local special agents in charge across the country, most of whom did not listen to the program, were deluged with tips about fugitives sent to them by *Gang Busters* listeners, often without the fugitive's name attached. Those SACs then contacted Bureau headquarters, where officials tried to figure out which clue related to which fugitive in each reported sighting. Once again, what *Gang Busters* producers saw as a combination of promotion and public service became a logistical headache for the FBI.

As the Bureau's relationship with *Gang Busters* was settling into a continuing, contentious pattern, another unwelcome radio dramatization was being developed by a former Bureau collaborator in the media. Frederick L. Collins's Bureau-authorized book, *The FBI in Peace and War*, had been completed with extensive assistance from Nichols and other FBI public relations officials, including a final line edit of the book and a ghostwritten foreword by Hoover. The book was a best seller in 1943. In the summer of 1944, Collins approached Nichols with the idea of developing a radio program based on the book, tentatively titled "This Is the FBI." Collins had already sold the concept to the Biow advertising agency, a fact he withheld from Nichols. The author requested FBI cooperation and even proposed that Hoover participate in the program. Nichols said the Bureau would consider his proposal, but he offered several conditions that had, between 1935 and 1944, become intrinsic to the Bureau's PR policies for cooperating with outside authors and producers: "I told him what the conditions were, namely, having to review the script and having control of the script."[51] Collins told Nichols that the advertising agency he was working with, Biow, would not agree to those conditions.[52] Nichols said he was surprised when, on September 18, 1944, Collins forwarded a wax platter of a test version of the new show, titled "This Is the FBI," and again offered to include Hoover. Nichols, Tolson, and Hoover listened to the show and found both the quality and the story line lacking.[53] "In each case the program has been offered [to potential sponsors] without any suggestion that Mr. Hoover might be willing to appear on it," Collins wrote. " . . . but if, at any time, he decided that his participation would add to the public service afforded by the program, he would be most welcome to appear as my guest in accordance with our previous talks."[54]

Three days later, Collins forwarded Nichols a copy of his contract with Biow, noting that he was to be paid $1,000 (equivalent to $13,500 in 2015) each week the show ran and reiterating his request for FBI authorization of and cooperation in the production of the program. "I simply wanted the Director and all of you to be familiar with the terms of the contract, in which I have done my best to protect the interests of all concerned," Collins stated. "I would, of course, be glad to have your criticisms and corrections on [the radio program] as soon as conveniently possible, as several most desirable sponsors are bidding for it."[55]

Five days later, after conferring with Tolson via phone, Nichols delivered bad news to Collins. Nichols understood the value of maintaining cordial business relationships with people like Collins, and he was far more diplomatic in his discussion with the author than Hoover or Tolson would likely have been. Not surprisingly, given the *Gang Busters* context of the request, the FBI refused to participate in the program. Nichols reported his conversation with Collins in a memorandum to Tolson: "I told him definitely the name of the FBI was not to be used, or any indication given which might give rise to the opinion that the Bureau had given its official approval of the program," Nichols added. "I pointed out that the title of the program ["This Is the FBI"] was likewise misleading, and it could not be used or any title that would give official Bureau approval." He then touched on the Bureau's frustration with Lord's program. "I told him also that we did not like the whole idea, it had a gang-buster approach and we could just not go along with him in any respect or phase of approving or cooperating with a radio series."[56]

With a lucrative contract depending on his relationship with the FBI, Collins did not give up. He forwarded a revised script to Nichols and Hoover. "I offer the enclosed script as a sample of what these first thirteen programs will be like, and I give you my word not to depart from this dignified formula," Collins said, noting that Biow had signed Procter & Gamble's Lava Soap as a sponsor. The sponsor had turned control of the show over to him, Collins added, and had "enthusiastically agreed that the best way to make the program a huge success is to differentiate it as much as possible from the crime programs now on the air by substituting FBI atmosphere and technical skill for the usual blood and thunder." The first broadcast was set for late November, he said. "Since radio time is at such a premium—good time, I mean—I should like to accept this offer at the earliest possible moment, but not, of course, until I have heard definitely from you or Louis."[57]

Again, Nichols maintained his contact with Collins, characteristically keeping lines of communication open. Nichols's successors as supervisor of Crime Records, men such as Cartha DeLoach or Thomas Bishop, would undoubtedly have cut Collins off immediately. In early October, Nichols called Collins again and reported the conversation in a memorandum to Tolson. Once more, the agent raised an objection to the "This Is the FBI" title, to which "[Collins] stated that since we would not approve 'This is the FBI' they would probably use the name of the book, 'The FBI in Peace and War.'"[58] Collins, by then clearly planning to proceed without the Bureau's blessing, asked if Hoover would "disown him" in that instance.[59] A few weeks later, a promotional item placed by the Biow agency appeared in the *New York Daily News*. According to the promotion, "This is the FBI, a dramatic series from the official files of the Federal Bureau of Investigation [redacted] bows over WEAX Saturday, November 25th." Nichols again spoke to Collins and then, as a pressure tactic, called an official at Procter & Gamble whose name was redacted in the file. "I told [redacted] that he, of course understood Collins was not authorized to speak for us, that we, of course had no control over the use of Collins' book, but that we were determined that the reputation of the Bureau should not be injured in any way by a radio program, regardless of who put it on."[60] In an aside to Tolson, Nichols noted that it would be difficult for Collins to stick to the material in his book: "There is not enough news in Collins' book to last for any long length of time, and he is going to find himself out on a limb."[61]

Collins's program, by then called *The FBI in Peace and War*, went on the air as scheduled in November without Hoover's blessing. After hearing nothing from the FBI in two months, Collins wrote to Nichols twice in late December. In one letter, on New York Hotel St. Regis letterhead, he took a conciliatory tone. "Frankly I had been a little hurt to receive no word from you at Christmas or any other time, especially as I knew that you had been in New York and had seen [redacted] and others without giving me a call," Collins wrote, ending with an offer to meet and discuss their differences.[62] In a second, undated letter bearing the same FBI file serial number, indicating it was part of the same series of correspondence, Collins was more defiant, citing the popularity of the program as a reason to avoid any changes. "We are up against a problem, however, that I think you should consider," he wrote. "Far from the lack of commendation that you report, we have been overwhelmed by commendatory mail not only from the usual radio listeners but from individuals of a very high class, the keynote of which is not only that it is an excellent program as it now stands, but that it is a much needed one."[63]

Collins claimed that Procter & Gamble was determined to make sure the public knew that *The FBI in Peace and War* was not an official FBI program. "The public is sick of official programs and films and is turning the dial and walking out all over the country," Collins said. "Moreover, the suspicion that it is an official propaganda program interferes with what is known as 'sponsor identification' and thus defeats the commercial effectiveness of the investment."[64] Nichols was unimpressed, describing the tone of Collins's December correspondence as "mealy-mouthed" in a memorandum to Tolson.[65] In his polite response to Collins, Nichols was unequivocal about what the FBI expected, and he even issued a subtle threat:

> The fact remains that so far nothing has been done to disassociate the FBI officially from the program, and everybody who hears the program feels that it is absolutely authentic. I was glad to hear of the success of the program, but I do think some consideration should be given to the FBI and as I told you yesterday, it will be incumbent upon you folks to take positive steps to insure that the listening audience disassociates the FBI from the program.[66]

The distancing of Collins's relationship with the FBI turned into a complete break with his next letter to Nichols. "Frankly, the tone of both letters puzzles me," he wrote, referring to Nichols's veiled threat of January 9 and to another letter reiterating the FBI's position that same week. "They would seem to be the letters of an angry and unreasonable man, which I know you, under normal circumstances, not to be."[67] Once again, Collins was defiant, citing his program's ratings in a handwritten note added to the letter: "The program has jumped another four points in the ratings as of this date."[68] Nichols responded by forwarding his January 9 letter to Collins's sponsor, Procter & Gamble, and to the Biow agency.[69] The act of forwarding his complaints to the two organizations paying Collins's $1,000 weekly salary could hardly be viewed as anything other than an attempt to intimidate him. Brought up to date on the situation, Hoover responded as if the FBI had no further options. "We might as well 'bring curtains down' on this controversy," he declared in a handwritten note. "However, after the 'run' of 13 weeks on this series, no one in future is to use name FBI in any presentation unless it is handled and supervised by us."[70] That declaration restated the public relations policy of the FBI, created by Nichols, that was scrupulously adhered to even after Hoover's death in 1972.[71]

In a memorandum to Tolson, Nichols summarized yet another phone call between himself and Collins, who clearly was becoming desperate to renew his relationship with the FBI. Collins told Nichols "he had come to the conclusion that he was not very successful in acting as an intermediary," Nichols reported. "To this I replied that frankly we were pretty much fed up with the radio program. . . . Collins stated that he frankly would like to go back to Cape Cod, that he could make more money writing than he could trying to run the radio program."[72] Their next phone conversation, on February 2, 1945, reflected the pressure Collins was feeling from his sponsors, who themselves were being pressured by the FBI. "Collins . . . in a very confidential-like manner, asked why we couldn't deal like we used to deal and why couldn't I call him on the phone and tell him what to do and what not to do in order to give him guidance," Nichols reported. "I told him that what he did with his book, of course, was none of our business."[73] Again, Nichols did not cut off Collins completely but maintained contact.

As with *Gang Busters*, complaints about Collins's show quickly began arriving at FBI headquarters. A writer whose name has been redacted urged Hoover to take the show off the air: "Last week's program, dealing with juvenile delinquency, made it seem that the FBI was helpless to do anything on its own account about young criminals." In a handwritten note on the letter, Hoover told his correspondence team to tell the letter writer the FBI had no connection to the program and then added, ominously, "We should write to the sponsors."[74] One special agent was mocked by Utica, New York, police officers, who greeted him by saying, "Here comes the soap salesman," referring to Lava Soap, the sponsor of *The FBI in Peace and War*.[75] Even when a letter writer praised the program as a positive influence on young people, he received a terse denial of involvement from Hoover, via Nichols's correspondence staff. "The fact of the matter is that the FBI has not given its cooperation or approval at any stage in this series of broadcasts, and as a result of the protests which has [sic] come to our attention, it was necessary for

Producer Jerry Devine (left), Louis B. Nichols, producer Jack Warwick, and producer Lee Meyers with Hoover in his office. Devine wrote and produced the authorized This Is Your FBI *radio program. (National Archives at College Park, Md., Record Group 65, Series H, Box 16, Folder 1060, #1.)*

the FBI to insist upon a disclaimer clause being made during each broadcast to the effect that the program is not sponsored by the FBI."[76]

The ongoing success of *Gang Busters* and the emerging success of *The FBI in Peace and War* represented a significant challenge to efforts made by both Nichols and Hoover to control the Bureau's public image. Rather than reinforcing the restrained, scientific FBI image the director preferred, the shows presented crime stories focused on the romanticized and sensational exploits of criminals whose capture came as the result of sometimes intrusive and overzealous investigations by local police or federal agents.

The success of the two unauthorized programs was undeniable, and the temptation for the FBI to assert control and capitalize on its own reputation proved irresistible. By mid-February 1945, Nichols was finalizing plans for the Bureau's own competing radio drama, *This Is Your FBI*, sponsored by the

Equitable Life Assurance Society of America and airing on the ABC radio network.[77] Nichols warned his colleagues to anticipate "some rather violent repercussions" from Collins, in part because the proposed title of the Bureau's program was so close to the original title he had proposed in 1944 ("This Is the FBI"). "In the event they get too nasty, I would refer them to their ad in the February 17th issue of the Washington Star, wherein they advertise the program as 'tense, exciting dramatizations of actual cases,'" Nichols wrote to Tolson. "They convey the impression by their advertising that it is an FBI sponsored program; contrary to [Collins's] promises, both orally and in writing."[78]

The rationale for the authorized program was detailed in an internal FBI memorandum intended for distribution to special agents in charge around the country who would become local promoters, touting the program to opinion shapers in their regions. "The radio program will be one hundred per cent [*sic*] entertainment," the memorandum's author (almost certainly Nichols) stated. "The educational points will be made by dramatic incident so that the listener will suddenly realize that the incident portrayed could effect [*sic*] him, or he could be guided by a lesson."[79] Further, the memo's author explained, "unlike other radio programs, this program will emphasize the FBI's work and not the work of criminals."[80] The best type of cases to dramatize in the program, according to the memorandum's author, were those where a crime was committed and the FBI was called in by local authorities, starting the investigation with little or no information. Those sorts of cases would best demonstrate the Bureau's methods. The memo then outlined the information to be provided to producers and writers, including the statement of a theme, a synopsis of the action, a detailed outline, and descriptions of the principle characters.[81] Whereas the FBI's involvement in other radio programs ended with the provision of case information (as with *Gang Busters*) or in the provision of assistance with a book upon which the program was based (*The FBI in Peace and War*), the new show, *This Is Your FBI*, would be a creative partnership between producers and Bureau officials in which Nichols, Tolson, and Hoover maintained complete control over content.

This Is Your FBI premiered on ABC on April 6, 1945, and though it reflected FBI policies and generated solid ratings, it only increased public confusion about the Bureau's role in the competing crime dramas. A column in William Randolph Hearst's *San Francisco Chronicle* was headlined TWO PROGRAMS ABOUT THE FBI—WHICH IS THE OFFICIAL ONE? and exemplified the confusion. The columnist's name was redacted in the FBI file, but the article was likely authored by Pulitzer Prize–winner Herb Caen. In his piece, the columnist presented "a letter to J. Edgar Hoover" asking about the programs, which seemed very similar:

> Both speak with authority. Both seem to advance the views of your department with equal impunity. Both give evidence of ready access to your files. What I want to know, Mr. Hoover, is this, do [*sic*] either of them bear the unqualified seal of approval of the FBI? And if one is so favored, and not the other, which one should we listen to if we want the cold dope on the methods used by your men in tracking down our public enemies? . . . One program is true to the FBI and one is not, or both are true, or neither is true. I am relatively certain the listeners themselves would be deeply grateful for any light you might be able to shed on this problem.[82]

In addition to public confusion, the addition of a third highly rated crime drama to the airwaves produced a new round of complaints by individuals and organizations that believed the shows' action-packed dramatizations promoted crime among young people. The complaints became significant enough that in 1947, Hoover (in a letter likely authored by Nichols) wrote Attorney General Thomas C. Clark to explain how *This Is Your FBI* was different. Hoover summarized the "broad argument" opponents made about the detrimental impact of crime dramas on children and then launched into his defense of the FBI's authorized program as a public service:

> I feel, however, that the program "This [I]s Your FBI," is different. It is produced for the avowed purpose of illustrating the responsibility and the duty of law enforcement in protecting society, showing how citizens may best cooperate with law enforcement, illustrating the need of crime preventive measures and of combatting juvenile delinquency, portraying lawlessness in its proper light, illustrating how law enforcement can best be effective and pointing out how citizens may protect themselves from crime.[83]

In June 1947, the American Bar Association (ABA) Committee on Motion Pictures, Radio Broadcasting and Comics in Relation to the Administration of Justice met in Washington, D.C. Chairman Arthur J. Freund defined a two-part problem with entertainment portrayals of crime and criminals, including both the depictions of the legal process itself and "the emphasis placed by the media upon the depiction of crime and the portrayal of the manner in which crimes of violence were committed, detected, and prosecuted."[84] That declaration was followed by the announcement, at the American Bar Association national meeting in Cleveland in September 1947, of a proposed National Association of Broadcasters (NAB) policy, part of a new comprehensive code of conduct for broadcasters; it stated that "the vivid, living portrayal of crime has an impact on the juvenile, adolescent or impressionable mentality that cannot be underestimated."[85] That same month, NAB members approved the new code of standards, including a prohibition on crime programs starting before 9:30 p.m. One network, NBC, quickly pledged to adhere to the 9:30 p.m. standard,[86] but ABC president Mark Woods described NBC's move as "hokum" because the network had not scheduled any crime programming before 9:30 p.m. prior to announcing its ban.[87]

Subsequent media coverage highlighting concerns about crime programming prompted Woods to write to Hoover requesting a statement "which we may release to the newspapers, to the effect that you consider 'This [I]s Your FBI' a vital force in combatting crime in the United States and that, in your opinion, you think it desirable that it be broadcast at an hour when maximum listening is available."[88] Hoover responded three days later with a statement written by Nichols declaring the FBI's program was, in contrast to others, educational and essential to maintaining law and order. "The emphasis [on *This Is Your FBI*] has always been placed on realism and the problems confronting all law enforcement as well as the FBI," Hoover wrote. "The criminal is always portrayed in his true light and in this, I think, there is a real object lesson, the lesson that decency and adherence to law and order are the only way."[89] Hoover's statement appeared in an ABC news release on October 7, 1944.[90]

When Freund contacted the attorney general to complain about the FBI's participation in an authorized radio crime program, Nichols's Crime Records staff compiled a four-page memorandum refuting Freund's charges as applying only to programs such as *Gang Busters* and *The FBI in Peace and War*. "The crime shows, in my opinion, which cause the harm are those which are unsupervised and which are portrayed in an unrealistic manner," Hoover asserted in a memo to a Justice Department public information officer.[91] He did not note the fact that producers of both *Gang Busters* and *The*

FBI in Peace and War had repeatedly requested FBI supervision and participation in their productions but had been rebuffed.

Freund's crusade against crime shows continued when he singled out *This Is Your FBI* for criticism at the 1949 American Bar Association meeting in his hometown, St. Louis. In his remarks, he cited *Gang Busters* as "one of the most evil of radio programs because of its blueprinting of crime," then he added that *This Is Your FBI* was "quite as offensive in so far as it educates youths in the methods of crime."[92] Nichols, tipped off to Freund's intentions, was at the meeting that day and defended the FBI. "We believe that law enforcement must be properly portrayed if it is to counteract the effects of some of the more harmful types of programs," he said. "I challenge any fairminded [*sic*] observer to find a 'blueprint' of crime in any program of 'This [I]s Your FBI.'"[93]

Despite painstaking efforts to distinguish *This Is Your FBI* from other crime dramas, even FBI agents became confused at times. In November 1947, for example, the SAC of the Los Angeles office, apparently unaware of the Bureau's position on *The FBI in Peace and War*, forwarded a request that he be allowed to promote the program on the air. "Under no consideration should we have anything to do with any advertising except to interpose objection to the use of the name of FBI," Hoover replied.[94] Nevertheless, *This Is Your FBI* remained on the air under Equitable's sponsorship until January 30, 1953. *Gang Busters* bounced from network to network, airing on NBC, CBS (two separate runs), NBC Blue, and the Mutual Broadcasting System. The program was shown almost continually from 1936 until 1957. Collins's *FBI in Peace and War*, which had aroused the most disdain within the FBI, actually outlasted the others, airing on CBS from November 25, 1944, until September 28, 1958.

The long-running saga of FBI disdain for radio crime dramas shows Nichols's unique skills at work. From the beginning of his career leading FBI public relations, Nichols developed a network of opinion shapers drawn from a broad spectrum of society. When former collaborators Lord and Collins stepped out of line with the Bureau's control policies, they were cut off from FBI information—but Nichols maintained the relationships nonetheless. He understood the strategic value that existed even in contentious relationships. For him, the relationships of public "relations" were less contingent on cooperation than they would be under subsequent generations of Hoover's PR men. When it came time to answer off-message portrayals of the FBI, Nichols's relationships with potential sponsors and radio networks quickly yielded a competing radio program, its content entirely controlled by the Bureau.

Nichols's value to Hoover and the Bureau, however, extended beyond his work with the news and entertainment media. It extended as well to government relations, where Nichols was similarly successful as the Bureau's primary liaison to members of Congress and other government officials. In 1946, for instance, several appalling incidents of racial violence and intimidation, many including African American World War II veterans, prompted President Harry Truman to issue an executive order establishing a committee to investigate civil rights. In February 1946, what was described as a race riot but was actually an orgy of white violence against African Americans in Columbia, Tennessee, was sparked by a disagreement over the price of repairs on a broken radio. In July, four African Americans, two married couples, were murdered by a lynch mob in Monroe County, Georgia. One of the two men, a World War II veteran, had bailed the other man, accused of a stabbing, out of jail. On their way home from the jail, the men and their wives were grabbed by the mob, tied to trees, and shot sixty times. The wives, who were sisters (one was pregnant), were killed because one of them recognized a member of the mob.[95] Georgia governor Eugene Talmadge had allegedly offered immunity to anyone who lynched the African American charged with the stabbing that prompted the mob violence.[96] The FBI investigated the murders, compiling a file of more than 3,000 pages on the case, but no one was charged in the brutal murders.[97] Announcing the civil rights committee, Truman said that the federal government was hampered by poor civil rights statutes and that the government had "the duty to act when state or local authorities abridge or fail to protect these constitutional rights."[98]

Hoover and the FBI had not, by 1946, made civil rights investigations a particular priority. For more than a decade since its authority and jurisdiction was expanded by Congress in 1934, the Bureau routinely inserted itself into local criminal cases where its own officials had determined that a possible federal violation had occurred. In bank robberies, kidnappings, and other lower-profile cases, the Bureau made its own judgment about whether to investigate rather than waiting for orders from the Department of Justice, ostensibly the FBI's supervising agency. On civil rights cases, however, the FBI self-righteously deferred to the Department of Justice, awaiting orders from the civil rights division there before entering into investigations.[99] The selective acceptance of Justice Department supervision can only be interpreted as an indication of Hoover's priorities. Civil rights investigations were not a priority in his FBI in 1946. Thus, the President's Committee on Civil Rights posed a significant threat to public perceptions of the Bureau's work. As in many instances when a complex outside entity held the potential to embarrass the FBI, Hoover turned the day-to-day management of the agency's interaction with the committee over to Nichols.

Nichols had already established relationships with several committee members, among them the chairman, General Electric chief executive officer (CEO) Charles E. Wilson, and committee members Charles Luckman, an architect turned president of Lever Brothers, makers of toothpaste and soap; Morris Ernst, a New York attorney and ACLU general counsel; Francis P. Matthews, national director of the Chamber of Commerce; and Franklin D. Roosevelt, Jr. Others on the committee were less likely to be sympathetic to the FBI, including Dartmouth president John S. Dickey; University of North Carolina president Frank P. Graham; labor leaders James B. Carey and Boris Shishkin; attorney Sadie T. Alexander, the first African American woman in the United States to earn a PhD; civil rights activist Channing Tobias; anti-lynching activist Dorothy Tilly; Episcopal bishop Henry Knox Sherrill; Rabbi Roland B. Gittelsohn; and Catholic bishop Francis J. Haas. Dartmouth civil rights scholar Robert K. Carr was selected as executive secretary of the committee.

The first indication that the committee would be turning some of its attention to the FBI came in March 1947 when Hoover was invited to testify in a closed session.[100] Prior to the questioning, he read a statement, no doubt authored and approved by Nichols's Crime Records staff, in which he asserted the Bureau struggled in civil rights investigations because it was stonewalled in southern communities, was hamstrung by weak federal laws, and could not trust local police officials. Hoover claimed that after World War II, the Bureau was deluged with requests from "patriotic groups" that wanted to help root out subversion in the country; he stated that he "tenaciously resisted that request" in order to protect civil liberties.[101] In fact, Hoover had agreed to work with the American Legion, establishing the American Legion Contact Program (ALCP)—a massive, nationwide network of "patriotic" informers. Hoover further bolstered his civil liberties bona fides by quoting ACLU chairman Roger Baldwin, and then he turned to the Bureau's civil rights investigation successes. Ignoring the FBI's policy of selective deferral to Department of Justice guidelines, Hoover claimed that the slow pace of decisions in the DOJ's Civil Rights Section hampered the FBI's investigations in civil rights cases. "The delay of even a day or a week can be fatal to an investigation," he told the committee. "If we had to wait, for instance, in a kidnapping until the matter could get reviewed by a group of lawyers in Washington, by the time we got to the place of the kidnapping there might be a delay of a week, and fingerprints and all those things have disappeared."[102]

Finally, in response to questions from Carr, Hoover misleadingly claimed there were "a number" of African American FBI agents. "We have," he stated, "utilized the Negro agents to great value in the metropolitan areas; they have been doing excellent work. In Los Angeles we have agents who have done excellent pieces of work there."[103] Hoover was likely referring to paid FBI informants, clerks, and typists rather than actual agents, a distinction he would have typically insisted upon. There were no African American FBI field agents during Hoover's forty-eight-year tenure. (His limousine driver was given the title of special agent but had no investigative responsibilities.) Later, under questioning, Hoover again emphasized the work of African American agents and the egalitarian nature of the Bureau's workforce. "So far as the Bureau is concerned there is no problem involved because colored agents in our large metropolitan offices are respected and accepted just like any other agent is respected," he said.[104] Three times during his testimony, Hoover's request to testify off the record was granted by Carr. All three instances were in response to questions about working with local police.

In April, Turner Smith, head of the Department of Justice's Civil Rights Section, noted that there was no specific policy stopping the FBI from investigating possible civil rights violations. Further, there was no requirement that the Bureau wait for DOJ approval before starting civil rights investigations, he pointed out. "Mr. Smith stated that so far as the Department was concerned, if the Bureau desired to go into these cases without obtaining clearance, it had no objection," J. C. Strickland, who spoke to Smith, reported to D. M. "Mickey" Ladd. Smith told Strickland it was the FBI, not the DOJ, that initiated the Bureau's practice of staying out of civil rights cases until ordered to investigate. "[Smith] was of the opinion that the Bureau preferred to have the matters cleared with the Department before starting investigation," Strickland reported.[105] He left little doubt that it was Hoover's preference to steer clear of racially charged civil rights investigations despite his claims to the Committee on Civil Rights. At the same time, the Department of Justice had shown no interest in expediting its decision-making process. Neither organization had distinguished itself with its work on civil rights cases.

As far as Hoover and Nichols were concerned, the director's testimony had inoculated the FBI from serious criticism by the committee. They were mistaken. On September 10, 1947, the Bureau obtained a draft copy of the committee's report, and Nichols and Ladd were immediately pressed into action. Ladd was assistant director in charge of the Security Division, which later became known as the Domestic Intelligence Division. A North Dakota native and the son of a US senator, he had joined the Bureau in 1928.[106]

Ladd analyzed the report, and Nichols wrote a letter from Hoover to Wilson objecting to several of the report's anecdotes and conclusions involving the FBI. The Bureau specifically objected to the conclusion that "FBI investigations in Civil Rights matters sometimes do not measure up to the Bureau's high standard of work in other areas." The report also concluded that "a number of [FBI] case files disclosed superficial or un-intelligent work by particular FBI agents." Two examples were cited to support those conclusions. In one, an FBI agent learned of the disappearance of an African American man who was later found dead, yet the agent did not inform the Department of Justice. In another case, it was claimed that in the Bureau's investigation of an alleged incident of police brutality, the sheriff-suspect was included in interviews with witnesses, intimidating them into silence.[107] Those mild criticisms were enough to spark a near-hysterical response from the FBI, in which Nichols led the effort to alter the committee's draft before its final release.

In a letter authored by Nichols, Hoover complained to Wilson, stating, "I was extremely surprised to note this criticism because when I appeared before your Committee, no member thereof questioned me as to the specific instances upon which the criticism of the Committee is based." He continued by criticizing members of the committee: "I know from experience that there are many individuals, some well meaning but misinformed and others with more sinister purposes, who have made charges against the Federal Bureau of Investigation, which charges when thoroughly investigated have been found to be completely unsubstantiated."[108]

Wilson called to speak to Hoover, but his call was directed to Nichols, who subsequently reported on the conversation in a memorandum to Tolson. Wilson told Nichols he was "concerned [to] no end" by the critical language in the draft report, and he suggested that the FBI review the same Department of Justice records that committee investigators had seen. Wilson, very reasonably, also suggested that the FBI might not agree with the interpretations made by the investigators. According to Nichols, Wilson "stated he was further concerned with that section of the Director's letter which referred to individuals criticizing the Bureau having sinister purposes."[109] Wilson indicated that he felt the section of criticism was innocuous and that Carr had already "tried to tone down" the report; in addition, he said he personally supported the FBI's position that obstacles outside its control had impeded civil rights investigations.[110] Hoover, however, did not feel the criticism was innocuous. In a handwritten note, he made clear the Bureau's position in opposition to the report: "Their attitude is amazing particularly for a Committee which makes a fetish of fairness & tolerance & yet when it will serve the purpose of some left-wingers they cast all conception of fairness away."[111] Whereas Ladd's initial memorandum outlined the mild criticism of the Bureau in the draft report, Nichols's letter was more pointed and reflected Hoover's personal feelings as expressed in his handwritten note. Parroting the tone of the director's reactions to events was a vital skill required for success in the FBI.

On the same day he spoke to Wilson, Nichols called on Carr at the committee's temporary offices in Washington. His goal was to identify specifics about the two incidents of poor investigative tactics cited in the draft report. "[Carr] impressed me as being a little bit on the dopey side," Nichols reported. Carr was clearly circumspect in his dealings with Nichols, deferring a response until after he was able to consult with Wilson. When Nichols pressed Carr to give him the information or to speak to his investigators to find out, Carr "happened to remember that he had been called out of a committee meeting in his office and stated that at the time he would not have time to do so but he would check the facts."[112] Nichols's networking paid dividends a few days later when Peyton Ford, assistant attorney general in charge of the Civil Division, reported that the committee's deliberations about the FBI criticism had been divisive, with Charles Luckman rising in "righteous indignation" to make a thirty-minute speech denouncing that section of the report.[113] There is no record in available FBI files that Nichols spoke to Luckman, but it seems highly likely that he did so, prepping the Bureau's friend "Charley" to denounce the report in the committee hearing. Nichols did meet with committee investigators Nancy Wechsler and Charles Whiting on September 12. Wechsler (whom Nichols identified as the wife of journalist James A. Wechsler, a frequent FBI critic) and Whiting provided the information Nichols sought. With the case specifics identified, Nichols then set out to determine whether the charges were true.

The instance cited in the report as a failure of an FBI agent to report a possible racial murder involved the murder of Sam McFadden in Jacksonville, Florida, in 1945. McFadden was murdered by a law enforcement officer, Tom Crews, who was later convicted in federal court after a local grand jury refused to issue an indictment. McFadden had been arrested and beaten by Crews in "June or July 1945" and was reported missing on September 21, 1945. His body was found a month later, on October 29. The local FBI agent was instructed by the Department of Justice to investigate on November 30, but no investigative report was filed until January 8, 1946.[114] Nichols told Tolson that the FBI was "weakest in our defense on this one."[115] The second instance cited in the committee's report involved an allegation of police brutality. In 1945, an FBI agent investigating allegations against Sheriff Willis McCall in Leesburg, Florida, allowed the local chief of police, Floyd R. Morgan, to participate in the questioning of the alleged victim. The agent claimed there was no evidence that Morgan "was known to entertain racial prejudices."[116] Apparently, it did not occur to the agent that the presence of a local policeman might cause the alleged victim of police brutality (albeit by the local sheriff) to feel intimidated. The analysis provided to Nichols by the Crime Records staff concluded that "the actions of the Agent in accepting the invitation of the Chief of Police and not 'the Sheriff-suspect' appear reasonable and do not appear subject to criticism in this case."[117] Even Hoover could see through that claim. "I think it is bad policy to have local officers accompany our agent in such cases," he wrote on Nichols's memorandum. "If a witness [to the questioning] is necessary then 2 agts should be sent."[118] Tolson, also tacitly admitting the Bureau's defense in both cases was weak, suggested that Nichols and Ladd speak to Turner Smith of the Civil Rights Section and get him to make a statement "that [the section] approved the Bureau's work in these cases."[119]

The fact that the report's authors, charged with investigating civil rights enforcement rather than defending the FBI's public relations image, might simply have interpreted the same set of facts differently did not seem to occur to Hoover, Nichols, Ladd, and Tolson or to Peyton Ford of the DOJ or to Hoover's defenders on the civil rights committee. For the FBI, there was only one interpretation of the facts, and that was that they were exculpatory. The truth was that an FBI agent had included a local police officer in the questioning of an alleged victim of brutality perpetrated by a sheriff. The Bureau's official interpretation of that choice was that it was reasonable. Likewise, the FBI and the Department of Justice had delayed investigating the murder of a black man by a police officer. The Bureau's position in that case was that it was the DOJ that caused the delay. The judgment of the committee investigators was that those two instances portrayed unintelligent and superficial investigation by the FBI—a judgment that Hoover would not allow to stand without a battle.

Nichols made sure that a copy of the Bureau's explanatory statement was provided to the committee chairman and FBI ally, Wilson.[120] A few weeks later, as the divided committee (with Wilson, Luckman, and Ernst as the FBI's most outspoken champions) struggled to reach a compromise, Nichols called Wilson. Afterward, Nichols reported to Tolson that Wilson had said "he hoped the Director realized that the Committee for practical purposes was a committee of minorities." Further, Wilson said that he, Luckman, and Ernst were "the only three who can agree and there has been a constant fight among all the others; that personally he thought that if he had his way he would take the whole section pertaining to the Bureau out of the report."[121] Wilson argued that 90 percent of the objectionable material had been removed and that the remaining critical material was "offset by a ton of honey." Nichols countered with some FBI boilerplate, ignoring the Bureau's own analysis that showed the committee had most of the facts correct and simply disagreed in its interpretation of them: "If the Bureau was at fault we frankly would expect them to criticize us, but we did not want to be criticized for something we didn't do,"[122] Nichols said.

Under pressure from a top Bureau official, Wilson backpedaled. Previously, he had felt that most of the objectionable material had been removed, but he was "now convinced that the report was not too honest and that he would call Mr. Carr immediately and make Carr put up specific facts."[123] Nichols promised Wilson that the Bureau "would vigorously fight for that which is true."[124]

That fight included direct attacks on the committee's staff. In July, Assistant Attorney General Theron L. Caudle requested FBI file checks on five committee staff members, among them Nancy Wechsler.[125] The resulting memorandum, which was not turned over to Carr or Wilson, was forwarded to the DOJ on August 25, 1947. Wechsler was the only staff member found to have had a past connection to any subversive organizations. She and her husband, James, had briefly been members of the Young Communists League (YCL) during college in the 1930s. Both left the YCL after one year, and both renounced communism; in fact, James Wechsler became an extremely outspoken anticommunist journalist. That information had apparently languished in DOJ files. As the Bureau's frustration with the mild criticism contained in the committee report grew, Nichols and Tolson decided to use the information to pressure the committee. On September 29, Tolson authored a letter for Hoover's signature in which he shared the information about Nancy and James Wechsler's YCL membership with Wilson.[126] Nancy Wechsler was fired that same day.

The threat to the committee's public reputation was not lost on Wilson, who told Nichols that "he hoped that nothing leaked out about this."[127] Nichols claimed that Hoover had "frankly debated whether to send the letter to Wilson for fear that he, Mr. Wilson, might entertain a thought that this was a subtle attack on the report since Mrs. Wechsler had reviewed files in the Department of Justice."[128] Nichols noted that "the Director had finally come to the conclusion that he would be unfair to Mr. Wilson not to call this information to his attention because sooner or later some southern Congressman who might take exception to the report would find out about Mrs. Wechsler and would subject Mr. Wilson to attack. Wilson said he certainly appreciated this."[129] The October 3 conversation with Wilson showed Nichols at the peak of his skills as a persuader, tacking back and forth, refusing to compromise, and ultimately commiserating with and threatening the CEO of General Electric. Eight days after his conversation with Wilson, the committee met in New York and agreed to significant revisions in the few paragraphs criticizing the FBI.[130] Nichols reported to Tolson that the changes had been "adequately taken care of."[131]

The final report still contained mild criticism of the Bureau, however, and recommended that the FBI create a civil rights squad of agents specially trained to handle the complexities of civil rights investigations. When a publicist assigned to coordinate Wilson's appearances promoting the report called Nichols to ask if Hoover would appear with Wilson, he was not so gently rebuffed. Nichols told the publicist that Hoover was too busy and that "in view of the shabby treatment of the Bureau they might not want the Director [to participate]."[132] Hoover added a handwritten note to the memorandum: "I want nothing to do with or for this lousy outfit. It is steeped with intolerants, subversives & outright liars."[133]

The recommendation that the Bureau create a special civil rights squad captured the imagination of New York Democratic congressman Emanuel Celler, who wrote to Hoover asking if he could sponsor a bill to that effect. Hoover was not interested, claiming that all FBI agents were well trained in civil rights investigations. "Tell him we already have it & had it at the time the recommendation was made," he said, "but the committee never checked to ascertain the facts."[134] In December, a Truman aide named George Washington contacted the Bureau requesting language for the president's State of the Union address regarding progress in setting up the civil rights squad in the FBI. The aide was told that "in the light of all the circumstances the Bureau was opposed to any untrue statement relating to increased coverage because of our sincere belief that the Bureau had been doing an efficient and effective job within its jurisdiction prior to the time the Committee was set up."[135] And finally, in August 1949, the Library of Congress contacted Nichols to ask about the status of the special squad. As Nichols told Tolson, he "explained that all Agents are trained in handling civil rights investigations."[136] Again, Nichols's network had spared the FBI significant (and well-deserved) embarrassment. In addition, the incident displayed Nichols's ruthless side. Even as he pressured the Bureau's friends on the committee to push for revisions, he acted as a hit man, delivering information from FBI files that led to the resignation of Nancy Wechsler, a committee staff member considered hostile to the Bureau.

Even as he maintained control of high-level relationships with Congress and the media, Nichols was also called upon to manage local or regional controversies that carried the potential to embarrass the FBI or its strategic allies. In late 1953, at the height of McCarthyism and the pinnacle of the reign of terror of the House Un-American Activities Committee (HUAC), a minor controversy erupted in Cincinnati that obliquely involved the FBI but became potentially threatening to the Bureau when it expanded to include a key member of Congress. Three Cincinnati municipal officials had been forced out by the city council. The moves were based on information that City Planning director Sydney Williams had, in 1945, attended a Marxist study group in San Francisco. Williams resigned, and two members of the City Planning Commission, Henry Bettman and Wallace Collett, were accused of disloyalty and publicly disgraced. Bettman and Collett, citizens serving on the committee, eventually resigned not because they were accused of affiliations with communist organizations but because they knew about Williams's 1945 transgression and failed to let other committee members know.[137]

First-term congressman Gordon H. Scherer, an FBI ally and an acquaintance of Nichols, was a Cincinnati Republican and a member of the HUAC. He became embroiled in the controversy after he was accused of providing city officials with FBI reports that led to the resignations. Under siege from members of the Charter Party, a local third-party organization founded in the 1920s by Republican reformers, Scherer asked the FBI to issue a statement denying it had provided the information to him. Through its top public relations official, Louis Nichols, the Bureau refused to comment publicly on the situation.[138] To do so would be to confirm one of the key elements of critics' suspicions about the Bureau—namely, that it maintained files of political intelligence and used those files to discredit or undermine public officials. The notion that Hoover could reach into city government in Cincinnati of all places and rearrange the chess pieces there would, in some ways, be a stronger indictment of the Bureau than a higher-profile incident of political intrusion. The Bureau, after all, presented itself as only a reluctant participant in local issues. The idea that it actively involved itself in the politics of a city council in the heart of the Midwest actually held enormous potential to embarrass the agency and unmask its work in political and domestic intelligence.

The FBI first learned of the controversy when a local Charterite political party official contacted Robert Wick, Nichols's top deputy, and asked whether the Bureau might have provided derogatory information about Williams to City Manager Wilbur R. Kellogg. Wick reported that he was caught off guard by the local official's questions and answered with Bureau boilerplate, stating that "FBI files are confidential and available for official use only. . . . The FBI is not empowered to make FBI investigative reports available to city officials."[139] In a handwritten note on Nichols's memorandum recounting the case, Hoover said he wished Crime Records staff would simply say nothing. "I can't understand why Wick or anyone else must reply to every ragtag who calls up & asks obviously 'loaded' questions," he said. When Nichols recommended that he call Frank and clarify the situation (by blaming the release on Scherer), Tolson and Hoover wrote that they could see no way around Wick's unequivocal responses. "I shudder to think what Nichols will say," Hoover noted. "He & his whole staff suffer from diarrhea of the mouth."[140]

A few days later, the possibility of embarrassment for the FBI increased when Kellogg, a friend and political supporter of Scherer, announced that the agency had turned the information over to him, not to Scherer. In a memorandum discussing the case, Nichols demonstrated his masterful ability to reconcile a lie in order to maintain the Bureau's public image. "We, of course, had given [Kellogg] the information under a cooperative program worked out with the Governors a few years ago, and Kellog [sic] has simply violated a confidence," he told Tolson. "I do not propose to either confirm or deny that we furnished the information to Kellog, make any explanations whatsoever and will decline to issue any statements to the press to the effect that we did not give him the information." Instead, Nichols would let Kellogg take the heat: "My position will be that he knows we did not give him the information and he can say what he wants to."[141]

The provision of derogatory information about municipal employees was an extension of a program of bureaucratized McCarthyism—the Responsibility of the FBI in the Internal Security of the U.S. Program. The Responsibilities Program was originally established to provide state governors with the information they needed to purge communists from their administrations, but it was eventually expanded to include municipal and other levels of local government. On September 17, 1953, the Bureau's Cincinnati special agent in charge walked into Kellogg's office and handed him a one-page "blind" memorandum outlining the alleged communist connections of Sydney Williams and his wife. Kellogg made copies of the document, which was a violation of Bureau policy in regard to its blind memoranda—messages that contained derogatory information without indicating the FBI was the source. Kellogg then confronted Williams, who said he had told Collett and Bettman about the meeting he attended in 1945. The end result, in addition to costing Williams his job and Bettman and Collett their committee positions, became a political problem for both Kellogg and Scherer. "Scherer stated that the FBI, by stating that Bureau files are not made available to city officials, are in effect discrediting Kellogg," Nichols reported to Tolson. Scherer complained to Nichols that the Bureau's denial put him, a member of the HUAC, in the crosshairs as the likely source of the information, a charge that actually took the FBI off the hook for the disclosure. Ever the networker and cajoler, Nichols tried to take advantage of the situation, urging Scherer to lie and "admit" providing the information. "I then told him I thought he could take some pride in exposing the Communists," he wrote. "Scherer felt that we had an obligation, in good conscience, to state that we had furnished the information to Kellogg. . . . He stated this would be the only way the record could be cleared, it would be the truth, and to merely state it was not furnished to him (Scherer) would not be sufficient."[142] Nichols continued to give "no comment" responses to media questions.

On October 23, he explained to Deputy Attorney General William P. Rogers that the Bureau could not admit to providing the information because of the political costs and embarrassment that would result. If the agency admitted it provided the information, Nichols told Rogers, "every left-wing group in the country would not only be after us but would be after the Attorney General."[143] The controversy spilled over into the pages of the *Nation*, a left-leaning opinion magazine. In its November 28, 1953, issue, *Nation* editors assumed correctly that the FBI was the source of the information provided to the Cincinnati officials. "We don't know whether the F.B.I. simply volunteered the information," they wrote. "What we do know is that if the F.B.I. reports are hereafter going to be made available to Republicans in order to throw opponents out of office, or to discredit them, then this country has become a police state and its chief executive is not the President, but J. Edgar Hoover."

Luckily for Hoover and Nichols, the *Nation* was generally not seen as a particularly credible publication by mainstream, agenda-setting media such as the *New York Times*. The *Times*, with its vast power to set a news agenda that filtered across the country as if by osmosis, did not cover the Cincinnati controversy. Nichols's strategy of stonewalling the story—issuing no comment and working his network to neutralize the story behind the scenes—succeeded. The Cincinnati incident, with its outsized potential to confirm critics' fears and humiliate the FBI, was essentially kept local, and the embarrassment was confined to Scherer, who ultimately forgave Nichols and continued to be an outspoken defender of Hoover and the Bureau. In 1958, for example, he came to Hoover's defense during what the Bureau labeled a smear campaign that included critical comments from a wealthy industrialist, a subsequent critical article in the *Nation*, and another critical series on Hoover in the *New York Post*. "Can he [industrialist Cyrus Eaton] not see that the Federal Bureau of Investigation far from being a 'Hitler-like Gestapo'—as he describes it—is the principle bulwark of our liberties and the chief weapon of the nation against internal subversion?" Scherer asked a Hunter College audience on May 8, 1958. "There are those like Eaton and his sponsors who are giving aid and comfort to the enemy in this struggle, particularly when the [*sic*] attempt to discredit one of the greatest Americans of our time, J. Edgar Hoover, and the Federal Bureau of Investigation which he heads—our chief bulwark against infiltration and subversion which is the new and effective weapon of modern warfare."[144]

In addition to leveraging relationships with ideological allies, Nichols also cultivated relationships with the natural enemies of Hoover and the Bureau on the political Left. The FBI leveraged those kinds of relationships, for instance with ACLU general counsel Morris Ernst, to inoculate the Bureau from left-wing criticism. At about the same time Nichols was managing the

Cincinnati controversy, he began his courtship of a pair of left-leaning academics and authors, Harry and Bonaro Overstreet. The courtship and ultimately the co-opting of the Overstreets as liberal defenders of the FBI showcased Nichols's talents at their height. In order to build and maintain the Bureau's relationship with the Overstreets, he first had to convince Hoover and Tolson to accept them, and he had to defend the Overstreets from external attacks from the political Right, primarily from the FBI's allies in the American Legion. Nichols was unlike Hoover and Tolson in that he could genuinely imagine that a liberal academic like Harry Overstreet could become a sympathetic FBI defender. Later Crime Records supervisors such as Cartha DeLoach would show themselves much less open than Nichols to discussion with those labeled opponents of FBI orthodoxy. In the Overstreets, Nichols—the man who admired Hoover so much that he named a son after him—recognized the potential power of liberal insiders who were also anticommunist. No doubt, the model of ACLU counsel Morris Ernst, who became Hoover's mole in the liberal intellectual community, influenced Nichols's thinking. Although Ernst had credibility in legal circles, Nichols recognized that the Overstreets—academics with credibility in adult-education circles—could become powerful advocates for Hoover and the FBI among that typically skeptical crowd.

Nichols's first contact with the Overstreets came, in fact, as the result of their being blackballed by powerful right-wing groups, including an FBI ally, the American Legion's National Americanism Commission, and its local affiliates. After one of their frequent lectures was canceled because the organizers "discovered" their alleged communist ties, the Overstreets visited FBI headquarters in Washington, D.C., asking to see Hoover. Instead, they met with Nichols and made themselves available to him "for interrogation and cross-examination." Nichols advised them that the FBI did not "clear" anyone but said that he would be happy to place their statements in Bureau files.[145] Harry and Bonaro Overstreet were already established authors and experts on adult education when they visited Bureau headquarters in 1953. Harry Overstreet, by then a retired professor of psychology, was widely known as a popularizer of modern psychology and sociology. His book *The Mature Mind* was a best seller in 1949, with hundreds of thousands of copies sold. None other than Morris Ernst reviewed the book for the *Saturday Review* and declared that Overstreet "has garnered and presents in simple language some of the advances and new techniques developed in the fields of psychology and psychiatry for dealing with the interrelationships of individuals. . . . He fills the interstices with wise, temperate and calm observations."[146] Overstreet was born in San Francisco in 1875. Educated at the University of California and Oxford, he joined the faculty at City College of New York in 1911 and retired after his best-selling book was released. He married Bonaro Wilkinson in the 1930s, and together, they wrote a series of books, articles, and opinion pieces and made television and radio appearances from the 1950s until Harry's death. Bonaro Overstreet taught at Claremont College, the University of Michigan, and the University of California. She died in 1985.[147] Most of their work explored issues of adult education and parent-teacher relationships until the late 1950s, when they became outspoken anti-communists.[148]

After the meeting with Nichols in 1953, the Overstreets provided a lengthy statement on past affiliations to both the FBI and the House Un-American Activities Committee. In the statement, Harry Overstreet said he was not a communist nor a communist sympathizer, and he requested an opportunity to testify before the full HUAC. He said he and his wife had gotten themselves "tangled up" in organizations they now understood to be suspect. "It does not give me satisfaction, you may be sure, to feel that I have thus brought support to Communist causes or put innocent people on the spot," Overstreet wrote.[149] In his statement, he listed the organizations and explained his involvement in each of them. The "subversive" organizations the Overstreets had been affiliated with included the Consumers Union, the American Committee to Save Refugees, Friends of the Abraham Lincoln Brigade, and the National Federation for Constitutional Liberties.[150] Illinois Republican congressman Harold H. Velde, chairman of HUAC, wrote to Overstreet that his statement served to complete the committee's records—coded language that meant the Overstreets would not be called to testify.[151]

Despite their efforts to clear themselves, the Overstreets were frequently dogged by local American Legion officials when they arrived for speaking engagements. A Tucson speech in December 1953, for example, drew crowds of protesters after the local Legion published an advertisement, headlined AN OPEN LETTER, in the *Tucson Daily Citizen* listing their alleged connections to communist-affiliated groups and urging their host, the Tucson Mental Health Board, to cancel the appearance.[152] Another scheduled speech in Dallas was canceled after the local American Legion pressured organizers of a mental health conference.[153]

Even as the Legion disrupted their public appearances, Bonaro Overstreet maintained a frequent correspondence with Nichols. In December 1954,

Nichols wrote a memorandum to Tolson in which he attempted to clarify for Hoover and Tolson the Overstreets' anticommunist credentials. "There is no question in my mind but that if any one was ever duped through naievety [*sic*], it is the Overstreets and I think they are doing their utmost in trying to redeem themselves," Nichols told Tolson. "Certainly, in my opinion, such actions as that taken down in Dallas cannot help but hurt the anti-Communist fight among liberal-minded people, particularly if the Overstreets were the type (which they are not) for airing their treatment."[154] Nichols also ordered his top deputy, Cartha DeLoach, the Bureau's liaison to the Legion, to urge the organization to back off its criticism of the Overstreets. DeLoach met with Lee R. Pennington, a former FBI agent who was the executive director of the Legion's National Americanism Commission, and urged him to "lay low on the attacks against the Overstreets." DeLoach did not view the action as an effort to recruit the Overstreets as friends of the FBI but instead said that "such action on Pennington's part may have the effect of preventing the Overstreets from corresponding further relative to their problems."[155] DeLoach's preference for containment rather than recruitment would characterize much of his work after he succeeded Nichols as supervisor of Crime Records, public relations, and liaison in 1959.

After an April 1955 meeting with the Overstreets, Nichols reported that he had urged them to become the Bureau's "missionaries in the educational field," particularly within the American Association of University Professors (AAUP) professional association and labor union. Nichols told Tolson that "we have now developed a very potent friend and these people can be instrumentalities of great good."[156] About a month later, he met with them again and reported that the "old couple" agreed to launch a campaign within the AAUP. To prepare them for questions they would get from AAUP members, Nichols invited the Overstreets to dinner at his home, where they talked until early in the morning. "I really feel very enthusiastic about what these two folks can accomplish," he told Tolson.[157] His continued courtship of a controversial couple like the Overstreets, including multiple exchanges of letters and phone calls, meetings at FBI headquarters, and even dinner at his home, exemplified his approach to potentially valuable relationships. Whereas later Bureau public relations managers such as DeLoach were effective in many ways, they were not patient cajolers willing to work even with those from subversive "lists," as was Nichols. During their long postdinner conversation, Nichols even convinced the Overstreets that the Bureau's relationship with their intrusive nemesis, the American Legion, was harmless. "Don't worry too much about us and the Legion," Bonaro Overstreet told Nichols. "We hadn't known anything about that past and couldn't seem to avoid a certain sense of hurt about what appeared to be an inexplicable tie-up between FBI requests and Legion behaviors. But that's all disposed of now."[158]

Nichols's courtship of the Overstreets resulted in his long-term, close relationship with the "old couple." In October 1955, he even hosted Harry Overstreet's eightieth birthday party at his home. Bonaro Overstreet asked seventeen of her husband's friends, all liberal educators, to attend. Nichols listed their names in a memorandum to Tolson and asked that Assistant Director William Sullivan attend to help him persuade attendees of the FBI's goodwill. Nichols also made a joke that Sullivan would be his witness in case the party became "a subject of a Security of Government Employees investigation because of associations" made there.[159]

Hoover and Tolson, however, began to have doubts about the Bureau's budding relationship with the liberal Overstreets after another effort by antcommunists to portray them as possible subversives. The Overstreets were scheduled to speak to a Phoenix, Arizona, meeting of the Mental Health Institute in December 1955. Shortly before the meeting, a letter to the editor in a Phoenix newspaper, written by the wife of a prominent businessman, repeated the old charges regarding the Overstreets' affiliations with allegedly subversive groups. In her letter, Mrs. Verland M. Haldiman, the wife of a local insurance business owner, lumped the Overstreets with such "infamous names" as Communist Party USA chairman Earl Browder, British socialist Harold Laski, and Freda Kirchwey, editor of the left-wing political journal the *Nation*. "The bringing in of the Overstreets indicates a sad lack of information among the leaders of our community," she wrote.[160] Exacerbating the situation, local SAC Francis Crosby, acting on orders from Nichols, had lunch with the Overstreets, a fact that was reported in local newspapers. State senator Lottie Holman O'Neill of Arizona wrote Hoover to complain about Crosby's lunch, which she claimed allowed the FBI to be "drawn into the controversy" surrounding the Overstreets' visit.[161]

Tolson, always quick to cut off embarrassing controversies, urged a total break with the Overstreets. "I think we should have nothing more to do with these people," he wrote on a memorandum. "They are using us for their own benefit. Crosby should be alerted not to get further involved. They should not be introduced to other SACs."[162] Nichols pushed back against Tolson's recommendation, arguing there was clearly a potential benefit for the FBI in the relationship. "Their subsequent actions [after early affiliations with subversive groups] to any reasonable person would establish their true loyalties," Nichols, one of the few people in the Bureau who would stand up to Tolson, said in a memorandum. "Quite frankly, I have sought to use the Overstreets in the last couple of years in seeking to break down an antagonism which has developed against the Bureau in certain intellectual and academic circles. I frankly think we have been making some progress because wherever they go, they talk about the Bureau and there is no question but that they do have considerable following."[163] Hoover sided with Nichols, stating, "I am not taking a stand for or against them but I see nothing to be gained by being injected into such a turmoil as has arisen in Arizona."[164]

Instead of easing, though, the Arizona controversy intensified when local businessman Verland M. Haldiman, whose wife started the campaign against the Overstreets, wrote to Hoover and complained about Crosby's lunch. Haldiman charged that the Overstreets had taken advantage of the Bureau "in attempting to establish innocence by association."[165] The Bureau received perhaps a half dozen complaints from Phoenix area residents, hardly a torrent but enough to get Hoover's attention and enough to discourage Nichols. "I have lost my enthusiasm for this project," he wrote on a memorandum.[166] His expression of frustration with the situation, however, did not last, and when the Overstreets started publishing articles in support of the Bureau, his original goal of establishing a credible liberal voice in academe in support of the FBI began to be realized. In addition, the Overstreets provided inside information about the groups they had formerly been affiliated with, essentially acting as the Bureau's liberal moles within those organizations. In July 1956, they sent Nichols copies of a letter and mailing list for a petition drive to urge a grant of amnesty for Smith Act violators, accused of advocating the overthrow of the US government or of being members of a group that advocated such an action.[167] Nichols took that opportunity to urge them to write the organizers of the petition drive expressing their opposition and to make the letter public. "Perhaps we can start a little counter-propaganda in the right places," he told Tolson.[168] The Overstreets agreed, and Nichols helped them edit and publicize their draft letter to A. J. Muste, the organizer of the petition drive.[169]

The Overstreets penned a series of glowing reviews of journalist Don Whitehead's authorized history of the Bureau, *The FBI Story: A Report to the People*, which was conceived, written, and edited by the two-time Pulitzer Prize–winner in collaboration with Crime Records staff, a fact Whitehead denied in claiming it was an "objective" study of the Bureau. "It is not enough for us to learn [from Whitehead's book] that—in spite of all irresponsible, calculated, or anxious words to the contrary—the FBI is a very different kettle of fish from the Gestapo," the Overstreets wrote in the *Detroit Free Press*. "As working citizens, we need to know what Whitehead's book can teach us about the patterns of crime that have marred our national life in this century."[170] In addition to running in the *Detroit Free Press*, their reviews of Whitehead's authorized history appeared in education journals such as the *AAUP Bulletin, National Parent-Teacher*, and *Adult Leadership*.[171] Access to those kinds of publications was the payoff Nichols had hoped for when he convinced Hoover and Tolson and the American Legion that the Overstreets were not merely radical communists who should be dismissed and blacklisted. "I started urging them to take the offensive in the educational field," Nichols told Tolson. "This they have done in an excellent manner against considerable obstacles which they had to overcome."[172]

Even after Nichols left the FBI for a lucrative job with Schenley Industries in 1957, the Bureau's relationship with the Overstreets continued to pay dividends; Assistant Director Sullivan managed the relationship, and Nichols urged on the Overstreets from outside the Bureau. In 1959, the ever-petulant Tolson again tried to cut off the relationship when the Overstreets requested FBI help with a new book defending the FBI from its critics. "I am opposed," Tolson wrote on Sullivan's memorandum. "I think we have done enough for the Overstreets. We should concentrate on our work and problems."[173] Sullivan nevertheless continued to work with the couple. Nichols, still defending them from Legion attacks, publicly vouched for their anticommunist credentials.[174]

The biggest payoff for his efforts to promote the Overstreets inside the Bureau and defend them against threats from inside (Tolson) and outside (American Legion) in the 1950s came a dozen years after he retired from the FBI. In 1969, the Overstreets' comprehensive defense of Hoover and the FBI, *The FBI in Our Open Society*, was published by W. W. Norton. With Sullivan as ghost editor, the volume was both a recounting of Bureau history and a defense against several high-profile critics. Boasting chapter titles such as "Out of Communism's Lexicon" and "The Exploitive Adulators," *The FBI in Our Open Society* was an academic, analytical, and sometimes pedantic take on the same classic FBI history and themes that were covered journalistically by Whitehead. "Especially now that President Nixon has declared war on organized crime, it would be helpful to have a thoughtful, objective study of the F.B.I.," *New York Times* reviewer Charles L. Mee, Jr., wrote. "This volume comes nowhere near answering that need." Still, Sullivan and Hoover were very pleased that the book focused on the director as the leader of a scrupulously cautious, limited investigative agency and protector of civil liberties. According to Harry Overstreet's obituary in 1970, the reputation for liberalism that he and his wife once had "withered in recent years" after the publication of *The FBI in Our Open Society*, which one reviewer referred to as "an apologia" for J. Edgar Hoover. The transformation of Harry and Bonaro Overstreet from suspect liberals to reliable Bureau defenders demonstrated the effectiveness of Nichols's engagement efforts, which stood in stark contrast to the instincts for isolation favored by Hoover, Tolson, and to some extent Nichols's successor as the Bureau's most important public relations official, Deke DeLoach.

Nichols's surprising retirement from the Bureau at the age of fifty when he became eligible for a federal pension foreshadowed the early 1970s departures, also at preretirement ages, of several of Hoover's top advisers, including DeLoach and communism expert William Sullivan. Also intriguing is the amount of coverage given to Nichols's post-FBI career in his Bureau personnel file. Almost half of the more than 4,500-page file is devoted to communicating with Nichols and monitoring his activities after he left the FBI. On October 15, 1957, he wrote Hoover to inform him of his decision to retire, referencing a discussion he had had with the director on September 30. The circumstances of the conversation are not mentioned in the file, but it seems likely that their talk covered questions of personal health and family concerns. Nichols had been a tireless worker, and sixty-hour workweeks were not uncommon for him. In 1936, just two years after joining the Bureau and shortly after moving to the Washington Seat of Government, he had suffered what one supervisor described as a "breakdown" and was away from his job for months. The correspondence in his personnel file suggests that his 1936 health problems involved both physical symptoms and mental exhaustion.[175] Nichols reported that the breakdown had taught him a "rather bitter lesson," and he pledged to exercise more and eat better.[176] Photos of him in 1957 suggest that those changes had not been entirely successful. He remained overweight and still had a pallid complexion. Responding to Nichols's resignation in a statement likely written by the agent's successor, Gordon Nease, Hoover said of Nichols, "No one has ever given more unselfishly of his time and strength to the service of the Nation."[177] In his resignation letter, Nichols announced that his "future plans will be determined after a prolonged vacation."[178]

The wide variety of congratulatory retirement letters in his personnel file testifies to the breadth of his network. Fred Belen, chief counsel of the House Committee on Post Office and Civil Service, wrote with his congratulations.[179] Leslie C. Stratton, director of the nonprofit Theodore Roosevelt Association, thanked Nichols for his "loyalty and devotion" to the country.[180] American Bar Association president Charles S. Rhyne called Nichols a "great man."[181] Numerous newspaper editors, publishers, and reporters added their congratulations.[182] Democratic senator James Eastland of Mississippi, chairman of the Senate Judiciary Committee, wrote that he knew of no one in Washington who "did his job better" than Nichols.[183] One of Hoover's congressional enemies, Tennessee Democratic senator Estes Kefauver, stated coolly that he regretted Nichols's retirement.[184] Texas Democratic senator Lyndon B. Johnson wrote that Hoover was a "genius in selecting loyal, dedicated, able men to be his trusted advisors."[185] There were letters from Hollywood studio moguls, broadcasting executives, US Supreme Court justices, CEOs, and members of the clergy. Nichols's friend and sometime collaborator Rex Collier editorialized in the *Washington Star*: "That [Nichols] was able to walk the tightrope between national security and publicity without a tumble is a tribute to his intelligence, judgment, and tact."[186]

Yet Nichols's ultimate choice of employers in his post-FBI career no doubt caused a few FBI supporters to question his judgment. Just a month after writing his resignation letter, he became executive vice president of Schenley Industries, Inc., a massive liquor distillery and distribution company headed by ultraconservative chairman Lewis S. Rosenstiel. Nichols's job with Schenley Industries (at a reported salary of $100,000 a year plus a furnished apartment in Manhattan) raised eyebrows because of Rosenstiel's bootlegging past and alleged ties to organized crime, stemming in part from his company's quick and dramatic expansion after Prohibition was repealed in 1933.[187] "I went up and talked the matter over with Mr. Hoover, and left it solely up to him," Nichols said in an interview published in 1975. "I told him about the offers I had received, and it was Mr. Hoover who pretty much caused me to go with Mr. Lewis Rosenstiel at Schenley Industries . . . because Mr. Hoover thought that would be a greater challenge and it would be financially remunerating."[188] Although Rosenstiel always denied any business relationship with organized crime, Nichols testified before a New York state joint legislative committee on crime that Rosenstiel was "social friends" in the 1930s with several organized crime figures, including Joseph Linsey of Boston, Joseph Fusco of Chicago, and Robert Gould of Miami. Linsey and Fusco were associ-

Former FBI assistant director Louis B. Nichols (left) and his boss, businessman Lewis S. Rosenstiel, visit J. Edgar Hoover in his office on May 8, 1968. (National Archives at College Park, Md., Record Group 65, Series H, Box 45, Folder 2445, #2.)

ates of underworld leader Meyer Lansky. Other than that, Nichols testified, Rosenstiel "shunned any connection with the underworld like the plague."[189] Some of the charges against Rosenstiel were sparked by a dispute with his estranged ex-wife, Susan Rosenstiel, who dismissed Nichols's denials, remarking, "Once again, [Nichols] is doing Lewis Rosenstiel's dirty work."[190] She also later claimed to have seen J. Edgar Hoover dressed in drag, a claim that most historians have deemed almost certainly false.

Whenever charges that Rosenstiel had organized crime ties arose, news stories noted Nichols's former affiliation with Hoover and the FBI. In addition to the questions raised about Rosenstiel, Nichols was also criticized for using his FBI connections inappropriately. For example, in 1958, he used the contacts he had developed at the FBI to lobby Congress to adopt a bill that changed the excise tax code, saving Schenley between $40 million and $50 million.[191] Nichols told the New York legislative committee that he worked so hard for the passage of the changes that he suffered a heart attack but continued lobbying from his hospital bed.[192] William Sullivan, who was forced out of the Bureau after serving as the assistant to the director, the third-highest rank in the agency, believed that Hoover was angry with Nichols for using his FBI contacts in that way. "Hoover was furious, because when Nichols left he [Hoover] called for a list of Nichols' key contacts on the Hill and there was no such list," Sullivan said in an interview published in 1975. "Nichols kept them to himself. Nichols used the Bureau to promote himself and get himself a big job with Schenley."[193] There *is* evidence that the continual references to Nichols's former affiliation with the FBI annoyed Hoover. One example occurred in 1968 when Nichols was hired by the Nixon presidential campaign to monitor the election for voter fraud. Nichols told reporters he would personally head a "force" of 20,000 trained observers, including former FBI agents, to monitor Democratic precincts.[194] In the margin of the printout of a United Press International (UPI) story, Hoover wrote, "I wish Nichols would stop throwing around the FBI name."[195]

Questions about Nichols's boss and about his former FBI affiliation were raised again when, in 1969, Rosenstiel donated $1 million to the J. Edgar Hoover Foundation. The foundation was formed on June 10, 1965, by Nichols and other agents to "[combat] communism and promote Americanism, law and order and good citizenship," Nichols told the *New York Post*. Prior to Rosenstiel's donation, Nichols claimed that the foundation had raised $200,000.[196] Yet the expenditures of the foundation between 1965 and 1968 were $11,125. In a story that enraged Nichols, *Washington Post* reporter Maxine Cheshire highlighted the connections between Rosenstiel and controversial McCarthy subcommittee attorney Roy Cohn, who was then under federal indictment. "Rosenstiel has been described as a 'father figure' to Roy Cohn," Cheshire wrote. The story listed all of the contributions and quoted the foundation's secretary, FBI assistant director Cartha DeLoach, and its president, Nichols.[197] Nichols was furious. "The story intimated that Mr. Hoover was in league with the underworld," he said in an interview published in 1975.[198]

Nichols's relationship with Cohn continued after he left the FBI in 1957, and at times, it became an embarrassment to the Bureau. Cohn had been a person of intense interest within the FBI ever since he had emerged as an assistant US attorney in New York in the early 1950s. Through his subsequent work with the Department of Justice and Senator Joseph McCarthy's Permanent Subcommittee on Investigations, the FBI had maintained its monitoring of Cohn, noting primarily his tendency to self-promote, his propensity to identify himself with the FBI, and his frequent outbursts in the media, many of which were embarrassing to Hoover and the Bureau.[199] From 1952 to 1957, Nichols was the Bureau's primary contact man handling Cohn, whom Nichols himself described as "temperamental" but "smart beyond comprehension." Referring to Cohn's work with Senator McCarthy's subcommittee, Nichols complained that Cohn talked too much, including to the press, but added, "I think we have got to get along with him as long as he is in his present role."[200] Handling the temperamental Cohn required that Nichols essentially act as a parent. In 1953, Cohn told Nichols he was "hurt" not to have been invited to the New York FBI Christmas party, prompting a flurry of memoranda as Nichols attempted to learn why he was excluded.[201] The answer—that the New York SAC only specifically invited federal district judges and not assistant US attorneys and that Cohn usually attended without an invitation—speaks volumes about Cohn's sense of entitlement and his grandiose sense of importance.[202] That he renewed his Christmas party complaint in 1956 merely highlights his petulance.[203] Cohn frequently claimed a closer relationship to the Bureau than Nichols and Hoover were comfortable admitting. In 1954, as the Army-McCarthy hearings led to McCarthy's censure by the Senate, Cohn was accused by the secretary of the army of petulantly claiming he had access to FBI documents whenever he wanted them.[204] For Hoover, any suggestion that FBI files might have been compromised was a major concern. "Cohn gets nothing from us & anyone having contact with Cohn should be most circumspect so he (Cohn) can't enlarge on it," the director wrote on a memorandum.[205]

After leaving the McCarthy subcommittee in 1954, Cohn returned to New York, where he joined the Saxe, Bacon & O'Shea (later Saxe, Bacon & Bolan) law firm, bringing in high-paying clients, including alleged mob figures. He frequently found himself under investigation by the federal government, and he was tried and acquitted on charges ranging from fraud to conspiracy three times in federal court, in 1964, 1969, and 1971. The Internal Revenue Service (IRS) audited Cohn's taxes for twenty consecutive years, collecting more than $300,000 in back taxes and placing liens on his earnings ultimately totaling $3.18 million. In 1986, he was disbarred for a series of unethical dealings, charged, among other things, with coercing Lewis

Rosenstiel into signing a codicil to his will that would have benefited Cohn, as the man lay on his deathbed in 1976.[206]

In 1968, Nichols and three FBI agents became embroiled in a controversy involving Cohn and his friendship with Nichols and Hoover. At the time, Cohn was under federal indictment in New York for bribery, blackmail, and conspiracy based on an investigation by the Securities and Exchange Commission (SEC). That year, New York US attorney Robert Morgenthau solicited affidavits from three New York FBI agents. Those affidavits refuted a pivotal point of Cohn's defense. Nichols gained access to the affidavits (probably from Cohn) and forwarded them to the FBI. Hoover immediately transferred the three agents out of New York, ostensibly because they had violated Bureau policy by furnishing affidavits without authorization. The unflattering media coverage, suggesting that Hoover had placed his friendship with Cohn first and justice for the accused second, was one concern. The second concern was Morgenthau's claim to the New York FBI special agent in charge that Nichols, in his work for the Nixon presidential campaign, had pledged that "if Nixon were elected, he would see to it that Morgenthau was fired as [US attorney] and that would be the end of the case against Cohn." Morgenthau told Hoover that lawyers handling witnesses in the Cohn case were afraid of "what will happen to witnesses if they testify. They are afraid of L. B. Nichols' connection with the Bureau."[207] Morgenthau's implication was that Hoover and Nichols conspired to remove potential prosecution witnesses from New York in order to assist their friend Cohn. In a lengthy *Life* magazine article, journalist William Lambert explored the relationship between Cohn and Nichols and concluded that the reassignment of the three agents "not only added to the Cohn legend but thoroughly shook up some of Morgenthau's witnesses. If Cohn through Nichols could bring about the arbitrary transfer of three FBI agents, what chance had an ordinary citizen?"[208]

Hoover was concerned about the negative media attention caused when Cohn allowed the notion to stand that the director had acted to transfer the agents to assist him. He was also concerned that Nichols continued to involve himself in FBI affairs. "Nichols must have a pipeline into the Bureau," he wrote.[209] On another memorandum, Hoover noted that he had transferred the agents for administrative policy violations and not to assist Cohn: He added, "I have no interest in Cohn & less in Nichols."[210] Although Nichols continued to provide information to the Bureau and to advocate on Hoover's behalf, his controversial affiliations seem to have soured the relationship. After Hoover died, Nichols scolded Acting Director L. Patrick Gray for not engaging the "old timers" to help with his rocky transition both internally and externally.[211] Nichols's own health issues in the mid-1970s kept him from advocating on Hoover's behalf, and he died after a heart attack in 1977.

Nichols's influence over FBI public relations policies began with his work in Crime Records in the 1930s and continued through the production of the Bureau's authorized history by Don Whitehead in the late 1950s. In fact, Nichols's policies continued to shape Bureau PR into the 1970s. His interactions with the news media and others were characterized by a long-term perspective and a willingness to maintain contacts with critics such as author and radio producer Collins and potential critics such as the Overstreets or Morris Ernst. Nichols's standard mode was that of the networker inside the FBI, always willing to listen to proposals and generally blunt in his assessments but rarely closing the door to additional conversations. Over time, he gained enough authority within the Bureau hierarchy to be able to moderate the reactionary tendencies of Hoover and Tolson and finesse their agreement when he needed it to pursue a potentially helpful relationship with an outside opinion leader. Though Nichols did not create the Crime Records Section, his work in the late 1930s and throughout the 1940s defined Bureau public relations policies for decades. He has been cited as among the most prominent FBI officials during the Hoover era, and his value to the Bureau was never more obvious than in the years after he left to pursue a more lucrative living with Schenley Industries. Nichols's successor, Gordon Nease, was ill prepared to handle the public relations crisis of 1958 created by a critical article about the FBI in the *Nation*. Nease lacked Nichols's savvy ability to manage relationships with friends and enemies of the Bureau. He also lacked Nichols's ability to manage Hoover and Tolson, who became more intransigent as they aged. In his post-Hoover career, Nichols remained a staunch defender of his former boss and the FBI, even as his own associations became, at times, embarrassments to the Bureau. From his affiliation with controversial figures such as Rosenstiel and Cohn to his leadership of the J. Edgar Hoover Foundation, Nichols became the subject of sometimes critical stories that could anger Hoover. Still, Nichols's legacy as the founder and, for two decades, the enforcer of FBI public relations policies and as the one person able to moderate Hoover's reactions earns him a rank among the most important individuals behind the creation and maintenance of the iconic FBI image of the Hoover era.

Chapter Three

Speaking with One Voice

By late 1943, Joseph P. Kennedy's efforts to land a new position with the FDR administration were going nowhere, halted by Kennedy's unrepentant isolationism and behind-the-scenes scheming for political power. In a letter to their children, his wife, Rose, wrote of the family patriarch's disappointment about his failure to find a role in the administration's war effort. "[He] gets very depressed at times about the whole war situation," she stated.[1] The former movie mogul, SEC chairman, and US ambassador to Great Britain was so anxious to contribute to the war effort that he telegrammed British prime minister Winston Churchill's minister of supply, offering his services "in any capacity here that would be of any value to England and to you."[2] Rebuffed at every turn, Kennedy focused his attention on growing vegetables for the family at his Osterville, Massachusetts, farm.

Despite the fact that Kennedy's influence in the Roosevelt administration had evaporated, his experience and connections were valued by one person ostensibly working for FDR—J. Edgar Hoover. On September 7, 1943, Edward A. Soucy, the special agent in charge of the Boston FBI office, wrote to Hoover requesting permission to establish Kennedy as one of the Bureau's 300 or so Special Service Contacts (SSCs). "[Kennedy] considers the Naval and Army Intelligence Services 'amateurs' in comparison to the Bureau and regrets that they have often meddled in investigations coming within the jurisdiction of the Bureau," Soucy wrote.[3] Five weeks later, Hoover gave his approval to developing Kennedy as a Special Service Contact. "The Bureau should be advised as to the nature of the information he is able to provide or the facilities he can offer [for] the Bureau's use," the director wrote. "Every effort should be made to provide him with investigative assignments in keeping with his particular ability and the Bureau should be advised as to the nature of these assignments, together with the results obtained."[4]

The language of Hoover's agreement reveals the nature of the Special

Service Contact Program. SSCs were prominent people in strategic positions who, because of their past or present work, were able to provide informal intelligence or investigative services to the FBI. The program, which was at times referred to as the SAC Contact Program, included everything from routine public relations contacts to contacts with individuals in sensitive positions who were willing to discreetly ask questions the Bureau could not ask and provide the information to the agency. SSCs were either nominated by special agents in charge, who were required to investigate the nominees' backgrounds and request approval from headquarters, or identified as possible contacts through their outspoken support of the FBI. The program was managed by the SSC Contact Desk at headquarters, where an index of SSCs was maintained; contacts were given symbol numbers as identification, similar to the way the Bureau identified confidential informants in criminal and domestic intelligence cases.[5] Thus, the SSC Program was more than a Rolodex of PR contacts—it was also an effort to develop informers in strategic places such as the news media, government, business, and even the clergy.

Field agents understood that establishing relationships with opinion shapers in their local areas was part of the job. They also understood that the messages they were to communicate were largely defined in Washington, primarily by staff in the Crime Records Section. Finally, they knew that monitoring their environment for potential embarrassments was a key part of their responsibilities. Hoover understood that certain kinds of relationships with certain kinds of people and organizations held potential value for the FBI.

The SSC Program was just one of several massive contact programs, including the Responsibilities Program and the American Legion Contact Program. In each case, building relationships with the people who would be contacted under these programs offered the FBI an investigative, political, or public relations advantage (or some combination of the three). The ALCP and, later, the Responsibilities Program were formed to create relationships with individuals who shared Hoover's xenophobic and paranoid worldview. Through these programs, the FBI was able to provide information to local individuals and gather information from them as well. With the Responsibilities Program, in which governors and other local officials were given information about allegedly subversive people in state and local government, the Bureau was able to craft an ongoing connection with policy makers and opinion shapers to foster long-term relationships. The American Legion

Contact Program, by contrast, was primarily a public relations effort to mollify a group of patriotic veterans who without the guidance of the FBI might actually become a hindrance to Bureau domestic intelligence work.

According to Soucy, Joseph Kennedy could provide information on the liquor business, the motion picture industry, the financial industry, South America, and the Catholic Church. In addition, Soucy told Hoover, Kennedy's service as ambassador to Great Britain left him with contacts in the international diplomatic field.[6] Between 1943 and 1946, when the program was put on hiatus, Kennedy provided special services to Soucy and the Bureau on two occasions, although the nature of the information he provided was redacted in his FBI file. In 1950, the Bureau restarted the Special Service Contact Program, and Kennedy was again identified as an SSC.[7] Between 1950 and 1955, he was frequently contacted by the Boston SAC, but he was not given any investigative assignments. He did, however, speak to a journalist, whose name was redacted in the file, about a series of stories that criticized the Bureau's civil rights investigations.[8] By 1953, the Bureau had identified 174 SSCs nationwide, an average of 3.5 per field office.[9] FBI records indicate that most SSCs were, like Kennedy, primarily public relations contacts and seldom provided investigative services. The SSC Program was dissolved again in 1956 and apparently continued only as an informal PR contact program after that.

The most significant, enduring, and far-reaching of the FBI's public relations–oriented contact programs was the American Legion Contact Program (ALCP), established in 1940 and continued as a formally defined set of procedures through 1966. Like the Special Service Contact Program, the ALCP was designed to enlist people in strategic positions as informants, but it ultimately yielded few investigative leads and instead served primarily as a PR program. Cartha DeLoach, who became the third most powerful man in the FBI in the 1960s, served as liaison to the American Legion and thus was deeply involved in the ALCP. DeLoach's connections to the Legion and his relationship to the ALCP were important elements in his rise to a leadership position within the Bureau.

The American Legion was founded after World War I by in-service and discharged members of the American Expeditionary Forces who found themselves marooned in Europe with long waits for return trips home. Lt. Col. Theodore Roosevelt, Jr., son of the twenty-sixth president, conceived of a new organization composed of Great War veterans from Europe as well as those who served stateside during the war. The concept of a veterans' service organization was not new. In the wake of the American Civil War, former Union soldiers established the Grand Army of the Republic, and southern veterans founded the United Confederate Veterans. Following the Spanish-American War, the American Veterans of Foreign Service, now known as the Veterans of Foreign Wars (VFW), was founded. The American Legion, once it began accepting veterans of all wars, became the largest and most influential veterans' group during the last half of the twentieth century. After World War I veterans finally returned home, a founding convention for the Great War veterans' group was held in Minneapolis in 1919, and the American Legion was formed. At its founding, the Legion worked through a national legislative committee to promote legislation favorable to Great War veterans. During the Legion's first two-plus decades of existence, its membership was limited to veterans of World War I. But in 1942, the organization began allowing World War II veterans to join. Officially nonpartisan, the Legion concentrated on spreading the "ideology of Americanism" and lobbying on behalf of veterans.

By 1940, it had become increasingly clear that the United States would eventually be forced into the wars raging in Europe and the Pacific. With conflict spreading across the globe, members of the American Legion conferred with Attorney General Robert H. Jackson in a meeting arranged by FBI assistant director Edward A. Tamm to discuss what Legion leaders felt was a natural role for the group's members—domestic intelligence gathering. Tamm was no doubt motivated to facilitate the meeting by a desire to engage the Legionnaires in the war preparation effort then under way.

The American Legion had the potential to be a very useful organization for the US government. Legionnaires, affiliated with 11,700 posts in all corners of the country, were members of a highly structured and disciplined organization and boasted powerful patriotic ideals that motivated them to assist in the World War II home front effort and, postwar, in marginalizing the perceived communist threat. The question was: How would they contribute? In late 1940, American Legion leaders were confident that their overtures to the government would be welcomed. They met with Attorney General Jackson in an attempt to formalize a home front role in helping protect defense industries and monitor subversion in their local communities. The meeting did not go well. According to FBI special agent in charge B. Edwin Sackett of the New York office, Legion officials told him that "the Attorney General indicated to them that he did not want the American Legion support; that he did not want them to do any investigating or take any action."[10] Jackson advised the Legionnaires that they could best help by stabilizing the situation, in an effort to "reduce and prevent mob violence and hysteria which appeared to be cropping up in various parts of the country."[11] Jackson's advice, though legally prudent, could not have been more tone-deaf in terms of public relations concerns. Confronted with the desires of a highly motivated and influential group, Jackson simply dismissed their interests out of hand.

His unequivocal rebuke created both a significant PR problem and a possible opportunity for Hoover's FBI. The director faced a choice. He could, like Jackson, reject the Legionnaires' offers to help. Yet he knew from his ongoing relationship with American Legion leaders that if spurned by the FBI, the Legionnaires would either create their own investigative force or become affiliated with another organization such as a congressional committee, thereby essentially competing with Bureau investigators.

Hoover had played a part in motivating Legionnaires to seek a role in the fight against communism, and he knew they would need an outlet for their efforts. Speaking to the American Legion National Convention in September 1940, two months before Legionnaires approached Jackson, Hoover described a dire security situation for the United States and urged Legionnaires to act. "Action is necessary to prevent the bloodstream of America from contamination," he told the Legionnaires gathered in Boston on September 23, 1940. "Born of devotion and sacrifice, the American Legion is a reassuring force in the preservation of our internal security. There is a need for your program in every community in the land."[12] Hoover closed his speech by issuing a call for Legionnaires to join a "crusade for America."[13]

As a result of their failure to gain the attorney general's support, Legion leaders, meeting as a national executive committee in Indianapolis, hatched a plan to affiliate themselves with another domestic intelligence organization, the Dies Committee or military intelligence.[14] The option of setting up internal investigating committees in each Legion office was also considered.[15] In either case, the Legion's natural inclination to affiliate with Hoover's FBI would be thwarted, and, of course, the Bureau would miss out on a potential torrent of information. Perhaps most important, if the Legionnaires affiliated with the Dies Committee or military intelligence, the FBI would find itself with a formidable rival in its domestic intelligence investigations.

Confronted with a public relations and investigative problem, Hoover moved quickly. His liaison with the American Legion, Sackett, was in Indianapolis attending the group's executive committee meeting. Sackett had headed the Bureau's New York office for less than a year when he was sent on special assignment by Hoover to serve as liaison to the American Legion's various annual meetings. A Columbia Law graduate, Sackett formerly served as special agent in charge in New Orleans, Milwaukee, Phoenix, Buffalo, and until mid-1940 Indianapolis, home of the American Legion. Upon learning of the Legion leaders' plans to affiliate elsewhere and create their own investigative apparatus, Hoover immediately adopted Sackett's alternative plan of setting up a close relationship between the Legion and the FBI. Sackett proposed that SACs around the country could contact local Legion posts, gathering and, to a lesser extent, sharing information with them in the same way that the FBI worked with local police departments. Essentially, he proposed deputizing the entire American Legion organization as a quasi–secret police force, passing intelligence information to the FBI through an organized and formalized process. Legionnaires would become confidential informants for the agency, transmitting possibly subversive information as they encountered it in their own unregulated investigations.[16] In addition to potentially providing a vast amount of intelligence information to the Bureau, Sackett's plan would forestall Legionnaires' plans to affiliate with a competing intelligence-gathering organization.

The only problem with the plan was that Attorney General Jackson needed to be convinced. Hoover quickly dispatched a memorandum identifying the problem at hand and offering Sackett's solution as an alternative. "The American Legion membership feels that the offer of the services of the Legionnaires to the Federal Government and particularly to the Department of Justice was not adequately answered by the treatment afforded the Legion representatives," Hoover wrote. "I have hoped that this resentment would not crystallize and take form in any action which would be detrimental to the interests of the Department."[17] The damage, he told the attorney general, could be significant when "large groups of inexperienced men undertake investigations of cases which should in the interest of national defense be handled by experienced investigators."[18] Hoover told Jackson that he preferred Legionnaires be treated as informants rather than investigators, a distinction that made little difference in practice because, for the most part, they neither informed nor investigated. The director did not, in his efforts to sway the attorney general, mention the public relations issues at hand. For the FBI, there would be value in an affiliation with Legionnaires beyond the information they provided, if any. Upon creation of a contact program, Hoover would have at his command a literal legion of public relations defenders spread throughout the country to rally to the Bureau's side and promote its agenda.

Hoover followed his memorandum with a phone call to Jackson, and within a few minutes, he had his answer. The attorney general, Hoover reported in a memorandum, "said it would be all right to go ahead with the plan although personally he would much rather not have to do this but apparently something must be done so he will approve the plan."[19] Something had to be done, from Hoover's perspective, to repair the PR damage the attorney general had caused and to salvage the investigative and public relations value contained in a relationship with the American Legion. Attorney General Jackson's understanding of the scope of the program, however, differed from Hoover's intent. Jackson believed that Legionnaires of German, Italian, French, and Russian descent would monitor their ethnic groups, and workers in defense plants would watch for signs of sabotage at the plants. Hoover, though, asked Legionnaires to provide information about any situation where un-American sentiments existed. One memorandum to Seat of Government administrators issued orders for classifying the types of information American Legion contacts could provide. The memo listed ethnic categories such as German, Japanese, and Italian, along with political categories such as communist, fascist, Nazi, and nationalist. Finally, a catchall category for information not falling into any of those groups essentially freed the Legionnaires/informants to vacuum up information on any topic that they judged germane to the war effort.[20] Hoover planned on using his American Legion informers for much broader purposes than he let on in conversations with the attorney general.[21]

The details of what became known as the American Legion Contact Program were formalized and communicated in an issue of the *Bureau Bulletin*, a newsletter produced by the Crime Records Section's Publications Unit and sent to all FBI offices and resident agencies across the country. The bulletin and a letter to all SACs that followed it presented the program as having been concocted by the American Legion itself and not, as it was, by the FBI as a response to a public relations and investigative problem. The bulletin told SACs that they would receive a list of initial contacts, typically state and district Legion leaders, from FBI headquarters and that they should "discuss with The American Legion official the vital need of the Bureau to know conditions in various localities throughout the country." SACs were further instructed to make clear the importance of the relationships between the FBI and the American Legion. "The Bureau cannot emphasize too strongly the necessity for handling these conferences [with regional Legion officials] in such a manner as to impress upon the American Legion official the reliance which the Bureau is placing upon their assistance and cooperation in participating in the national defense program."[22] That paragraph contained as much a public relations message as an investigative one. Not only did the FBI plan to call upon Legionnaires to assist in domestic intelligence-gathering activities, it also planned to rely upon those Legionnaires as partners in the national defense program, particularly in promoting the FBI's role in that program.

With a goal of enlisting 15,000 American Legion contacts, SACs across the country held conferences with regional Legion officials during the first four months of 1941.[23] On April 29 of that year, an FBI official compiled statistics showing that Legion representatives had recommended the names of 38,677 possible Legionnaire sources, of whom 16,670 had actually been contacted. When the regional leadership was included, FBI agents had interviewed 23,519 Legion members in just four months. What was unclear was how many of those sources would become regular informants for the Bureau. Hoover was disappointed in the productivity of several FBI offices. In a handwritten message, he urged his managers to press the issue. "It is interesting to note that the inaction has occurred in offices manned by least competent SACs," Hoover wrote. "Get after them at once."[24]

Meanwhile, Sackett's public relations liaison with the Legion leadership, specifically with the American Legion's National Americanism Commission, continued. Founded in 1919 with the Legion itself, the commission had a goal of realizing "one hundred percent Americanism, through the planning, establishment and conduct of a continuous, constructive educational system." That system was designed to counter anti-American propaganda, educate immigrants, promote the principle that "the interests of all the people are above those of any special interest or any so-called class or section of the people," spread information "about the real nature and principles of American government," and promote Americanism curriculum in schools.[25] Sackett attended the commission meeting in Indianapolis in early May and reported that the group was pleased with the progress of the contact program. In keeping with the Bureau's liaison with various organizations, Sackett's work with the commission, though, included building relationships and gaining an assessment of the group's aims. That sort of "listening" function has long been established as a key part of organizational public relations, designed to build relationships and issue persuasive messages. Persuasion requires insight into the target audience; thus, monitoring audiences has become an essential function of organizational public relations. Sackett delivered the message that the FBI had interviewed nearly 24,000 Legionnaires to the commission, and then he delivered feedback on various other topics to Hoover.

The relationship bore fruit immediately. The National Americanism Commission adopted a resolution commending the FBI for its war preparation work, a statement that would carry tremendous influence with Legionnaires around the country. Moreover, it was clear from the commission's meeting that the effort to head off any competing alliance, with the Dies Committee or military intelligence, had been thwarted. "It is interesting to note," Sackett reported to Hoover, "that this is the only resolution adopted by the Commission concerning any law enforcement or investigative agency."[26] As indicated by that resolution, Sackett reported that the group had become less enamored of the work of the House Committee on Un-American Activities led by Democratic congressman Martin Dies of Texas. Hoover spoke with Sackett, who reported that Dies's name did not even come up at the meeting and that the chairman of the Americanism Commission, Homer Chaillaux, "did not seem to be as ardently in support of Dies as he has been in the past."[27] Obviously, the public relations aspect of the American Legion Contact Program had succeeded in building a stronger relationship with the FBI, turning Legion attention away from Dies and toward the Bureau just as Hoover had hoped. Sackett did report that one member of the National Americanism Commission, whose name is redacted in the released version of the FBI's file for the ALCP, expressed opposition to the Bureau and Hoover. In case others shared that view, Sackett made a public relations recommendation: "It is my suggestion that the Agents in Charge of the districts in which the National Americanism Commission reside be instructed to call upon these men in person if they have not already done so in the immediate future."[28] Sackett further suggested that he attend the Legion's annual convention in Milwaukee in September 1941 in order to forestall any efforts by rank-and-file Legionnaires to create additional investigative programs. "If we are there on the scene," he pointed out, "we can possibly prevent or minimize the damage before the action is taken, rather than trying to accomplish this with much greater difficulty afterwards."[29]

Progress on initiating American Legion contacts continued, albeit too slowly for Hoover's preference, and in July, Percy Foxworth reported that contact had been made with 37,042 Legionnaires.[30] A month later, when the initial contacts were complete, Hoover reported in an SAC letter that 42,578 total contacts had been made.[31] Once again, considering the public relations value of such an effort, it seems evident that those individual meetings with special agents made a substantial impact in convincing the rank and file of the American Legion that they were in partnership with Hoover's FBI as part of the war effort, even if the contacts were cursory and ultimately failed to provide anything of investigative value. Sackett's report from the Legion's national convention in Milwaukee confirmed the impact of those contacts. He noted that "a great many more Legion leaders in different parts of the country have come in contact with the Special Agents in Charge of the Bureau than was apparent from my previous contacts with these men . . . and it was very apparent that we are much closer to the Legion now than we have ever been."[32] In an SAC letter, Hoover characterized the purpose of the program and included a mention of public relations. The program would collect information, of course, but it would also "satisfy [the American Legion's] desire to be of assistance."[33]

Yet the program's secrecy caused problems when individual local Legion post commanders who had not been among the more than 42,000 Legionnaires contacted set out on their own to initiate cooperation with other federal investigative agencies, potentially undermining both the domestic intelligence and PR purposes of the contact program. Despite the nationwide scope of the ALCP, commanders of just 4,000 of the Legion's 12,000 local posts had been contacted. The remaining 8,000 posts were considered to be located in remote areas where surveillance of war production plants and other facilities would be unnecessary. Sackett worked with the National Americanism Commission to draft letters to those post commanders, informing them of the Legion's cooperation with the FBI and discouraging any local efforts to affiliate with other investigative organizations. In the letter, intended to be sent from Legion department commanders to post commanders, the recipients were urged to keep the program confidential, withholding word of its existence from any Legionnaires who would not be contacted by the FBI.[34]

Although the letter informed local commanders of the program and mentioned that the contact program was confidential, the Bureau could not expressly prohibit Legionnaires from working with other federal agencies. Hoover used a *Bureau Bulletin* issue to inform all special agents of the new complication. "I am greatly concerned over the fact that recently several American Legion Post Commanders, being unaware of this Bureau's leadership in the national defense field, have pledged the facilities and assistance of their posts to Federal investigative agencies other than the Federal Bureau of Investigation," Hoover wrote. "For this reason, it appears that the coverage already obtained is not sufficient and that it will be necessary to immediately take steps to see that all American Legion Post Commanders are informed of the Federal Bureau of Investigation's responsibility in national defense matters."[35] The last paragraph of the *Bureau Bulletin* notice included the operative phrase, from the perspective of the Bureau's interest in limiting Legion cooperation to working only with the FBI, "as it is most important that these Post Commanders be apprized [*sic*] of the Bureau's work so that their activities can be directed along the proper channel."[36] The proper channel, of course, was cooperation solely with the FBI. The renewed effort yielded 10,000 additional potential American Legion contacts. In a 1942 *Bureau Bulletin*, Hoover again offered an expansive view of the utility of those sources who were listed on individual index cards in local FBI offices: "With this vast informant coverage, each Special Agent can readily note sources of information which will give an entree in almost any locality for any type of investigation."[37]

Liaison work with the National Americanism Commission continued in 1942 when Special Agent Lee R. Pennington attended the group's annual meeting. A World War I–era US Army veteran and an engineering graduate of the University of Maryland, Pennington joined the Bureau in 1929 as an accountant. Within a few weeks, he had gained a reputation among supervisors for being overbearing and tactless.[38] In a special review, ordered by Hoover, Pennington was warned against "talking too much and becoming too personally acquainted with persons with whom he comes in contact in his investigations."[39] But despite his rocky start, Pennington proved himself a capable accountant, although his personality conflicts continued throughout his FBI career and beyond.[40] By 1934, he was assistant special agent in charge in the Washington, D.C., field office, and late that year, he was assigned to the Investigative Division in FBI headquarters.[41] There, he developed into a capable public speaker, addressing numerous civic and professional groups.[42] In 1940, Pennington was elected first vice commander of the Department of Justice Post of the American Legion.[43] He joined Sackett as liaison to the American Legion during its 1941 meetings. Sackett reported that Pennington took to his liaison duties "like a duck to water" and "was instantly liked" by the Legionnaires he met during the meeting.[44] In January 1942, Pennington was initiated into the Grande Voiture, La Société des 40 Hommes et 8 Chevaux, commonly known as the "40 et 8"—an honor society of select Legion members. He described it in a letter to his supervisor as the "inner circle of the Legion."[45] He later served as commander of the Department of Justice's Legion post,[46] and in 1944, he was elected commander of the District of Columbia American Legion.[47]

After attending the 1942 meeting of the National Americanism Commission as Hoover's liaison, Pennington reported that several resolutions adopted by the commission praising the director and the FBI would be introduced at the next American Legion national convention. Pennington also reported, however, on signs of frustration from several commission members, who told of instances in which individual Legionnaires felt that the FBI had failed to follow up on the initial contacts—essentially unmasking the reality of the program as a superficial public relations effort rather than a serious investigative collaboration. "I had a few other instances called to my attention where the Legion was prepared to cooperate fully with the Bureau and then nothing happened," Pennington wrote.[48] Hoover, always mindful of any budding counternarrative that could undermine the official cooperation story, scrawled instructions on Pennington's memorandum: "Get after this at once."[49]

In mid-1943, Hoover sent all special agents in charge a letter noting that many statewide American Legion organizations had requested FBI officials to speak at their annual conventions. Apparently, with 59,865 American Legion contacts identified, keeping the program secret from the rank and file was no longer paramount, or perhaps it was no longer possible.[50] In SAC Letter No. 243, Hoover urged SACs to attend and speak if invited, and he began working on a PR message for their speeches. "It is, of course, important at these state meetings that we be in a position to point out to American Legion groups specific instances in which the assistance of the American Legion has been valuable," he wrote. "In citing particular cases, we are then in a position to express the Bureau's appreciation of their past assistance and point out ways and means by which they can be of assistance to us in the future, particularly in our Internal Security and Selective Service programs."[51]

Interestingly, the FBI's American Legion Contact Program file contains very few responses to the request for specific cases in which Legion assistance was invaluable. In other words, the reality of the program as a public relations contact effort was revealed by the inability of Bureau officials to identify any substantive intelligence-gathering results from the nearly 60,000 contacts it had made. G. C. Callan of the Washington Field Office reported on a case in which a young woman "who lived very near a United States Army Arsenal" had addressed suspicious telegrams to an elderly German man in a nearby city. The telegrams expressed thanks for gifts the man had sent the woman. For some reason, those telegrams were considered suspicious "in their wording," and it took contact with a Legionnaire to determine that the potentially incriminating telegrams were not written in code and were, in fact, thank-you notes for items the elderly man had sent the younger woman. In another instance, Callan wrote, a Legionnaire reported that a man paid for a car with $75 in silver half-dollars. The FBI was able to link that purchase with an earlier bank robbery where a great many half-dollars were stolen.[52] Though the file does not indicate so, it seems unlikely, given that the purpose of the contact program as it was officially stated was to contribute to the war effort, that the confirmation of the authenticity of several thank-you notes and the identification of a bank robber were success stories deemed worthy of note in speeches to American Legion audiences. The program apparently yielded little useful information, a reality that again suggests the primary value of the contact program lay in the development of relationships with individual Legionnaires, both in leadership and among the rank and file, around the country.

Hoover alluded to the lack of reports citing concrete results in an SAC letter sent in late 1943. "On several occasions I have asked the field to furnish the Bureau cases in which the Legion has been of service to the Bureau," Hoover wrote. "The results of my inquiries have been most disheartening."[53] Early in its run, the ALCP had been confronted by concerns from within the Legion that contacts were not being fully utilized. In his SAC letter, Hoover noted that his agents felt the same way. "Occasionally, I have heard it said by Bureau personnel that the Legion program has not justified the efforts expended by the Bureau," he wrote. For that, he blamed the agents for failing to contact Legionnaires in the course of their investigations. Then, Hoover turned to the public relations context of the program. "Certainly the potential value to the Bureau in future times of possessing the good will and cooperative effort of such a rapidly growing organization as the American Legion should not have to be called to your attention."[54] In other words, whether or not the program yields anything useful for an investigation, there is public relations value there.

The question of continuing the program during the postwar era was considered by the Bureau's Executive Conference, which was led by Associate Director Clyde Tolson and included many of the top officials in the Seat of

Government. Among the considerations was the enormous workload that was required to continually identify new contacts. The conference determined that the growth in the number of American Legion posts and the greatly expanding number of Legionnaires after the war made continuing the program as it had been operated unsustainable. On November 1, 1945, the Executive Conference approved a memorandum discontinuing the American Legion Contact Program.[55] The *Bureau Bulletin* informing agents that the program was halted included a caveat about the public relations value of maintaining relationships with the Legion. "Rather, it is more vital than ever at this time to retain the continued support and active cooperation of this ever-increasingly important organization," the *Bulletin* reported over Hoover's name. "Every effort should be made to take advantage of invitations to attend, in the role of speakers, American Legion gatherings. Special Agents in Charge will be held accountable to maintain contact with policy-making American Legion officials."[56]

Five years later, as the world situation drifted again toward war in Korea, the FBI's Executive Conference debated restarting the ALCP. The Bureau's top administrators considered several advantages and disadvantages to reviving the program. The disadvantages included the considerable administrative and contact work required of agents in the field and concerns that other veterans' organizations might take offense if they were left out. But the most significant disadvantage cited hinted at the relative failure of the prior program as an investigative tool: "It is doubtful whether the number of cases reported to us through this source in the past warrants the time and effort involved in developing the program."[57] Given that unequivocal indictment of the program's investigative effectiveness, it is not surprising that all three potential reasons for restarting the program mentioned in the Executive Conference memorandum to Hoover were related to public relations and the Bureau's interest in maintaining its exclusive relationship with the American Legion:

1. The American Legion is a powerful, numerically large group of citizens in active participation in the affairs of this country. From the standpoint of public relations alone and having the backing of such a group, the time and effort involved in the program is well worthwhile.

2. Through a contact program, the American Legion can be held in mind in so far as investigations involving security matters is concerned. Unless the program is installed, the American Legion can

well embark on its own investigative activity which would conflict with that of the Bureau.

3. The backing of an organization such as the American Legion can be of great assistance to the Bureau in carrying out its duties from the standpoint of entree to persons and organizations in all walks of life.[58]

The Executive Conference recommended that the program be restarted, arguing that it was unnecessary to seek the approval of the attorney general for a public relations program.[59] Pennington was dispatched to Indianapolis to gauge the interest of national and state American Legion commanders. "[National Legion] Commander [George] Craig and the attending Legionnaires were all enthusiastic in desiring to cooperate in making our internal security program a success," Pennington reported.[60] In August 1950, a *Bureau Bulletin* ordered special agents around the country to restart the contact program. The procedures were similar to those instituted in 1941, with SACs responsible for conferencing with American Legion national officials, post commanders, and adjutants in order to identify key individuals and posts for contact, followed by selected interviews with rank-and-file Legionnaires. More than 17,000 American Legion posts were available for contact in 1950.[61] Within a year, nearly 50,000 individual Legionnaires had been contacted by the FBI.[62] That was an enormous amount of effort for a public relations–oriented program that was not expected to pay investigative dividends.

In August 1951, Joe Deutschle, state adjutant for the Ohio American Legion, informed FBI liaison Pennington, who by then was also a member of the National Americanism Commission, that an editorial criticizing the Bureau would appear in the *Ohio State Legionnaire* magazine that month. The editorial faulted the FBI for its failure to support other agencies' anticommunist crusades and cited the disappearance a few weeks earlier of several accused communists prior to standing trial in New York. Deutschle told Pennington that he had spoken to *Ohio Legionnaire* editor M. M. Carrothers in an attempt to kill the editorial but that the paper had gone to press nonetheless. Further, Deutschle said he would introduce a resolution at the Ohio convention of the American Legion to counteract the editorial. In response to the criticism, Hoover hastily ordered the Executive Conference to consider whether to end the ALCP in Ohio, where nearly 2,000 contacts had been identified.[63] The Executive Conference recommended that the program be continued, but Hoover asked for further investigation of the circumstances behind the editorial. It is remarkable how much effort was expended to clarify the situation that led to the publication of one anti-FBI editorial in an isolated American Legion publication.

Upon further investigation, the FBI discovered that Deutschle himself had authored the critical editorial "for the purpose of needling Washington headquarters of the FBI."[64] He had also worked behind the scenes to thwart the introduction of the counteracting resolution at the state convention. "Deutschle stated he feels no animosity toward the FBI and meant for his article to be considered as a 'friendly needle,'" according to the investigating agent. "He said the FBI is the only agency which receives a list of all of the officers and Posts of the American Legion and he felt that a friendly relationship exists between the FBI and the American Legion."[65] Hoover issued a handwritten order on the memorandum: "Deutschle should not be dealt with at *any* time."[66] On a routing slip for the memorandum, he ordered further investigation of Deutschle, stating "I think we should try & find out motivation in back of the American Legion official in Ohio who has been shooting at the FBI."[67] When informed that the national American Legion would consider resolutions praising the bureau at its November 1951 conference, Hoover showed his thin skin regarding criticism of any kind. "OK, but such resolutions are hollow compliments when such coyotes as the Legion representative in Ohio openly attacks us in the official journal."[68]

By October 1951 and with nearly 63,000 contacts made, the reinstated ALCP had exceeded the contact numbers of the World War II–era program.[69] Three months later, the number exceeded 73,000 contacts.[70] The public relations value of those contacts, cementing a "personal" relationship with tens of thousands of like-minded people who held positions in all walks of American life, was no doubt considerable. The investigative value, however, remained less clear to the Bureau. In March 1952, in fact, Hoover ordered SACs to discontinue contacts with program informants for one year. "You will be advised when the recontact program for the American Legionnaires should be reinstituted,"[71] he announced. Given the cultural and political context of 1952, with Joseph McCarthy at the peak of his fear campaign, the mounting threat posed by nuclear weapons, the Korean War at a stalemate, and a US presidential campaign under way, it seems unlikely that Hoover would have suspended the contact program had it been yielding any significant amount of useful intelligence. Most probably, the program had, as in World War II, provided limited useful information and was worthwhile primarily for its public relations value.

Though second contacts were suspended, the FBI reported nearly 82,000 total initial contacts with Legionnaires by late April 1952.[72] That same month, the Executive Conference considered another proposal to relax the requirements of the program, recommending that in rural areas with small populations and no significant national defense installations, agents should be required to contact only the commanders or adjutants of local American Legion posts but not necessarily both. The proposal would save time and cost little in terms of sources of information, according to its supporters on the Executive Conference.[73] Hoover agreed to limit the contacts in rural areas. Several other conference actions during 1952 further limited the contacts and eased the administrative burden of maintaining records for the program.[74]

Further evidence of the lack of investigative return on time invested came in October 1952 when field agents from Charlotte, North Carolina, recommended that the contact program be terminated. In a memorandum evaluating the suggestion, FBI assistant director Alan H. Belmont recommended continuing the program despite its modest investigative return, highlighting the public relations value of maintaining the contacts. "The American Legion is a powerful, numerically large group of citizens in active participation in the affairs of this country," Belmont wrote. "From the standpoint of public relations value alone and having the backing of such a group, the time and effort involved in the continuance of the program is believed well worthwhile."[75] Belmont did include some statistics regarding the relative investigative value of the ALCP and the separate (Defense) Plant Informant Program. In the three months prior, Belmont reported, there were 167 instances when informants from the two programs provided useful information.[76] He intended the statistics to bolster the case for a positive return on investment of the two programs, but it could be argued that the provision of 167 pieces of useful information in three months represents a dismal return on nearly 90,000 contacts in the American Legion program alone and an untold number in the parallel contact effort, the Plant Informant Program. The number of initial contacts made in the ALCP would grow to almost 100,000 by January 1953.[77]

In July 1954, FBI inspector C. W. Stein recommended that the American Legion Contact Program be terminated. Stein estimated that recontacting each of the approximately 100,000 Legionnaires required, on average, one hour of agent and/or clerical work annually. He cited the Philadelphia SAC's report that Legion contacts yielded no information of value during the prior year. Stein cited several reasons for discontinuing the program, including the time savings, the likelihood that most Legionnaires were already aware of the contact program, and the claim that the program had "contributed no information of value."[78] As an alternative to the full ALCP, Stein recommended a limited public relations contact program to keep Legion support. Under that alternative plan, SACs would maintain contacts with national, state, and district Legion officials, much as they maintained relationships with other key opinion shapers in the regions they served. Furthermore, SACs would explain FBI responsibilities in national security and domestic intelligence to the leaders, who would then keep their subordinates informed. Stein noted that under such a program, the "estimated potential value of contacts justifies [the] amount of Agent time which will be expended."[79] His recommendation was ignored by Hoover.[80]

As the American Legion Contact Program was winding down, an up-and-coming FBI agent, Deke DeLoach, was assigned as the Bureau's official liaison to the Legion. On October 27, 1953, Pennington met with Hoover to announce his decision to retire and join the American Legion as director of the National Americanism Commission.[81] In his resignation letter, Pennington pledged to assist the FBI. "On the outside, I will be in an even better position to fight those trying to smear you and the Bureau than I could as a Bureau employee, which definitely limited my activities," he wrote.[82] His installation as director of the National Americanism Commission was a public relations coup for the FBI, and within days of starting his new job, Pennington was providing inside information to his former FBI masters.[83] The Bureau reciprocated by sending information to Pennington—for example, providing content for articles in *Firing Line*, the American Legion magazine.[84] Ladd even offered to devote an entire issue of the magazine to debunking attacks on the FBI.[85] Bureau officials discussed the idea but recommended against it. "Scarcely a day passed during which some subversive publication did not avail itself of the freedom of the press to cast aspersions upon the conduct of the Bureau with the obvious intent of embarrassing or harassing the Bureau and the Director; . . . we should expect such attacks," agent Joseph A. Sizoo told Belmont in a memorandum. "It was pointed out that the compilation of such data might serve as the basis for additional attacks."[86] On another occasion, Assistant Director Louis Nichols reported that Pennington had fired one of his employees who "made statements in some bars around Indianapolis that he is coming to Washington to expose Pennington to Hoover."[87] The FBI ran name checks for Pennington on prospective employees.[88]

J. Edgar Hoover presents Assistant Director Cartha D. DeLoach with a lifetime membership in the FBI's American Legion Post 56, August 31, 1961. (National Archives at College Park, Md., Record Group 65, Series H, Box 31, Folder 1699, #1.)

On May 14, 1954, Nichols recommended that two agents from his public relations division, DeLoach and Donald G. Hanning, be designated as American Legion liaison agents to replace Pennington.[89] DeLoach made his first appearance in this position at the National Americanism Commission meeting in Indianapolis on July 1, 1954.[90] He and Hanning then worked the crowds at the Legion's 1954 national convention in Washington, D.C. The FBI worked tirelessly to make the convention a success—expanding Bureau headquarters tours; monitoring city police preparations; engaging confidential informants and sources of information in hotels to track small-time criminals who might wish to prey on Legionnaires and their families; and even providing, at no cost, more than 30,000 reprints of anticommunist news media reports for Pennington to distribute to convention attendees.[91]

With thousands of Legionnaires across the country preparing to journey to Washington, Bureau leaders sought input from field offices about the viability of the American Legion Contact Program. SACs were surveyed for their opinions of the value of the program and unanimously recommended its discontinuation. Belmont reported the survey results in a memorandum, noting that SACs believed the program was a public relations success: "Thousands of Legionnaires have been made cognizant of our jurisdiction in the internal security field."[92] In his assessment, Belmont said the program had kept the Legion from undertaking its own internal security investigations, and he alluded to its PR success as well. On August 17, 1954, the Bureau issued an SAC letter discontinuing most of the program except for contacts with national and departmental officers and members of the Legion's National Americanism Commission.[93] From more than 100,000 contacts annually, the revised ALCP would require just 140 contacts each year.[94]

As one historian has described it, the program "limped along" until 1964,[95] when an attempt was made to revive it with a goal of developing sources during the civil rights unrest of the mid-1960s.[96] The broad expansion of the program was rejected, but a 1965 mention of it indicates it remained in effect in its diminished form.[97] Even that scaled-down program was finally discontinued in 1966, in part because two high-ranking FBI officials, Assistant to the Director DeLoach and Hanning, a supervisor in the Crime Records Division, held prominent positions in the national American Legion hierarchy. DeLoach was chairman of the Legion's National Public Relations Commission, and Hanning served on the National Americanism Commission. By the time of the ALCP's discontinuation, there was no pretending that it was anything but a public relations effort. "With Bureau representatives holding positions of importance such [as] these, it is inconceivable that the American Legion could embark upon any program contrary to the Bureau's interest without these representatives first becoming aware of the contemplated program," headquarters official Fred H. Baumgardner wrote in a memorandum to his supervisor, Assistant Director William Sullivan.[98]

The American Legion Contact Program and Special Service Contact Program were but two of many similar, systematic, relationship-building efforts that were undertaken during the Hoover era. Although media relationships were managed by Crime Records staff, relationships with other constituencies (such as the American Legion) were often left to others, led by Hoover and Tolson with assistance from headquarters and field office staff members such as Sackett, Pennington, Hanning, and DeLoach. A similar program intended to provide information to public and private organizations outside the executive branch was the Responsibilities Program, which funneled information about allegedly subversive citizens to friendly governors around the country. The Special Service Contact Program enlisted the support of prominent Americans, among them Joseph P. Kennedy, as quasi investigators, but the program yielded primarily public relations value. A small program, including at its peak perhaps 300 contacts, the Special Service Contact Program was focused on Americans in government, finance, the news media, and the clergy. The American Legion Contact Program, by contrast, was a massive undertaking that focused on ordinary Americans who happened to be Legionnaires. It was designed to build relationships with Legionnaires and thus eliminate the Legion's threats to undertake its own investigations of subversives. Similarly, the Responsibilities Program sought to limit encroachment onto the FBI's investigative turf by state governments and others. "The FBI provided information to local and state officials so that public employees deemed subversive could be terminated from their jobs," historians Cathleen Thom and Patrick Jung concluded. "This, the FBI reasoned, was better than allowing legislative committees to conduct reckless loyalty hearings. . . . The effect, however, was that while the program originally was intended to curb McCarthyite excesses, ultimately it added to them."[99]

The specter of an army of conservative Americans informing on their fellow citizens and others has, rightly, struck FBI historians as an alarming development. "While FBI officials received little information of value from the American Legion contacts, the ability to recruit thousands of 'confidential informants' radically expanded the FBI's surveillance of American dissidents," historian Athan Theoharis observed.[100] The FBI's zeal to develop an army of informants without Department of Justice oversight, Theoharis suggested, "captures the most searing impact of the cold war on American institutions—its contribution to the evolution of a quasi-autonomous internal security bureaucracy administered by individuals indifferent to the legal and constitutional restrictions central to a federal system of divided government."[101]

Hoover repeatedly pushed his field offices to develop more and more American Legion contacts. Yet he did not overrule the findings of his field office staffers in 1954 when they urged him to shut down the program because it had required an overwhelming amount of work with very little payoff in terms of investigative leads. Anyone who has read many FBI files has noted that Hoover often complained about the overwhelming workload of the Bureau and used that excuse to parry requests from other federal agencies for intervention—or requests from news media wanting information or authors seeking access to cases. Hoover must have seen value in the American Legion Contact Program, at least from a public relations standpoint.

That the ALCP had failed in its domestic intelligence purpose was an opinion expressed repeatedly by field agents and Seat of Government officials over the history of the program, which existed for more than twenty-five years. But the public relations value of maintaining contact with tens of thousands of like-minded, disciplined, and patriotic Legionnaires cannot be overstated. Hoover well understood the importance of the work of Nichols's PR team in Crime Records in terms of augmenting the FBI's cultural, jurisdictional, and logistical footprint in the 1930s. Clearly, the director believed that avoiding competition in domestic intelligence while cementing strong relationships with a patriotic, activist group like the American Legion was well worth the Herculean public relations effort the program required.

Chapter Four

The Editor and the Professor

On January 18, 1968, Lady Bird Johnson hosted a luncheon in the Family Dining Room at the White House for fifty women leaders who were invited to discuss President Lyndon Johnson's proposals to address "What Citizens Can Do to Help Insure [*sic*] Safe Streets." The guest list included wives of Johnson administration officials, wives of wealthy businessmen, governors' wives, women journalists, authors, and artists.[1] All of the attendees were cleared by the FBI at the request of the First Lady's staff in late June 1967. The event was one of a series of "Women Doers" luncheons hosted by Mrs. Johnson that started in 1964. "Mrs. Johnson didn't want to have luncheons of people to sit around and talk about their ailments and their bridge games," the First Lady's press secretary, Elizabeth Carpenter, said in a 1969 oral history interview. "So to get a more vital type of woman, we just started calling them Women Doers Luncheons. . . . And you tried to get activists in different fields to be there and have one person speak on the subject. . . . An interesting thing that develops—some of these women were the professional career woman types, not always an attractive lot, vital, but not always an attractive lot, and not always the kind that the average woman can identify with."[2]

The January 18 Women Doers luncheon featured three speakers in addition to the First Lady. After lunch was served and the dessert course was under way, President Johnson arrived as a surprise guest. He spoke briefly, calling for the public to support police and adding, "There's a great deal we can do to see that our youth are not seduced, and the place to start is in the home."[3] As Johnson made his way out of the room, one of the invited guests, African American singer and actress Eartha Kitt, blocked his way. "Mr. President, what do you do about delinquent parents?" she asked. "Those who have to work and are too busy to look after their children."[4] Johnson, described in newspaper accounts as "startled," responded that the Social Security Act included money for child care centers. "But what are we going to do?" Kitt asked. "That's something for you women to discuss here," Johnson said, abruptly leaving the luncheon.

Kitt's inclusion on the panel came only after Carpenter "checked her out with two or three people at Justice and so forth, and asked if her name had ever shown up on any kind of ad protesting the president on Viet Nam. It had not."[5] Kitt was recommended to Carpenter because of her testimony before a congressional committee on the issue of juvenile delinquency.[6]

Later, after three speakers formally addressed the gathering, the First Lady asked for comments from the group. Kitt raised her hand, and Mrs. Johnson recognized her. "Miss Kitt puffed on a cigarette and her eyes flashed," according to the *Washington Post* reporter covering the event. The melodramatic depiction of Kitt as an out-of-control interloper at a proper luncheon came to characterize media coverage of the event. Both Kitt's approach and the substance of her statement became a national sensation for several days after she connected the problem of juvenile delinquency with the grim prospects poor men faced as potential draftees who were "snatched off from their mothers to be shot in Vietnam":[7]

> I think we have missed the main point at this luncheon. We have forgotten the main reason we have juvenile delinquency. The young people are angry and parents are angry because they are being so highly taxed and there's a war going on and Americans don't know why. Boys I know across the Nation [*sic*] feel it doesn't pay to be a good guy. They figure that with a (crime) record they don't have to go to Vietnam.[8]

Then Kitt directly addressed Mrs. Johnson. "You are a mother, too, although you have had daughters and not sons," she stated. "I am a mother and I know the feeling of having a baby come out of my gut. I have a baby and then you sent him off to war. No wonder the kids rebel and take pot, and Mrs. Johnson, in case you don't understand the lingo, that's marijuana."[9]

Two of the attendees, both wives of Democratic politicians, rose to Mrs. Johnson's defense before the First Lady, reportedly shaken by the actress's confrontational statement, spoke. "Because there is a war on, and I pray that there will come a just and honest peace, that still does not give us a free ticket not to try to work on bettering the things in this country that we can better," she said.[10] The First Lady then addressed Kitt directly. "I cannot identify as much as I should," she admitted. "I have not lived the background you have nor can I speak as passionately and well. But we must keep our eyes and our hearts and our energies fixed on constructive areas and try to do something that will make this a happier, healthier, better-educated land."[11] The luncheon guests applauded.[12]

Later, at a meeting of a Washington youth group dedicated to combating juvenile delinquency—Rebels with a Cause—Kitt, who gained fame as an actress by portraying Cat Woman on the original Batman television series in the mid-1960s, reflected on the confrontation. "I should put out my claws because I am the cat woman of America," she said. "If Mrs. Johnson was embarrassed, that's her problem. . . . The fact that Mrs. Johnson wants to put flowers in the street or trees on the side of the road is not going to prevent juvenile delinquency."[13]

The confrontation between the isolated and genteel Lady Bird Johnson and the outspoken African American singer and actress made front pages the next day and sparked editorial and columnists' discussions for the following week. It also became the topic of conversation within the FBI, which, after all, had cleared Kitt to attend the event, potentially opening the Bureau up for criticism among what may have been its most important constituency, the Johnson administration. The day after the luncheon, the Secret Service requested a second check of Kitt's record and of the Rebels with a Cause group. The timing of the request for a recheck of FBI files clearly pointed the finger of blame at the Bureau for its prior recommendation that Kitt be vetted to attend the luncheon.[14]

News media coverage of the incident focused largely on the perceived incivility of Kitt's statement interrupting a proper luncheon and causing the First Lady distress, rather than on the substance of her critique of the administration's Vietnam policy. In his *Washington Examiner* column, Damon Runyon, Jr., son of the flamboyant journalist and author he was named after, addressed Kitt's White House performance a few months before he leaped to his death from a Washington, D.C., bridge. He declared that Kitt was "out of her depth": "She was off-key, hit more sour notes than you could wave a baton at, and her phrasing was irrelevant, incompetent and immaterial."[15] A January 20, 1968, editorial in the *New York Times* again ignored the substance of Kitt's comments, instead highlighting her "rude" behavior and tying her "emotional outburst" to issues of race, attributing similar "rude and irrational" outbursts to "psychic scars of centuries of injustice."[16] One attendee, NBC-TV reporter Nancy Dickerson, who was seated with Kitt at the luncheon, privately informed the president in a letter that "Miss Kitt told me during the luncheon that she was teaching manners to children in Watts because, as Miss Kitt said, 'without manners you are nothing.'"[17] Kitt, meanwhile, defended her remarks by asking, "How can the truth be construed as rudeness?"[18]

In her 1969 oral history interview, Carpenter claimed that Kitt was possibly drunk that day, definitely a fading starlet, and a desperate headline seeker who may have been under militant control. "I wondered if militant blacks got hold of her before she came to the White House or afterwards," Carpenter recalled. "She has a lot of problems. One of them was she was dieting and she didn't eat a bite at the lunch. She had had some drinks. The second thing is she is a declining actress looking for publicity."[19] According to Carpenter, letters and telephone calls to the White House following the luncheon ran 95 percent in favor of Mrs. Johnson. On January 29, 1968, the First Lady issued a statement saying she was sorry that the constructive ideas discussed at the luncheon were not heard but "only the shrill voice of anger and discord."[20] Mrs. Johnson's public statement was relatively restrained, but it is fair to assume that her feelings—and her husband's—hewed more toward Carpenter's vituperative and race-tinged criticism of Kitt.

In the aftermath of the confrontation, White House officials set out to discover where the vetting process that allowed Kitt to attend the event had gone wrong. On January 19, the FBI provided an updated memorandum to the president and the Secret Service. When it became evident that Kitt's attendance should not have been approved according to White House standards that avoided controversial guests (particularly entertainers), Carpenter wrote her own memo to President and Mrs. Johnson, reiterating what they already knew—the FBI had cleared Kitt to attend and had failed to identify her as a "peacenik."[21]

In his 1972 novel, *Don't Embarrass the Bureau,* former FBI agent Bernard E. Conners described a paranoid culture within the agency, referencing bugged training rooms, Hoover's disdain for sweaty recruits, and an environment that encouraged blending in rather than standing out. Conners's fictional agent, Harvey Tucker, was taught that "the underlying code, like a strong, unrelenting conscience, which guided the agent in all things, whether making an apprehension of a dangerous fugitive, . . . or merely engaging in cocktails with a neighbor—the main rule, indeed the one that seemed to prevail over all others, was, 'Don't embarrass the Bureau.'"[22] In his critical memoirs, former FBI agent M. Wesley Swearingen described a similar situation during his real-life Bureau training. According to Swearingen, the very first meeting of his training in 1951 included a speech by Assistant Director Hugh Clegg, "a large strapping man who was overweight, out of condition, and out of breath."[23] Clegg, known to street agents as "Troutmouth" according to Swearingen, swore the new agents in and then warned, "Always remember, you are a personal representative of Mr. Hoover. Please, for your own sake, try not to embarrass the Bureau."[24]

Swearingen and Conners were referring to the tendency of the FBI's central administration in Washington to second-guess agents' actions and even their intentions and loyalty when errors that led to public relations crises occurred. Officials within the so-called Seat of Government in the capital found themselves under even more stringent and constant scrutiny from Hoover and his top associate and chief defender, Clyde Tolson. The two men communicated their wishes to the bureaucracy below them largely through their written comments on memoranda. Often, Tolson would receive a memorandum first and then offer his action notation, which would receive an "OK" or "Yes" from Hoover's blue pen. Officials in high-profile positions, such as Milton Jones, chief of the Bureau's public relations section, found that their work was a daily struggle to avoid public mistakes—or at least to avoid having their mistakes become the subject of a memorandum weaving its way up to Tolson and Hoover and then back down bearing their handwritten judgments. Within the highly centralized and hierarchical FBI, a dictum such as "Don't embarrass the Bureau" also meant "Don't do anything that gets Mr. Hoover and Mr. Tolson involved." In his 1976 testimony before the US Senate Select Committee to Study Governmental Operations with Respect to Intelligence Activities—generally referred to as the Church Committee after its chairman, Democratic senator Frank Church of Idaho—former attorney general Nicholas deB. Katzenbach noted Hoover's thin skin. "It is almost impossible to overestimate Mr. Hoover's sensitivity to criticism of himself or the FBI," Katzenbach said. "It went far beyond the bounds of natural resentment to criticism one feels unfair. . . . In a very real sense there was no greater crime in Mr. Hoover's eyes than public criticism of the bureau."[25]

By 1968, Jones had led the Crime Records Section (by then renamed the Crime Research Section) for nearly twenty-five years. He was such an institution in the Bureau and such a stickler for accuracy that agents working for him fondly referred to him as "Ma" Jones.[26] Each day, the Bureau's public relations technicians in Crime Records processed thousands of documents, responding to letters and telegrams on Hoover's behalf, and they produced the daily accounting of the Bureau's work along with numerous special projects and publications such as the *Investigator*, the FBI's official internal newsletter, and the *FBI Law Enforcement Bulletin*, a magazine distributed to hundreds of police departments nationwide. As chief of the section, Jones proofread and approved essentially everything produced by agents and supervisors working for him. Yet ultimately, it mattered not whether he had personally approved an item produced by his section because his bosses, including Tolson and Hoover, held Jones responsible for any errors that emerged. Kitt's very public confrontations with LBJ and Mrs. Johnson did not occur until January 1968, but the White House had requested name checks on Kitt and the other attendees the prior June. And in a letter produced in Jones's section, based on FBI file information his agents reviewed, all of the luncheon guests were cleared to attend.

The public confrontation between Kitt and the Johnsons, extensive media coverage of the event, and the request for further information from the Secret Service added up to a potentially embarrassing situation for the FBI. The general public had no idea that the Bureau was in any way involved in the verbal fracas between Kitt and Johnson. But others, including powerful people whose favor Hoover relied upon, were well aware of the Bureau's responsibility for vetting White House guests. In particular, the fact that the perception of failure within the Bureau's name-check apparatus had impacted the president made the potential fallout even more serious. In May 1964, Johnson, through an executive order, had waived Hoover's retirement at the federally mandated age of seventy. However, the waiver did not indicate a specific time period for the exemption, and thus, it could be rescinded at any time. In their groundbreaking biography of Hoover, historians Athan Theoharis and John Stuart Cox pointed out the significance of the order, which reduced Hoover's power over the presidents he served during the last seven years of his life: "Johnson's qualified extension required Hoover to continue to curry favor and, furthermore, reduced whatever leverage Hoover might have commanded from his Johnson dossier."[27] Within the framework created through a combination of circumstance and Johnson's savvy executive order, embarrassing mistakes could have significant consequences for Hoover's ability to serve.

Although there is no record that either Hoover or his White House liaison, Deke DeLoach, discussed the incident with Johnson, the president did receive both the Bureau's second report on Kitt and Carpenter's memorandum that laid blame for the fiasco at the feet of the FBI. The president spoke by telephone with Chicago mayor Richard Daley on January 20, the arc of their conversation indicating that the incident was very much on his and Mrs. Johnson's minds. Immediately upon being connected to the president, Daley delivered the news that his own wife had met with "500 women" in Chicago's South Side Bridgeport neighborhood, the historical center of the Cook County Democratic Party. The women in attendance at that meeting had passed a resolution supporting Mrs. Johnson, the mayor reported. When Daley brought up the resolution, the president thanked him and then immediately put Mrs. Johnson on the phone. "I just wanted to tell you, Mrs. Daley had a meeting of 500 women, housewives, in our ward last night and they adopted a resolution complimenting you upon your great patience and particularly your demonstration that you are a real First Lady of our land in the recent incident," Daley told her. "These women were all up cheering you and, above all, your great lady-like conduct in the face of a very very trying incident." Mrs. Johnson struggled to speak over Daley's monologue, but she managed to inject her thanks and added, "Mr. Mayor, the bad thing was there had been so many sensible suggestions made there."[28] The tone of her comment again suggests that the prevailing feeling in the White House was that Kitt had, by mentioning Vietnam in a strident tone, ruined the event and embarrassed the First Lady and the president.

In the aftermath of the incident and in response to the Secret Service request for a renewed name check on Kitt, FBI official Joseph Sizoo had produced a two-page memorandum summarizing the Bureau's files on the singer. He reported that Kitt had been an affiant in support of a passport application for singer and songwriter Joshua Daniels White, a friend of Franklin Delano Roosevelt who, because of his antisegregationist views, was presumed by the FBI to be a communist. In 1963, actor and reliable right-wing Hollywood FBI informer Charlton Heston had included Kitt's name on a list he provided to the FBI of movie stars planning to participate in the March on Washington on August 28, 1963. The Bureau was unable to confirm her attendance at the march, an effort to focus attention on fair housing and employment laws that took several thousand marchers from Lafayette Park to the Justice Department. In addition, Kitt "reportedly" expressed an interest in joining another march protesting the shooting of civil rights activist James Meredith after he was shot on the second day of his March against Fear from Memphis to Jackson, Mississippi, in 1966. Finally, Sizoo noted that an informant, whose name is redacted in the file, told the Bureau of an alleged Kitt affair that led to another couple's divorce. He pointed out that Kitt's possible participation in the March on Washington and Meredith protests along with her vouching for White's passport application were not mentioned in the June 28, 1967, letter to the White House that cleared the singer to attend the luncheon.[29] The tone of the memorandum was largely speculative—for instance, Heston reported she *might* participate in one march. Sizoo's memorandum suggested that Kitt should have been kicked off the invitation list because she had vouched for someone the FBI watched on a passport application, because she may or may not have participated in one march, and because she may or may not have said she intended to participate in another. It was upon such revelations that the Bureau's assumptions of subversive intent were often based. Presumably, the details about Kitt, had they been taken into account before the meeting, would have derailed her clearance to attend the event. The first letter clearing Kitt—and ignoring those details—was produced by an unnamed Correspondence Unit agent on Jones's Crime Research staff.

Jones's work as Crime Records chief involved everything from authoring complex reviews of critical works for the upper administrators of the Bureau to scrutinizing minute details such as the specific spelling, grammar, and usage in hundreds of letters that went out over Hoover's signature daily. Jones was trusted to produce lengthy reviews of critical manuscripts, often summarizing hundreds of pages in a brief memorandum so Hoover, Tolson, and other key Bureau officials were spared from reading the many books that mentioned the FBI. In 1953, for example, Jones was assigned to review controversial FDR administration official Harold L. Ickes's *Secret Diary of Harold L. Ickes*, which included a single reference to Hoover and the FBI. In the executive summary of his detailed, forty-five-page, typewritten review, Jones concluded, "One gathers the idea that [Ickes] was pretty well convinced that he was the indispensable man of the Administration."[30] Similarly, in 1966, Jones was asked to review *Look* magazine excerpts from William Manchester's account of the Kennedy assassination, *The Death of a President*. He highlighted Manchester's critique of FBI procedures but dismissed the book as appealing to "gossip-artists and others with small minds."[31] Like his other analytical pieces, both reviews demonstrated Jones's unwillingness to match some of his colleagues' hysterical reactions to published criticism of the FBI. His sober, careful analysis was unlike that of more practiced Hoover pleasers such as DeLoach and Assistant Director William Sullivan. Even as he was entrusted with complex analyses, Jones was also expected to take responsibility for catching minor typographic or grammatical errors in the work of his correspondence and special projects teams. When

Sizoo's memorandum pinned the blame for allowing Kitt to appear at the luncheon on three sketchy details left out of a name-check clearance letter produced by the Crime Research Section, Jones was asked to explain why the singer had been vetted. In the FBI bureaucracy, such explanations took the form of administrative memoranda that were then circulated through appropriate divisions within headquarters. When they ultimately reached Tolson and Hoover, these men usually added their orders and then sent the memos back down the chain of command.

In a factually dense, three-page memorandum addressed ostensibly to his supervisor at the time, Assistant Director Thomas E. Bishop, Jones explained that in his opinion, the June 28, 1967, name-check letter to the White House had included all pertinent negative information about Kitt, centering mainly on the reports of her participation in an extramarital affair. Jones's affirmative defense, arguing that no error was made, was rare within the FBI, where agents, knowing that Hoover and Tolson would ultimately determine their fates, typically stipulated that errors had been made and argued for leniency.

Rather than plead for mercy, Jones argued that he (and his subordinates) were not to blame because the June 1967 letter was complete as written. Kitt's civil rights activities were not included, Jones said, because her participation in the March on Washington and the Meredith protest had not been verified, a point Sizoo had confirmed. The Bureau had only Charlton Heston's claim that Kitt would be among possible Hollywood attendees at the March on Washington and only an unsourced report that she had "expressed interest" in the Meredith march. Moreover, Jones argued, even if Kitt's participation in those protests had been proven, she would have done nothing wrong. "These two affairs have been identified as legitimate civil rights activities, supported by many respectable Americans including Congressmen and Senators," he asserted—a statement at odds with the long-held beliefs of Tolson and Hoover, to whom civil rights advocacy and subversion were generally synonymous.[32] Hoover had always been deeply suspicious of the motivations behind any and all civil rights activities, and he believed that the movement was driven and financed by communist influences. When he reviewed Jones's memorandum, the director underlined the claim that certain civil rights activities were recognized as legitimate by the Bureau and then offered a handwritten assessment: "This is not completely accurate."[33] Jones further argued that FBI policy (perhaps "Crime Records procedure" would have been a more appropriate phrase in this instance) was to report civil rights activities in name checks only when arrests resulted.

Regarding Kitt's inclusion as an affiant on White's passport application, Jones argued that White was not a proven communist and that the singer and onetime FDR acquaintance had always claimed his contact with alleged "front" groups had been innocent. Jones noted that White had voluntarily appeared before the House Committee on Un-American Activities in 1950 and had voluntarily submitted to an FBI interview as well. Moreover, Jones asserted, in a rare moment of FBI nuance and clarity on the nature of personal relationships with alleged communists, "It is realized that an individual has no control and frequently no knowledge that another individual has listed him as a reference."[34]

Vietnam had been the topic of Kitt's outburst, so Jones reported that because the actress had never "popped off" about Vietnam before and because there was no information in Bureau files about her antiwar stance, there had been no reason for further investigation of her feelings about the conflict.[35] He concluded: "Based on the policy of summarizing pertinent derogatory data in FBI files for the White House in connection with their voluminous requests, it is felt the communication to the White House of June 28, 1967, setting forth pertinent derogatory data was correct in light of all factors considered."[36]

Jones's affirmative defense is particularly remarkable considering his own understanding, as chief of the public relations–oriented Crime Research Section, of the importance of the Bureau's relationship with the Johnson administration and of Hoover's personal relationship with LBJ. It is also a stunning statement because Jones, having served in Hoover's dissent-free FBI for two decades, must have known that his argument would not sit well with the director or with Tolson. Not surprisingly, Hoover disagreed with Jones's explanation, especially with his assertion that the Kitt name check had adhered to FBI policies. "I totally disagree," he wrote. "I never knew of any such policy." One might argue that Jones, whose section completed thousands of name checks each year, was actually in a better position to know how the Bureau decided what information to include and exclude in those name-check letters. Unless there was a problem in the aftermath of a clearance, Hoover rarely got involved in the policy or procedures in common name checks. However, given the context of a potential embarrassment to the Bureau and Hoover with a key constituency at the White House, Jones was in no position to press that point.

Tolson and the charming pleaser DeLoach echoed Hoover's disdain for Jones's explanation, joining Hoover by scrawling their own notes on the last page of the memorandum. DeLoach wrote, "I think we should have furnished *all* information re Civil Rights." Hoover, in his second of four notes on the page, added his agreement to DeLoach's point: "I most certainly do. It was gross bad judgment not to have done so." Tolson's handwritten comment recommended that the unnamed agent from the Correspondence Unit who wrote the June 28 letter be censured and placed on probation. Hoover agreed with that suggestion, and he added Jones and his immediate supervisor, Bishop, to the list of officials to be so punished, writing, "Yes & to Bishop & Jones for approving recommendation in this mess. They can't realize the fallacy of such an alleged policy." Hoover added one more notation to the document, an expression of his general feelings about the relationship of civil rights and subversion. Referencing Student Nonviolent Coordinating Committee (SNCC) member Stokely Carmichael, he stated, "Also note Carmichael escorted the Kitt woman to the airport after the 'explosion.'"[37] Hoover did not need to elaborate. Agents who read the note would instantly understand the director's point. Carmichael was a civil rights advocate and therefore a communist. So by association, "the Kitt woman" was likely a communist, too.

Jones was placed on probation, meaning he was ineligible for raises for the open-ended duration of the punishment. Though the letter Hoover sent informing Jones of his probation alluded to the failure to provide pertinent information to the White House, it was obvious that President and Mrs. Johnson's embarrassment was secondary to concerns about potential Bureau embarrassment and damage to FBI interests at the White House. "Hereafter, you should manifest more concern for the Bureau's interests in connection with the performance of your supervisory duties," Hoover wrote.[38]

The Kitt incident with its censorious outcome for Jones illustrated the peril of working in the Washington headquarters in general and in the high-profile Crime Records Section in particular. Agents assigned to the units in Crime Records found themselves under enormous pressure to perform perfectly. Letters from the Correspondence Unit had to be flawless, with no typographic, grammatical, or syntactic errors. Scripts for entertainment programming had to be completely on-message, showcasing the Bureau at its best while avoiding embarrassing or taboo topics. Publications such as the *Bureau Bulletin*, the *Investigator*, and the *FBI Law Enforcement Bulletin* had to be engaging for the audience, on-message, and free of errors. Any contact with media was expected by Hoover and Tolson to result in only laudatory coverage. If criticism did emerge, Crime Records was expected to engage media and other contacts to counter the critical message. Only a handful of agents who joined Crime Records, often chosen because of their undergraduate journalism degrees or demonstrated writing skills, stayed for long. The steady and capable Jones, as Crime Records chief, and his close friend and colleague Fern Stukenbroeker, a brilliant writer and talented public speaker, were among the few agents who managed to successfully navigate the Washington Crime Records bureaucracy for decades, establishing themselves as vital, behind-the-scenes players in the public relations successes of the Hoover era.

Jones's FBI career featured a halting start followed by a fast rise into his key position at Crime Records. A Kentucky native, he was a graduate of Western Kentucky State Teachers College in Bowling Green, where he was editor of the school newspaper, the *College Heights Herald.*[39] Jones first wrote to Hoover in October 1937, requesting information about becoming a special agent in the FBI. His interest no doubt resulted from the enormous growth of the Bureau's cultural footprint during the mid-1930s. Public fascination with the agency's work in the thirties was sparked by sensational media reports on high-profile outlaw cases such as the arrest of George Barnes, Jr., better known as Machine Gun Kelly, in Memphis in 1933 and the shootings of John Dillinger in Chicago and Pretty Boy Floyd in Ohio in 1934. The killings and capture of many members of the Barker-Karpis gang in 1935 and 1936 followed, and by 1937, Hoover and the FBI had become household names, with a heroic public image created and maintained by the Bureau's PR agency, the Crime Records Section, itself created in 1935. That same year, Jones graduated from Western Kentucky, where he received the Ogden Scholarship Medal recognizing the student with the highest grades.[40]

From Western, Jones moved on to Harvard Law School, where he studied under famed legal scholars including Roscoe Pound and Felix Frankfurter. "It gradually dawned on me that I was treading in deep water," Jones wrote in his unpublished memoir. "I had led my class in high school and college, but now I was in faster company competing with graduates of colleges such as Yale, Princeton, Stanford, Amherst and Harvard. From hearing some of the better students recite in class I could see that I just did not have the native ability of many of my classmates."[41] At Harvard, he suffered bouts of anxiety but struggled his way through and finished in the middle of his class with slightly below average grades.[42] While those in the upper reaches of his cohort fielded job offers from major law firms, Jones struggled to attract employers' interest. He interviewed with a few less prestigious firms but never received a job offer. As he waited for the FBI to respond to his request for information, Jones applied for other federal jobs.

He was still a student at Harvard Law in 1937 when Hoover wrote back urging him to recontact the FBI when he graduated with his LLB degree the following June. He did so, and his application arrived at the Washington offices of the FBI on December 23, 1938.[43] In the meantime, Jones had used a connection with Democratic US senator Marvel M. Logan of Kentucky to get a job as a file clerk at the US Department of Agriculture in Washington, D.C. In September 1938, having passed the bar exam in Kentucky, Jones accepted a position with the regional office of the Farm Security Administration (FSA) in Raleigh, North Carolina.[44] His boss there, Wright Strange, the regional attorney for the FSA, attempted to dissuade him from joining the FBI, recounting the gory details of the Kansas City Union Station Massacre of 1933 in which an FBI agent and three local police officers were gunned down in a failed attempt to free fugitive Frank "Jelly" Nash. Nash was also killed in the melee.[45]

On January 15, 1939, Jones and several other prospective special agents were interviewed by Special Agent in Charge Edward Scheidt in Raleigh. Scheidt, who later became SAC at the FBI's largest field office in New York City, filed a report mentioning Jones's graduation from Western Kentucky State Teachers College and Harvard Law School. Jones told Scheidt that he had been a member of his high school debating team, editor of the student newspaper and member of the yearbook staff, and president of the Baptist Sunday school class at Western Kentucky. He reported that he was employed by the US Department of Agriculture in the Solicitor's Office in Raleigh. Scheidt offered a favorable recommendation.[46] Investigators found that Jones was studious, neat, and well liked by his roommates and landlady in Raleigh.[47] Dozens of other neighbors, teachers, professors, colleagues, and friends similarly described Jones as an intelligent, reliable, upstanding citizen—a "genteel" southern gentleman, according to his former pastor.[48] His Harvard professors reported that, despite his C average and middling 214th rank in a class of 365, Jones had a "brilliant mind and a well-rounded personality."[49] As part of his interview, he was given a test in which he was told to locate and interview another special agent candidate—actually, FBI special agent Milliard Schaeffer, who was posing as an interviewee in a Raleigh hotel. "Suspecting that this was a fake interview designed to test my ingenuity . . . I cased the lobby carefully and spotted a man in the far corner behind a newspaper," Jones recalled. "I approached him and, sure enough, he was the man I was seeking."[50] Having completed the interview, Jones hoped he would have some time to consider his options, but he did not. On January 28, 1939, he was offered an appointment as a special agent with a salary of $3,200 annually.[51]

In a letter to his fiancée, Fannie M. Ferris, Jones admitted his ambivalence about the FBI. "Some of the good features seem to be: the money, the investigative experience, a chance to see the country, etc.," he wrote on January 31, 1939. "The bad features are: the danger, the lack of much legal work, and the idea of being far from you."[52] Three days later, Jones sought to defer his appointment, telegraphing Hoover twice. "Learned of parents [*sic*] bitter opposition during week," he wrote in his first telegram, offering an incomplete explanation for his reticence. "Advise if matter can be deferred until I satisfy parents of nature of work."[53] The telegrams were sent two hours apart, suggesting that the situation caused him significant anxiety. Jones followed his telegrams with a letter the next day, further detailing his parents' concerns but also mentioning his own. "They learned of my having applied for the position when an agent from your department investigated my standing, etc., in my home town," he reported. "I trust that my declining an appointment at this time will not be construed to mean that I do not want to be a Special Agent. I do, but at the same time I feel that I owe a duty to my aging parents not to do anything which will cause them to worry about me constantly."[54] After sending the second telegram and letter, Jones recalled that he did not sleep the following night. "A feeling of shame crept over me, and I said to myself, 'What is the matter with you anyway? Don't you have any guts?'"[55]

Even before Jones's letter, his third communication with the Bureau on the matter, arrived in Washington, Hoover's second-in-command, Clyde Tolson—who was his boss's chief defender and the resident curmudgeon of the headquarters staff—issued a reply via a handwritten note on Jones's telegram: "Must report Feb'y 6 or appt canceled—advise not known when another class will be called."[56] Jones was notified by telegram, and on February 1, he reconsidered and accepted the appointment as a special agent.[57] He traveled to Washington, signed his oath, and entered service in the FBI on February 6, 1939, one of twenty-four new agents who began training school that day.[58]

For the FBI, the period from 1935 to 1940 was a time of explosive growth and dramatic change. A war on crime was a central feature of President Franklin Delano Roosevelt's New Deal. The Kansas City Union Station Massacre occurred two months after FDR's inauguration and was followed by extraordinary media coverage of kidnappings and bank robberies, exemplified by the pursuit of John Dillinger. Historian Tony Poveda has characterized media coverage of the Dillinger case as a farce, "emphasizing police bungling in the various phases of Dillinger's criminal career."[59] Police failings in the Dillinger case, a perceived (but not statistically significant) "crime wave," and well-publicized law enforcement (primarily FBI) successes versus the other famed gangsters of the day provided a useful backdrop for FDR's efforts to engage in a war on crime, which would be spearheaded by Attorney General Homer Cummings. In 1934, Congress passed most of Cummings's proposed "twelve point crime program," making previously local crimes such as bank robbery, racketeering, and extortion federal crimes and expanding FBI agents' authority to arrest and carry weapons.[60] In the years that followed, FBI appropriations grew dramatically, from $2.8 million in 1933 to nearly $8.8 million in 1940. The ranks of special agents expanded from 343 to 896 over the same years. Support staff, including file clerks, typists, secretaries, messengers, and others, similarly boomed, from 422 in 1933 to 1,545 in 1940.[61] Like Jones, many of the men and women who eventually joined Hoover's public relations unit entered the Bureau either as agents or support staff during the FBI's prewar and World War II growth spurts from 1933 to 1945.

After three months of training in the Washington area, new special agents like Jones typically bounced around several field offices before receiving a permanent home. Jones spent a few uneventful months each in Des Moines, Iowa, and Cleveland and Youngstown, Ohio, before being transferred to FBI headquarters—the Seat of Government in Washington, D.C.—in late February 1940. There, his three-month training assignment stretched into a posting that lasted nearly thirty-three years. It was Jones's two journalism courses and his yearlong stint as editor of his college newspaper during his junior year at Western Kentucky State that landed him a position in the Seat of Government. During his three-month in-service training class in Washington, he was interviewed by the "grand old man of the FBI," Assistant Director Harold "Pop" Nathan, who predated Hoover in the Bureau, entering service in 1917.

In his report to Hoover, Nathan described the young agent as neither "bumptious or aggressive" despite his Harvard pedigree. He urged Louis Nichols, whose supervision included the public relations–oriented Crime Records Section, to interview Jones for a possible position there and concluded, oddly, that "[Jones] has a rather academic aspect, but not displeasingly so. His outstanding feature is a rather large mouth. A large mouth to me has always been an indication of outstanding mental ability. I thought he was attractive."[62] Nichols interviewed Jones and concluded that though he needed more field experience, he should be contacted whenever there was an opening in Crime Records.[63] "He is of the scholarly type," Nichols noted.[64] Jones's opportunity came just five weeks later, on February 20, 1940, when he was officially transferred to the Crime Records Section, then led by Robert C. Hendon.

In his initial evaluation of Jones, Hendon noted he was quiet and unassuming, intelligent, and a hard worker. "[He] has a personality which is not at all flashy or effusive but could better be described as definitely substantial and lasting," Hendon wrote. "I am particularly impressed with the expeditious manner in which he handles any assignment."[65] Jones quickly learned that the expectations in Crime Records were nothing short of perfection. An error report for February through early April showed that Jones had made seven errors in correspondence he authored or edited. During the same period, another Crime Records agent, J. J. Starke, made forty-nine errors, including twenty-seven that were caught not by Hendon but by Hoover's secretary, Helen Gandy.[66] A few weeks later, in Jones's first official annual evaluation in Crime Records, Hendon gave him a "good" rating. As part of their training, new agents in Crime Records were shuffled through the various units—Correspondence, Special Projects, Research, Tours, and Publications. Hendon noted that Jones was not well suited as a "contact man" responsible for working with authors and reporters outside the Bureau. "He needs to develop more outward friendliness and animation to improve as a contact man," Hendon wrote.[67] To aid in his development, Hendon assigned Jones to do some public speeches and to lead Bureau tours.[68] But despite those efforts, Jones never developed into a contact man or public speaker. He was an editor and analyst.

Jones learned quickly that Crime Records operated under the watchful eyes of Hoover and Tolson. Errors they found significant, no matter how seemingly meaningless, were chased down through the bureaucracy until a culprit was found, and thereafter, an explanation or apology was sent back up the line. In 1942, Jones was forced to explain why he accidentally discarded a piece of evidence from the investigation of Michael William Etzel, an employee of the Glenn L. Martin Company who sabotaged bombers under construction in Baltimore. Etzel pleaded guilty to charges that he cut wires in B-26 bombers under construction and left a cardboard sign lettered

J. Edgar Hoover marks Milton A. Jones's twenty-year service award in 1964 with the Jones family: (left to right) Keith, Fannie, Hoover, Muriel, Milton, and Leland. (FBI photo courtesy Muriel Jones Cashdollar.)

in blue and red pencil with "Heil Hitler" in two of the planes.[69] In early 1942, Nichols ordered Jones to contact the Baltimore FBI office and retrieve the signs. When the envelope arrived from that office, Jones accidentally discarded one of the signs. "It so happened that a second sign containing almost identical wording and appearing on a piece of pasteboard was wrapped around the first sign which I removed from the envelope," he wrote in a memorandum to Nichols. "This was discarded under the belief that it was placed in the envelope to keep the other sign from being crushed." Jones had learned that Hoover and Tolson could be forgiving if agents admitted their errors and offered a clear mea culpa.[70] However, he noted only that "photographic copies of the destroyed sign are available."[71] Nichols recommended that Jones be suspended for three days for the mistake.[72] Hoover reduced the penalty to a letter of censure, urging that the young agent "use more care in the future."[73] The "Heil Hitler" incident was only the first in which Jones was asked to explain himself. During his thirty years in Crime Records, he became the master of the mea culpa, not because he was incompetent but because he was very good at his job and extremely productive. On February 10, 1944, Jones was named chief of the Crime Records Section. From that date until January 1, 1973, he was responsible for every one of hundreds of thousands of letters, memoranda, articles, scripts, name checks, and analyses produced by the Crime Records Section.[74] A June 13, 1944, memorandum summarized his duties as chief: "Special Agent Jones as head of the Crime Records Section reviews all outgoing mail, the proof copies of the 'Investigator' [magazine], 'FBI This Week' radio scripts, prepares certain memoranda for the Assistant Director in charge of the Division [Nichols] and for the Director."[75]

In addition, Jones supervised the work of a team of eight to ten supervising special agents who wrote press releases and interesting case memoranda (narratives of high-profile cases), prepared statistical and other material for distribution to reporters, wrote articles and scripts, answered correspondence from the public, led tours of the Bureau, wrote and produced the *FBI Law Enforcement Bulletin* and other publications, reviewed books of interest to the Bureau, and authored speeches for Hoover and others.[76] Jones signed off on everything created by the Crime Records Section, reviewing and editing every piece of paper. Nichols also relied on him personally for key research and analysis projects, declaring that he was "one of the best research men the Bureau has ever had."[77]

It was an enormous set of responsibilities, and Jones worked in close proximity to Hoover and Tolson, increasing the pressure to be perfect. A missing word in a letter or a misspelled name of a police chief could prompt a flurry of memoranda as Nichols sought to explain the error to Tolson. Jones was repeatedly censured for errors made by his staff that he failed to catch in the blizzard of paperwork that emerged from Crime Records.[78] In 1948, three censures resulted in Tolson and Hoover rejecting Nichols's recommendation that Jones be granted a promotion.[79] In a handwritten note, the director criticized Nichols for recommending a promotion for Jones: "Nick made a gross mistake here."[80] When Nichols rated Jones "excellent" on his 1949 annual review, Hoover took the unusual step of reducing that to "very good," and he censured Nichols. "You should give more care in the future to your preparation of efficiency reports on employees of your Division," Hoover wrote.[81]

Jones earned his first probation and nearly lost his position as chief of

Crime Records when he was blamed after two names were transposed on letters addressed to the newly installed officers of the International Association of Chiefs of Police (IACP). Probation rather than mere censure was necessary, Hoover wrote, because Jones had noted and fixed an error in one IACP letter but had not then withdrawn the other two for review.[82] While on probation, Jones's work was scrutinized more carefully, and he was ineligible for any pay raises or promotions. The situation was exacerbated by the way Hoover and Tolson learned of the error. The police officials contacted Hoover's office and reported the mistake. Nichols, fully understanding that the circumstances would be viewed as a major embarrassment by Hoover and Tolson, engaged in some hyperbole in his explanatory memorandum. "This is one of the most embarrassing situations which has ever come out of my Division," he stated, "and the facts disclose a comedy of errors which would be humorous if they were not so tragic."[83] In a second memorandum, Nichols said he had considered removing Jones and recommended that, in addition to probation, he should be demoted and his salary should be reduced.[84] In their handwritten notes, Tolson and Hoover again reduced the penalty to mere probation, allowing Jones to remain in rank at the same salary. Tolson also recommended an inspection of Crime Records.[85] Just three months later, Nichols recommended—and Hoover and Tolson agreed—that Jones be removed from probation.[86] The IACP fiasco illustrated how serious Hoover and Tolson were about enforcing a standard of perfection. It also showed their motivation, which was to avoid embarrassing situations or PR crises. Finally, Nichols's talent in finessing the situation was apparent in this incident. He understood that he should not attempt to minimize the importance of what were, frankly, two relatively minor and (given the volume of work in Crime Records) understandable typographic errors. Perhaps Nichols understood that if he admitted that dismissing Jones was a possibility, Hoover and Tolson would likely agree to a lesser punishment. In the end, they consented to an even more moderate punishment— probation without a demotion—than Nichols had recommended. Nichols's hyperbolic response in the IACP situation reflected both his understanding of how Hoover and Tolson viewed embarrassing situations and his skill at moderating or manipulating the two men.

When the Bureau needed careful analysis of critics' work, though, Nichols turned to his best researcher and analyst, Jones. In 1950, a credible liberal critic, Max Lowenthal, published his book *The Federal Bureau of Investigation*, a meticulously documented study of the Bureau's history. Lowenthal was a well-connected Washington lawyer and a longtime confidant of President Harry Truman. Nichols knew that Lowenthal's book would be taken seriously by the mainstream media and that it thus presented a serious challenge to the Bureau's carefully crafted public image. His response to Lowenthal's rigorously documented book was to recommend a thorough review of the author's sources. "I feel that it is necessary, as quickly as possible, to check the sources quoted by Lowenthal in his book and to have in one place what Lowenthal says, what the sources actually show, and the facts along with any possible explanation necessary to justify the Bureau's action," Nichols told Tolson. "I have in mind that we will find in the sources referred to by Lowenthal, statements not used by Lowenthal which would contradict and cast a reflection upon his objectivity."[87] On November 20, 1950, Nichols assigned the job to Jones, who worked full-time on the project for weeks, ultimately supervising the work of six Crime Records agents who produced the review.[88] Nichols reported on the progress two weeks later. By then, Jones and his team had checked 1,110 of 3,346 citations in Lowenthal's book. "On the whole Lowenthal has been most accurate in his quotations and we have not found anything really outstanding wherein he has misquoted," Nichols told Tolson. "The chief thing it appears will be the accumulation of matters, which in themselves, standing individually, do not mean much."[89]

The citation review and analysis work was not completed until mid-January 1951, and there is no indication in either Jones's or Lowenthal's files indicating how it was used. Hoover did, however, offer Jones a rare commendation for his work on the document, which he felt was "excellent." "I also want you to know I am not unmindful of the many hours of your own time which you devoted to this project and the personal sacrifices that were necessary in order to complete this work as promptly as you did," Hoover wrote. "I know that your leadership, supervision, inspiration and enthusiasm were responsible for this splendid achievement."[90]

Yet the commendation for his work on Lowenthal's book was the exception, for Jones was censured almost monthly and placed on probation almost annually during the early 1950s. He absorbed blame for everything from minor errors or delays in letters and memoranda to unhappy FBI tour patrons. When a memorandum to the attorney general included the wrong date in the text (August 24, 1955, was typed by a stenographer as April 24, 1955), Jones was censured after an almost comical number of detailed memoranda were exchanged to determine the source of the error.[91] Hoover's handwritten note on one memo indicated the kind of pressure the director and Tolson were exerting on Jones and his Crime Records staff: "Is there no way to get over [to Jones and his staff] the *need for accuracy!*"[92] In addition to writing comments, Hoover frequently underlined passages or placed hash marks next to text in memoranda to indicate information he found particularly important.

On November 13, 1956, Jones received a rare letter of commendation from the director for his work on Don Whitehead's book *The FBI Story: A Report to the People*.[93] But one week later, he found himself demoted and transferred to the Newark office. Two letters produced in Crime Records had been sent back from Hoover's office with a note from the director's secretary, Helen Gandy, stating that they contained grammatical errors. Jones, who had approved the letters, expressed his frustration, penciling a note on the routing slip intended only for Nichols: "This one takes the prize. We break our necks getting it out and get this type of stuff back."[94] In fact, Gandy's "corrections" were incorrect. The two letters were grammatically correct as written and approved in Crime Records.[95] Somehow, Tolson's assistant, Gordon Nease, intercepted the routing slip before Nichols could remove it and informed his boss. Tolson called Jones to confirm he had written the note. Then, in a memorandum to Hoover, Tolson indicated that Jones had apologized and "stated that I could be assured and could assure you [Hoover] that this was not typical of his attitude." "I told him I thought it was and I thought you would think so too," Tolson informed the director, adding, "I think he has outlived his usefulness at the Seat of Government."[96] Hoover agreed, writing, "When suggestions are made, whether by my office as is in this case, or from some other source, they are constructive & not captious. Any such attitude as herein manifested is not only unwarranted but is insubordinate."[97] He expanded on that theme in a comment he added to a Nichols memorandum two days later. "The note was a culmination of many complaints about his difficult manner & uncooperativeness," Hoover wrote. "I discounted these previous complaints assuming that there might be clashes of personalities but when I saw this in black & white, the actual expression of hostility frankly stunned me & confirmed all previous reports I had received about his attitude."[98] In that same memorandum, Nichols reported that Jones was "taken-aback and stated that this was the biggest blow to him in his life."[99] Once again, though, the director was swayed by a heartfelt apology. Jones met with Hoover on November 23 and apologized. "As soon as I took my seat in Mr. Hoover's office, he jumped on me with 'four feet' and ripped me up one side and down the other," Jones recalled. "Never before or since have I had such a tongue lashing."[100] Hoover filed his own memorandum on the meeting. "I told Mr. Jones that I could not understand how a man forty-three years of age and who had been in the Bureau eighteen years and at the Seat of Government fourteen years was not the master of his temper," he wrote. "Mr. Jones pleaded for another chance. . . . I told Mr. Jones that I would be willing to give him one more chance, but that I hoped that he had learned his lesson because he would not have an opportunity again to be afforded another chance if he manifested any display of temperament, indicating rank immaturity."[101] Jones kept his job in Crime Records, but he was placed on probation for seven months.[102]

Prior to 1957, Crime Records staff members were censured for every error that Hoover or Tolson became aware of. Under a new error program, implemented by Tolson's assistant Nease in April 1957, censures resulted only after a series of "nonsubstantial" or simple typographic or grammatical errors occurred, and total errors charged to individuals were tracked. Rather than a letter of censure from Hoover, a notification was sent indicating that an error had been charged to a staff member. Jones was still held responsible for every error made under his supervision.[103] In his unpublished memoirs, he said he felt the censure system for errors and the formal error program were "vicious and unfair." The error program "hit hard the employee who handled a big volume of paper work and made the person who handled scarcely none look good by comparison," Jones wrote. "The argument I always made to the head of our division was that as in all other walks of life a man should be judged on his batting average and on this alone. In my case, I was at bat all day long because of the huge volume of work turned out by my section."[104]

One instance in September 1957 showed the unfair nature of the error program and highlighted Tolson's intolerance for excuses. Jones had urged Nichols not to censure an agent who had made a significant error in a letter. He noted that the agent had suffered an allergic reaction to a flu vaccine, had seen a doctor that day, and was ordered to go home. "I do feel that perhaps some consideration could be given him," Jones wrote in a memorandum to Nichols. "Today, his eyes are swollen almost completely shut and he is wearing dark glasses, but he is still turning out work."[105] Tolson, who in the 1960s would be shown extraordinary consideration for his own health issues, was unmoved: "He should have taken care of himself, suggest probation."[106]

When Nichols retired in 1957 to take a position with a liquor distillery, Tolson's assistant and Jones's nemesis in the routing slip incident, Inspector

Gordon Nease, was chosen to replace him as assistant director in charge of what was by then known as the Records and Communication Division, which included the Crime Records Section. Nease and Jones had been in conflict on multiple occasions, and Jones blamed Nease for intercepting the routing slip that had nearly landed him in Newark. As Tolson's assistant, Nease had been in a position to be a lightning rod for frustration. Tolson's office managed the Bureau and oversaw the work of inspectors who were dispatched to field offices (and different sections in the Seat of Government) to enforce written and unwritten policies and procedures.

Nease quickly discovered that the Records and Communication Division in general and the Crime Records Section in particular were pressure-packed assignments. When two letters Hoover requested were four hours late in arriving in the director's office, the usual inquisition ensued, complete with a series of memoranda. In his explanation, Jones noted that the delay occurred when he sent the letters back to the supervising agent who wrote them to be corrected.[107] Hoover expressed his displeasure with the delay in a handwritten note on Jones's memorandum. "These things are happening all too frequently in Nease's office," he wrote. "Nease is to be censured also."[108] Three weeks later, Nease wrote to Tolson recommending that Jones be removed as head of Crime Records. "[Jones] has not demonstrated his ability to properly administer the Section under the fast-moving conditions and circumstances facing the Bureau today," Nease stated. "Mr. Jones is an introvert, and while he makes a very good personal appearance, he is lacking in the personality qualities which make a good contact man."[109] Of course, Jones had, under Nichols, been primarily an editor and was not responsible for contacting individual reporters and editors; Nichols had managed those relationships. Nease contended that the fifty-three letters of censure received by Crime Records employees during the previous ten months were evidence of Jones's "administrative weakness."[110] He admitted Jones was a capable editor and researcher, and he wrote that Jones had "on occasion presented good ideas," damning his rival with faint praise.[111] Nease recommended that SAC Scott J. Werner of Denver replace Jones.[112] Tolson in turn recommended that the matter be considered after completion of an inspection of Crime Records that was already under way. When Jones learned of Nease's recommendation, he met with several trusted members of his staff. The ongoing inspection involved the physical examination of paperwork and workspaces but also included lengthy interviews with staffers, who praised Jones's work. "I don't know what they did," Jones wrote in his unpublished memoirs. "I never asked. It is enough to say they were effective."[113] He used his positive relationships with his staff to outmaneuver Nease.

It was during the three-month inspection that an article by little-known New York journalist Fred J. Cook was published in the *Nation*, an opinion journal of the political Left. In it, Cook dismantled the mythology of the FBI, specifically answering the hagiography of Don Whitehead's book, *The FBI Story*. Cook's piece prompted a hysterical response from Hoover, who requested that the article be deconstructed by Crime Records, with an eye on countering Cook's laundry list of charges.[114] Hoover was also frustrated that the article was published without the Bureau receiving any advanced notice—an implicit criticism of Nease, who lacked the extensive network of relationships with reporters, editors, and publishers that Nichols had developed over the years. "I can't understand how with all our alleged contacts & informants we had no inkling of Cook's article in the Nation," Hoover wrote, referring to the article as a "planned literary garbage barrage."[115] When the Bureau did learn about the article, from a source in its Madison, Wisconsin, office, Nease assigned Jones to do an initial review. Jones sent Nease a 10-page memorandum analyzing the article on the same day he received the assignment.[116] His more complete, 443-page memorandum on Cook's 60-page piece followed on December 5, 1958. Hoover found the Crime Records review inadequate and assigned the task of reviewing the article in detail to William Sullivan's Central Research Section, asking that Sullivan "bring order out of chaos."[117] The director called the Crime Records review "inept" and lamented, "It should not have been necessary to have the review redone at considerable expense."[118] Tolson termed one chapter of Jones's massive review "valueless," and Hoover told Nease that the Crime Records memorandum was "a sad commentary on our staff."[119] Hoover and Tolson were fond of the pseudo-scholarly "monographs" produced by Sullivan's section. In April 1959, six months after Cook's article appeared in the *Nation*, Sullivan's section finally forwarded its 173-page monograph, "The Smear Campaign against the FBI," and included the warning that it was not to be distributed outside the Bureau. The six-month lapse was far too long for Nease's Crime Records Section to mount any sort of affirmative defense.[120]

The so-called smear campaign of 1958 involved the sort of embarrassing attention that Hoover and Tolson sought to avoid at all costs. And the timing of the supposed smear could not have been worse for Nease and Jones, coming as it did during the annual inspection of Crime Records. Inspector John

F. Malone submitted his inspection report in mid-January 1959. He found the Crime Records offices were messy, as publishing offices tend to be, but Jones's performance was rated good by Malone. It was Nease who received the most negative review. "He is definitely trying to do a good job but seems to lack administrative and supervisory know-how to meet the challenge of the present assignment," Malone wrote.[121] "Mr. Nease's main weakness lies in administration and supervision."[122] The inspector recommended—and Hoover approved—censure and probation for both Jones and Nease. Malone further recommended that Jones delegate more responsibilities to his staff.[123] In a separate memorandum addressing the question of morale in Crime Records, Malone's supervisor, Quinn Tamm, again cited Nease's shortcomings and Jones's failure to delegate responsibilities.[124] Tamm pointed out that three agents in Crime Records had resigned since the inception of the error program in 1957.[125] In his comments, Tolson cited both Nease's and Jones's failures and issued a threat: "Unless there is an immediate improvement, they will have to be replaced."[126]

Hoover wrote Nease on January 27, 1959, summarizing the inspection report. One week later, Nease resigned, claiming financial hardship as the reason.[127] The reality, though, was that he had been outmaneuvered by Jones. The inspection report that Nease had expected to justify his recommendation for Jones to be replaced instead included a tough critique of his own performance. Hoover and Tolson were already angry over the way Nease's division first failed to warn them that Cook's broadside was forthcoming and then botched the Bureau's response. The implication of the director's angry response to the handling of the Cook article was that Nichols's Crime Records Section would not have let the Bureau down. As a result of that failing plus an unsuccessful coup, Nease was rendered a transitional figure. Jones had won. "It seemed evident that I won the battle," he later remarked, "for I stayed around in relative peace and quiet until my retirement in 1973."[128]

Jones's new supervisor was Cartha DeLoach. A few months later, the Records and Communication Division was renamed the Crime Records Division, and the former Crime Records Section was renamed Crime Research Section. Jones's duties changed very little after the reorganization. In Jones's first full-year annual review, DeLoach mentioned that the nature of the work in Crime Research/Records made him "vulnerable to error and possible criticism to a degree, I believe, far in excess of the average Bureau Supervisor or Section Chief." According to DeLoach, Jones was "one of the hardest workers ever to come to my attention. He works under a considerable amount of pressure and performs his duties smoothly."[129] One year later, DeLoach again praised Jones and highlighted the pressure he worked under. "In view of the considerable volume of mail crossing his desk, which he must approve personally, the four censures (in 1959) are not considered to be any reflection upon his efficiency or ingenuity," DeLoach wrote, and he mentioned Jones's "concise, analytical mind."[130]

For Jones, the 1960s comprised a decade when his talents for editing and analysis were again recognized by a supervisor, DeLoach, who, like Nichols, understood that he was a "desk man" and not a "contact man." Isolated from the cultural shifts roiling the Bureau and its public relations efforts, Jones was able to concentrate on enforcing narrative, language, and style discipline in Crime Research/Records during the sixties. In addition, he was able to focus on promoting the career of one of his Crime Records agents, Fern Stukenbroeker. The two men were close friends, and their families spent considerable time together outside work.[131]

Stukenbroeker's unusual—for an FBI agent—background included a PhD in history with an emphasis on modern Europe from Washington University in St. Louis. During his time at the university, Stukenbroeker, a Missouri native, earned a bachelor's degree in journalism and worked for the school's news bureau.[132] In April 1942, two months before he earned his doctorate, he was interviewed by St. Louis special agent in charge Gerald B. Norris, who recommended that Stukenbroeker not be offered an appointment.[133] Two weeks later, however, Norris changed his mind and forwarded a positive recommendation to Hoover. Norris described Stukenbroeker as youthful but "intelligent, aggressive and sincere," and he recommended him "because of his apparent energy, ambition, intelligence."[134]

Stukenbroeker completed his PhD in June 1942; his dissertation title was "British Public Opinion upon Austria-Hungary, 1900–1914."[135] Before being offered an appointment to the Bureau, however, he was required to take a French translation test.[136] Ultimately, it was his imminent induction into the military that prompted the Bureau to offer him an appointment, after his local draft board notified the FBI that he would be more valuable there than in military service.[137] Stukenbroeker reported for duty with the FBI on November 16, 1942, one month before his twenty-fourth birthday. After brief training in Washington, he was sent to Baltimore, then to the Washington field office, and then to Cleveland. On June 20, 1948, Stukenbroeker was assigned to Jones's Crime Records Section, where he would serve for twenty-four

FBI special agent Fern C. Stukenbroeker, ca. 1950s. Stukenbroeker became a reliable surrogate speaker for Hoover and authored many of the director's law journal articles and a significant portion of his book, Masters of Deceit. *(National Archives at College Park, Md., Record Group 65, Series HN, #5136.)*

years.[138] On a routing slip attached to one of Stukenbroeker's early perform-ance reviews at headquarters, which included praise for his initial public speaking engagements, Hoover gave him a handwritten endorsement. "This man should be kept in mind," the director wrote. "He has an excellent back-ground and did a fine job on the speech & if properly guided & given the opportunity should be most valuable on preparation of material for public use."[139]

Nichols, who always showed respect for agents with unique abilities and impressive educational credentials, said in a 1950 review that Stukenbroeker was among the best writers of "original composition" in Crime Records: "He is outstanding as a research man and is able to turn out a far above average volume of work of uniformly excellent quality."[140] Just two years into his tenure in Crime Records, Stukenbroeker was already serving as a ghostwriter for Hoover—for example, authoring a twenty-three-page article, "The Civil Investigations of the FBI," for the *Syracuse Law Review*.[141] In a memo to Nichols, Jones described the article as a "scholarly masterpiece."[142] Hoover was so pleased with the law journal piece that he recommended Stukenbroeker be promoted early, a reward seldom offered by the famously parsimonious director and rarely approved of by Tolson.[143] The early promotion offer was withdrawn a few days later, however, when Stukenbroeker made an error in a speech he wrote for Hoover, a rebuke that demonstrated Tolson's status as a remorseless perfectionist.[144] Another legal article by Stukenbroeker, "Civil Liberties and Law Enforcement in Mid-Twentieth Century America," appeared in the *Iowa Law Review* in 1951. "Law enforcement is a protecting arm of civil liberties," he wrote, channeling Hoover's voice. "Civil liberties cannot exist without law enforcement; law enforcement without civil liberties is a hollow mockery. They are parts of the same whole—one without the other becomes a dead letter."[145]

The civil liberties message in Stukenbroeker's law review articles was undoubtedly intended as a response to the publication in 1950 of an anti-FBI book, Lowenthal's *Federal Bureau of Investigation*. In keeping with the strategic focus of work in Nichols's Crime Records Section, the audience for the articles—legal scholars, law students, and a few practicing attorneys—must have been seen as a prime location of opinion and agenda setting for the Bureau. In Stukenbroeker's *Iowa Law Review* manuscript, which also appeared under Hoover's byline, the director cast himself as the protector of freedom. "The FBI, which I have had the honor of heading for over a quarter of a century, is dedicated to this proposition: to protect both the security of the nation and the liberties of each individual," Stukenbroeker wrote for Hoover. "Along this path—the path pointed out by the founding fathers—lies the eventual solution of this historic problem. The state and the individual can and must exist as cooperating and mutually interacting entities."[146]

Stukenbroeker's law review articles focused squarely on the elements of the Bureau's public relations template, developed in the 1930s. The Bureau was portrayed as a scientific, reluctant, and careful agency guided by the great protector of civil liberties, Hoover. "Law enforcement, however, in defeating the criminal, must maintain inviolate the historic liberties of the individual," Hoover (Stukenbroeker) wrote. "To turn back the criminal, yet by so doing, destroy the dignity of the individual, would be a hollow victory."[147] FBI training, including the training of the Bureau's own agents and the FBI National Academy programs for local police, was held up as a defense against the tendency of law enforcement to overstep the bounds of civil liberties.[148] The FBI Crime Laboratory was touted as a protector of civil liberties because it employed dispassionate science (and, by implication, not the passions of human beings) to determine innocence or guilt.[149] The Bureau's security investigations were given special notice. Communists, both inside and outside the United States, would, Hoover (Stukenbroeker) wrote, "obliterate, completely and ruthlessly, everything we cherish."[150] In a jab at criticism of the Bureau as an American gestapo, the article concluded that "free government cannot be defended by dictatorial methods—in so doing the defender will devour the very thing that is to be defended."[151] According to the law review article, the Bureau was still a "small" agency: "By no stretch of the imagination is the FBI a vast, colossal bureau, growing with uncontrollable speed."[152]

Stukenbroeker's articles, countering as they did most of the criticism of the day, showed that Nichols's confidence in him was well founded. Although his work was cloaked in scholarly language and published in scholarly journals, Stukenbroeker was a public relations practitioner, after all. What was viewed from inside the FBI as "education" was clearly an attempt to persuade a key set of agenda setters that the Bureau was a responsible, cautious, scientific organization and not the out-of-control gestapo cited by critics such as Cook and Lowenthal. Tolson was pleased with the result and urged that Stukenbroeker receive a letter of commendation from Hoover (it would be the first of many) for capturing the director's voice in a persuasive public relations document presented with scholarly credibility.[153] In ensuing years, Stukenbroeker's value to the Bureau as a "research man" (Bureau parlance for "ghostwriter") was such that Nichols had to repeatedly fend off efforts to promote him to a supervisory position outside the Records and Communication Division. "While Special Agent Stukenbroeker is doing an outstanding job and should be kept in mind for possible advancement," Jones wrote in Stukenbroeker's 1954 evaluation, "I do feel that his services are much more valuable at the Seat of Government than they would be elsewhere. This Special Agent is primarily a research man and it is felt that it would be best for him to remain in this capacity."[154] By 1955, however, Stukenbroeker had added contact man to his duties, providing an eighty-page memorandum on bank robbery and otherwise assisting a *Saturday Evening Post* reporter, a man named Beverly Smith, with his article "Return of a Bank Robber," published in the November 12–13 issue of the *Post*.[155] Typically, Nichols himself would have worked with Smith due to the high-profile nature of the article. That Nichols and Jones entrusted the work to Stukenbroeker is evidence of the confidence they had in his work, his knowledge of FBI messaging, and his ability to avoid embarrassing the Bureau.

In 1956, Stukenbroeker was one of several Crime Records agents who assisted two-time Pulitzer Prize–winner Don Whitehead in the preparation of the best-selling authorized history of the Bureau, *The FBI Story: A Report to the People*. Whitehead's manuscript was based entirely on information provided to him by Crime Records. It appears that drafts of significant portions of the manuscript were also prepared by Stukenbroeker and other members of Jones's Crime Records staff. "At one time or other practically every employee in Mr. Jones's section was involved in this project," Nichols wrote in a memorandum to Tolson. "In addition to the research the typing of the manuscript and all of the proofreading were done in the Crime Records Section."[156] Stukenbroeker "initiated the documentation procedure" for the book, compiled the index, played the role of devil's advocate, and proofread much of Whitehead's manuscript. Initiating the "documentation procedure" meant that Stukenbroeker most likely provided a draft outline and possibly even draft chapters to Whitehead.[157] In all, seventeen agents, most of them from Crime Records, assisted Whitehead.[158]

Stukenbroeker's next major assignment was the production of a book manuscript for publication as Hoover's own. The working title for the manuscript was "Communism in the United States," but the book was ultimately published, in 1958 by Henry Holt and Company, as *Masters of Deceit: The Story of Communism in the United States and How to Defeat It*. Stukenbroeker wrote the first draft of the manuscript in 1954. Hoover had very little to do with the production of "his" book. At one point as the manuscript was being prepared, Hoover made a note on a draft chapter, prompting Nichols to respond: "I was frankly very pleased when Mr. Holloman conveyed your inquiry because I was glad that you had read the chapter this encloses."[159] Jones reviewed the manuscript, and then Stukenbroeker revised the book in 1957.[160] *Masters of Deceit* sold 250,000 copies in hardback and 2 million in softcover. Former assistant director William Sullivan later charged that Hoover, Tolson, and Nichols pocketed the many thousands of dollars earned by the book, a charge that has never been clearly proven or disputed.[161] Sullivan was in charge of the Domestic Intelligence Division, and he and his staff had authored an 815-page draft of a book on communism. In an interview conducted after he left the Bureau, he claimed that "Nichols turned it over to a Ph.D. in the Crime Records Division, Fern Stukenbroeker, to jazz it up, to put in what Nichols called anecdotal material, and it was jazzed up." "If you read it now," he remarked, "you have to admit that it is a pretty light, frothy damn book."[162] Stukenbroeker did not get any of the royalties for the book, Nichols noted.[163]

A colleague assessed Stukenbroeker's value to the Bureau in proposing that he receive an incentive award for his work on *Masters of Deceit* and multiple other publications. "The extent and value of the data produced through his creative efforts have far surpassed any similar previous performance by FBI employees engaged in similar work," H. L. Edwards wrote.[164] Tolson and Hoover approved a $300 incentive award for Stukenbroeker.[165]

During the late 1950s and into the 1960s, Stukenbroeker began giving public speeches, first in and around Washington, D.C., and then adding remote locations around the country. A public speaking program coordinated by Crime Records had been part of the Bureau's PR efforts since the section's beginnings in the mid-1930s. Just as the so-called Four Minute Men of the World War I Committee for Public Information were dispatched to speak to civic organizations and other gatherings nationwide during the Great War, special agents in charge around the country and top headquarters agents maintained active public speaking calendars. The Bureau carefully monitored feedback on those speeches, making note when letters of praise came in and sometimes sending other agents to monitor first-time or inexperienced speakers. Agents in the Crime Records Section often provided information or even authored speeches for local agents around the country. In a 1961 inspection report on the Crime Research Division, Hoover highlighted the importance of the public speaking program to Bureau PR. "I note that the number of speeches given by Crime Records [*sic*] Division personnel during 1960 again exceeded the number given in the previous year," the director wrote in a letter to DeLoach. "I am sure that you are aware of the value of a well-planned speech program and will continue to afford the speeches given by selected personnel constant evaluation to insure that they are kept at the highest possible standards."[166] In 1964 alone, Bureau agents and officials, using speeches vetted through the Crime Research Division, delivered 8,000 public addresses.[167]

From the time Stukenbroeker arrived in Crime Records, reviews of his speeches had been positive. By all accounts, he was an engaging and dynamic speaker, and he was definitely able to channel J. Edgar Hoover's voice and deliver the Bureau's preferred public relations messages in his speeches. In November 1959, Stukenbroeker delivered two speeches in Georgia, including an address at Abraham Baldwin Agricultural College.[168] "One of the most effective ways to combat the Communistic influences in this country is to teach the young people to appreciate their American heritage and American way of life," Stukenbroeker told his audience. "To combat [communism], Americans must have a greater purpose of creating a better America under God, a better program for overcoming Communistic influences such as voting, service to community, etc., and must have faith in the dignity of man and faith in God."[169] J. Edgar Hoover could not have said it better—or even much differently since Stukenbroeker frequently wrote the director's speeches as well. Reviews of his Georgia appearances were positive. "This Special Agent is being used more and more for speeches before major groups throughout the country," Jones reported in Stukenbroeker's 1960 annual review. "Several weeks ago, he delivered 2 addresses before college groups in Georgia and numerous letters have been received commenting on his outstanding performance. In fact, as a result of this speech, requests were received for comprehensive tapes on the subjects of the FBI and communism which will be distributed to Georgia schools."[170]

Stukenbroeker continued his normal duties, receiving an official commendation for his article entitled "The Federal Bureau of Investigation: The Protector of Civil Liberties," which appeared in the *American Bar Association Journal* in August 1960.[171] His public speeches, though, became more frequent. In September 1960, he substituted for Hoover in addressing 500 attendees at the Midwest College Placement Association convention in Minneapolis. One attendee, representing the conference sponsor, the Minnesota Mining and Manufacturing Company, wrote that the reception for Stukenbroeker's speech—a discussion of how to remain an individual while working for a large organization—"couldn't have been more enthusiastic."[172] Between October and December 1960, Stukenbroeker delivered speeches in Washington, D.C., Virginia, Maryland, Oklahoma, Nevada, and Texas, and he ghostwrote a series of three articles for Hoover that were published in

Christianity Today.[173] In 1961, he spoke in Tennessee, Virginia, Colorado, Montana, Ohio, Florida, and Idaho. He also ghostwrote articles for Hoover that appeared in *Notre Dame Lawyer* and *Syracuse Law Review*. Stukenbroeker's appearance in Memphis included newspaper, radio, and television interviews in addition to his speech at the Memphis Civitan Club.[174] The *Memphis Commercial Appeal* reported that club members gave him a standing ovation after his speech on communism.[175] Following a speech in Cincinnati, Special Agent in Charge E. D. Mason reported to Hoover that Stukenbroeker was an engaging presenter. "His platform poise is excellent. Enunciation perfect," Mason told the director in a letter. "Voice modulation has superior qualities. He used force and vigor and made a masterful presentation in accord with the high standards you have set."[176]

In May 1961, Jones summarized Stukenbroeker's public speaking successes in a memorandum highlighting the value of such speeches. He noted that the agent's speeches had been well received, with no critical responses at all. His speeches succeeded even on college campuses, Jones noted, and had generated substantial local publicity. Jones recommended that Stukenbroeker's speeches on communism were most effective when presented to ministers and teachers. "Our speech program can be highly productive and beneficial," he wrote in a memorandum to DeLoach. "However, we should appear only before highly selective groups (with proper advance preparation by the field office). In this way we not only can gain favorable reaction from the public but influence key intellectuals, such as teachers, clergymen, professional people, etc."[177]

Stukenbroeker's public appearance schedule continued to fill. In one week in November 1961, he addressed more than 2,500 people in five groups in four different states.[178] In four days in 1962, he spoke to more than 8,000 students in six different high schools in Texas.[179] A Rotarian who attended one of Stukenbroeker's speeches to students wrote to Hoover. During his speaking tours in 1962 and 1963, Stukenbroeker promoted Hoover's *Study in Communism*, the high school textbook version of *Masters of Deceit*.[180] After a speech to Texas teachers, one attendee wrote to Stukenbroeker stating, "Anyone who can hold the rapt attention of 1,800 school teachers on the subject you had [communism] can be rated as one of the top speakers in the country, and that is where you are in my opinion."[181] Over time, the variety of groups addressed by Stukenbroeker expanded from church and civic organizations to include high school and college student groups; American Legion meetings; and even gatherings of the media, such as the National

Religious Broadcasters and the Middle Atlantic Association of Industrial Editors.

The content of Stukenbroeker's addresses varied little. Under the broad umbrella of communism, he typically cited the Bureau's protection of civil liberties, the public's role in reporting possible subversive activities, and the danger posed to young people by the lure of communism.[182] He gave eighty-six speeches in 1962 and sixty-three in the first nine months of 1963. Jones recommended that Stukenbroeker's writing duties be reduced so he could spend more time on the road as a speaker. "These out-of-town speeches are vitally important to the Bureau's best interest but by the very nature of their importance they do demand more time for extensive and comprehensive research than SA Stukenbroeker with his other assignments and time spent out-of-town can afford them," Jones told DeLoach in a memorandum.[183]

By the mid-1960s, Stukenbroeker's speaking tours had become a prominent element in FBI public relations, and he had become Hoover's most prolific public speaking stand-in. His audiences grew and were enthusiastic about his speeches. In Seattle in April 1965, Stukenbroeker gave five television speeches, fourteen public speeches, and fourteen radio appearances in the space of one week.[184] Later that year, he participated in the Indianapolis American Legion "anti-communism seminars" for high schools, made twenty-three speeches, and was interviewed on two radio and three television stations. Organizers estimated he addressed 12,000 high school students during the visit, which became an annual event on Stukenbroeker's calendar.[185] The local American Legion adjutant reported that Stukenbroeker had "made a host of friends" for the FBI through his appearances. "Each year he seems to make new friends and keep all the old ones," Norman R. Booher reported in a letter to Hoover.[186]

Over the years, Stukenbroeker added criticism of the New Left to his public speaking repertoire, and despite his heavy public schedule, he accumulated just a handful of censures on his written work from the error program czar, Tolson. In his 1968 annual review, for instance, Stukenbroeker was rated, by Jones, as "one of the best speakers in the entire nation on the subject of communism." Jones also noted that Stukenbroeker made only one mistake under Tolson's error program during the entire year: "The only thing to occur during the rating period which reflects in any way unfavorably on the work of this Special Agent was the inadvertent use of the word 'possible' for 'possibly' [in an outgoing letter written for Hoover]."[187] That same year, Jones himself was censured four times and placed on probation for six months after the Eartha Kitt fiasco.[188]

In between speaking engagements, Stukenbroeker continued to produce law review and popular journal articles under Hoover's byline. In 1970, for example, he wrote two articles on the Students for a Democratic Society: "The SDS and the High Schools: A Study in Extremism" appeared in the *PTA Magazine*, and "A Study in Marxist Revolutionary Violence: Students for a Democratic Society, 1962–1969," was published in *Fordham Law Review*.[189] "A disease afflicts America today—the disease of extremism," Stukenbroeker wrote, for Hoover, in the *Fordham Law Review*. "We see extremism of several varieties: left wing extremism (Old Left and New Left); right wing extremism (Minutemen); black extremism (Black Panther Party); white extremism (Ku Klux Klan and anti-Negro hate groups)."[190] The tone of this and other Stukenbroeker articles of the era is reminiscent of Courtney Ryley Cooper's *10,000 Public Enemies* from the 1930s. Cooper's thesis was essentially that outlaws and other lawbreakers were hiding in plain sight. For Stukenbroeker (channeling Hoover), extremism of all kinds had mainstream America surrounded. Typical of his writing for Hoover, the *Fordham Law Review* article cited a wide variety of sources to support its narrow thesis, everything from Thucydides to Oliver Wendell Holmes to the *Guardian* newspaper, Theodore Roosevelt, and even the *New York Times*. "America must face up to the challenge of extremism—lest, step by step, the foundations of law are eroded to the detriment of all of us," Stukenbroeker wrote for Hoover. "No cement more durable to hold together a free society has ever been found than the law and all the majesty it represents."[191] The *PTA Magazine* article, given the audience, offered a similar message presented in less scholarly, more populist terms. "Let's remember when we talk about student extremism, that it exists in many forms," Stukenbroeker wrote under Hoover's byline. "In addition to SDS extremism, we have black extremism—a growing problem—as well as extremism from Old Left groups. Perhaps never before have our schools on all levels been so subjected to extremist pressures of all types, white and black, left and right."[192] The two articles demonstrate Stukenbroeker's ability to communicate the Bureau's message in a variety of styles and in a variety of publications with different audiences. His article in the *PTA Magazine* may be seen as a direct extension of the sort of speech he frequently gave to student groups.

College campus audiences did not respond as well to Stukenbroeker's FBI message. As civil unrest, particularly protests on college campuses, swept across the nation in 1970, Stukenbroeker conceived and authored an "open letter to college students" under Hoover's byline. In a paternalistic tone that could not have gone over well with a college audience, he told students, "You do have ideas of your own—and that's good. You see things wrong in our society which we adults perhaps have minimized or overlooked. You are outspoken and hate hypocrisy. That is good, too." Dissent is also acceptable, he wrote. "But there is real ground for concern about the extremism which led to violence, lawlessness, and disrespect for the rights of others on many college campuses during the past year."[193] Stukenbroeker then warned about eight ways radicals would try to "lure" students with their own ideas into subversion. "Along with millions of other adults," he declared, "I'm betting on the vast majority of students who remain fair-minded, tolerant, inquisitive, but also firm about basic principles of human dignity, respect for the rights of others, and a willingness to learn. I am confident our faith has not been misplaced."[194] As usual, Stukenbroeker had captured Hoover's worldview perfectly. Unfortunately, that worldview was, by 1970, hopelessly out of step with much of society and, perhaps most evidently, out of step with America's outspoken youth, who indeed had "ideas of their own."

Hoover's death on May 2, 1972, marked the beginning of the end of the Crime Research (formerly Crime Records) Section and of the careers of Jones and Stukenbroeker. In late 1972, the Crime Research Section was disbanded by Acting Director L. Patrick Gray III, its functions parceled out to several sections within the Crime Research Division. The remaining leaders of the public relations section were transferred. Jones saw the writing on the wall, and on December 20, 1972, he submitted his resignation to Gray, effective January 5, 1973. "I made the decision that Gray would not give me the Bishop [transfer] treatment," Jones wrote in his unpublished memoirs. "I would get out in a hurry."[195] The media reported his retirement, along with the transfers of Bishop and others, as "a purge of old J. Edgar Hoover hands."[196] A few months later, Jones wrote to the new FBI director, Clarence Kelley, to congratulate him on succeeding Gray. "It is truly a triumph of real professionalism over rank amateurism and ineptitude," Jones stated. He continued:

Undoubtedly you will want to consider reconstituting the Crime Records Division. Under such Bureau greats as L. B. Nichols, Deke DeLoach, Bob

Wick and Tom Bishop, this Division, perhaps more than any other, made the Bureau what it was in the Hoover days. It is most ironic that this Division, which could have helped Mr. Gray succeed more than any other if he had only let it, was the one he was "down on" from the beginning.[197]

On December 14, 1972, as part of Gray's elimination of Crime Records/Research, Stukenbroeker was reassigned to the Police Training and Research Section of the Training Division.[198] His duties there cannot be determined by a review of his personnel file. His annual review merely said that "during the extremely difficult period of reorganization in this Section, he made most valuable contributions, giving of his time and efforts in all phases of the operations."[199] A few aimless months later, he was reassigned as unit chief of the Research Section of the Records and Communication Division and then to the External Affairs Division, which was Kelley's version of a revived Crime Records Section.[200] Essentially, Stukenbroeker took over one aspect of Jones's job, overseeing research and article production. His speaking role was greatly diminished. He retired on January 3, 1975.[201]

Jones and Stukenbroeker were not the only behind-the-scenes Crime Records figures worthy of particular note. Because of their positions—Jones the editor and Stukenbroeker the public professor—they wielded enormous influence as Bureau PR messages were shaped and delivered. Although historians have rightly noted the contributions of major figures such as DeLoach and Nichols to Hoover's nearly forty-year PR campaign, behind-the-scenes figures such as Stukenbroeker and Jones have been relatively infrequently mentioned. In Crime Records chief Jones's daily struggle for perfection, all too often a failing one, we see how the influence of Tolson and the looming figure of Hoover created a pressure-packed atmosphere in the public relations section. As the Bureau's resident editor, Jones was viewed by his immediate supervisors and by his staff as an enormously capable analyst and tireless, detail-oriented worker. He maintained the cantankerous facade of the classic editor who sometimes did not suffer fools gladly. Jones demonstrated astonishing self-control in the face of almost weekly censures and annual stints on probation, penalties often assessed for simple typographic errors by the agents and stenographers who worked for him, and errors he simply failed to catch. Every piece of paper—tens of thousands of letters annually, hundreds of articles edited or written by the Crime Records staff, radio and television scripts, memoranda for Hoover and Tolson, analyses of published books and articles—found its way to Jones's desk before moving up the hierarchy to Tolson or out to reporters, editors, publishers, and producers. Perfection was the standard all staffers were held to, and Tolson's error program most frequently ensnared Jones, who was almost weekly forced to write a memorandum (which had to be perfect as well) explaining the context of the most minor mistakes.

Even as Jones was nitpicked from above, his immediate supervisors, Nichols and DeLoach, relied on his analytical and research acumen. Transitional figures Gordon Nease (who preceded DeLoach) and Robert Wick (who came after) failed to rely on Jones, and Nease even attempted to remove him, but neither of them lasted very long in the high-pressure, high-profile position of assistant director supervising Crime Records/Research. In the end, Jones outlasted them and managed to remain a central figure in FBI public relations—a managing editor of sorts—for nearly three decades, which was a remarkable tenure given the stress inherent in that position.

As Jones was dealing with the petulance of Hoover and Tolson almost on a daily basis, he was also running interference and promoting the career of his friend Fern Stukenbroeker, who managed to succeed despite his un-FBI-like academic affect and his high public profile. Others who achieved notoriety under Hoover found their careers cut short. When Melvin Purvis became famous as the man who got Dillinger, Hoover purged him from the Bureau and from FBI history. Much later, when William Sullivan and Cartha DeLoach began to rival Hoover and were talked about as potential successors (whether they sought the job or not), they were removed (Sullivan) or retired (DeLoach). Yet Stukenbroeker, the ghostwriter of Hoover's law journal articles and of *Masters of Deceit*, became a trusted surrogate for the director on the speaking circuit, gaining considerable acclaim and media attention. Stukenbroeker spoke to all types of groups across the country, appearing before tens of thousands of people in person, being interviewed on radio and television, and having his picture appear in newspapers.

Stukenbroeker's speaking tours began as the FBI was weathering what it termed a smear campaign of criticism over its domestic intelligence-gathering activities. Previous smear campaigns in 1940 and 1950 were countered primarily by activating defenders in the news media to attack critics and amplify the Bureau's preferred messages about itself. Stukenbroeker's speaking successes began to mount in the late 1950s, shortly after the 1958 smear that began with industrialist Cyrus Eaton's public criticism and escalated with Fred J. Cook's rebuttal of Don Whitehead's book that appeared in the *Na-*

tion. The 1958 smear also came shortly after the retirement of Louis Nichols as the assistant to the director who oversaw Crime Records. His replacement, Nease, lacked access to Nichols's network of media contacts, and perhaps Hoover, Tolson, and Jones saw Stukenbroeker's speeches as a way to work around the media and take the inoculative message of civil liberties restraint directly to audiences. Stukenbroeker's professorial appearance and demeanor lent gravitas to his presentations, and as a professor, he was not a heroic rival to Hoover but instead appeared to lend scholarly credibility to the director and the Bureau. Unlike the tall, slim, and charming DeLoach or the shorter but intense Sullivan, Stukenbroeker was mild-mannered, bald, and unimposing. Few observers were likely to mistake him for an aspirant to Hoover's chair. Whatever the reasons, Stukenbroeker's notoriety never earned him the director's jealousy or Tolson's long-term wrath. Instead, his speeches were viewed as a valuable addition to the Bureau's public relations tool kit, something very different and more powerful than the typical speeches delivered by local special agents to Rotary or Kiwanis Club meetings. Stukenbroeker's presentations, with their scholarly implications, obviously enhanced the credibility of Hoover and the FBI among certain groups.

Like most men who were successful in Hoover's FBI, Stukenbroeker internalized the director's worldview. His value to Crime Records was his ability to translate that narrow worldview for a variety of audiences, from high school students to readers of law journals. As the audience broadened to include other voices and views, though, Stukenbroeker and his colleagues in Crime Records failed to create a message that resonated with them. The messages of Stukenbroeker's articles and speeches in 1970 were nearly identical to the topics he had covered in 1959 when he began his public speaking tours. By 1970, America was a different place, bursting with new voices and perspectives that had been considered unworthy and outside the bounds of "respectable" debate in 1959. Jones's promotion of Stukenbroeker's public speaking campaign as a critical element in FBI public relations was correct in 1961, but as the culture shifted out from under Hoover, his PR staff failed to create messages that resonated outside the Bureau's shrinking base of support.

That Stukenbroeker received fifty-seven commendations and five cash awards or incentive salary increases demonstrated that the way to succeed in Hoover's FBI was to ape the director's worldview. Jones, meanwhile, looked back on his rocky, nearly thirty-year tenure as chief of Crime Records, with its hundreds of censures and multiple probation periods, and wondered in his memoirs whether he "really had anything on the ball when in the FBI." Obviously, anyone who managed to remain in such a high-pressure position so close to Hoover and Tolson had something "on the ball." Jones spanned the tenures of two giants in FBI public relations, Nichols and DeLoach. He outlasted two other supervisors, Nease and Wick, and retired under a third, Bishop. Jones even outlasted J. Edgar Hoover himself. It would be easy to ignore the contributions of an editor such as Jones in a review of FBI public relations. Yet anyone who peruses FBI files from the 1940s to the 1970s will repeatedly encounter Jones's work, from analyses of situations to recommendations for action. The agents who worked for him, Stukenbroeker being the highest-profile example, were the FBI's communication technicians, drafting the narratives and collecting the information to provide to other authors that became the Bureau's "story" during that nearly three-decade period. The supervision and management functions of Nichols and De-Loach, of course, were significant, as was their service as contact men working with important individuals outside the FBI. It was Jones and the staffers in his unit, however, who provided those men with the raw materials of the Bureau's story in narratives and reports geared to external audiences. In his unpublished memoirs, Jones concluded that he did, in the end, have an impact. "Maybe I did have a little something," he wrote, "for how else can one explain my staying for so long in a strategic spot which was continually getting the 'heat.' I was not a relative of any top FBI official, and I made no effort to curry favor with any of them." He added that one former clerk who worked for him "still can't resist saying, when she receives a compliment on anything, 'You know, I am Jones-trained.'"[202]

Chapter Five

Taming the Octopus

On July 31, 1957, William Randolph Hearst's *New York Daily Mirror* attacked gadfly power broker, activist, and ACLU-affiliated attorney Morris Ernst in an editorial headlined, HOW EARNEST IS ERNST? The editorial captured precisely the FBI's escalating frustration with Ernst, a longtime friend and key public relations adviser and contributor who once boasted that he had served as Hoover's personal attorney: "Morris Ernst has for years been on all sides of every situation but he has been most vocal in the noisome campaigns for what are generally called civil liberties, but which can be understood, if one is so minded, as special privileges for those left wingers who got caught."[1]

Mirror editors attacked Ernst for his statements suggesting that alleged State Department spy Alger Hiss was innocent and for his work as an agent for Dominican Republic strongman Rafael Trujillo. It was perhaps not surprising, given Hoover's close relationship with Hearst and his newspaper empire, that the editorial recounted the very reasons that the Bureau had begun by 1957 to distance itself from Ernst. A casual glance at the situation might lead one to believe that it was no surprise at all that Hoover viewed Ernst as an untrustworthy leftist. For almost twenty years prior to 1957, however, he was Hoover's "mole" in the liberal community, providing information and cover for the director and the FBI based on Ernst's credible position as a well-known, outspoken author and attorney affiliated with the American Civil Liberties Union.[2] Because of his influential status in liberal circles, Ernst was both an audience for Bureau public relations messages and a public relations contact who, working primarily with Louis Nichols, helped amplify the FBI's civil liberties message. It was, in fact, Ernst's status as a reliably liberal voice, as he injected himself into practically every possible public controversy, that made his support of the FBI so striking and so powerful. Hoover and his PR advisers were not shy about engaging Ernst as a defender and bludgeoning critics with the ACLU counsel's claims that the FBI was a civil liberties advocate, protecting the political Left against abuse.

Ernst was born in Uniontown, Alabama, in 1888 and moved with his German Jewish family to New York City in 1890. His father entered the real estate business and once owned the land upon which Macy's Department Store was later built. After failing entrance exams for Harvard College, Ernst enrolled in Williams College in Williamstown, Massachusetts, and graduated in 1909. After graduation, he joined his grandfather's shirt business located along the Gowanus Canal in Brooklyn and then moved into furniture sales.[3] As he jumped from job to job, Ernst attended law school at night, earning an LLB from the New York University School of Law in 1912.[4] Three years later, he became a partner in the fledgling Greenbaum, Wolff and Ernst law firm, which grew by 1944 to include thirteen partners and a staff of forty-five at a Madison Avenue office.[5]

Ernst was described as the "man about town" of the trio of partners, frequenting popular clubs such as 21, Sardi's, and the Algonquin and socializing with the leading literary lights of the day.[6] "He kept his nose in politics, relished the latest gossip and was a confidante of every New York Mayor from Jimmy Walker on," Harrison Salisbury wrote in the *Nation* a few years after Ernst's death.[7] In addition to his relationships with intellectuals and politicians, he had strong connections to organized labor. He was a lifelong friend of *New York World* columnist and American Newspaper Guild founder Heywood Broun; the two met in grade school in New York. He was involved in the National Lawyers Guild (NLG) until he and the group had a falling out over Ernst's outspoken anticommunism. Most famously, Ernst was a leader in the first decade of the American Civil Liberties Union and served as general counsel for the ACLU from 1929 to 1955.[8] That position offered him credibility as a spokesman for civil liberties, and that, in turn, created an opportunity for the FBI to enlist his help, both as a prop in a public relations campaign and as an informal PR adviser.

A smallish man who was usually attired in a Dagwood bow tie and steel-rimmed glasses, Ernst was, like Nichols, a talented and charming networker. A breathless *Life* magazine profile of him, written by Yale Law professor Fred Rodell, described an incident in which the New York attorney had come to the aid of the 1940 Roosevelt presidential campaign, offering to intervene with a highly placed friend to solve a problem. "The entire incident," Rodell wrote, "was Morris Ernst in normal form; refusing to cry over spilt milk, snapping up the personal equation and projecting himself into the middle of

New York attorney Morris Ernst (center), May 10, 1939. (Library of Congress, Harris & Ewing Collection, Call Number LC-H22-D-6549.)

it, bouncing back with a bright idea, an angle, a plan of action. And, inevitably, advertising his intimacy with the great—an intimacy that was no phony. . . . No living man can compete with Ernst when it comes to first-naming the famous."[9] The article listed a sampling of Ernst's great "friends," including FDR; Wendell Willkie, Roosevelt's 1940 opponent; powerful Treasury secretary and Roosevelt confidant Henry Morganthau; and journalist Walter Lippman.[10] A partial list of Ernst's eclectic portfolio of legal clients followed, including the *New Yorker*, the *Nation*, the Macaroni Workers Union, the *New York Post*, the Sauerkraut Workers Union, and the New York Gents Furnishing and Hatters Association.[11]

Ernst gained national fame in the 1930s for a series of legal victories in censorship and obscenity cases, many of which involved access to literary works and to information about birth control and human sexuality. One historian noted that although Ernst was not the first civil libertarian to take on censorship and obscenity in the twentieth century, "he was the most systematic and successful by far until a new generation of lawyers took on these issues in the late 1950s."[12] In general, Ernst rejected the distorted moral absolutism that often led to censorship. "If we try hard enough to look for dirt, everything begins to look dirty,"[13] he asserted. His most famous legal victory over censorship came in 1933 when he represented Bennett A. Cerf, president of Random House, in the publisher's attempt to clear the way for sales of James Joyce's novel *Ulysses* in the United States. The court battle over *Ulysses* was just the most famous of Ernst's contributions opposing censorship and blunting the hangover that remained from the outmoded moral Comstockery of the late nineteenth century.

Joyce's novel, originally published overseas in the early 1920s, fell prey to the Comstock obscenity laws in the United States, named for their inspiration and enforcer—moral crusader turned US postal inspector Anthony "St. Anthony" Comstock.[14] A dry goods salesman, Comstock morphed into a moral crusader in the early 1870s after a friend became "diseased by reading a filthy book."[15] In 1873, he took his traveling pornography exhibit to Congress and lobbied for antiobscenity bills that were ultimately passed at 2:00 a.m. on a Sunday. The Comstock Laws substantially expanded an already vague definition from previous laws, creating a ten-year prison sentence for anyone found guilty of mailing or receiving "obscene, lewd, or lascivious" material. Comstock was named a special post office inspector to enforce the law and immediately turned his attention to Victoria Woodhull and the sexual reform press of the 1870s; in the process, he effectively bankrupted Woodhull and jailed other editors of the press. He later clashed with anarchist Emma Goldman (who referred to Comstock and his followers in her memoirs as "moral eunuchs")[16] and with birth control advocate Margaret Sanger. Comstock served forty years as a postal inspector, convicting 3,000 men and women on obscenity charges.[17]

Though St. Anthony himself was gone from the scene by the 1930s, his eponymous laws remained on the books. Supporters of the *Ulysses* ban in the thirties based their arguments on the definitions in the Comstock Laws, arguing that Joyce's narrative could spark "impure and lustful thoughts" among readers.[18] Ernst argued that the book had literary merit and that adult readers should be allowed to choose whether to read the book on their own. Employing his connections, he managed to maneuver the case into the court of the relatively progressive federal judge John W. Woolsey. After carefully reading the novel and listening to the arguments in the *U.S. v. One Book Called Ulysses* case, Woolsey agreed with Ernst, ruling that individual passages could not be isolated from their context in determining whether the whole work of fiction was obscene. "In many places, it seems disgusting,"

Woolsey wrote, but he noted that it was not simply "dirt for dirt [*sic*] sake."[19] His opinion was included in the Random House edition of *Ulysses* that appeared in bookstores six weeks later.

Ernst next stood in the national spotlight when, representing the American Newspaper Guild, he argued before the Supreme Court in favor of the constitutionality of the Wagner Act as it applied to the press. The New Deal's Wagner Act, named after New York's Democratic US senator Robert F. Wagner, established the National Labor Relations Board (NLRB) and guaranteed the rights of workers to organize into trade unions, bargain collectively, and take collective action. Ernst, on behalf of the Newspaper Guild, argued that the Associated Press had improperly dismissed reporter Morris Watson in 1935 because of his efforts to organize his coworkers, a point of fact that the AP did not contest. Watson was among the first organizers of the Newspaper Guild and served as treasurer of the organization in New York.[20] The national wire service instead argued that it was not engaged in interstate commerce and thus could not be regulated by Congress. The NLRB heard the case and ordered the AP to cease and desist its efforts to discourage employees from unionizing, and it further ordered that Watson be reinstated with back pay. The AP refused to comply with the NLRB order, and the matter moved into federal court where, as part of its argument in favor of its action, the Associated Press urged the court to find that the Wagner Act did not apply to the press.[21] The Supreme Court's ruling in 1937 upheld the lower court's decision and effectively upheld the right of journalists and, by extension, workers to organize under the Wagner Act.[22] Watson returned to the AP for two weeks and then left by choice. Later, he became active in the American Labor Party and ran unsuccessfully for Congress before becoming publicity director for the International Longshoremen's and Warehousemen's Union in San Francisco. He retired in 1966 and died six years later.[23]

The FBI opened a file on Ernst in 1935 when he was considered for an unspecified Department of Justice position. The Bureau's applicant investigation included interviews with Ernst's friends and colleagues, several of whom noted his leftist politics. Judge Martin L. Manton of the US Circuit Court of Appeals in New York told an FBI agent that though Ernst's ability as a lawyer was "outstanding," his politics were "somewhat radical."[24] A New York Bar Association official noted that Ernst's clientele included very prominent New Yorkers and that his friends included Governor Herbert Lehman (FDR was also an Ernst acquaintance).[25] Ultimately, Ernst was not offered an appointment in the Department of Justice, but the judgments of that initial applicant investigation, particularly Manton's "somewhat radical" assessment, became part of the Bureau's ongoing evaluation of him, appearing in periodically updated summaries for almost four decades.

No doubt, Hoover and his PR team were aware of Ernst's very public break with the National Lawyers Guild over the issue of communism. The guild was founded in Washington, D.C., in 1937 as a Left-liberal alternative to the American Bar Association, and it quickly grew to include more than 3,500 members. Among the organization's founders were labor attorneys Harold I. Cammer and Frank P. Walsh, former Roosevelt administration official Jerome Frank, and the ACLU's Ernst. Their motives for founding the organization varied and included labor advocacy, civil liberties advocacy, and objections to the ABA's refusal to include African American members. Within months, the guild had enrolled 3,000 lawyers nationwide. The organization's second president, Minnesota Supreme Court justice John P. Devaney, said the group's prime objective was to convince "the ordinary citizen that all the members of the bar are not working to defeat the legitimate demands and aims of the great masses of the people for a better and fuller life."[26] As historian Christopher H. Johnson noted, "A network of 'peoples' lawyers' thus rapidly emerged. Almost immediately, however, it was labeled a 'Communist front.'"[27]

At the NLG's 1939 convention in Chicago, New York State Supreme Court justice Ferdinand Pecora, a past president of the organization, criticized members for failing to adequately condemn communism and "other isms." In response, Ernst offered a strongly anticommunist resolution that affirmed the guild's support of democratic processes and bluntly stated, "We are opposed to dictatorship of any kind, left or right, whether Fascist, Communist or Nazi."[28] The NLG's executive board refused to consider the resolution, asserting that it would divide the organization and thus undermine both sides' shared opposition to fascism. A separate resolution, similar to Ernst's, was offered by another New York attorney, Ernest Cuneo, and was rejected. The board then adopted a resolution generally endorsing Pecora's views, a resolution perceived by some in the organization, including Ernst, as suggesting a less than clear consensus on the topic of communism. The entire episode served to place the NLG on the defensive, and the New York chapter issued a statement denying any communist influence. "We are, and always have been opposed to all dictatorships, whether Communist, Nazi or Fascist," the statement said.[29]

A few months later, the division in the NLG was again highlighted after the stunning news of the August 23, 1939, signing of the Molotov-Ribben-trop Pact, a treaty of nonaggression between Josef Stalin's communist Soviet Union and Adolf Hitler's fascist Germany. News of an agreement between communists and fascists further isolated American communists, many of whom were aghast at the Soviet Union's tacit endorsement of Hitler's fascist regime. In response, anticommunist NLG members—including SEC commissioner Jerome Frank, Assistant Secretary of State Adolf A. Berle, New Dealer and future Supreme Court justice Abe Fortas, and Ernst—proposed a reorganization of the NLG executive board, presumably to facilitate passage of a stronger anticommunist resolution. When that effort failed, Ernst and the others resigned from the National Lawyers Guild, in May 1940.[30] With that decisive and very public move, Ernst cemented his anticommunist credentials with Hoover and the FBI.

It is not clear when Ernst and Hoover (or, actually, Hoover's public relations team, who authored most of his letters) began their decades-long correspondence. Ernst initiated an exchange in October 1941, using the excuse of having received a PR mailing from the Bureau as an opportunity to offer his services as Hoover's mole in New York's liberal and literary circles. In his October 14 letter, he told the director that the *New Republic*, a progressive publication that was frequently critical of the Bureau, was "getting an article written about the FBI." Ernst noted that he was scheduled to receive an advance copy of the article from the author, his friend and ACLU director Roger Baldwin, and he volunteered to forward a copy to the Bureau. Ernst even offered to author a response for Hoover: "I should think you would want to then and there answer whatever criticism there is, and in this connection, I would be honored if you would let me write you a letter containing parts of the answer, to the end that you could incorporate parts of my letter in your answer." Regarding Baldwin's article, Ernst said, "I am convinced that he has got nothing in the way of factual evidence to rely on."[31] Hoover replied on October 17, in a letter written by Nichols. The letter reflected Nichols's instincts to allow contacts to prove themselves, rather than dismissing them as later Crime Records supervisors sometimes did. In the letter, Nichols (for Hoover) asked Ernst to forward a copy of the article and any suggestions he might have for a response. "I would like to impose upon your friendship to the extent that, prior to submitting the [FBI's] answer to the New Republic, you would carefully go over it and make any changes which you think would be desirable," Nichols wrote for Hoover. "If similar situations arise at any time, I trust it will not be an imposition if I ask for your counsel and advice."[32]

It appears that the Japanese attack on Pearl Harbor on December 7, 1941, caused a change in the *New Republic*'s plans to publish Baldwin's article on the FBI. Instead, the magazine published a short piece in its weekly "Washington Notes" column. The short piece—headlined WHAT HAS THE FBI BEEN DOING?—criticized the Bureau for failing to uncover the Pearl Harbor plan through its political intelligence work focused on unmasking spies and saboteurs. The article noted enormous growth in the FBI's budget, from $1.6 million annually prior to World War I to $35 million for the two-year period following President Roosevelt's authorization of FBI domestic surveillance in 1939: "The record so far suggests that Hoover has not overcome his penchant for chasing liberals up blind allies while Axis sympathizers are barricading the streets and while the Marxist secret-society boys and girls promote their devious projects without interference."[33] The article ended with a question about how Hoover would handle his temporary duties as the nation's censor, controlling messages from the press.

Ernst and Hoover met in the Director's Office on December 5, 1941, two days before the Japanese attack on Pearl Harbor. Ernst outlined the meeting topics he hoped to cover in a letter on December 2:

1. Is all your work directed to threats from the Left and none through threats from the Right,—meaning only being concerned with Communists and not with Nazis?
2. Have you gotten specific complaints as to the behavior of local authorities?
3. Can you let me see your synopsis as to all "isms"?[34]

Hoover's staff produced a four-page memorandum for the director, responding to Ernst's questions. Regarding the first, about whether the Bureau focused only on the political Left, Mickey Ladd wrote that the response was obvious from the FBI's record: "Very definitely the Bureau has always given the same consideration to threats from Fascist elements as it has to threats from Communist groups." Ladd suggested that Hoover discuss the Bureau's investigations of the German American Bund as an example supporting that point.[35] Regarding "complaints as to the behavior of local authorities," Ladd surmised that Ernst was referring to complaints leveled by ACLU director Roger Baldwin regarding the FBI's conduct of raids in Detroit in 1940, where the Bureau arrested a dozen American citizens, charging them with recruiting other Americans to fight for the Loyalist cause in the Spanish Civil War. In those raids, critics claimed, the Bureau arrived at 5:00 a.m., knocking down doors and searching homes without warrants. The FBI was roundly criticized by politicians and news media for its "gestapo" tactics in conducting the raids.[36] Ladd further speculated that Ernst could also be concerned that local police practiced even less "finesse" in security investigations than the Bureau did. "His attention might be directed to the fact that the Bureau has conducted numerous investigations of [overzealous] officers under the Civil Rights Statutes," Ladd suggested.[37]

Finally, regarding Ernst's request to review Bureau reports on the "isms," Ladd noted that the FBI kept close track of individual Americans involved in various isms and maintained a catalog of subversives called the Custodial Detention Index (CDI), a list of American citizens to be monitored or arrested without charges in case of a national emergency. Those citizens arrested under the CDI would be subject to a Justice Department tribunal, rather than a hearing in a court of law. In 1943, Attorney General Francis Biddle declared the CDI illegal and ordered Hoover to discontinue its use. Hoover responded by changing the name of the CDI to the Security Index, thus cynically complying with the attorney general's order.[38] Ladd, understanding the controversial nature of such an FBI enemies list, suggested that Hoover "may or may not care to mention" it to Ernst.[39] The two men met, and things apparently went well, although there is no report on the December 5 meeting in Ernst's file. The fact that their cordial correspondence continued unabated suggests that their meeting was positive. What is likely is that Ernst was able, in that face-to-face meeting, to convince Hoover of the sincerity of his anticommunist views and of his willingness to be publicly supportive of the FBI's work.

Denied his opportunity to provide feedback on Baldwin's aborted article by the Japanese attack, Ernst instead offered his public relations advice as a champion of anticensorship causes. President Franklin Roosevelt appointed Hoover as temporary coordinator of censorship in the wake of Pearl Harbor. On December 11, Ernst wrote to Hoover enclosing a two-page press statement to help the FBI director shape and explain his censorship policy. Ernst presented his recommendation as a statement, "drafted to aid you in your basic point of view, and maybe your utterances." The statement offered a strong defense of dissent, focusing instead on censorship as a protection against any compromise of military tactics. "This job is not one of censorship," he wrote in his proposed statement. "It is a job of preventing the loss of American property and lives through divulging to the enemy valuable information. There is no intention to limit in any way opinion and criticism."[40]

Hoover responded with a letter he wrote himself, praising Ernst's statement of censorship principles but noting that "fortunately . . . I am not to be the censor." Roosevelt would instead appoint a permanent director of censorship, Hoover reported. He said, as well, that he would recommend a system of voluntary press censorship, adding, "For the few days that I have been operating in the field of censorship I have found a most hearty and earnest desire upon the part of the press and radio to cooperate." He alluded to the canceled Baldwin article and said he hoped to soon "be back in my groove so that I may be able to continue alert [*sic*] to the rumblings of our mutual friend, R. B."[41] Hoover's quick response so soon after Pearl Harbor, when he was undoubtedly extraordinarily busy, and the fact that he chose to author the letter himself suggest that he sensed value in creating and maintaining a relationship with a liberal icon like Ernst.

On December 31, 1941, Ernst met with Assistant Director Percy Foxworth in New York and again offered PR advice on countering several critical articles that had appeared that month. "Mr. Ernst stated that he would like to be of assistance in countering such material," Foxworth reported in a letter to Hoover. Ernst outlined possible responses to three critical articles. In each case, he said he was a close friend of the writer, editor, or publisher or with a peripheral figure who could put pressure on one of those individuals.

Within a few months, in March 1943, Ernst wrote Hoover again, once more demonstrating the reach of his personal network. He enclosed a letter he wrote to Roosevelt aide Marvin McIntyre. After a salutation of "Dear Mac," which demonstrated his close personal relationship with someone in proximity to FDR, Ernst noted that he had urged that "subversive" groups such as the America First Committee, the Bridges Committee, the Nonpartisan League and others be required to give the Department of Justice their federal income tax documents so that authorities could determine who financed those organizations. In a statement that Hoover undoubtedly cheered (and that would likely have left the attorney's fellow ACLU officials aghast), Ernst justified his position: "There is no civil liberties in anonymity and these bastards can only gain headway through stealth and secrecy."[42] Hoover forwarded a copy of Ernst's enclosure to Attorney General Biddle.[43]

In addition to acting as an informant on the political Left, Ernst became a public relations defender of the FBI in print, frequently penning letters to the editors of publications such as the *Nation*, to counter critical stories about the Bureau. In July 1943 in two articles written by "XXX" (likely the alias for iconoclastic liberal I. F. Stone), the *Nation* attacked the Bureau for its "gestapo" tactics in its loyalty investigations of federal employees. The articles included the account of a ridiculous interview in which agents asked one man why he grew a beard, why he was referred to by a childhood nickname, and why he listened to Russian composer Pyotr Tchaikovsky. Moreover, the agents conducting the interview, according to XXX, wanted to know why the man read the *Nation*, implying that it was a subversive publication. The articles portrayed FBI agents as oafish buffoons asking loaded questions and misunderstanding basic historical and cultural facts.[44] On August 2, 1943, Ernst wrote Hoover to ask if he could help in answering XXX's charges. His suggestion was to make clear that XXX was conflating the work of the Civil Service Commission and the FBI, which shared responsibility for the investigations. "The least that ought to be done," he wrote, "is to separate investigators from the two different departments."[45] The next day, in a letter that must have crossed Ernst's in the mail, Hoover wrote to ask for his help in countering the articles. In his letter, the director included an oft-repeated lie that had become part of his personal story, namely, that he had no role in the Red Scare Palmer Raids of 1919 and 1920. The raids, in which thousands of alleged radicals were rounded up and jailed (most were ultimately released), came to symbolize the Bureau's tendency to overreach. As head of the Bureau's General Intelligence Division, Hoover actually had organized and spearheaded the raids.[46] Ernst's public relations recommendation more directly addressed the problem of XXX's articles, whereas Hoover's letter was a rehash of old FBI PR themes. Apparently greatly motivated to help, Ernst traveled to Washington before he even received the request for assistance and met with Associate Director Clyde Tolson.[47]

After forwarding the FBI a copy for comment, Ernst notified Hoover that his letter to the editor in response to XXX's broadside was being published. In typical Ernst fashion, his letter, addressed to the *Nation*'s editor, Freda Kirchwey, included a personal postscript: "And let's see something of each other this Fall and Winter. It's not right that we have wandered far apart."[48] An edited version of his letter (minus the postscript, of course) appeared in the September 25, 1943, edition of the *Nation*, alongside a letter written, surprisingly, by Ernst's ACLU colleague, Director Roger Baldwin. Baldwin's response, misleadingly headlined IN DEFENSE OF THE FBI, instead defended the Department of Justice's War Policies Unit for its "level-headed" work dealing with allegations of subversion. Ernst, of course, offered a full-throated defense of Hoover and the Bureau, asserting that he had not heard of a single violation of basic civil liberties by the FBI and highlighting his own personal relationship with the director. "The FBI is not perfect, nor is The Nation," he wrote. "But in every case in which I have brought a complaint involving matters of this nature to Edgar Hoover, the complainant and myself have felt that we received sympathetic understanding and proper administrative treatment of the situation."[49] (Ernst's FBI file includes no mention of any such queries to Hoover.) He further argued that the investigations in question were performed by the Civil Service Commission, which was sharing responsibility for loyalty investigations with the FBI. Ernst ended his letter with an unequivocal endorsement of the Bureau, declaring, "I believe its protection of personal liberty is one of the outstanding contributions to the cause of civil liberties in my time in the United States."[50] Nichols authored Hoover's thank-you note to Ernst: "I thought your letter to the editor of The Nation magazine was a classic."[51]

In a response in the same issue, I. F. Stone claimed that Ernst's declaration that he knew of no civil liberties violations by the FBI was "close to a miracle," and then he listed several cases in which the Bureau crossed the line.[52] Never one to concede a point, Ernst penned a response to Stone's response and forwarded copies to the *Nation* and to Hoover. In it, he argued that Stone, in two of his "miracle" examples of FBI civil liberties violations, had "indicted the wrong bureau," a point Stone conceded, though he noted that the other examples clearly involved the FBI.[53] In a letter penned by Clyde Tolson, Hoover thanked Ernst: "I do feel that you have very properly pointed to the defects contained in Stone's most recent effusion."[54]

Ernst continued to act as Hoover's mole in the liberal movement, informing the director in 1943 that a scholarly journal, *Public Administration Review*, planned to publish a piece by a Cornell professor examining investigative procedures of government agencies. The letter prompted a lengthy memorandum compiling FBI and public source information on the professor and the publication.[55] Check marks next to the professor's name and the publication's title indicate that copies of the letter and summary memorandum were indexed in the files of the professor as well.[56] When the article appeared in print later that year, the FBI obtained a copy; the Bureau was mentioned several times, it was noted, although "none of the references can be considered in any sense derogatory."[57]

In 1943, a summary memorandum on Ernst was produced for the Department of Justice. The memorandum is particularly interesting for what it did not include. The five-page document noted Ernst's work for the Newspaper Guild, for New York mayor Fiorello La Guardia, and for Governor Lehman. It repeated Judge Manton's concerns about his radical politics. The writer cited several affiliations considered important, including Ernst's service on boards and committees and his support of the socialist Norman Thomas. Special mention was made of his work for the ACLU, his alleged attendance at Communist Party meetings, and the mention of Ernst in several *Daily Worker* stories.[58] The memorandum does not read like a document concerning someone who became a friend of the FBI, and the information it contains certainly does not indicate the subject was a person who became a highly valuable Bureau PR prop and sometime adviser on PR matters. Considering the audience for the memorandum, Attorney General Biddle, the failure to note Ernst's relationship with the FBI, including his willingness to act as a liberal mole for the Bureau, suggests the value that the agency placed on his cooperation. Outlining his willingness to work with the FBI could have damaged Ernst's credibility within the political Left and thus damaged his value to the Bureau.

Ernst left no doubt about his anticommunist beliefs. When his letter attacking communist influence in labor unions appeared in the *New York Times* on January 18, 1944, Hoover himself wrote a congratulatory letter. Ernst's letter argued that the evil of communism lay in its centralized control structure: "The evil, however, stems from the fact that heads of unions and surreptitiously planted executives of social and liberal organizations must take orders from the executive committee."[59] A few days later, Hoover authored his own letter to Ernst, praising him for having "hit the nail on the head." Ernst's letter was a "masterpiece," Hoover said, and he urged the lawyer to "give him a ring" when he was next in Washington.[60]

Ernst again displayed his ingratiating nature on August 30, 1944, when he forwarded a draft chapter on Hoover from his autobiography, *The Best Is Yet: Reflections of an Irrepressible Man*. By that point, Ernst's letters to Hoover opened with either "Dear John" or "Dear Edgar," and FBI correspondence responded with "Dear Morris." The enclosed draft chapter echoed Ernst's letters to the *Nation* and previewed the themes in a *Reader's Digest* article— "Why I No Longer Fear the F.B.I."—that Ernst would later write and that

Hoover would cite repeatedly over the years as evidence of his civil liberties bona fides. The first paragraph of the draft chapter foreshadowed the title of the later *Reader's Digest* article:

> I started with suspicion. I listened to the blank indiscriminate attacks on him by my civil liberties friends. It was fitting that fringe [*sic*] should be on guard. A national police force carries implicit dangers within itself. But after listening to repetition of assaults on the FBI at Civil Liberties Union meetings and elsewhere I took the time to look into the facts. At that time the FBI had made close to 100,000 arrests, with a record of over 95% of convictions of all cases brought to trial—a higher percentage by far than that [of] headline crime-buster Tom Dewey. Of all the cases there was not one single instance of proven violation of civil liberties. No duress, no holding incommunicado, no rubber hose, no third degree— practices common to police of most big cities.[61]

Ernst included a request that Hoover's staff offer suggestions, and he quipped, "If you think I am completely wrong on my conclusions and judgments, I will give you a chance to be heard provided you buy the drinks."[62] Nichols edited the article, adding his handwritten comments and adjusting some of the statistics. Then he wrote a letter for Hoover's signature. Since Ernst's draft essentially channeled the FBI's line on civil liberties and its claims in the 1940 Detroit cases, it is not surprising that all the suggested changes were minor and not substantive.[63] When the book was released in 1945, Hoover even provided a blurb to promote it: "It is interesting, illuminating and entertaining. It touched me deeply."[64]

The reviews of Ernst's autobiography were harsh, particularly those from liberal and legal circles. Reviewing the book for the *Harvard Law Review*, Fred Rodell, author of the 1944 *Life* magazine hagiography of Ernst, judged it a superficial and poorly written ode to famous friends: "Mr. Ernst cannot resist bombarding the inevitably bored reader with gratuitous references to his intimacy with important and influential people."[65] An anonymous and petulant review in the *New York Guild Lawyer*, a publication of the Lawyers Guild, was forwarded to Hoover. The review began by declaring Ernst an egotist, argued that he was a "source of merriment" for members of the guild, and described the book as "inchoate, confused maleficence of a puny dabbler in things of unconsidered moment." The FBI agent who forwarded the review to Hoover circled one paragraph that excoriated Ernst for defending the Bureau after the Detroit raids. It read, "Was Ernst in hiding then because those were times that tried men's souls and it required firm courage to come out and be counted?"[66] The nature of those reviews would not have pleased FBI public relations officials, but thereafter, the Ernst and Hoover shared the distinction of being attacked by the political Left. The harsh reception for his autobiography likely enhanced Ernst's credibility within the FBI.

Like many of Hoover's "friendships" with opinion shapers such as Ernst, their relationship began in fits and starts, with long periods between letters early on. Then, once Ernst had sufficiently established himself as a faithful defender, liberal mole, and public relations adviser, the correspondence increased in frequency. In November 1945, Ernst forwarded to Hoover a copy of a letter he wrote to President Truman in which he urged action against labor leaders involved in the Communist Party of America.[67] In late 1945, he included Hoover on the mailing list for his daughter's wedding announcement.[68] He provided a report on his trip to Europe in 1946.[69] And in 1947, Ernst offered Hoover some unsolicited PR advice, urging him to temper his endorsement (which was mailed to the FBI mailing list) of a *Memphis Commercial Appeal* article, written by the director's friend Jack Carley, that attacked communists. "I would suggest that in the future any statements that you make endorsing the splendid article of the Memphis Commercial Appeal be restricted so that you do not appear to endorse everything proposed by the Commercial Appeal," Ernst wrote. "I don't like to see you become vulnerable by appearing to endorse all of the positions taken by the Commercial Appeal."[70]

In 1947, Ernst inserted himself into Bureau public relations when he attempted to broker a deal for an FBI movie with movie mogul Samuel Goldwyn. "I am very excited by Sam's approach—a kind of life of an average FBI agent," Ernst wrote. "It will not conflict with your other movie commitments and should be the answer to the millions of kids who have been more affected by the FBI legend than any other force during the past twenty years in our society."[71] Crime Records supervisor Nichols, who brokered the Bureau's movie deals, authored Hoover's response, pleading—as often happened when others attempted to engage the FBI in entertainment deals—that the press of daily business prevented the Bureau from undertaking a film project.[72]

Later in 1947, an Ernst misstep jeopardized his relationship with Hoover. In December 1946, President Harry Truman had established the Committee on Civil Rights, with a broad mandate to review the topic. The fifteen-member committee was headed by General Electric chairman and president Charles

E. Wilson and included Franklin Roosevelt, Jr., and Ernst. The committee's report, issued in October 1947, offered a mild criticism of the FBI, stating that the agency's civil rights investigations had, "upon occasion . . . not measured up to the Bureau's high standards in the handling of other types of cases." Specifically, the report stated that the FBI found enforcement of civil rights laws burdensome and difficult and that investigations were sometimes not as fully pursued as they should have been. And the committee cited the Bureau's relationships with local police as a potential detriment to civil rights investigations: "Having in general established such a wholly sound relationship, it is sometimes difficult for the FBI agent to break this relationship and work without, or even against, the local police when a civil rights case comes along."[73] In its coverage of the report's release, the *New York Times* made no mention of the FBI in its front-page story.[74] The *Times* did print the committee's recommendations on an inside page, including a recommendation that the FBI create a special civil rights unit.[75]

Ten days later, Ernst called Assistant Director Edward A. Tamm, a frequent public relations adviser to Hoover himself and a future federal judge, to explain why he had been out of touch. Ernst stated that he had avoided contacting Hoover for three months while the committee completed its work to avoid providing ammunition to critics of the FBI. He apparently left unsaid just how or why anyone would know if he had written or called Hoover. In a memorandum to the director, Tamm reported, "He said he wanted you to understand why he had not been in touch and that he hoped you had found the Committee's report on civil liberties entirely to your satisfaction."[76] When Tamm told Ernst the director was very disappointed in the report, "Ernst interrupted to say that he had personally eliminated from the report all derogatory references to the Bureau . . . and that this had taken a little 'pushing.'"[77] Tamm also told Ernst that Hoover particularly objected to the finding that the Bureau was reluctant to take on civil rights investigations. "At this point," he noted, "Ernst interrupted again to state that he wanted you to understand the whole picture with reference to the President's Committee."[78]

Ernst's participation in the civil rights report is not mentioned further in his file, but Hoover was not one to forget instances when the Bureau was publicly embarrassed. The discussion reported by Tamm demonstrates that Ernst fundamentally misunderstood his relationship to the FBI. He viewed the modest measures called for by the report as minimal and sought to gain favor with Hoover based on his efforts to eliminate critical references to the

Bureau. He believed he was the director's confidant and secret adviser on public relations and other matters. For their part, however, Hoover and his PR team viewed Ernst as a useful toady. Ernst never understood that Hoover expected total fealty and adherence to the Bureau's worldview as conditions for entry into his circle of "friends."

On March 22, 1947, President Truman issued Executive Order 9835, establishing a program to investigate the loyalty and intentions of all executive branch federal employees. Under the order, the attorney general was charged with creating a list of "totalitarian, fascist, communist or subversive" groups and organizations. The FBI was charged with conducting investigations to establish whether existing federal employees had any connection to such groups or causes; the Civil Service Commission would handle investigations of job applicants for federal positions.[79] The entire program would be overseen by the Loyalty Review Board, which was created to provide political cover and to limit the role of the FBI in order to avoid charges of conducting an anticommunist witch hunt.[80] The board included twenty lawyers and scholars and was led by Seth W. Richardson, a New York attorney. Despite the Bureau's limited role, investigating only existing employees and reporting to the Loyalty Review Board, Truman's loyalty program was reviled by FBI critics as an opportunity for political purges and intrusive investigations—in other words, an anticommunist witch hunt.

In a remarkable note handwritten on a routing slip in early 1948, Hoover expressed his concerns about the criticism being leveled at the Bureau based on its loyalty program investigations:

> I am getting concerned about our public relations situation. We seem to be "going to seed." The attached is an interesting article but we ought to be getting out some items like this ourselves. The CSC [Civil Service Commission] & Seth Richardson [head of the Loyalty Review Board] have been giving out a lot about loyalty inv[estigations] whereas FBI which does the real work has been unusually silent. During the Hiss Chambers case we have not made any effort thru our contacts to protect our position. All of this quiescence on part of FBI in all its fields results in public & Congress losing interest in us. By the time we make up it may be too late to regain our prestige.[81]

Hoover may have been reacting, in part, to another bit of advice from Ernst after a January 24, 1948, article appeared in the *New York Times*. It reported on a debate between the attorney general, Tom Clark, and a former assistant attorney general, John Lord O'Brian, before the New York State Bar Association. Clark's defense of the program likely was not staunch enough for Ernst. And O'Brian's statement that there was no way to justify "this radical departure from historic policy" was too much for him. "For God's sake get Edgar to get out a complete statement in accordance with the interview appearing in today's *New York Times* showing that there is no basis for hysteria," Ernst wrote.[82] A review of the *Times* from December into January demonstrates that Hoover was right in being concerned about public relations.

It was rare for Hoover to have to prod his Crime Records Section supervisors and agents to seek out publicity. The director was likely reacting to a pair of stories in the *New York Times* that appeared in late December 1947 and early January 1948. In a front-page story on December 28, Richardson promised that the program would not degenerate into a witch hunt.[83] The January 4 story, buried deep in a Sunday edition, restated Richardson's "frank" pledge and again presented him and the Loyalty Review Board, instead of the FBI, as the focal point of the loyalty program.[84]

At about the same time, Hoover requested from his correspondence team a letter to Ernst in response to his request for information about the director's appearance before the Loyalty Review Board. It is very likely that the letter was at least edited by Milton Jones in the Crime Records Section. When it arrived in the director's office, however, Hoover attacked it with his blue pen, stating the language lacked "punch & virility" and describing the work as a "'namby-pamby' epistle."[85] Though the language of the letter did not appeal to Hoover, the subject matter—the FBI's take on Hoover's appearance before the Loyalty Review Board—is interesting given Hoover's concerns that the board was overshadowing the FBI. In the letter, Hoover noted the relatively small role the board would play in the program. "To my knowledge, the Loyalty Review Board has not been called upon to hear a single case and if I may judge from the results already obtained, they will hear few, if any, cases," the original letter said. Paradoxically, Hoover was frustrated that the FBI was not given credit for its large role in the loyalty program, but he then complained about the so-called smear campaign being waged against the agency because it was conducting the investigations. "I am concerned, however, when otherwise loyal, patriotic citizens are duped by the propaganda emanating from the dishonest kinds of subversive individuals," he stated. As an addition to that sentence, Hoover scrawled in the margin: "& parrot the statements & phrases of these subverters of democracy."[86]

Ernst was ready to provide public relations advice and, whenever possible, to issue his own defense of the Bureau. On February 2, 1948, he urged Hoover to begin releasing a weekly report tallying the total number of employees still to be investigated, the number already checked, the number of employees found loyal, and the total resignations and prosecutions resulting from the program. "I know you are not concerned about such criticism any more than you are about the commies whipping up a witch-hunt," Ernst wrote. "As a matter of fact, we will get to the non-hysterical stage when one side balances out the other in their exaggeration and your Department will come out on even keel with the public esteem, which it deserves."[87] In the bottom margin of the page, sometime public relations adviser Assistant Director Tamm wrote: "I think weekly is too often. How about once a month?"[88] Hoover and his PR team took Ernst's advice. The director wrote to inform Ernst of the plan to provide monthly reports on the loyalty program, noting, "This should furnish the information to the reading public in order that the so-called witch-hunt cries will be dissipated."[89]

A few days later, Ernst again offered public relations advice related to the loyalty program, urging Hoover to call off his Crime Records team, which had been issuing dozens of requests for corrections and letters to the editor from Hoover as the witch hunt charges arose. "If you don't mind my being impertinent, may I suggest that I think you are getting a little thin-skinned, and I think you are probably writing too many letters making corrections of attacks on the FBI," Ernst wrote. "I don't blame you for being sore, but I think there must be some better strategy than having you answer these attacks."[90] He may have been right, but the FBI operated under the principle of scrupulously avoiding embarrassment. Whenever the Bureau had been subjected to widespread criticism that threatened to become a meme such as the prior gestapo claims, the Crime Records Section repeatedly worked to counter those notions, with Hoover being the only public spokesman for the FBI.

In late 1948, Hoover again penned a highly critical evaluation of FBI public relations efforts. When Nichols reported that Ernst had renewed his attempts to put Samuel Goldwyn to work on an FBI motion picture, Hoover, no doubt still stinging from the smear related to the loyalty program, replied in a note on Nichols's memorandum: "I would very much like to have a really good picture on the Bureau—I don't consider the last one [*The Street with No Name*] as a class 'A' one. However we *can't* do it because we are not equipped for it. Our *whole* public relations has been in the doldrums for the last 9 months. We must get the *essential* things working properly first before embarking on such a project as this."[91]

Once again, Ernst was prepared to offer a public defense of the FBI's loyalty investigations. In a 1949 article in the *Saturday Review*, he decried the "hysteria" of critics of the program who had not explored the statistics. Ernst once more offered the argument that the loyalty program only harmed those who had not behaved themselves. Echoing the public relations message he had suggested to the FBI, he argued that few federal employees had been dismissed under the program and that the investigation of millions of people was thus fully justified: "The question I now ask," Ernst wrote, "is, isn't it possible that the hysteria was increased because the people who were shouting hysteria never looked or were given occasion by the press to look at the facts?"[92] He noted that of 2.6 million employees investigated, all but 10,724 were immediately cleared and just 91 were dismissed. Then he offered a few lines of boilerplate from the FBI's PR template. "Keep in mind that the FBI can't fire or hire," he said. "It only investigates and reports. . . . Bear in mind also that the FBI must as a constabulary, put everything it gets into its files—facts, rumor, garbage, whatnot, because the greatest danger freedom can face is a police force granted power to screen its files."[93] Hoover could not have authored a better defense, and Ernst, mimicking a line frequently used by the director, had again proven his public relations value to the FBI.

Many of Ernst's contributions to Bureau PR were facilitated by the FBI's own internal networker, Nichols. Ernst's value as a credible liberal defender led Nichols to work hard to maintain a relationship. Later, after Nichols retired, the relationship began to fall apart. In November 1949, Nichols took the unusual (for the FBI) step of asking Ernst to edit the Bureau's annual report. Ernst responded with a letter and a three-page memorandum of edits and recommendations, including suggestions for clarifying the agency's work on the loyalty program that continued to be a source of critical commentary. "I think you must make clearer than you have the distinction between the loyalty program and the investigations that you conducted outside of it in relation to employees' loyalty," he wrote. He added that the Bureau should clarify under what circumstances it tapped wires "and the Hoover position on indiscriminate wire-tapping."[94] Nichols's handwritten comment on that recommendation and most of the others was simply "No."[95] Such responses indicate that asking Ernst for his opinion was merely a performative exercise. In most instances, the value of the FBI's interactions with Ernst lay in what amounted to flattery, which the "liberal mole" paid back by providing advocacy and inside information.

There was one instance in which Ernst's contribution was of significantly greater value to the Bureau than even to Ernst, and it marked the high point and start of the decline of their relationship. By the time Ernst's *Saturday Review* article appeared in print, the Bureau already had a plan in mind for him to author a civil liberties defense of the FBI that would be printed in the nation's most-read magazine, *Reader's Digest*. The editor of *Reader's Digest* was Hoover's close friend Fulton Oursler. For years, the Crime Records Section and its Correspondence Unit had maintained a friendly relationship with Oursler that had frequently paid PR dividends for the Bureau. Oursler was a Baltimore native whose relationship with the FBI began when he was editor of *Liberty* magazine in the 1930s. Moving to *Reader's Digest* in 1942, Oursler was also an author and freelance writer; his 1949 religious best seller, *The Greatest Story Ever Told*, sold 1.5 million copies. His friendship with Hoover included several in-person meetings, but it was primarily maintained via frequent letters. The director's correspondence team even maintained a relationship with Oursler's wife, Grace.[96] In return, Oursler became a reliable defender and promoter of Hoover's agenda.

The idea of a *Reader's Digest* article endorsing the FBI as a protector of civil liberties came from Nichols in October 1949 and no doubt was related to Hoover's critical evaluations of the Bureau's public relations "doldrums." Ernst was the perfect author for such a testimonial, given his position with the ACLU and his credibility in liberal circles. The first mention of asking Ernst to write an article for *Reader's Digest* occurred on October 18, 1949, when Nichols told Tolson that he had taken the idea to Oursler.[97] On November 2, Nichols reported to Tolson that Oursler and *Reader's Digest* publisher DeWitt Wallace responded favorably and that Ernst was pleased and enthusiastic but was concerned that "the field was so broad that unless he pinpointed his subject his article would lose its effectiveness."[98] In a handwritten comment, Hoover worried that Ernst could not be trusted to cover the issue effectively and would do a "loop de loop" and address another topic entirely.[99] Specifically, he worried that Ernst would use the opportunity to defend actor Fredric March, a friend of his who was one of several Hollywood figures named in an FBI report released in June 1949 identifying alleged communists in the film industry. The report was read aloud in court as part of the espionage trial of Judith Coplon, accused of stealing government secrets for Russia.[100]

Ernst, meanwhile, continued advocating for the FBI to "take the offensive" against loyalty program critics. He recommended that Hoover attend one of his weekly dinners in New York, where members of the media mixed socially with Hollywood actors, Washington and New York political and government officials, and other luminaries. Nichols demurred, arguing that Hoover was too busy.[101] Hoover again expressed his concern that Ernst had ulterior motives, commenting, "No. I don't want to do this. I anticipate he would include such individuals as [actor and outspoken liberal] Fredric March et al."[102]

Ernst's work on the *Reader's Digest* article continued with a rambling letter to Oursler offering possible topics; it could not have been heartening to an editor seeking a coherent publication. Ernst said he wanted to "tell the story of the FBI to the American public," but he offered an outline that would be more suitable for a book than a magazine article. The topics he proposed covered everything from enemy aliens and Pearl Harbor to wiretapping. "I have a lot of other angles that might be worth going into, and as a matter of fact, I would welcome your editorial guidance because the difficulty of the piece, as I see it, is in limiting the material," Ernst told Oursler.[103]

As he worked with the editor to perfect the civil liberties article for *Reader's Digest*, Ernst was drawn into a dispute with a fellow ACLU member, former Federal Communications Commission (FCC) chairman James Fly. A Texas native, Fly graduated from the US Naval Academy in 1920 and earned his law degree from Harvard in 1926. Prior to being named FCC chairman by President Roosevelt in 1940, he served as an antitrust lawyer in the Department of Justice, as general counsel for the Electric Home and Farm Authority, as solicitor for the Tennessee Valley Authority (TVA), and as general counsel for the TVA. Fly served as chairman of the FCC from 1940 to 1944 and as chair of the Defense Communications Board during that same period. Republican Wendell Willkie once said of Fly, "He is the most dangerous man in the United States—to have on the other side."[104]

As chairman of the FCC, Fly staked out a position critical of the industries the agency regulated, objecting to backslapping cronyism between regulators and the radio industry, asserting that the major networks were seeking a monopoly, and charging that the National Association of Broadcasters was a "stooge" organization. During Fly's tenure, the National Broadcasting Corporation was forced to divest itself of one of the two radio networks it established in 1926. After leaving government service in 1944, Fly returned to private practice and became a director in the ACLU. In a letter to the *New York Times*, published in 1948, he warned of the dangers of reactionary politics. "It is ever so important that in our country democratic principles be harnessed in the interests of the people as a whole," he wrote. "With a soundly progressive government, democracy cannot fail. But more witch-burning will never cure sorcery."[105]

In 1949, Fly turned his attention to the subject with perhaps the most potential to embarrass Hoover and the FBI—wiretapping. On June 14, 1949, he wrote to Attorney General Tom Clark, stating his intentions while praising Hoover for his apparent restraint in the use of wiretaps. "I am sincerely and deeply interested in the social, philosophical and constitutional principles involved in wire-tapping," he wrote. "I am going to do my best to see it wiped out. This is probably unnecessary, but I want to make explicit the fact that this—and other debates—are without any personal feeling on my part."[106] Fly said he harbored no ill feelings for Hoover, noting, "I would still stand ready to acknowledge the tremendous job he has done for law enforcement, and his signal achievement in building an effective agency."[107] Hoover was unimpressed, scrawling a comment on the routing slip attached to Fly's letter: "This fellow Fly certainly misrepresents the FBI position & activities."[108]

Fly's critique of wiretapping was based on solid legal ground. The Communications Act of 1934 banned the interception and disclosure of the contents of telephone conversations. Hoover believed the law did not apply to the FBI as long as it did not disclose information gained by wiretapping or provide it to prosecutors. In other words, he intended to continue using wiretapping for intelligence-gathering rather than evidence-gathering purposes. In 1937, though, the US Supreme Court, in *United States v. Nardone*, ruled that the ban included the activities of federal agents. In 1939, Hoover was forced to admit, in testimony before a House committee, that the Bureau had continued wiretapping even after the Nardone ruling.[109]

Wiretapping by the FBI did not cease at that point, however, thanks to a secret 1940 order from President Roosevelt, who, ignoring the Communications Act and the high court, authorized Hoover and the FBI to continue wiretapping subversive activities. For twenty-five years after that secret order, Hoover used it to justify at least 6,769 illegal wiretaps.[110] The September 27, 1949, issue of *Look* magazine included Fly's article, "The Case against

Wiretapping." In it, Fly singled out the FBI as being the "most extensive of wire tappers." "We have no way of knowing how much tapping FBI agents do," Fly wrote. "There is complete concealment on those statistics: the number of persons whose conversations were heard; the charges involved and the convictions obtained."[111]

The Fly charges represented a significant public relations challenge for Hoover and the FBI. At several points during the agency's history, critical voices emerged challenging the Bureau's image as a protector of civil liberties. Wiretapping was a longtime concern among civil libertarians, and Ernst—the Bureau's liberal mole and a key prop in its campaign to convince the public that Hoover was a protector of freedom—was prepared to step in and defend the FBI. On October 24, 1949, he wrote a plea to the ACLU, urging it to condemn Fly's criticism and issue a statement supporting the Bureau. In response, Fly wrote to Ernst, agreeing that the organization should be fair to the FBI. "At the same time your own close personal relation to Mr. Hoover has blinded you to the fairness of the fair critics," Fly stated. "You appear long since to have lost your judicial poise on any issue involving this one agency, and I think it is about time you were taking inventory."[112] Fly tied the issue of wiretapping to the FBI's role in the loyalty program. "With so much power lodged in a single agency—coupled with a great aura of secrecy and the refusal to account to the public—certain excesses are the normal result," he asserted.[113] Next, Fly obliquely criticized those who provided the FBI with "blind support" and urged Ernst instead to "support or to criticize as specific issues emerge."[114] Finally, Fly suggested that Ernst had abdicated his responsibilities as a civil libertarian. "Mr. Hoover needs criticism," he wrote. "That is not only part of the democratic process, but with an institution of this power and character criticism is well nigh essential. . . . More danger comes from the fear to criticise [*sic*] than from criticism itself. It must be not only tolerated but welcomed."[115]

Ernst provided Hoover with a copy of the letter, which the director turned over to his public relations staff with a note: "Fly's letter should be carefully gone over. I know he is a stinker & a liar, but nevertheless I want it carefully digested to determine any truth in it from which we may benefit in improving & correcting our procedures."[116] Fly urged Ernst to ask his friends at the FBI "to pull out any sizable stack of reports" as evidence that the Bureau was focusing on surveillance of the political Left.[117] Hoover viewed that as an effort to get access to FBI files "so as to have a Roman holiday."[118]

Look publisher Mike Cowles disavowed the Fly article, claiming it had slipped through while he was vacationing in Europe.[119] He also asked journalist Leo Rosten to contact Nichols about producing an FBI response. Nichols suggested that Ernst could write it, but Cowles and Rosten vetoed that idea; in his memorandum to Tolson, he remarked, "They thought that in the long run the reaction might be adverse except in a very small circle of liberals who know Ernst."[120] Instead, Nichols urged Hoover to consider the idea, stating, "I think that this offers excellent opportunities and I certainly would be in favor of doing it." Hoover refused. "I thought it was understood *we* (FBI) would not pursue Fly matter," he scrawled on the memo. "Of course Look or any other group would like to get me into a public controversy re wire-tapping. If Fly is to be taken on it will have to be by someone other than us."[121]

Hoover's very bad 1949 continued in October with yet another broadside in the press. On October 19, *Harper's* magazine published an article, "Due Notice to the F.B.I.," written by influential scholar and writer Bernard DeVoto. In it, DeVoto described a fictional interrogation by a government agent who inquires about a neighbor. The agent, a Mr. Craig, asks whether the neighbor has ever gone swimming in the nude at Bay View, whether he has suffered indigestion, and whether he reads the *New Republic*. "Do you think the questions I have put in Mr. Craig's mouth are absurd?" DeVoto asked *Harper's* readers. "They are exactly like the questions that are asked of every government employee about whom a casual derogatory remark has been unearthed, even if that remark was made twenty years ago, even if a fool or an aspirant to the employee's job made it."[122] DeVoto argued that the FBI's conduct of loyalty investigations was turning the United States into a society of hunters and the hunted: "There is loose in the United States the same evil that once split Salem Village between the bewitched and the accused and stole men's reason away."[123]

Hoover ordered a review of Bureau procedures to determine whether questions like "Do you read the *New Republic*?" were allowed as part of loyalty investigations. Nichols reported to Tolson that Bureau manuals "do not contain a specific admonition that the question 'Do you read the New Republic' not be asked."[124] The director telegraphed all offices in 1941, Nichols reported, ordering that "questions may not be asked concerning membership in non subversive [*sic*] organizations, periodicals or publications, unless admittedly official organs of Communist Party."[125] In 1947, Hoover issued a *Bureau Bulletin*—a statement of policy to local FBI offices—specifically noting that "[questions like] 'Do you read the New Republic?' or 'Do you read

The Nation' or similar periodicals, [should] not be asked."[126] Those statements were provided to Ernst.[127] Hoover also wrote to Daniel Mebane, publisher of the *New Republic*. Before sending that letter, in which he argued that DeVoto had put the *New Republic* and the FBI in the same boat, "faced with unproven, undocumented attacks,"[128] Nichols showed the Mebane letter to Ernst, who recommended several edits.[129] Ernst also met with Mebane and the *New Republic* staff to press the FBI's public relations message of restraint; he reported that he had done the Bureau some good and that *New Republic* staffers were angry with DeVoto.[130] "He stated that if the Director were to sit down with the *New Republic* group, the Director's first impressions would be pity for their almost abject stupidity."[131] Ernst recommended that Nichols meet with the *New Republic* staffers to try to take advantage of the opportunity of them joining the FBI in the "same boat."[132] There is no record that Nichols followed up on Ernst's recommendation.

The public relations peril for the FBI deepened when, on December 5, 1949, the United States Court of Appeals reversed the espionage conviction of Judith Coplon. Coplon had been convicted of passing secrets to the Soviet Union through her co-conspirator, Valentin Gubitchev. The conviction had been complicated by revelations that FBI wiretaps were employed in the investigation of Coplon. The appeals court held that the government failed to prove that those wiretaps did not lead to any of the evidence introduced in the trial. Chief Judge Learned Hand mentioned the illegal FBI wiretaps in his opinion: "By hypothesis, the evidence [against Coplon] should not be introduced, and would not have been found, if officials had not violated the laws designed to deny them access to it."[133] Fly wrote Ernst, in another letter the recipient turned over to Hoover, that "I am wondering if even you do not have your stomach turned by the recent exposures of various illegal activities of the FBI."[134] In a handwritten note, Hoover agreed with Ernst's evaluation of the PR problem posed by the Coplon decision: "I certainly agree with Ernst that the record looks *very* bad but I seem to be alone in that view within the Bureau. I do wish our own officials would not be so blind & stop whistling in the dark. Let us face realities & facts."[135]

Nichols met with Ernst to strategize an FBI response to Fly. Ernst reported that arrangements for the *Reader's Digest* article had been settled and that he would be paid $1,000. The Bureau strategy, he advised Nichols, should be to demonstrate that FBI wiretapping was limited and that other agencies did their own wiretapping. Ernst then suggested taking the offensive by looking into an incident in Fly's past that had generated criticism. In the wake of the attack on Pearl Harbor, several officials, including FCC chairman Fly, had been criticized for hampering the intelligence agency's work. In its report, the Roberts Commission, led by Supreme Court justice Owen Roberts, found that restrictions on wiretapping had hampered the FBI's efforts to uncover the plot to attack Pearl Harbor: "The United States being at peace with Japan, restrictions imposed prevented resort to certain methods of obtaining the content of messages transmitted by telephone or radio telegraph over lines operating between Oahu and Japan."[136] In 1943, a special congressional committee, led by Representative Eugene E. "Goober" Cox, investigated the Fly-led FCC; among other things, the committee looked into rumors that Fly was partially responsible for the Pearl Harbor attack because his FCC refused to shut down Japanese-language radio stations in Hawaii before December 7, 1941. The Cox investigation was described by one historian as "the most vindictive, legally questionable, unethical, and embarrassing investigation conducted by the House of Representatives."[137] Nevertheless, Hoover agreed with Ernst that using the investigation against Fly was an option to silence his criticism. "Maybe Fly's obstructionist tactics in Hawaii might be worked in," he wrote.[138]

Two weeks later, Ernst's personal public relations campaign continued with a letter he wrote to Phillip Graham, publisher of the *Washington Post*, in which he tried out his recommended strategy, minus the references to Pearl Harbor. "I assume you are aware of the fact that the FBI's use of wiretapping is limited and is under the written directive of the Attorney General," Ernst wrote. "Take a look at Internal Revenue or military tapping. It is my impression that no Cabinet officer approved in those cases and that is where the number of taps takes place."[139] In the meantime, the attorney general issued a news release stating that the FBI had less than 170 active wiretaps, a release that Ernst thought was helpful in combating Fly.[140] Ernst's next recommendation was for Hoover to release the 1940 FDR memorandum that authorized continued FBI wiretapping despite the Nardone decision.[141] On February 8, he called Nichols to report that he had met with Fly, who agreed to withdraw from the campaign against the Bureau—a report Nichols told Tolson was "almost too good to be true."[142] It was. Ernst shared a copy of Fly's February 8 letter with Hoover. It included no fewer than twelve provisions he felt had to be included in any policy or law addressing wiretapping. "Fly is very clever," Hoover wrote. "He tries to appear he is yielding yet his so-called accession is so restricted it is his same old proposition."[143]

During February and March, Nichols and the public relations staff in

Crime Records turned their attention to Ernst's *Reader's Digest* article, which would be the most important and by far the most widely read response to wiretapping and loyalty program critics. In early February, Oursler called Nichols to discuss the article. Oursler was disappointed in the draft and said he had not forwarded it to the Pleasantville, New York, editorial offices of *Reader's Digest* for fear the article would be killed. Oursler asked Nichols to look the article over and suggest changes. Nichols told Tolson he believed the article was good and that Oursler was becoming more and more difficult to work with. He also said he would provide a few more anecdotes to sway Oursler's opinion, commenting, "Fulton is a great one for these dramatic incidents."[144] Nichols turned the article over to Crime Records chief Jones, who recommended several strategies to improve the manuscript by adding the kinds of dramatic incidents that Oursler liked. "The article, 14 typewritten pages in length, contains very few illustrative stories," Jones wrote in a memorandum to Nichols. "This, of course, makes readability more difficult and also, to a certain extent, may make the article less effective."[145] Jones provided narratives of several suggested incidents related to Ernst's main points on wiretapping and the FBI's loyalty investigations.

Oursler contacted Ernst directly to urge that he rework the article to more firmly emphasize the main concept, "that of a famous liberal who viewed the FBI with great suspicion and some fear, investigated it for himself, and emerged as one of its most enthusiastic champions." The editor recommended that Ernst focus on that point, illustrating it with "potent anecdotes." Oursler added that a "great deal of work" was necessary before the manuscript could be published.[146] Nichols was left to act as intermediary, translating Ernst's intentions for Oursler and Oursler's recommendations for Ernst. The two men finally agreed to meet to fix the article.[147] Nichols's willingness and ability to mediate demonstrated why he was so effective. He knew both men personally and very well because of his constant efforts to maintain a network of FBI supporters. (Later occupants of Nichols's position were far less flexible and more dogmatic, and they were often unwilling to massage the egos or mediate disputes among authors and editors.) Nichols continued his mediation until a satisfactory version of the article was finally produced in late summer 1950. Hoover, in a letter written by Nichols, thanked Ernst for persevering: "You have been a real source of encouragement and a tower of strength over the years and this is but another evidence of your many efforts to be helpful."[148]

Even as he continued to advise Hoover on public relations matters, Ernst remained in his other role as the Bureau's mole inside the ACLU. When Fly proposed that the ACLU make a public statement condemning wiretapping, Ernst provided Hoover with a copy of that statement and with an alternative version authored by ACLU staff counsel Herbert M. Levy.[149] Agents in the Crime Records Section produced a seven-page memorandum countering the much shorter Levy proposal, and the Bureau memorandum was provided to Ernst.[150]

As Ernst and Oursler labored to prepare the perfect liberal defense of Hoover and the FBI, yet another PR crisis emerged. The August 28, 1950, issue of *Publisher's Weekly* included a notice that a book by longtime FBI foil and liberal Washington insider Max Lowenthal, *The Federal Bureau of Investigation*, would be published later that year.[151] Nichols reported that same week that *Reader's Digest* editor Oursler had done some research with his contacts in the publishing industry, who recommended that "a conspiracy of silence is the most effective manner in killing off a book."[152] The book was a ten-year project for Lowenthal, a close confidant of President Truman. The FBI had monitored him for years and rightly expected the book to be highly critical. Hoover engaged Ernst, the well-known censorship opponent, to contact the publisher, William Sloane Associates, and urge that the book be canceled. Ernst recommended against direct intervention of that sort, arguing that it could backfire. As Nichols reported to Hoover and Tolson, "He is still reluctant to contact the publishers as he is fearful that they might seize upon any contact and issue a statement that the Director, through his attorney, had approached them on the book." Oursler's advice to Nichols for dealing with the book included a recommendation that "if something could be done to get the word out as to who Lowenthal is this would probably force the reviewers to be cautious and force editors and publishers to be more skeptical."[153] Ernst was willing to do just that and began intervening with friends in the media, arguing that the book was inaccurate and thus planting a seed of doubt with book review editors. On September 18, 1950, Nichols reported on a meeting with Ernst, who had called a book review editor (the name is redacted) at the *New York Times*; Ernst told Nichols that the editor "will be careful as to just whom he would assign [the review]."[154]

Ernst next proposed that the Bureau issue a booklet titled *The Federal Bureau of Investigation* to confuse the issue and then urge the Library of Congress to contact William Sloan Associates to ask "if the publisher knows that they have indexed a writing under a similar title and that considerable confusion on the public might occur unless the title is changed."[155] Hoover intervened through a handwritten note: "Just tell Ernst to drop it. There is no use of pressing more on it."[156] Instead, the Crime Records Section labored to prepare critical reviews of the book and planted them with journalist friends such as syndicated columnists George Sokolsky and Fulton Lewis, Jr.

Ernst's *Reader's Digest* article finally appeared in the December 21, 1950, issue. It has been cited as a direct response to Lowenthal, but of course, the article was in the works for almost a year before the Bureau was aware that Lowenthal's book existed. Headlined WHY I NO LONGER FEAR THE F.B.I., the article was presented as an unsolicited testimonial from a credible liberal who endorsed Hoover and the Bureau wholeheartedly. Ernst told readers he had been carefully studying the FBI and had learned that "lies were being spread against it." He concluded that "nothing oppressive" had been done by the Bureau in its loyalty investigations. "Those who feared the bureau—as I once did—will be glad to know the facts. The FBI is unique in the history of national police. It has a magnificent record of respect for individual freedom. It invites documented complaints against its agents. It has zealously tried to prevent itself from violating the democratic process."[157]

Hoover was pleased with the Ernst article. The Bureau immediately mailed 375 reprints to its mailing list of opinion leaders, including journalists, members of Congress, police officials, members of the clergy, and others.[158] That was just the beginning. In his autobiography, former FBI assistant director William Sullivan said the Bureau "mailed out copies by the thousands."[159] Meanwhile, Ernst's article earned him praise in several FBI-authorized books. Even more than fifty years later, Ernst's name was dropped by former FBI assistant to the director Mark Felt in his memoirs as evidence of Hoover's civil liberties credibility.[160]

The importance of Ernst's 1950 article from a public relations perspective can hardly be exaggerated. *Reader's Digest* boasted the largest circulation of any magazine in the world; each issue was read by more than 10 million people. Faced with credible and vocal criticism from the political Left regarding the Bureau's wiretapping and loyalty program investigations, Nichols maneuvered a credible testimonial from a famed liberal with connections to the ACLU and got it published in the most widely read periodical on the planet. Ernst's article became the Bureau's go-to citation on civil liberties questions for years afterward. It also marked the high point of his relationship with the FBI, a relationship that unraveled over the course of the succeeding years as Ernst's utility faded in a whirlwind of self-inflicted public relations damage and as another ACLU mole took his place.

From 1950 to 1957, Ernst's interactions with Hoover and Nichols became less frequent. In 1957, though, the relationship came apart completely over two issues, the Alger Hiss case and Ernst's advocacy on behalf of Dominican president Rafael Trujillo—advocacy that made Ernst a pariah in the eyes of the US media and thus a potential embarrassment to the FBI.

A former State Department official, Alger Hiss was convicted of perjury in an espionage case in 1950 after being accused two years earlier of passing secrets to the Soviet Union during the 1930s. He denied the charges, but the testimony of an admitted Soviet agent, Hede Massing, led to Hiss's conviction. He was sentenced to five years in prison. The FBI's analysis of a typewriter that was allegedly used to copy stolen documents became an issue in the trial and appeals. The issue was revived in May 1957 with the publication of Hiss's memoirs, *In the Court of Public Opinion*. Hiss asserted that it was possible to commit forgery by typewriter, calling the competence of the FBI Crime Laboratory into question at the very least and even suggesting a conspiracy in the Bureau to secure his conviction.[161] Hoover, of course, denied the charges. On May 13, the director received a letter from *Newsweek* reporter Ralph de Toledano, who enclosed a letter he had received from Ernst. The latter document is not included in Ernst's FBI file, but a copy of de Toledano's letter to Ernst is in the *Newsweek* reporter's file. In it, de Toledano expressed shock at Ernst's testimonial in an advertisement for Hiss's book that appeared in that day's *New York Times*. "Is the self-serving declaration of a convicted perjurer sufficient grounds on which to accuse the FBI of subornation?" de Toledano asked.[162] In the ad, Ernst was quoted as saying the book made him believe Hiss was innocent: "I have a hunch that the validity of the court processes in the Hiss case may one day be profoundly re-examined."[163] It came as a shock, de Toledano wrote to Hoover, to learn that Ernst would lend his credibility to "the shabby efforts of the pro-Hiss and pro-Communist forces." He added that the only pro-Hiss comments he had seen regarding *In the Court of Public Opinion* came from Ernst and the *Daily Worker*.[164] In a reply authored by Nichols, Hoover told de Toledano that his letter was the first he had heard of Ernst's apparent betrayal.[165]

It was Ernst's association with Dominican Republic strongman Rafael Trujillo, however, that ended his relationship with Hoover and damaged his credibility within liberal intellectual circles. Trujillo ruled the Dominican Republic from February 1930 until his assassination on May 30, 1961. As commander-in-chief of the Dominican army, Trujillo had facilitated a February coup that allowed him to be "elected" president with 99 percent of the vote; he was sworn in as president on June 16, 1930. Although "El Jefe," as he was known, stepped down from the presidency in 1938, he nonetheless remained the de facto leader of the Dominican Republic until he was reelected president in 1942. He served in that office until 1952, when he ceded the office—but not the power—to his brother Hector. Throughout his reign, Trujillo outlawed opposition and used violence to strengthen his hold on power. "There is nothing near a complete list of his victims," the *New York Times* reported the day after his assassination. "It is widely thought, however, that they number in the tens of thousands. Some were openly denounced as enemies and shot. But often bizarre and even wildly improbable charges were brought against the victims, or, just as often, the victims simply disappeared."[166]

Jesús de Galindez, a Basque scholar and lecturer at Columbia University in New York, was one of Trujillo's victims who simply disappeared. De Galindez had written a doctoral dissertation exposing the violence and corruption of the Trujillo regime, and he was seeking a publisher when he disappeared on March 12, 1956. Norman Thomas, a friend of de Galindez and former Socialist Party candidate for president, told the *New York Times* that de Galindez said he had been threatened. "He was very fearful," Thomas remarked. "I had a high regard for him as a man and a scholar."[167] In his book, de Galindez accused Trujillo of more than 140 political assassinations, as well as establishing a spy service abroad to check on Dominicans away from home.[168]

On July 11, 1957, Ernst informed Nichols that he had been hired by the Trujillo regime to investigate the de Galindez case. In fact, Ernst had been hired by Sydney S. Baron, an American public relations firm engaged by the Trujillo regime.[169] Hoover was skeptical, writing several notes on the related memorandum. In one, he accused Ernst of doing exactly what he always did: "Ernst is always maneuvering in his own interest." And then, at the bottom of the memorandum, Hoover indicated that his agents should not assist Ernst in his investigation. "If Ernst again contacts us re this," the director stated "he should be told to deal *directly* with the Dept. [of Justice]. I am surprised he would come near FBI after *concurring* with Hiss that FBI fabricated the 'typewriter' in the Hiss trial."[170] Hoover ordered Nichols to tell Ernst why the FBI would not cooperate with his investigation. "I told him we certainly did not appreciate the implications and the implied reflection upon the Bureau [of Ernst's statement that Hiss was innocent]," Nichols reported to Tolson.[171] That same day, Ernst wrote to Nichols that he was "bewildered" and "shocked" by the FBI's disappointment in him. "I have never found any per-suasiveness in the manufactured typewriter story," he wrote to Nichols. "In any event, you must know by now, if you ever will learn, my profound and publicly stated admiration and faith in the FBI."[172] The pleading tone of Ernst's letter would become a common theme in his correspondence with the Bureau going forward. That same day, Hoover cut off contact with Ernst. "He is a liar & I want no explanations from him," he wrote. "I will not allow any FBI contact with him."[173]

It seems Ernst never could understand why Hoover ended their relation-ship. Nichols, however, maintained contact with him as a protective mea-sure, given the sensitive nature of Ernst's Trujillo investigation. In fact, Ernst's position in that investigation—that he would turn over his conclu-sions to the FBI—was exactly what Hoover did not want. By accepting Ernst's investigative product, the Bureau would be tacitly admitting that its own investigation was flawed, something Hoover would never allow. Fur-thermore, Hoover knew something he hoped Ernst's investigation would not discover: de Galindez had been a Bureau informant and had been paid $10,500 in salary and expenses by the FBI's New York office between 1950 and 1956 for supplying information about the Dominican Republic—a fact with enormous potential to embarrass the Bureau.[174]

The tone of Ernst's communications with Nichols became increasingly petulant as his estrangement from Hoover became more obvious. In Octo-ber 1957, he wrote to Nichols claiming credit for obtaining a statement from the ACLU that supported the continued secrecy of FBI files. Nichols's hand-written notation offered the first indication that the FBI had by that time left its ACLU-affiliated liberal mole, Ernst, behind and had found a replacement: "This is funny when I started this move [to obtain a statement from the ACLU on the secrecy of FBI files] with Irving Ferman."[175] Ferman was the director of the ACLU's Washington, D.C., office and had begun providing intelligence to the FBI earlier that year.[176] Nichols's curt, boilerplate response to Ernst had none of the friendly and familiar language of past correspon-dence.[177] On the attached routing slip, Hoover reiterated his feelings about Ernst, stating, "the FBI will have no dealings with Ernst because 1. He is a Trujillo agent & 2. His review of Hiss' book indicates he believes FBI altered the evidence."[178]

The FBI officials did not need Ernst anymore. They had a new liberal mole. By 1955 when Ferman took over in the Washington ACLU office, he and Ernst were the only two remaining ardent anticommunists among the organization's leadership. Most of the anticommunists in the group left after a bitter battle over policy during the McCarthy years led to the adoption of what they saw as an insufficiently anticommunist referendum. Ernst remained in the ACLU but became vice chairman of the board in 1955, a relatively inactive position. Many other anticommunists simply left the group or were not reelected to leadership posts. Ferman was the only aggressive anticommunist left in the organization's staff.[179] And he took up where Ernst had left off with the FBI, working with Nichols and, after Nichols took a job outside the Bureau, with other Crime Records or Crime Research staff members.

Ernst, meanwhile, continued his de Galindez investigation on behalf of the Trujillo regime. He had become increasingly upset over FBI officials' refusal to talk to him. "After more than twenty years of what I have cherished as a thoughtful and frank relationship between the FBI and myself, I am disturbed at a situation that has arisen," he wrote to Hoover in February 1958. "I do not want to see you in order to convey information as to the fruits of our investigation in our search for the truth but I am most anxious to clarify what seems to me to be an odd kind of disturbance in my relations with the FBI."[180] Just four days prior to writing that letter, Ernst poured fuel on Hoover's simmering anger related to the investigation, claiming in a letter to New York special agent in charge Edward Powers that the FBI had been trying to intimidate him. "We have some reason to believe that our wires have been tapped and our employees tailed, and our investigators thwarted by people who said (whether truthfully or not) that their communication with us was subject to approval of the F.B.I.," Ernst wrote.[181] That his letter to Hoover and his letter to Powers were filed under the same serial number by the Bureau indicates that they were seen as linked. If Ernst believed he could charm the director while simultaneously threatening the FBI over alleged wiretaps, he was mistaken. Thereafter, most of his letters to Hoover would prompt an "in absence" reply from the director's secretary, with a promise to make the correspondence available to Hoover when he returned to the office.[182] In absence replies were used strategically when Hoover did not wish to shut off a source of information but also did not wish to engage the source directly.

Unsurprisingly, Ernst's investigation, funded entirely by Trujillo, found the dictator innocent in the de Galindez disappearance, a verdict shared by precisely no one and met with disbelief or ridicule by the press. Ernst's report, issued on June 2, 1958, cruelly even suggested that de Galindez might be alive and living in Spain. The report relied on the time-tested defense tactic of attacking the victim, painting de Galindez as a tax dodger who had used his status as a registered agent for the anti-Franco Basque government-in-exile to enrich himself and then arrange for his own disappearance.[183] In December 1958, the FBI confirmed that Ernst received $200,000 from the Dominican government for his services in the investigation, including a $75,000 retainer for himself, $40,000 for his investigator, and reimbursements for $85,000 in expenses.[184] The *New York Times* reported that between his payments to Ernst and public relations counselor Sydney S. Baron, Trujillo spent $562,855 on the investigation.[185]

If Ernst imagined that the end of his investigation would mark the renewal of his access to Hoover, he was mistaken. In December 1958, he contacted Nichols's replacement, Gordon Nease, requesting a meeting with the director. A few months earlier, Ernst had received a boilerplate response to one of his letters in which Hoover's correspondence author in Crime Records, apparently unaware that Ernst had been cut off, stated that the director would be happy to meet with him any time he was in Washington, schedule permitting. Reporting on his own recent contact with Ernst, Nease noted, "He stated that . . . thus far he had been unsuccessful in seeing the Director." Nease concluded, "Unless advised to the contrary, no further action will be taken."[186]

In an ironic twist, Ernst became the subject of an informant rather than an informant himself. In a 1958 report to his FBI contact, Special Agent J. J. McGuire, Ferman speculated on the motives behind a liberal offensive against Hoover in the press that year and on the activities of Democratic senator William Proxmire of Wisconsin. He also advised that he himself would be visiting with Ernst in New York. Ferman told McGuire that "he hoped to obtain some indication as to the current status of Morris Ernst's feelings toward the Bureau." He further hoped that Ernst could shed more light on who was behind the ongoing liberal smear campaign against the FBI.[187]

Ernst became so desperate that he called former FBI official Nichols in an attempt to clear his reputation with the Bureau. Nichols reported on his conversation to Tolson. Ernst told Nichols that his de Galindez report did not implicate the FBI but did implicate the Bureau's nemesis, the CIA. In what must have struck Hoover as a galling statement, Ernst—a man who had made himself bigger than the attorney generals who were his nominal supervisors—suggested that the director was being ordered not to meet with him, and he implicitly threatened to leak that message to the media. "Ernst indicated he was fearful that the story would break out that Mr. Hoover had been ordered by a superior not to talk to a citizen and that this might be embarrassing to us," Tolson reported. In his handwritten comment on Tolson's memorandum, Hoover chose a colorful metaphor to describe Ernst's constant self-promotion: "Ernst is still up to his 'octopus tricks' muddying the waters."[188]

The 1944 *Life* profile had noted that it was odd Ernst had not "risen by pure osmosis if nothing else, above the rank of near-celebrity . . . the man is neither well nor widely known."[189] In the 1940s, Ernst used his anticommunist credentials and ACLU, civil liberties, liberal credentials to ingratiate himself with Hoover and make himself useful as both a public relations adviser and a liberal mole. He lent his understanding of the civil libertarians he associated with to the development of FBI messages to counter their criticism of the Bureau's intrusive use of wiretapping and the bullying conduct of loyalty program investigations. He maintained his utility and credibility with the FBI through his willingness to inform on and publicly challenge fellow liberals such as James Fly. He defended the FBI in print, and his most famous defense, "Why I No Longer Fear the F.B.I.," was among the most important Bureau public relations messages of the 1950s, coming as it did in the midst of a series of credible attacks from the Left when the FBI was vulnerable. Ernst's naive *Reader's Digest* PR prop was employed for decades—and is still used today—as evidence that the Bureau's contemporary critics and the generations of historians that followed were wrong about Hoover's FBI. Working closely with Nichols, Ernst was among a very few outsiders Hoover consulted on public relations matters. In the 1930s, the director worked with promoter and sometimes journalist Courtney Ryley Cooper to develop a PR template that came to characterize the stories the Bureau, through its Crime Records Section, told about itself or allowed others to tell with its authorization.[190] Ernst's status as a bona fide liberal, well known among civil liberties activists, made him particularly valuable during the era of loyalty investigations and public concerns about wiretapping. Most of his associates actively opposed Hoover, making Ernst's dissidence even more striking to observers. In the end, though, Ernst's strengths, his "octopus" tendencies, and his inveterate networking and self-promotion were also the causes of his falling out with Hoover. When he spoke out off-message on Hiss, took up the cause of a brutal dictator, and was pushed aside by another credible liberal, he and his public relations advice and action became expendable.

Chapter Six

The Heir Apparent

On May 27, 1963, Assistant Director Cartha "Deke" DeLoach, head of the Crime Research Division that included the public relations–oriented Crime Research Section, wrote a memorandum to Assistant Director John Mohr, recounting another agent's conversation with Bell-McClure syndicated columnist Andrew Tully. The agent had spoken to Tully at the White House Correspondents' and News Photographers' Associations annual banquet for the president a few days earlier. Tully was an experienced reporter and was one of the first American journalists to enter Berlin in April 1945. He started his career as a sports reporter for his hometown paper in Massachusetts, the *Southbridge Press*, which he purchased at age twenty-one and sold two years later. He worked at the *Worcester Gazette* and the *Boston Traveler* before becoming a syndicated columnist in 1961.[1] Originally, his column was syndicated by Scripps-Howard, but he moved to Bell-McClure in 1963. Tully would go on to write sixteen books, including a critical book about the FBI that was published in 1980.

DeLoach reported that a top deputy in Crime Research, Robert Wick, was introduced to Tully at the May 1963 event. "[Wick] observed that Tully had been drinking considerably," DeLoach informed Mohr, and then told Tully that he was disappointed in the journalist's May 22 "National Whirligig" column. In that column, the reporter argued against FBI director Hoover's claim that the rise in crime was due to a "lack of interest and support" for law enforcement.[2] Tully cited statistics that he said showed the increase in crime had outpaced population growth, and he noted that "every year the people's representatives have given Hoover every penny he has asked for to seek out and arrest criminals."[3] He ended his column by praising the director's service but adding a twist: "Undoubtedly, Hoover and his men are doing their best, but the record would seem to hint that their best needs to get a lot better."[4]

Assistant Director Cartha D. DeLoach, ca. 1961. (National Archives at College Park, Md., Record Group 65, Series F, Box 1, Folder 9, #37.)

At the correspondents' dinner, Tully responded to Wick's confrontational critique of the column by walking away. On May 27, he contacted Wick's supervisor, DeLoach, to complain. DeLoach reported the substance of the conversation to Associate Director Tolson. "I told [Tully] I was well aware of his May 22, 1963 'National Whirligig' column containing as it does distorted material, untruths, innuendoes, etc.," he wrote. "I told him it was one of the worst attacks on Mr. Hoover we had seen."[5] Later, DeLoach rebutted Tully's 400-word column point by point, in a three-page, single-spaced letter. "We welcome any constructive suggestions you may have as to how the FBI can better serve the American people," he told the columnist. "Certainly the May 22nd edition of 'National Whirligig' contributed nothing toward this objective."[6] In his memo to Mohr, DeLoach reported that the FBI had learned more about Tully, undoubtedly through an investigative report that is not included in the columnist's file. "He has deserted his wife and has recently been living with a woman commonly classified as a prostitute. He recently has even broken up with her. He is a drunk. He receives little respect from his newspaper associates. The Tully column of 5-22-63 has caused little stir at all."[7]

DeLoach's full-throated defense of Hoover and the FBI may appear incongruent, given the nature of the situation. A few critical words in Tully's opinion column were hardly the equivalent of a *New York Times* editorial. In the same situation, Assistant Director Nichols might have offered a defense of Hoover and the Bureau as DeLoach did, but it seems likely that he would have matched that defense to the relative level of harm inflicted. Nichols's approach emphasized the long term, and he sometimes even attempted to rehabilitate critics through an ongoing campaign of calls. The consummate networker, Nichols recognized that mild criticism did not mean the writer was an enemy of the FBI forever. DeLoach, however, had internalized Hoover's focused rage at the news media. His tenure as Hoover's top PR adviser was marked by a combative, reactionary approach and subtle self-promotion rather than long-term relationship building.

A more serious challenge to the Bureau's public image in 1967 demonstrated how DeLoach's sharp elbows had developed during his tenure as one of the top officials at the FBI. In that year, New Orleans district attorney Jim Garrison's infamous and ill-fated investigation into the Kennedy assassination led to public claims that Clay Shaw, an army veteran and New Orleans businessman, was one of the district attorney's alleged shooters. As word spread, a media frenzy descended upon the FBI and Department of Justice. How was it possible, reporters asked, that the FBI had not identified Shaw as a suspect in the assassination? When Attorney General Ramsey Clark was asked about Shaw on March 2, 1967, his reported response was that the man had indeed been the subject of an FBI inquiry four years earlier but had been cleared by the Bureau. "On the evidence the FBI had there was no connection between Shaw and the assassination," Clark told a United Press International reporter.[8] Actually, the Bureau had not even encountered Shaw's name in its investigation; it had identified a Clay Bertrand, possibly an alias for Shaw, but had never been able to locate that individual.[9] Clark's statement suggesting the FBI had "cleared" Shaw led an exasperated Hoover to write on his printout of the story, "To be expected!"[10] Hoover later called Clark a "jellyfish" and a "bull butterfly," and he described him as the worst attorney general he had encountered as FBI director.[11] Ironically, Ramsey Clark was the son of one of Hoover's favorite attorneys general, Tom Clark, who served in that post from 1945 to 1949, when he was appointed to the US Supreme Court by President Truman.[12]

The day after Ramsey Clark was quoted as stating the FBI had cleared Clay Shaw, the attorney general called the Bureau and said he had been misquoted; he then turned the blame on the FBI, claiming that one of DeLoach's assistants had spoken to reporters off the record, telling them that Shaw had been cleared. After checking with his team, DeLoach called Clark back and denied that the story of Shaw's clearance had come from the FBI.[13]

The controversy was far from over with DeLoach's denial. Later that same day, Clark again summoned DeLoach and reported that two former Department of Justice press officials, Jack Rosenthal and Ed Guthman, both confirmed to him that FBI agents were speaking to reporters about Shaw. DeLoach, a charming southern gentleman who was nonetheless uncompromising and often strident in his defense of the FBI, would not allow those claims to stand unchallenged. "I told the AG this was obviously an attempt on the part of Rosenthal and Guthman to drive a wedge between the AG and the FBI," he reported to Tolson in a memorandum. "I stated that Rosenthal and Guthman had pulled many such tricks in the past." Clark quickly backed down but said he hoped the FBI would follow a "no comment" policy with regard to the Garrison investigation in the future.[14] Hoover, in a handwritten note that was not seen by Clark, turned the tables on the attorney general. "I wish A.G. would follow same 'no comment' policy in this Garrison matter," he wrote.[15]

The no comment policy worked to ease the pressure from the media for a few days, but Shaw's lawyers became aware of the attorney general's statement and its exculpatory value for their client. Shaw's counsel, Edward F. Wegmann, contacted the Bureau on March 9 and urged the FBI to release its secret reports potentially supporting his client's innocence. DeLoach's deputy, Wick, noting Hoover's instructions to stay out of the case, refused the request.[16] Hoover's handwritten note on Wick's memorandum again turned the blame on the attorney general: "A.G. made the statement so it is up to the Dept [of Justice] to wrestle with this."[17]

The issue of Clark's statement flared up once again, on May 15, 1967, when the attorney general summoned DeLoach to a meeting that included Assistant Attorney General Harold "Barefoot" Sanders and the Department of Justice's information officer, Cliff Sessions. Two days prior, Sessions fielded a call from *Washington Post* reporter George Lardner, who was working on an article stating that Clark had erred when he issued his statement claiming the FBI had cleared Shaw. In a telephone call prior to the meeting, Sessions informed DeLoach that Clark intended to issue a statement admitting his error. "I told Sessions that it would be a very serious mistake for the AG to issue a statement of any kind," DeLoach reported to Tolson in a memorandum. Sessions responded that a statement might forestall the embarrassment of Lardner's story. At the meeting, DeLoach reiterated the FBI's position, invoking Hoover's name to bolster his case. "I told the AG that the Director strongly recommended that no comment be made concerning this matter for several reasons," he reported. "I stated that obviously any comment by the AG would further put him in hot water."[18]

Clark agreed with DeLoach, but Sessions said that though Clark erred by making the Shaw statement, the FBI had erred as well. De Loach noted, "Sessions stated the second mistake was when the FBI told reporters on the same date that the FBI had never investigated Clay Shaw and that the AG was in error."[19] "At least four" reporters, Sessions said, had told him first on the record and later off the record that the FBI had made these statements. DeLoach, unwilling to allow any criticism of the Bureau to stand, denied Sessions's claim and challenged him to prove it. "I told Sessions that we should clarify this matter and if he would give me the names of the four reporters I would have them questioned immediately so that they could put up or shut up," DeLoach reported.[20] Ultimately, Clark stuck to his decision to refrain from issuing a statement. In his memorandum, DeLoach drew a clear distinction between himself and Sessions, a former journalist, observing, "Sessions has the 'reporter's point of view' and does not realize the implications involved."[21] In a note on the memorandum, Hoover agreed: "Sessions is no bargain & never was!"[22]

Incredibly, Clark's indecision returned when, on May 31, 1967, Shaw's attorney wrote him a strong letter urging the attorney general to back up his statement about the accused's clearance by the FBI. Clark told DeLoach he felt it was important to issue a retraction of the earlier statement. After reading the proposed retraction, DeLoach again urged Clark to remain silent, and he particularly objected to the suggestion in the statement that the FBI was the source of the erroneous information. "I told the AG . . . that it appeared he was trying to palm off trouble on someone," DeLoach reported to Tolson. Clark even suggested that it was DeLoach who had told him Shaw was cleared by the FBI. "I told the AG I could not possibly have made this statement inasmuch as the FBI never 'clears' anyone," DeLoach said, parroting oft-repeated Bureau boilerplate.[23] Clark continued claiming that the FBI's leaks and other public statements in the case put the attorney general in a "bad light." Again, DeLoach, the front line of the FBI's defenses, did not back down. "I told the AG it put him in a bad light only because the AG made a mistake in the beginning," he reported. "He made no reply." DeLoach's vituperative response to the attorney general's attempts to place blame on the Bureau was mirrored in Hoover's handwritten notes. "We are not going to cover up for the A.G.'s mistake," the director wrote on page 4 of the memo, and then he continued on page 5, "If he would talk less he would be better off."[24]

DeLoach's handling of Ramsey Clark offers insights into his personality as well as the Bureau's relationship with "superiors" in the Department of Justice. Born in Claxton, Georgia, in 1920, DeLoach was quite young when his father died. Family friend and US attorney J. Saxton Daniel of Savannah, Georgia, later wrote, "It became necessary that [DeLoach] scuffle along for an education and make his own way in life."[25] DeLoach attended three colleges, starting at Gordon Military College for one year and then attending South Georgia College for another year. He was an unremarkable student, earning marks "considerably below average" due to his failure to "study and apply himself."[26] Professors at Stetson College in Deland, Florida, where he graduated in 1941, reported that DeLoach missed being student body president by eleven votes. Stetson's president, William Sims Allen, added that DeLoach was friendly "but talks too much," that he would not have "received such good grades under old faculty," and that he "is talking his way through school."[27]

Because he had not earned a law degree when he applied with the FBI, DeLoach was hired on August 20, 1942, as a clerk/messenger working the midnight shift.[28] He was twenty-two, and his Selective Service classification was 1-A, meaning he was available for military service.[29] DeLoach immediately applied and was accepted for a commission in the Naval Reserve; he then applied to move up to special agent status in the FBI, a position where he could be assured of an occupational draft deferment. However, he was told that he could not be considered for a special agent position until he had worked for the Bureau for six months.[30] On November 2, 1942, DeLoach received word from his mother that the Claxton draft board would likely send him an induction notice "in the near future" but that the board would grant him a permanent occupational deferment if he was named to a special agent position in the FBI and resigned his Naval Reserve commission.[31] That week, Hoover wrote to the Claxton board to notify officials that DeLoach's training as a fingerprint technician was not complete and that "it is not felt that this Bureau can request an occupational deferment for Mr. DeLoach."[32] Just one month later and two months before his six-month probationary period was over, DeLoach was offered and accepted a special agent position with the Bureau.[33] His benefactor, US Attorney Daniel, wrote Hoover that because of his "special interest" in the young man, he was pleased a position had been found for him.[34] On December 30, 1942, Hoover notified the Claxton draft board and requested an occupational deferment for DeLoach.[35] On January 6, 1943, De-Loach was reclassified 2-B, a deferment "in support of war production."[36]

His first field assignment was in Norfolk, Virginia. Three months later, he was assigned to the Cleveland office as part of its Communist Squad.[37] In February 1944, DeLoach was appointed as resident agent in Akron, Ohio.[38] (Resident agents headed small suboffices that extended Bureau coverage.) A month later, he was notified that because of changes in executive branch policy, the Bureau could no longer request an occupational deferment.[39] He therefore applied for reinstatement of the Naval Reserve commission he had resigned when he became a special agent,[40] but his request was not granted as expected.[41] According to DeLoach, the navy was angry with him for resigning his prior commission to become an agent. He asked Democratic US senator Walter F. George of Georgia to intervene with the navy,[42] but either George declined to recommend DeLoach or his intervention was not successful. DeLoach finally received a notice from his local draft board, in late September 1944, and he voluntarily enlisted in the Naval Reserve as a seaman.[43] He served most of his seventeen months in the navy in Norman, Oklahoma, where he, having been a quarterback in college, played football and taught physical education. He was promoted three times, ultimately becoming a specialist second class, working in recreation and supply.[44] After his honorable discharge, DeLoach requested a return to FBI service on September 24, 1945.[45] He reported to the Cleveland office on April 1, 1946, and was again assigned as resident agent in Akron.[46]

DeLoach quickly distinguished himself as a public relations contact man, establishing relationships with an important audience for the FBI in Akron—the local police. His supervising SAC, E. C. Richardson, noted in a 1947 review, "[DeLoach] is very effective in his contacts with police officers and I have noticed a distinct improvement in the friendly relations existing between the Akron Police Department, as well as the Sheriff's Office and the Akron Resident Agency since his assignment there."[47] Also during that period, DeLoach married Barbara Owens and the first of their seven children (also named Barbara) was born.[48]

DeLoach's skillful contact work was rewarded in May 1947 when he was transferred to FBI headquarters in Washington as a supervisor in the Atomic Energy Section of the Bureau's Security Division. There, he replaced future rival William Sullivan, who was named to head the Communist Research Desk for the Bureau.[49] Again, DeLoach was recognized for his interpersonal communication and contact skills, and he was reassigned as FBI liaison to the US Navy and, more critically, to the Central Intelligence Agency (CIA).[50]

Hoover and Tolson maintained close supervision of the Bureau's liaison agents. Although these agents were not based in Crime Records, they performed tasks commonly viewed as part of public relations practice in most organizations. FBI liaison agents gathered information and feedback from the organizations and agencies they worked with. They built and maintained relationships with well-placed individuals within their target organizations. They also explained Bureau positions and policies to their contacts. By 1951, FBI agents were assigned as liaison to the air force, the National Security Council, the Atomic Energy Commission, the coast guard, the army, the Defense Department, the National Security Resources Board, the Treasury Department, and other "miscellaneous" agencies.[51] In a "pursuant to the Director's instructions" 1948 memorandum, Special Agent Victor P. Keay expressed Hoover's view of the work of the eleven liaison agents working out of the Seat of Government. "I have personally warned each of the liaison men that they should not engage in 'Politicing [*sic*]' for their own benefit in connection with liaison work," Keay wrote in a memorandum to Assistant Director Mickey Ladd. "I pointed out that they were primarily engaged in this work to promote the interests of the Bureau. I also warned them against viewing with awe the high positions in the various departments contacted by them and pointed out that if they desired to seek one of these positions, they should definitely inform the Bureau."[52]

Liaison with the CIA was a crucial role during the postwar period as various government agencies, including the military intelligence units and the

FBI, jockeyed with the CIA for position in the emerging Cold War intelligence superstructure. As liaison, DeLoach was responsible for developing information sources within the CIA in addition to managing more formal communications between the two agencies. By the end of 1948, he had developed "unusually close" relations with both Adm. Thomas B. Inglis, chief of the Office of Naval Intelligence, and Adm. Roscoe H. Hillenkoetter, director of the CIA.[53] DeLoach reached an agreement with Inglis that called for all secret navy material to be supplied to the FBI "for screening for matters of interest to the Bureau" before being turned over to the CIA.[54] At the same time he was interposing the FBI between Naval Intelligence and the CIA, DeLoach was praised by CIA director Hillenkoetter in a letter to Hoover.[55] In the competitive postwar intelligence atmosphere, where getting access to information first was considered crucial, DeLoach had scored a small coup for the FBI, and it earned him a meritorious pay raise. "He appears to have a facility for maintaining friendships with the highest officials of agencies he handles," supervisor Keay wrote in DeLoach's 1949 annual review.[56]

Despite the fact that he worked to build and maintain connections to the CIA, DeLoach told an FBI inspector reviewing the Security Division that he had "no respect whatsoever for CIA which he contacts regularly."[57] The inspector concluded that DeLoach was "very familiar with the Bureau's liaison problems and obviously protects the Bureau's interests when contacting other agencies."[58] A 1949 disagreement between the two agencies offered a glimpse into DeLoach's approach to problems. When James Andrews from the CIA's Office of Collection and Dissemination (OCD) requested access to Bureau technical manuals, DeLoach told him the request should come from the CIA's Special Operations Section, not OCD. Instead of technical manuals used by agents, DeLoach provided public source information from Crime Records. Andrews then showed DeLoach a CIA memorandum (the author's name is redacted in FBI files) criticizing the Bureau for its failure to share information with OCD. "We can get public source information any time that we want it, and do not need to obtain it from the FBI," the unnamed author wrote.[59] DeLoach claimed he told Andrews that "it seemed to be rather poor taste to exhibit an intra-agency memorandum to a representative of another agency, particularly one reflecting criticism of that agency." He then went to CIA director Hillenkoetter and "advised [him] that it was obviously unfair and ridiculous for the FBI to be criticized so sharply by [redacted]" because the CIA had already received the information it needed.[60] Hillenkoetter apologized, DeLoach told Keay.[61]

That relatively innocuous incident showed that DeLoach had become familiar with CIA procedures in a short time and knew when the Bureau was being dragged into an intra-CIA sectional battle. It also showed that though he could be ingratiating, when the FBI was criticized DeLoach responded with an uncompromising defense, a talent that would later serve him well as supervisor of Crime Records and the Bureau's liaison to the media and Congress. Hoover added his approval to the memorandum: "Well handled by DeLoach."[62] His approval of DeLoach's liaison work was the subject of a rare memorandum to Tolson and Ladd in 1950. The director said that CIA officials had told him they "liked" DeLoach. "Mr. DeLoach handles himself in a most mature and excellent manner," Hoover wrote. "He is well informed on the various problems [between the CIA and FBI] which have arisen in the past."[63] The agent's liaison work was again praised by Hoover in July 1951 when Assistant Director Mohr proposed that DeLoach be transferred to the Training and Inspection Division. The director wrote on the memorandum, "I don't want to remove him from CIA liaison at this time."[64] Hoover forestalled another effort to transfer DeLoach in October 1951 but then allowed a transfer in December of that year.[65] After a four-month training period, DeLoach became an FBI inspector.[66]

The transition from liaison to the inspection ranks was rocky for DeLoach. FBI inspectors reviewed personnel and policies in the agency's far-flung offices as well as within the Bureau's headquarters. Inspectors could be ruthless in their criticism of local offices, but their work was also intensely scrutinized by Hoover and Tolson; by July 1953, DeLoach had been censured three times for various shortcomings in his inspection reports. In addition, the travel was wearing on him and his family. In September 1953, he met with Hoover and requested a new assignment, telling the director that his family life was suffering. "He stated that as an Inspector he had been on the road for extended periods of time," Hoover told Tolson. "He stated that [redacted, probably referring to one of his children] practically does not know him because of his long absences from the city."[67] When Hoover suggested a special agent in charge position, DeLoach pointed out that he had just bought a home in Washington, D.C. Hoover's memorandum revealed the director's human side and seemed to encourage Tolson to find DeLoach a position that did not involve so much travel. Six weeks later, DeLoach was temporarily assigned to Tolson's office, where he handled correspondence and contacts with members of Congress.[68] Six months later, in March 1954, DeLoach found his permanent home at the Seat of Government—in the Bureau's Records and Communication Division under Assistant to the Director Louis Nichols.[69]

Under Nichols, DeLoach was made a Bureau liaison to the American Legion, and he worked as a supervisor in Crime Records, handling a variety of duties from correspondence to media and congressional contacts, name checks, and even tours and speeches. Like others working in the high-pressure Crime Records Section, which was closely monitored by Tolson and Hoover, DeLoach piled up a series of letters of censure for various errors, ranging from typographic errors to botched tour preparations to delays in notifying Hoover and Tolson of a negative news story. But DeLoach's frequent censures were balanced by equally frequent commendations, most of them citing his liaison work with the American Legion.[70] In October 1955, he was named to the American Legion's National Americanism Commission.[71]

DeLoach's talent for developing contacts included his work with members of Congress. Democratic congressman Jack Pilcher of Georgia became a close confidant, often inviting DeLoach to his Washington home. For instance, on March 6, 1956, DeLoach reported to Nichols that after a dinner at Pilcher's home, "the Congressman got in a talkative mood regarding the civil rights situation in the South."[72] DeLoach "deliberately steered" the conversation to attacks on the FBI from opponents of civil rights in Congress, particularly within the Georgia delegation. He "mentioned that apparently emotions had run away with logic, that [the FBI] had been unduly criticized for carrying out our duties under the very laws which Congress had seen fit to pass."[73] Pilcher told DeLoach that Georgia Democratic congressman James C. Davis "is a lunatic on the subject of white supremacy." Pilcher said he and First District congressman Prince Preston were supportive of the FBI's civil rights investigations. DeLoach took a fishing trip with Preston and Pilcher three weeks later and promised an update.[74] Hoover scrawled his approval on the memorandum: "Well handled by DeLoach."[75]

In 1956 and 1957, DeLoach continued his contact duties and added significant public speaking assignments, primarily addressing American Legion audiences. In six months in 1957, he addressed sixty-five Legion groups, all on weekends or evenings.[76] When Nichols retired in 1957, Gordon Nease was selected as his replacement and presided over a rough two years, including what Hoover and Tolson saw as mismanagement of a 1958 smear campaign against the Bureau. Nease resigned in early 1959 following a critical inspection report that largely blamed his administrative failings for the 1958 troubles. On January 28, 1959, Hoover selected DeLoach as Nease's replacement as assistant director, leading a reorganized Crime Research Division that included the public relations–oriented Crime Records Section (renamed the Crime Research Section).[77]

An early 1960 inspection of DeLoach's division cited problems with delayed handling of letters, noted improvements in the delegation of duties by Crime Research Section chief Milton Jones, and recommended that the Correspondence and Tours Units be split off so that Crime Research could concentrate solely on publicity and publications.[78] Inspector John Malone praised DeLoach, Wick, and to a lesser extent Jones for their contact work, particularly with newspapers, television and radio stations, and the motion picture industry. The implication was that those contacts had suffered under Nease and led to embarrassments such as the alleged smear campaign of 1958. "Contacts with public through communications media greatly intensified at SOG [Seat of Government] and in the field," Malone wrote. "Direction of contact program of officials at Seat of Government being given close attention by Mr. DeLoach."[79]

An April 1960 confrontation with a nine-member committee of juvenile court judges revealed DeLoach's willingness to leap to Hoover's defense as well as his ambitious nature and tendency to tout the significance of an assertive confrontation in a memorandum he knew the director would see. A New Jersey juvenile court judge invited DeLoach to a meeting of the National Council of Juvenile Court Judges Committee on Cooperation with Federal Agencies and Legislation. In a memorandum to Assistant to the Director Mohr, DeLoach portrayed the meeting as a setup. "Upon meeting the nine judges and two on-lookers and sitting down around the conference table, it was noted the air was very tense and the situation was formally stacked against us," he wrote. "Judge [Horace S.] Bellfatto led off by stating his organization had serious misgivings about the constant criticism leveled at it by Mr. Hoover. . . . He added that invitations had been extended to the Director for approximately ten years straight, however, this was the first time the Director had seen fit to honor such requests."[80] Another judge, Chauncey M. DuPuy of Chambersburg, Pennsylvania, brought up Hoover's ongoing efforts to allow more juveniles to be tried as adults. "He stated that the Director's philosophy went out the window with 'Gilbert and Sullivan' and was not in step with the times," DeLoach reported.[81]

As strident a defender of the FBI and Hoover as there was, DeLoach also had a tendency to portray himself in memoranda in terms that emphasized his ultimate loyalty to the director, often in ingratiating language that parroted Hoover's tone and terminology. This tendency was obvious in the following passage from his memo to Mohr:

> I stopped DePuy at this point and told him I wanted to make it plain that I took serious exception to his ridicule, that I had not been sent to this meeting to represent Mr. Hoover for the purpose of allowing sarcasm and scorn to be heaped upon him, but to the contrary was there as an invited guest to point out the factual basis of any charges they might desire to bring, plus mentioning in specific detail their organization's obvious lack of specifics when they attempted to cover up their own shortcomings by criticizing Mr. Hoover and the FBI.[82]

Hoover highlighted every paragraph of DeLoach's six-page memorandum with hash marks in the margins indicating his approval.[83]

Throughout the memo, DeLoach portrayed the judges as sarcastic antagonists and himself as a voice of reason, speaking on Hoover's behalf. At one point, he wrote, "DePuy sarcastically replied that the juvenile court judges were trying to save souls not condemn them to life in prison." He continued, "I told him that while he was saving souls he should give a little consideration for the preservation of society."[84] On another point, DeLoach used common Hoover terminology when he argued that names of "vicious youthful hoodlums" should be published.[85] Similarly, DeLoach addressed another of Hoover's common foils—the "bleeding hearts" of the parole and probation system.[86] When one judge criticized Georgia Fifth District congressman James Davis, DeLoach told him that "Jim Davis was a very good friend of the FBI and had been a personal friend of mine over the years, consequently I could not share his sarcasm for him." That "shut up" the judge, DeLoach reported.[87] The entire meeting, he wrote, was held for the purpose of "having a 'holiday' at the expense of the FBI. They did not succeed in doing this. I sincerely think that we converted their thinking to some extent and that we should continue to meet with these groups."[88] Not surprisingly, considering the nature of the report, Hoover approved. "DeLoach did an outstanding job," he wrote on the memo. "Nothing can be gained by appeasement—slugging it out toe to toe clears the atmosphere."[89]

There is no reason to believe that DeLoach embroidered the truth in his memorandum about the meeting, but his language choices and the tone of the message demonstrated that he shared Hoover's approach to dissenters.

DeLoach had eighteen years of experience in the Bureau, much of it in the Seat of Government. Like most officials there who found long-term success, he had internalized Hoover's worldview and could skillfully mimic the director's attitudes and language. DeLoach was an ardent and outspoken defender of both Hoover and the Bureau then and throughout his career at the FBI until his death in 2013. He was also a bright and ambitious agent who knew that the confrontational narrative in the memorandum would capture the director's attention and approval.

Unlike his predecessor Gordon Nease—whose tepid response to the 1958 smear campaign that began with Fred J. Cook's article in the *Nation* helped speed his retirement—DeLoach did not shy away from confrontations with the news media. In April 1969, he showed that when it came to Hoover, not even lighthearted criticism published in a regional newspaper would be ignored. In his April 7, 1960, "Anyone for Tennis" column, *Denver Post* reporter Jack Guinn mused that *Post* writers who had not been able to get Hoover on the phone were concerned that the director was missing. DeLoach responded with a combative letter "strongly protesting" Guinn's column. "It may interest you to know that even though Mr. Hoover's assistants are younger than he, he still maintains a heavier work load, longer hours, and a tougher schedule than his subordinates," DeLoach claimed. "I think the American public is far greater interested in the results obtained by the FBI under Mr. Hoover's leadership than they are in the drivel turned out by those who seek to besmirch his name."[90] Rather than silencing Guinn, though, DeLoach's strident response prompted another humorous column in which the reporter suggested that the only thing missing at the FBI was a sense of humor. "There's no cause for alarm now, but one of the fellows [*Post* reporters] telephoned the FBI in Washington only yesterday, asked to speak to Mr. Hoover and was told in the same calm voice that Mr. Hoover was not in," Guinn wrote in response to DeLoach. "Well, it may be that they'll never get to chat with him on the telephone and perhaps someday they'll make more jokes, but nobody here wants to hurt Mr. Hoover's feelings. Like Mr. DeLoach, all of us respect the Director for the fine job he's doing. (And thank heaven he's safe.)"[91] Unfortunately for DeLoach, the ribbing did not stop there; instead, the thread was picked up by a Hoover critic, *New York Post* editor James A. Wechsler. In an editorial two weeks later, Wechsler recounted the "rumor that J. Edgar Hoover is missing" and said, "His disappearance is an optical illusion which funny people, mostly reporters, experience when they try to look at him closely, as through a microscope."[92]

DeLoach's strategy of intimidation actually prompted other critics to chime in. Having come to his position from a strictly liaison perspective, he lacked Nichols's nuanced understanding of the workings of the media.

A few months later, DeLoach's sensitivity to criticism again embarrassed the FBI. In a speech to 750 delegates at the annual convention of the American Federation of Government Employees, held in Cincinnati, DeLoach told the audience, "Each government employee has the responsibility of being ever alert to individuals working with him who might display disloyal tendencies which make them possible dupes and foils for communists or espionage."[93] That sort of statement played into criticism that the Bureau had been overzealous in its loyalty investigations in the 1940s and 1950s. In a note on the wire copy, Hoover expressed his concerns that "such statements can be distorted to mean we want all govt employees to 'spy' for us."[94] The same DeLoach quotation appeared in a column in the *Washington Post*, prompting Tolson to ask, "Was the speech cleared?"[95] As was typical, any comment or question from Hoover or Tolson caused a flurry of memoranda as staff tried to answer questions or track down explanations. In his explanatory memorandum, DeLoach admitted that he was accurately quoted but argued that his comments were taken out of context.[96] "If the full text were used, it is not believed that a misinterpretation could be placed upon such remarks," he said.[97] Hoover and Tolson were unimpressed with the explanation. "This standing alone is subject to misinterpretation," Hoover wrote, "& we must realize the press by necessity can't print all the qualifying phrases which precede or follow it."[98] Tolson wrote that DeLoach had embarrassed the Bureau, and Hoover added a note questioning whether the FBI's public speaking program could come under Department of Justice scrutiny. "There is no other agency in govt which has had the freedom of speech making & expression as has the FBI," Hoover observed. "It is therefore imperative we be super cautious in what we say & alert to possibility of misinterpretation else we are likely to be shackled like other agencies & have to curtail our speech making in public relations work."[99]

DeLoach's combative attitude toward the news media, a perfect match for Hoover's views, was again evident in 1961 when another speech, this time before 300 editors attending the Georgia Press Institute in Atlanta, prompted public criticism from a prominent journalist. In his speech in Athens, Georgia, on February 24, 1961, DeLoach "made specific reference to the very proper belief that there should be definite freedom of the press," he reported to Mohr. "It was pointed out at the same time, however, the press should never allow itself to be unwittingly used by the communists. The need for straight reporting and not slanted reporting or distortion was expressed in the continuing scheme of what the press could do to fight communism."[100] DeLoach claimed that newspapers such as the *New York Times* had "idolized Castro."[101] That afternoon, Turner Catledge, managing editor of the *Times*, spoke to the same group and, according to DeLoach, "stated that a previous speaker this morning almost suggested there should be censorship of 'The New York Times.'"[102] DeLoach told his supervisor, Mohr, that he "made no such reference."[103] The remainder of his memorandum, playing right into the director's personal hatred of the *Times*, offered a critique of Catledge's comments. "Excellent," Hoover wrote in the margin.[104]

A series of segments on the NBC weekend radio program *Monitor* comprised one of DeLoach's media success stories. First aired in 1955, *Monitor* was a magazine-style program that included news, sports, comedy, music, and celebrity interviews. Originally conceived by NBC president Pat Weaver (father of actress Sigourney Weaver and the broadcasting executive who pioneered the creation of now-ubiquitous television commercials) as a "kaleidoscopic phantasmagoria," *Monitor* was NBC Radio's attempt to maintain a radio audience at the dawn of the television age.[105] In its early years, the program ran continuously for forty hours each weekend, from 8:00 a.m. on Saturday to midnight on Sunday. Later, it was cut dramatically but still aired four to six nights weekly. Dave Garroway, host of television's *Today* show, another Weaver creation, was perhaps the best known of the rotating band of early *Monitor* hosts, each taking four-hour shifts. Others included John Cameron Swayze, Monty Hall, Mel Allen, and Gene Rayburn. Described as "relaxed and ironic," Garroway was known for his television sign-off of "Peace."[106]

DeLoach conceived the idea of a two-segment weekend radio series produced for *Monitor*. One segment would highlight fugitives wanted by the FBI; the second would explain one part of the Bureau's operations, such as the Fingerprint Section or FBI Crime Laboratory. He successfully pitched the idea to NBC and oversaw the finished product. The Crime Research Section produced 231 five-minute *Monitor* segments between March and November 1963 alone.[107] Those "National Alert" and "Know Your FBI" segments were produced entirely in-house by Crime Research employees, and several were narrated by DeLoach himself. "Know Your FBI" topics included the Identification Division, the Disaster Squad, the FBI National Academy, and the FBI Crime Laboratory. Completed segments were reviewed by Tolson before being sent to NBC. After an initial run of several months wrapped up, NBC asked that the segments be continued indefinitely. "This is a most effective means of informing the public of the many facets of the FBI and I want to thank you for your outstanding foresight in initiating this series," Hoover wrote to DeLoach in a letter of commendation.[108]

The assassination of President Kennedy and ascension of Lyndon Johnson to the presidency brought DeLoach a new assignment. Just one week after JFK was killed, Tolson recommended that DeLoach be named as the FBI's liaison to the new president.[109] DeLoach had met Texas Democratic senator Johnson in the 1950s when he was sent to lobby the majority leader for a bill—which eventually failed to pass—granting Hoover his full salary for life.[110] DeLoach was tapped by the director, at Johnson's request, to replace agent Courtney Evans as White House liaison the day after the assassination. Evans's trajectory as White House liaison presaged the rise and fall of DeLoach and then Sullivan in their key positions. A graduate of the Detroit College of Law, Evans was appointed assistant director of the newly organized Special Investigative Division in 1961 after a twenty-year career, most of it in Washington. He had previously served as the Bureau's liaison to the US Senate Labor Rackets Committee, where he met the committee's counsel at the time, Robert F. Kennedy. Evans became the Bureau's liaison to the attorney general just after RFK assumed that position in 1961. Because of Kennedy's close relationship with his brother, the president, Evans also served as the Bureau's liaison to the White House.[111] Three years later, at age fifty, he retired suddenly. His replacement as FBI liaison, DeLoach, retired suddenly in 1970, also at age fifty. And Sullivan, then fifty-nine, publicly criticized Hoover and was ousted just one year later. "Sullivan was only one of many guys that Hoover brought along to the number two position [effectively, with Tolson's declining health] and then ultimately fired," *Washington Post* reporter Ken W. Clawson, who covered all three men and was particularly close to Sullivan, said in 1975. "Deke DeLoach is an example of a guy who got out before he was fired." All three men, Clawson said, were molded by Hoover in his own image, their careers helped along by their ability to flatter the director: "Hoover had conceived them, he'd brought them up, he'd matured them, he'd promoted them to the number two spot—and then it would happen, and it happened in various ways to each of them." Evans became too close to Hoover's enemies, Robert and John Kennedy, Clawson asserted. DeLoach became too close to LBJ, and his fortunes fell with the end

Assistant Director Cartha D. DeLoach (left) with National American Legion commander Eldon James and President Lyndon B. Johnson, March 3, 1966. (Lyndon B. Johnson Presidential Library, A2046-16.)

of Johnson's career in 1968. Sullivan was fired by Hoover when he cast his lot with Richard Nixon, who did not reciprocate by protecting him.[112]

Over time, DeLoach and Johnson developed a close relationship.[113] Much of Johnson's early political focus as president was on efforts to keep racial antagonisms from sidetracking his official coronation as the Democratic standard-bearer at the 1964 nomination convention. Johnson was concerned about white defections to the Republican Party that were reshaping electoral politics in the country that summer. The president was placed in a difficult position: he needed to appeal to moderate white voters while at the same time maintaining his support among African Americans, walking a fine line to appease both factions. The 1964 Democratic National Convention in Atlantic City, New Jersey, promised to be a focal point of civil rights leaders' efforts to push Johnson to move decisively to address their concerns by acknowledging civil rights as an issue in the election. Johnson, of course, hoped to avoid confrontations in general and specifically to avoid incidents that would direct moderate whites' attention to civil rights. A few weeks before the convention opened, he told Minnesota Democratic senator Hubert

Humphrey of the potential consequences if he was seen to endorse civil rights activists in Mississippi. "I don't want to do anything in Mississippi that will lose Oklahoma for me, and I don't want to do anything in Mississippi that will lose Kentucky for me, and I don't want Mississippi to lose Maryland for me," Johnson said in a phone conversation. "Most of all, I damn sure don't want to lose Texas."[114]

Concerned with the potential for civil rights disruption of his coronation as party leader at the 1964 convention, Johnson directed his aides Walter Jenkins and Bill Moyers to contact DeLoach and order the FBI to spy on civil rights leaders during the event. Hoover agreed and assigned DeLoach to lead the special squad.[115] DeLoach and his team of agents were tasked with spying on convention delegates and protestors to provide LBJ and his staff with information they could use to forestall any embarrassing, unplanned demonstrations at the event. Johnson's FBI spies, the special squad, used all means at their disposal, including bugs, wiretaps, and COINTELPRO-style infiltration, according to DeLoach: "By means of informant coverage, by use of various confidential techniques [likely meaning bugs and wiretaps], by infiltration of key groups through use of undercover agents, and through utilization of agents using appropriate cover as reporters, we were able to keep the White House fully apprised of all major developments during the Convention's course."[116]

DeLoach reported to Hoover and Tolson that his team had been able to prevent a sit-in planned by comedian and activist Dick Gregory. They advised Johnson campaign officials to tighten controls over admissions to the convention hall, thus forestalling a demonstration planned by members of the Mississippi Freedom Democratic Party (MFDP), a group of civil rights activists who challenged the legitimacy of the state's sanctioned Democratic Party. "Through our counterintelligence efforts [Johnson adviser Walter] Jenkins, et al., were able to advise the President in advance regarding major plans of the MFDP delegates," DeLoach reported to Hoover. "The White House considered this of prime importance."[117] The special squad also used "highly confidential coverage"—Bureau parlance for illegal bugs, break-ins, and wiretaps—to monitor Martin Luther King and Bayard Rustin along with the leaders of the Congress of Racial Equality (CORE) and the Student Nonviolent Coordinating Committee (SNCC). Because of those "confidential" methods, DeLoach told his superiors, "we were in a position to advise the White House in advance of all plans made by those two sources in an effort to disrupt the orderly progress of the Convention."[118]

DeLoach's squad also monitored the Mississippi Freedom Democratic Party delegation, hiring African American informants posing as sympathetic activists to sit in on the group's strategy meetings. Agents also posed as journalists, and they even had NBC press credentials provided by a contact at the network whose name is redacted in DeLoach's FBI file. "As an example, one of our 'reporters' was able to gain the confidence of Aaron Henry [leader of the Mississippi National Association for the Advancement of Colored People (NAACP)], [Redacted], Dick Gregory and [New York activist] Jesse Gray, the notorious Harlem riot leader," DeLoach told Hoover. "Our 'reporter' was so successful, in fact, that Henry was giving him 'off the record' information for background purposes, which he requested our 'reporter' not to print."[119]

DeLoach also told Hoover that the squad provided forty-four pages of intelligence data to Jenkins and Bill Moyers. "Additionally, I kept Jenkins and Moyers constantly advised by telephone of minute by minute developments," he wrote. "This enabled them to make spot decisions and to adjust Convention plans to meet potential problems before serious trouble developed."[120] Blind memoranda (essentially dossiers of the FBI's information on individuals, typed up without any identifying sources) on potentially problematic civil rights leaders were created prior to the convention and "proved most helpful." For example, DeLoach was able to provide Jenkins with a dossier on Aaron Henry, who also led the Mississippi civil rights group known as the Council of Federated Organizations (COFO), in less than fifteen minutes. "Jenkins was highly pleased and said this was of vital importance to their operation," DeLoach told Hoover. In all, the special squad monitored fifteen organizations at the convention.[121] In addition to a redacted number of official informants, the squad included fourteen special agents and two stenographers working full-time in Atlantic City and approximately fifteen special agents working part-time from Washington, D.C.[122] Hoover was pleased with DeLoach's work and recommended him for a meritorious cash award.[123]

DeLoach opened his memoirs, published in 1995, with a recounting of events at the convention. In his book, he said that when Jenkins requested the FBI form a squad to prevent disruptions, "I didn't like the sound of it."[124] He admitted that wiretaps were placed in CORE and SNCC headquarters, but he did not confirm the use of microphone surveillance. He said the special squad's work was legal under changes in the law after the Kennedy assassination that allowed the Bureau to be called in to assist with presidential security—certainly a stretch in the case of this sort of political surveillance.

"But, in the end, the line between national security and political activism had been blurred," DeLoach admitted. "We felt we had been compromised. At that point I resolved never to be used again in that fashion. But I found it was a resolution I could not keep."[125]

The reality of DeLoach's liaison with Johnson was that the president had the FBI in a significantly compromised position, starting in 1964. That year, Hoover would turn seventy and thus face mandatory retirement. Through DeLoach, working with Johnson aide Walter Jenkins, the director obtained a reprieve in the form of an executive order from Johnson that waived his mandatory retirement. Executive Order 11154 exempted Hoover from retirement "for an indefinite period of time."[126] Clearly, Johnson's choice of language was intended to send a message to Hoover and the FBI that the president expected cooperation from the Bureau on his requests for political surveillance and intelligence, as in the case of the Democratic National Convention that same year.

Although DeLoach quickly became part of Johnson's inner circle, he was still Hoover's top public relations adviser. But events of November and December 1964 would demonstrate the difficulty of advising a man like the director. That November, members of the Women's National Press Club (women were still not allowed in the all-male National Press Club) finagled a press conference with Hoover. By the 1960s, he only rarely met with the press, and he typically allowed only one-on-one meetings in his office. Those meetings usually degenerated into monologues, with few questions allowed, as Hoover read rapidly from a memorandum provided to him before the meeting. To DeLoach's surprise, the director agreed to meet with the group of eighteen Women's National Press Club members, including famed reporters such as Sarah McClendon and Miriam Ottenberg, for a press briefing. DeLoach said the Crime Research staff spent days preparing statistics and other material for Hoover to present at the briefing. "We knew 'briefing session' meant a monologue by the director in which he would give them a history of the agency and some highlights of current policy," DeLoach wrote in his 1995 memoirs.[127] Hoover began his monologue, and then, according to DeLoach, "eyes began to glaze. [Hoover] sensed he was losing his audience and decided to give them something juicier."[128] The director then launched into a blistering criticism of Martin Luther King, concluding by saying, "In my opinion, Dr. Martin Luther King is the most notorious liar in the country."[129] As the briefing continued, DeLoach later said, he passed the director three notes urging him to say his King comments were off the record, to no avail.

Hoover's criticism of King appeared on front pages nationwide. "It was a public relations fiasco," DeLoach said in 1995.[130] In an attempt to halt the daily stories that followed, Hoover agreed to meet with King. That meeting occurred on December 1, 1964, and DeLoach sat in on it.[131] Any gains in understanding between Hoover and King, though, were scuttled after King's wife, Coretta Scott King, received a blackmail package from the FBI that included an audiotape of her husband with another woman at the Willard Hotel in Washington, D.C. DeLoach later admitted the package—which also contained a letter urging King to commit suicide or else the tape would be publicly released—was the result of an FBI bug. In his memoirs, DeLoach blamed his rival, Assistant Director Sullivan, for sending the tape and letter.[132] "Hoover had no knowledge whatsoever of that," DeLoach claimed in 1995. That account is challenged by several other individuals, though, who have said DeLoach offered a transcript of the tape to Ben Bradlee of *Newsweek* and to other members of the media.[133] Bradlee recalled that DeLoach asked him to stay behind after a fruitless interview with Hoover in 1964, adding, "Pretty soon he [DeLoach] was talking about some King tapes and asking me if I would like to listen to them and read transcripts."[134] When Acting Attorney General Nicholas Katzenbach learned that the FBI had offered the tapes to the press, he confronted DeLoach, who denied the charge.[135]

The poisoned relationship between the FBI and King only enhanced De-Loach's position of influence at the White House, where Johnson worried that public support of civil rights would undermine his position with southern white voters.[136] Working through DeLoach, President Johnson made frequent use of the FBI's political surveillance and intelligence-gathering capabilities between 1963 and 1968. In later years, DeLoach was critical of what he viewed as the political abuse of the FBI by Johnson and others, citing in particular efforts during the 1964 Democratic National Convention and the election of 1968 as examples of that kind of abuse. The final days of the 1968 presidential election, pitting Johnson's vice president, Hubert Humphrey, against former vice president Richard Nixon, included claims that the Nixon campaign intervened to delay the peace process in Vietnam. That intervention, it was asserted, came through the relationship between Nixon's running mate, Spiro Agnew, and Anna Chennault, Republican activist and widow of World War II hero Lt. Gen. Claire Chennault. Johnson believed that Chennault intervened on Nixon's behalf with the South Vietnamese leadership to delay peace negotiations—negotiations that presumably would have benefited Humphrey's candidacy.

In the last week of the campaign and on orders from Johnson through DeLoach, FBI agents wiretapped the South Vietnamese Embassy in Washington and placed Chennault under physical surveillance. When Johnson, through presidential assistant Jim Jones, ordered the FBI to immediately obtain a list of toll calls from Albuquerque to Washington in an effort to pinpoint the date and time of calls to the South Vietnamese Embassy from a Nixon campaign plane, DeLoach urged him to wait until the next morning rather than harassing telephone company staff late at night. "[Johnson aide Bromley Smith] asked me to do this after 7 o'clock one night," DeLoach said in an August 21, 1995, C-SPAN2 interview. "I told him that would be the wrong thing to do, a terrible thing to do. It would lead to allegations concerning the FBI being a Gestapo."[137] In a follow-up call a few days later, Johnson asked DeLoach, "Who do you think is your commander in chief?" DeLoach said he told Johnson, "I'm trying to save you from embarrassment and also the FBI from embarrassment." That is not accurate. In his memoirs and in the recounting of those memoirs for C-SPAN2, DeLoach portrayed himself and the FBI as only reluctantly getting involved in the Chennault affair, and he cast himself as having stood up to Johnson, who he believed was seeking information to hamstring Nixon, then the president-elect. Recounting Johnson's call to him on November 12, 1968, DeLoach's memoirs present a far different picture than does the recording of the discussion with Johnson, which was made publicly available on the Internet years after the publication of DeLoach's memoirs. In his book, DeLoach recalled, inaccurately, that Johnson "screamed" at him and that, on behalf of the Bureau, he was intimidated into attempting to obtain the Albuquerque telephone exchange information. "The office [of president] confers a special power that adds several feet to the stature of anyone who holds it," DeLoach wrote in 1995. "Somehow when you're in the presence of the president (or even talking to him on the telephone) you feel the strength of millions of Americans in his eyes and voice and movements. You're not frightened of him, but it's difficult not to be intimidated by the millions of people whose will he embodies."[138]

What DeLoach left out in his telling of the tale was the context of the nine-minute phone call, more than half of which dealt with Hoover's ill health and DeLoach's desire to replace his boss. After Johnson asked DeLoach to get the Albuquerque toll call information, without screaming, their discussion turned to a lunch at the White House that same day, attended by Johnson, DeLoach, Hoover, and Tolson. Johnson said he had talked to someone (from the context, it is clear he was referring to President-Elect Nixon) about the FBI and Hoover. "I told this fella [Nixon] that I couldn't fire this man [Hoover] and didn't want to ask him to leave, that I was very happy with the services of the department, of the Bureau," Johnson told DeLoach; he also said that he would have replaced Hoover with DeLoach but he "did not want to humiliate or mortify the other fella [Hoover] until he was ready." Johnson added that he had recommended DeLoach as the director's replacement to Nixon as well. The president then asked, in reference to Hoover's failing health, "Why in the hell doesn't he act?"

DeLoach's response was very telling and stands in contrast to his later claims of complete loyalty to Hoover. "Well [he doesn't retire] because he doesn't know how to do anything for himself," DeLoach said. "Because he's a very selfish individual and frankly just feels like he's invincible and we can't get along without him and he just wants to be there until he dies." Johnson then raised the executive order he had issued in 1964 allowing Hoover to continue to serve past the federally mandated retirement age. "Does the new man [Nixon] have to issue an executive order, too?" he asked. DeLoach said yes, then continued with his evaluation of Hoover's health. "He doesn't know how to drive a car. He has never kept books, doesn't know anything about housework, doesn't know anything about anything outside of the office because everything is done for him," he said. "And I love him and have always done it and I've worked for him for 27 years. Time is moving on. It's my fault and Walter's fault [referring to Johnson aide Walter Jenkins] because we came to you and recommended this [the executive order]. It's my fault and I'll admit that. But now we've got to get moving. We can't stagnate. We're too important an agency for that."

Johnson then asked what was wrong with Hoover's arm. "I don't know sir, he's been shaking pretty badly for some time," DeLoach responded. "He also has a pretty bad back ailment. He has had great difficulty getting in and out of a car and standing up and getting in and out of a chair." DeLoach noted that Tolson was also very infirm, having suffered several strokes. "They just want to stay on, they just don't know any other thing in life and I want to support them and I want to help them, but I'm not going to wait for the rest of my life, either," he added. Johnson said he might still be able to help De-Loach, who was clearly hinting that he did not want to wait to be elevated to Hoover's position. DeLoach responded with gratitude to his benefactor. "I owe you everything and I'm very grateful to you for it," he said. Then, turning immediately back to the president's request for the toll calls, he said, "I'm not stalling this situation in Albuquerque. I'll get this information if I have to go to Albuquerque and get it myself for you. I'll do it."[139] Although De-Loach, in his memoirs and related interviews, portrayed his response to Johnson's request as an example of his standing up to presidential intimidation, what is striking is his candor about Hoover's ill health, his obvious desire to replace Hoover as director, and his complete fealty to his departing benefactor, Johnson. Rather than standing up to Johnson, DeLoach through his actions in the Chennault affair showed himself to be a man skilled at pleasing his powerful friends, engaging in public relations on behalf of his own interests. His rival for Hoover's favor, Assistant Director William Sullivan, attributed his own rise within the FBI to his ability to flatter Hoover. "The FBI was a great game, a game of playing up to the ego of Hoover, in writing him fancy letters, in praising him to the skies," Sullivan said. "We all played up to the ego of Hoover, and that was the way to get along."[140] Another top FBI official, Mark Felt, who later admitted he had been Deep Throat of Watergate fame, believed that DeLoach's ambitions to become FBI director died when Johnson announced he would not seek reelection in 1968. "If DeLoach had felt that he had enough pull with Nixon to keep that job, he would have stayed," Felt remarked in 1975. "He wouldn't have left."[141]

DeLoach's efforts at self-promotion were doomed by political forces outside his control, yet there can be little doubt that he was an effective public relations manager for the Bureau during his eleven years overseeing FBI relationships with the press, Congress, and the White House. Three years before the Chennault affair, in 1965, the public relations productivity of DeLoach's Crime Research Division was astonishing, given his relatively small staff of approximately 36 agents and 160 clerical employees and typists. During the first eleven months of that year, more than 588,000 people had taken the FBI's popular Seat of Government tour, which included stops in the FBI Crime Laboratory and the opportunity to gawk at John Dillinger's death mask and pistol, displayed in Hoover's outer office. In addition, nearly 7,000 letters were read and answered monthly that year. The Crime Research Section produced publications such as the *FBI Law Enforcement Bulletin*, which boasted a circulation of nearly 60,000 monthly. Bureau inspectors attributed the capture of seven of the nineteen "Top Ten" fugitives listed that year directly to publicity generated by Crime Research. DeLoach himself appeared weekly on national and local Washington, D.C., radio programs. Scripts for a prime-time television program, *The F.B.I.*, were rewritten in Crime Research, and two agents from the section advised and oversaw the production in Hollywood. Crime Research Section writers produced 75 published articles that appeared in national publications, among them *Look, Parade, Christian Science Monitor,* and *U.S. News & World Report,* as well as various legal journals. The section issued 238 "statements" from Hoover, both responses to media requests and general statements that prompted media coverage. Jones, DeLoach, and others assisted in the production of published books by Andrew Tully and David Sentner. Jones's section also performed more than 6,000 name checks for the White House. Thousands of speeches were vetted, and many of those were delivered by DeLoach and members of his staff.[142] In addition to external audiences, DeLoach had contacts within the government that continued to pay dividends for the FBI. In his 1966 review of the Crime Research Division, Mark Felt praised DeLoach for his effective liaison work. "Assistant to the Director's close personal contact with the White House on practically a daily basis has greatly strengthened the trust and confidence in the Bureau's operations," Felt wrote. "The unique liaison with the White House, together with added top-level contacts developed in Congress, has effectively protected the Bureau's interests and increased the esteem in which the Bureau and the Director are held by the Executive and Legislative Branches of the Government."[143]

Under DeLoach, the Bureau's public relations activities, already remarkable in scope, reached their peak. In January 1966, he was promoted to assistant to the director, making him the third-highest official at the FBI. He maintained liaison responsibilities with LBJ and other key government officials and still oversaw the Crime Research Division, although Robert Wick became assistant director in charge there.[144] Like Nease following Nichols, Wick was assured of a difficult tenure by the simple fact that he was not DeLoach, and his situation was further complicated because, unlike Nease, he did not see his predecessor immediately leave the Bureau; instead, DeLoach became his supervisor.

Four years later, in a move that surprised reporters who covered the FBI, DeLoach retired suddenly. One question remains regarding the reasons for his unexpected retirement from the Bureau at age fifty, when he became eligible for his government pension. Why would DeLoach, a man many believed would ascend to Hoover's position someday, suddenly announce his retirement? There are signs that a rumored scandal, one that would have been a great embarrassment to the Bureau if true, may have hastened his departure.

On December 29, 1969, *Los Angeles Times* reporter Ron Ostrow called De-Loach, ostensibly regarding a story about who might succeed Hoover as FBI

Director J. Edgar Hoover with the DeLoach family for Assistant Director Cartha D. DeLoach's twenty-year service award, January 29, 1964: (left to right) Theresa, Barbara, Sharon, Hoover, Gregory, Barbara, Thomas, Cartha D. DeLoach, and Dekle, Jr. (National Archives at College Park, Md., Record Group 65, Series H, Box 34, Folder 1878.)

director. Ostrow was a veteran reporter at the time, known for his accuracy and toughness. He started with the *Wall Street Journal* in 1956 and joined the *Los Angeles Times* in 1965, moving to its Washington bureau one year later. John E. Otto, who served as acting FBI director briefly in 1987, told author Ronald Kessler that he respected Ostrow. "[Ostrow] knows his business," Otto said to Kessler. "He's tough, he's got wonderful sources, but I never once saw him write something that was not accurate, that was not verified, no matter how hard-hitting it was or whom it affected. You deal with many in the press, and he will always stand out in my mind. He is a consummate professional."[145]

Ostrow told DeLoach that his name and several others had been mentioned as potential successors to Hoover. "I interrupted Mr. Ostrow to inform him that the Director had no intention of retiring, was in good health, and that any question of this nature was strictly a moot one," DeLoach wrote in a memorandum to Tolson that he knew would also be read by Hoover.[146] Ostrow turned to questions about DeLoach's future, including whether he had fielded job offers from PepsiCo. DeLoach said he had but had turned them down. Finally, Ostrow asked DeLoach how many children he had. DeLoach and his wife had seven children, including several of or approaching college age, and they also contributed to the support of two grandchildren. "He told me it must be a pretty tough job financially to support such a crew," DeLoach reported to Tolson. "I agreed with this, but stated we have been able to get along well over the years and have no apologies to make to anyone."[147] DeLoach continued, citing his job security and the reputation of the FBI as "the reasons why I intended remaining as long as the Director wanted me to."[148] Six months later, he announced his retirement plans.

Reporters' continued inquiries about his finances appear to have played a role in those plans. In March 1970, an American Legion official phoned DeLoach to inform him that a *Los Angeles Times* reporter (likely Ostrow or Jack Nelson) had telephoned a Legionnaire in Bismarck, North Dakota, digging for information. The reporter, whose name is redacted in FBI files, asked about an amount of $933 in expenses for DeLoach's wife that was paid by the American Legion in 1966 when she accompanied him on an overseas trip. DeLoach's expenses for the same trip were paid by the Legion because of his position as national chairman of public relations. He later reimbursed the American Legion for his wife's expenses, the reporter was told.[149] In his memorandum detailing the *Times* contact with the Bismarck American Legion official, DeLoach speculated that two men may have been behind the leak of information about his debt—former special agent Lee R. Pennington, a fellow Legionnaire who left the FBI to lead the National Americanism Commission, and another former special agent whose name is redacted in the files. In fact, there had been an effort to destroy DeLoach's reputation in 1968, when the Justice Department received an anonymous letter alleging Jimmy Hoffa's Teamsters had evidence that he participated in an affair involving a "blonde, liquor, and lavish hotel accommodations." DeLoach said at the time that a former special agent, whose name is redacted on the memorandum, was likely behind the effort to smear his character.[150] He said he had testified against that unnamed agent and one other individual, whose name is also redacted on the memorandum, at a hearing before the Civil Service Commission.[151]

Regarding the financial claims being investigated by *Los Angeles Times* reporters in 1970, DeLoach reminded Tolson that Ed Guthman, former press agent for Hoover nemesis Robert Kennedy, was the national editor of the *Times*.[152] And both Los Angeles SAC Wesley Grapp and former Pulitzer Prize–winning journalist turned Nixon administration official Clark R. Mollenhoff had warned the Bureau that Nelson was working on a critical story or a series of stories.[153] In a handwritten note, Hoover dismissed Guthman and Pennington as "jackals" and ordered that Pennington be removed from all FBI mailing lists.[154] Crime Research chief Milton Jones added his own note, pointing out that Pennington had already been blacklisted.[155]

On April 3, 1970, upon receiving his usual "Outstanding" efficiency rating, DeLoach wrote Hoover a letter of thanks, notable primarily for its sober tone. In prior years, his annual thank-you letters to the director were remarkably consistent and effusive, generally mentioning how much he appreciated the recognition, sometimes noting how the financial award associated with the outstanding performance rating would be helpful since he had children in college, and expressing hopes for a continued future with Hoover. In April 1966, DeLoach closed his letter with, "I will never be anything but a loyal, devoted employee to you and the Bureau."[156] In April 1967, he noted that the financial benefits of the outstanding rating would be spent on college costs for his children, and he again offered a hopeful message of something good "in the near future."[157] In April 1968, DeLoach thanked Hoover for giving him a boost "in this world of discouraging political 'Bobby-news,'" referring to Robert Kennedy's presidential campaign. That same year, he noted the "many needy drains that a man with seven children has to face!"[158] In April 1969, DeLoach's thank-you letter ended with a clear declaration of a future with Hoover in the FBI: "I will strive to accomplish the same results in future years."[159] DeLoach's 1970 letter acknowledging his outstanding performance rating—written in the wake of Ostrow's pointed December questioning about his personal expenses and a few weeks after an unnamed *Times* reporter was seeking clarification about another financial transaction—was decidedly less focused on the future, emphasizing instead his personal relationship with Hoover. "I wish to also thank you for the many opportunities given me during the past year to talk personally with you concerning the many problems that we face from an investigative standpoint."[160]

Agents at the Seat of Government understood that Hoover expected them to parrot his own confrontational tone in their dealings with critics outside the Bureau. They also understood that in a paternalistic bureaucracy like the

FBI, continuing success required unrelenting fealty to the director. If Hoover and Tolson believed that an error had been made, agents were expected to hoist themselves on their own petards. If Hoover and Tolson approved promotions or raises, agents were expected to respond with gratitude, often in the form of fawning letters to Hoover. DeLoach was a master of playing on the director's vanities, and his expressions of gratitude only became increasingly florid over the years. For example, responding to a positive annual review on April 18, 1951, he wrote: "I sincerely wish it were possible for every employee in the Bureau to have the opportunity to know you personally and to understand your feelings about the welfare of FBI personnel as well as I have since being assigned as Liaison representative."[161] When Hoover spoke briefly to a conference of FBI inspectors in 1953, DeLoach sent a thank-you letter stating: "The fact that you personally met with us and gave instructions, suggestions, and well deserved criticism, is indicative of the intense interest you show in our work and in the Bureau as a whole."[162] Promotions in grade, commendations, and annual reviews also prompted notes from DeLoach to Hoover. After being informed of a promotion in 1957, he wrote, "I am very grateful for your guidance and leadership and simply hope that a little of the greatness you are made of will in some manner 'rub off' on me through the years."[163] In 1960, DeLoach was commended for his work and wrote to Hoover that he possessed "a rather guilty feeling at taking advantage of 'riding your coat tails.'"[164]

A positive annual review in 1960 also prompted DeLoach to write Hoover and express his feelings. "To be absolutely truthful, I feel so very inadequate at times because of the fact there are so many things I want to do for you and the Bureau that either cannot be done or else there is just not enough time, even with considerable overtime," he wrote.[165] A policy change increasing the travel per diem to $30 gave him an opportunity to thank Hoover (the letter salutation was "Dear Boss"): "I certainly hope and trust that it will not be necessary to use this amount. However, the satisfaction of knowing that you personally have arranged for us to receive this will certainly be a great solace and comfort."[166]

Was DeLoach considering retirement at that point? It is impossible to say. What is clear, however, is that the *Los Angeles Times* was working on a story about him and that the story involved allegations of a financial scandal that had the potential to be an embarrassment to the FBI. On April 8, 1970, DeLoach reported to Tolson that *Times* reporter Jack Nelson spoke to Warner Brothers executive vice president Bernard Goodman about royalties from

The F.B.I. television series. Nelson, again delving into personal finances, asked whether DeLoach received part of the proceeds from the series, which aired in prime time from 1965 to 1974 on ABC. DeLoach did not receive any of the royalties, which were deposited in the FBI Recreational Association fund (itself a slush fund for Hoover and Tolson).[167] In his memoirs, Nelson noted his frustration with his editors when they suddenly killed a major story he and Ostrow were working on involving a top FBI official—almost certainly DeLoach. "The FBI man's mortgage was being paid by a businessman, and to make the arrangement even fishier, the businessman sought and received an appointment as a roving ambassador from the president," Nelson wrote. "We, of course, wanted to press ahead with our investigation, but editors were swayed by the FBI's pleas that the official was about to retire and faced financing the college tuitions of several children."[168]

The businessman in question was Miami real estate magnate Maurice Gusman. Gusman arrived in New York City as a teenager at the turn of the twentieth century, fleeing the Ukraine and the czar. In New York, he took a job in a drugstore for $3 a week. Within a few years, he had moved to Ohio, where he first became a millionaire in the wholesale drug business. He diversified into banking before losing much of his fortune in the Great Depression. Gusman then moved to the suburbs of Akron, the rubber capital of the United States, and his condom business boomed during World War II. He sold his company for $10 million in 1947 and moved to Miami, where he dealt in real estate, property management, and philanthropy.

In 1964, Gusman, a lifelong Republican, was named a special envoy (or, in Nelson's term, a "roving ambassador") to Africa by President Lyndon Johnson.[169] In November and December of that year, he traveled to Dar es Salaam, Tanzania, to represent the United States at the Plastics USA trade fair.[170] In a letter thanking Johnson for the opportunity, Gusman made it clear who had recommended him for the appointment. "I am grateful to my very good friend, Deke DeLoach, and to you, Mr. President," Gusman wrote."[171] Obviously, DeLoach, serving as the FBI's liaison to the White House and having become a close confidant of Johnson, had suggested his friend Gusman for the appointment.[172]

According to mutual friend Efrem Zimbalist, Jr., star of *The F.B.I.* television show, Gusman and DeLoach met in 1944, during DeLoach's first posting as resident agent in Akron. According to Zimbalist, Gusman, then the owner of a plastics and rubber goods company, contacted the Akron FBI office and spoke to Resident Agent DeLoach about the theft of a railroad car loaded with condoms, just the latest in a series of condom heists. "Deke was able to retrieve the precious cargo," Zimbalist wrote in his memoirs, "and, as a result, the two men developed a liking for each other which in time ripened into a deep friendship."[173] Gusman wrote to Hoover on September 26, 1944, touting the help DeLoach had provided. "Mr. DeLoach was instrumental in apprehending those fellows," he stated. "I can not [sic] abstain from expressing to you the fine work done by Mr. DeLoach in this case."[174] In a 1976 biography, Gusman recalled that DeLoach discovered the missing condoms, a shipment of defective goods intended to be recycled, were being sold as first-quality merchandise in Chicago. According to Gusman's biographer, Lillian Erlich, DeLoach set a trap and captured the thieves, cementing a friendship (DeLoach described it as being like a father-son relationship) that lasted for decades.[175]

Although there is no independent evidence to support Nelson's claim that DeLoach left the FBI under the cloud of a potentially damaging financial quid pro quo arrangement with Gusman, a framework of plausible facts surrounds the charge. If DeLoach was being undermined by enemies, former FBI agents Pennington and the unidentified individual, they had created a credible fiction. Gusman and DeLoach were close friends. A lifelong Republican, Gusman had an opportunity to be a presidential envoy as a direct result of DeLoach's friendship with a Democratic president who had never heard of the Miami mogul. As for DeLoach, he did have seven children, and he did ultimately leave the FBI unexpectedly after more than twenty-five years of service and after rising to a position where he was even discussed as a potential replacement for Hoover. He freely admitted that he left seeking financial security for his family. In any event, the *Los Angeles Times* dropped the story, according to Nelson, after learning of DeLoach's sudden retirement plans, but the *New York Times* picked it up and attempted to piece it together. Obviously, the claim regarding a potential scandal was credible enough that two top-notch reporters, including one at the nation's most prominent agenda-setting newspaper, were willing to work the story.

Just days before his end-of-service date, DeLoach was visited at the FBI by an experienced *New York Times* reporter, Walter Rugaber. Then in his early thirties, Rugaber had joined the *Times* in 1965 after short stints at the *Atlanta Journal* and *Detroit Free Press*. In 1967, the *Times* sent him to Atlanta as its southern correspondent, and in 1969, he moved to the paper's Washington bureau. (He later served as executive editor of the *Greensboro [N.C.] Daily News & Record* and then as president and publisher of the *Roanoke*

Times & World News in Virginia.) On July 2, 1970, Rugaber rushed to his appointment with DeLoach to ask him about several items his editor had wanted him to check out.

DeLoach's memorandum describing Rugaber's visit appears to offer a significantly embellished version of events that day. Reviewing the memo decades later, Rugaber remembered the visit very differently. "There's a lot in the memo that really befuddles me," he said after looking it over.[176] If, in fact, DeLoach's memorandum mischaracterized Rugaber's visit, that again raises the question of why. There were only two people in the audience for the memo, Tolson and Hoover. Thus, the next question is why DeLoach might have wished to embellish the message. It is possible that he was attempting to polish his reputation and protect his relationship with Hoover, inoculating himself against past and/or future charges (whether true or not) as he exited the Bureau. Though DeLoach had significant executive experience at the FBI, his relationship with the director was a key point on his résumé that led to a high-level, high-paying position at PepsiCo. DeLoach knew the value of that relationship, and he knew that Hoover had frequently undermined former officials who had fallen out of favor. When Pennington lost Hoover's support, for instance, he was quickly demoted from his position at the American Legion. No doubt, DeLoach felt the pressure to stay in Hoover's good graces.

According to Rugaber, he was late for his appointment with DeLoach and had to run across the Mall on a warm July day in Washington to get to the Justice Department building on time, arriving redfaced and out of breath. DeLoach offered him a glass of water. "I was obviously playing a very weak hand," Rugaber recalled. "This tip, as I remember it, came into the [*New York Times* Washington] bureau editor and I got assigned to sort of check it out and did check it out. . . . He has obviously written this [memo] to accomplish something."[177] Rugaber's detailed recollections, down to the circumstances of arriving late and out of breath for his appointment with DeLoach, add credibility to his version of events, even more than four decades after the fact.

In his memorandum, DeLoach characterized Rugaber's visit as a surprise and claimed the reporter prefaced the interview by saying that he wanted to "discuss several 'old vague rumors.'"[178] He then asserted that Rugaber opened the interview by stating that his *New York Times* colleagues often criticized Hoover for his conservative politics and for "constantly talking about the dangers of communism."[179] Rugaber disputed that characterization of his first-ever meeting with anyone at FBI headquarters. According to him, DeLoach's account did not match his recollection, and it seems unlikely that an experienced reporter would make such an overture on meeting a top-ranking official in a powerful government agency. Why would he, a news reporter interviewing a source he had not met before, critique a Washington institution like J. Edgar Hoover upon meeting the director's second-ranking lieutenant? Rugaber asked. "I can't imagine any reporter starting off by saying his associates considered the director to be staunchly conservative. I can't imagine ever doing that."[180]

It is likely that DeLoach intended that paragraph in his memo to catch Hoover's attention, restating the director's expectations of what a presumably liberal reporter for the hated *New York Times* would say or believe. In addition, the scene setter placed DeLoach in the position of a beleaguered public servant, fending off rumors from what Hoover frequently referred to as the jackals of the liberal press. The scene-setting paragraph allowed for the remainder of the conversation to be presented in more aggressive terms. Instead of sounding defensive, DeLoach, claiming he had been confronted out of the blue by a *Times* reporter armed only with rumors, could play the martyr. According to him, Rugaber then stated that representing Hoover would have likely created enemies on the outside of the FBI, another comment that could be viewed as DeLoach's own, self-serving inoculation against charges from outsiders.[181] Rugaber denied that statement, noting that he had never written about the FBI before and was unfamiliar with DeLoach until an editor presented him with the news tip that led to the interview that day.

The two accounts agreed on the next point. Rugaber's primary purpose in visiting DeLoach had been to chase down the facts regarding the 1 percent financial interest that DeLoach's wife held in a building in Arlington, Virginia. The tip received by the *Times*'s Washington bureau was that the building had once housed an FBI office, which, if true, would have created at least the appearance of a conflict of interest for DeLoach. As any savvy reporter would do, Rugaber checked the Fairfax County records before visiting DeLoach and knew that the FBI never leased space in the building.[182] DeLoach confirmed that.[183] "I told him, knowing that he undoubtedly had the information anyhow, that the return on this investment paid $83.34 per month, and that I was using this to supplement my pay check [*sic*] in paying heavy college expenses for my children," DeLoach reported to Hoover and Tolson.[184]

The two accounts agreed further that Rugaber then asked about De-Loach's service on the board of a small savings and loan company and about his relationship with Baltimore contractor Victor Frenkil. In the 1960s and early 1970s, Frenkil's Baltimore Contractors, Inc., built the Dirksen-Hart Senate Office Building and the Rayburn Office Building parking garage, and it was the general contractor for the construction of the FBI Academy structures in Quantico, Virginia. In 1970, Frenkil's company was indicted by a federal grand jury regarding cost overruns on the Rayburn garage project, but Attorney General John Mitchell refused to approve the indictment.[185] Again, a relationship with the controversial Frenkil or service on the board of a troubled financial institution would have at least created the appearance of potential impropriety for DeLoach. In his memorandum, he said he told Rugaber that he had briefly served on the savings and loan board but that he had never attended a board meeting and knew of no allegations of impropriety against the institution. With regard to Frenkil, DeLoach admitted he was acquainted with the man but asserted that the contractor "had not asked me for any favors and that I had never been of assistance to him in any manner."[186] According to Frenkil's authorized biography, however, DeLoach was an "FBI contact" for the contractor and had, on at least one occasion, provided inside information. When Walter Jenkins, an aide to President Johnson, was arrested in 1964 for indecent sexual behavior in a Washington YMCA men's room, Frenkil contacted DeLoach, who confirmed the arrest was legitimate.[187] DeLoach was cited as a primary source for an entire chapter of Frenkil's biography. Given DeLoach's wide circle of contacts and Frenkil's own network of powerful people in Washington, it seems quite unlikely that the Jenkins incident was the only time the two discussed insider information.

DeLoach next claimed in his memorandum that Rugaber went on to raise the issue of Maurice Gusman. "Rugaber stated he had one more bit of gossip he wanted to ask me about," he wrote. "He added that I had probably gathered by this time that all of these allegations were based upon an old anonymous letter which several reporters had told him he should disregard, inasmuch as it had obviously been written by a disgruntled ex-agent who had either been fired, or else felt he had been mistreated while in the FBI."[188] Rugaber said that claim was a fiction: the reporter was not chasing down rumors from an anonymous letter but was, instead, conducting a scheduled interview of an FBI official about specific information received by the editor who assigned him to check out the story.[189]

DeLoach's inclusion of Gusman in the memorandum raises the question of why his name came up at all. Rugaber's interview had nothing to do with any Miami connection to DeLoach. Nor had the reporter ever spoken about Gusman with his *Los Angeles Times* competitor, Nelson, who later became a very close friend. "I have no recollection whatsoever about asking him about Gusman," Rugaber said. "It is possible, it was 45 years ago, but I do not remember and that name rings no bell with me at all."[190] Rugaber said he would not have raised the Gusman matter without first looking into it, and had he done so, he was certain he would have recalled the name: "I'd have done a lot of research on Gusman and I certainly would have remembered trying to track the guy down."[191] In his memorandum, DeLoach said he told Rugaber the record with regard to Gusman was quite clear. "I stated Mr. Gusman had been quite close to me and my family; had stayed in my home on numerous occasions, yet the fact remained there had never been any business transactions between us which had not been a matter of record and which had always been completely satisfied in every respect," he reported.[192] Left with competing claims in the historical record, one must consider each person's motivation to alter the record. Rugaber's involvement with DeLoach ended after one brief interview. DeLoach's memorandum would be read by Hoover and Tolson, two men who essentially held the keys to his future. Given the relative stakes involved, Rugaber's account rings true whereas DeLoach's assertions appear to be intended to shape the perceptions of his powerful benefactors.

Rugaber's final question, according to DeLoach (and disputed by Rugaber), was an implied threat to continue pursuing the story should DeLoach's ambitions change. According to DeLoach's memo, Rugaber asked whether he would ever consider a return to government service. DeLoach said he doubted seriously that circumstances, "financial or otherwise, would allow a return to Government service."[193] But Rugaber was sure he did not ask that question. "Why would I ask him whether he would reconsider entering government service?" he queried. "It would make no sense for me to ask that. I wouldn't give a hoot about whether he was coming back to government service."[194] Once again, it appears likely that DeLoach was sending Hoover a message, one that would help assure his own continued relationship with the FBI. Simply put, that message was: I don't want your job, Mr. Hoover. Given the fact that there had been media speculation that DeLoach hoped to become FBI director in the future, it would make sense for the departing official to circumvent that speculation with his boss. Perhaps Hoover knew that DeLoach had maneuvered with LBJ to push him out. If that was the case and if DeLoach wanted to maintain a close relationship with the powerful FBI director, it would be particularly important that he deny any such ambitions. He had seen how Hoover demonized Courtney Evans—the man DeLoach replaced as White House liaison—after Evans left the Bureau.[195] Similarly, DeLoach had witnessed the fall from grace of another top Hoover adviser, Quinn Tamm. After Tamm left to become executive director of the International Association of Chiefs of Police, Hoover came to view him as a traitor to the Bureau, referring to him as a "rattlesnake" and telling his top executives, "I made a mistake in keeping [Tamm] too long."[196] Now, there were signs that Hoover would make a similar break with DeLoach. Sullivan later said he was elevated to DeLoach's former position at the time of his retirement in order to humiliate the departing official. "DeLoach left under a big cloud," Sullivan said in 1975. "He had opposed Hoover, quietly behind the scenes, unlike myself—I fight out in the open. Hoover distrusted DeLoach and he wanted to get rid of him; he was very anxious that DeLoach resign."[197]

Even after editors at the *Los Angeles Times* spiked the story—and months after DeLoach resigned—Nelson continued pursuing the question of alleged financial impropriety. Two months after DeLoach's resignation, the reporter contacted former FBI special agent Charles Stine and asked if he had any information about DeLoach's finances. Stine reported the conversation to the Bureau. According to the agent who spoke to Stine, Nelson "commented that DeLoach and the American Legion had been engaging in 'mutual back-scratching.'"[198] Hoover scrawled "Nelson is a mental case!" at the bottom of the memorandum.[199]

In the absence of specific evidence to prove them, Nelson's charges that DeLoach benefited financially from his relationship with Gusman remain merely charges. Nonetheless, there is a record in the FBI files showing that serious questions were being asked by reporters in the weeks leading up to DeLoach's sudden retirement. Before his departure, his prospects, as the third-ranking official in an agency led by a less-than-vigorous man in his midseventies, were bright and included his potential, at least from the perspective of outsiders in the media, to become director of the FBI at some point. DeLoach's political capital, of course, plummeted after LBJ left the White House, and Sullivan claimed that Hoover knew of DeLoach's scheming to replace the director.

When assessing DeLoach's credibility, one must consider that he did, at times, lie, mislead, or misremember in recounting his work at the FBI. There is, for example, evidence that he misled Department of Justice investigators in 1977 about his recollections of the Bureau's use of wiretaps, break-ins, and bugs. He told a Justice Department Civil Rights Division attorney and testified before a federal grand jury on June 10, 1977, that he could not confirm that the Bureau had used wiretaps, "suicide taps," and "mikes." He told an aide to then–FBI director Clarence Kelley that when asked by federal prosecutors whether he had used illegal electronic surveillance methods during his tenure, "he had no recollection he had done so during his tenure as Assistant to the Director and he did not know of any such approvals given by anyone else during that time."[200] It is true that DeLoach's documented employment of bugs and wiretaps to spy on civil rights organizations for President Johnson during the 1964 Democratic National Convention occurred a few months before he was appointed "Assistant to the Director," as Kelley's aide put it. If DeLoach's characterization of his testimony given after the fact to an FBI official is accurate, he carefully parsed his response to avoid admitting his own deployment of illegal wiretaps and bugs in his special squad work for LBJ. His statement that he did not know of any approvals of wiretaps and microphones is contradicted as well by his own testimony before the Senate Select Committee on Intelligence Activities, the so-called Church Committee, in 1975. (During that hearing, DeLoach reported to Bureau legal counsel that he testified he had briefed [Attorney General Ramsey] Clark regarding wiretaps and microphones "at Clark's specific request."[201]) Clark served as attorney general from 1967 to 1969, and he did not trust DeLoach. In 1975, Clark said in an oral history interview that their relationship essentially ended when the FBI released news of the capture of King assassin James Earl Ray during Robert Kennedy's funeral, apparently in an attempt to upstage Hoover's deceased rival. Clark said he felt that DeLoach's explanation for the release—a claim that Scotland Yard could not withhold the information—was a lie. "I'd been told with some elaboration that they'd tried to hold up and couldn't do it when in fact it had been just the opposite, that they held up just to release it at that time," Clark said. "I called DeLoach in that afternoon and did what I don't do very often, that is, got upset and told him I didn't want to use him as a liaison with the Bureau because I didn't have confidence in him anymore, and that was the end of that."[202]

The incidents with Clark along with DeLoach's inconsistent responses before a federal grand jury and a US Senate committee suggest an effort to recast circumstances in order to defend his own and the Bureau's reputations. The circumstances of his sudden retirement suggest that unproven allegations of a financial arrangement with Gusman were at least plausible and had the potential to become an embarrassing story. DeLoach frequently mentioned his uncertain financial status, having seven children including some in college. The pursuit of a much larger, corporate paycheck may well have been the only reason for his departure from the FBI. Yet his retirement, following closely behind some probing questions about his own financial situation, at least begs the question of whether the Gusman relationship included a financial payoff. There is also a claim that, upon Hoover's death, three files from the director's "official and confidential" file were removed. All, the story goes, related to former FBI officials, and one of the files detailed a Hoover aide's financial improprieties.[203] Finally, it is intriguing to consider the possibility that DeLoach wrote the Rugaber memorandum with the understanding that Hoover would not know the reporter and would not question the veracity of whatever was asserted in the memo. Today, roughly half a century later, Rugaber has no incentive to alter the record, whereas DeLoach may have had an incentive to send his soon-to-be-former boss a series of messages as he exited the Bureau.

Just a few years before his sudden retirement at age fifty, DeLoach sent Hoover his annual thank-you letter, expressing clear satisfaction with his current and future prospects at the FBI and tying his continued service to Hoover's tenure as director: "I will be here as long as you want me or need me," he wrote on April 8, 1965. "When the day comes that I can no longer call you 'Boss,' then I will feel free to take a look elsewhere."[204] Instead, on July 20, 1970, six months after telling a reporter he would serve as long as Hoover would have him around, he left the "Boss" behind for a bigger paycheck at PepsiCo.

DeLoach continued to be an outspoken defender of the FBI and Hoover throughout the remainder of his life. In a 2001 telephone interview with the author, he said he was proud of his public relations work, and he bristled at the suggestion that effective public relations masked illegal or unethical practices by the FBI. Rather than masking the Bureau's work, DeLoach said, public relations helped people understand what the agency could and could not do. In that same conversation, he displayed the cordial charm and calm demeanor that had served him well as the director's top public relations assistant.[205]

Along with Nichols, DeLoach is generally seen as Hoover's most capable and successful public relations adviser. An amiable southerner with an unruffled demeanor and sonorous voice, he worked his way up from clerk to become the third-highest official in the Bureau, behind Hoover and Tolson. His loyalty to the director remained publicly unquestioned during his tenure at the FBI and after his retirement from the Bureau in 1970. Nichols viewed himself as an advocate for Hoover, working through his network of acquaintances in the media to forward the Bureau's agenda and essentially managing relationships from the inside out. DeLoach approached his work differently. Unlike Nichols, he had no public relations experience prior to joining the Bureau. Rather than being an inside-out advocate, DeLoach focused much of his attention on managing upward—promoting the Bureau among powerful people, most of them outside the news and entertainment media. His first public relations successes for the Bureau were in building relationships with the CIA and the American Legion as a boundary-spanning liaison agent. Whereas Nichols devoted considerable attention to the news media, including maintaining contacts with Bureau critics, DeLoach concentrated on embedding himself within other power structures as a Bureau representative. His American Legion ties helped the FBI maintain a link to a powerful group of patriotic veterans, spread throughout the country in a hierarchical organization that resembled the structure of the FBI. As liaison to the CIA, DeLoach was able to please his contacts there while working to promote the Bureau's interests and suppress, insofar as he could, the aspirations of a rival agency competing in the zero-sum game of establishing intelligence boundaries.

It was DeLoach's liaison to the Johnson White House, more particularly with President Johnson himself, that defined the arc of his career and the fortunes of the FBI. With Hoover and Tolson suffering from failing health, DeLoach was in a position to fill a power vacuum, and he had the world's most powerful man as his benefactor. His relationship to Johnson in many ways mirrored his relationship with Hoover during the late 1950s and early 1960s. During those years, DeLoach placed himself in a position of power through his dual abilities to promote the Bureau and promote himself. Beginning in 1963, his close relationship with Johnson played out similarly as DeLoach served the president's needs by leveraging the FBI's machinery for political purposes. Though he later said he was disgusted by the political use of the FBI, terming it an abuse in his memoirs and related publicity tour, DeLoach never expressed any significant reluctance to act when Johnson asked the FBI to intervene politically, as proven by the dozens of telephone conversations between the two men that are now publicly available. In fact, DeLoach transferred his loyalties from Hoover to Johnson even to the point of undermining the director and making a handshake agreement with Johnson to take over the FBI at some point. When Johnson chose to end his political career rather than seek reelection, DeLoach's frustration at the loss of his political benefactor was evident in his November 12, 1968, telephone conversation with LBJ. Under tremendous pressure to support a large family and believing himself a capable replacement for Hoover, DeLoach must have felt Johnson's departure from the political stage (compounded by the related setback of Humphrey's loss to Nixon) was a difficult blow.

Similarly—and following just over a year after the November 12 conversation with Johnson—the circumstances surrounding DeLoach's sudden retirement from the FBI demonstrated his tendency to manage upward. It is unclear whether the circumstances that immediately preceded his retirement, in particular the questions about his alleged financial arrangements with Maurice Gusman, contributed to his departure. The fictional memorandum about DeLoach's meeting with Walter Rugaber reiterated the message from his behind-the-scenes efforts to succeed Hoover as director. It seems likely that DeLoach, fearing that stories alleging financial impropriety could damage his future relationship with Hoover, placed himself in a position of martyrdom in the Rugaber memorandum. The document included hooks that would appeal to Hoover's disdain for the news media, and it offered DeLoach the opportunity to reiterate his denial of wrongdoing, even to the point of manufacturing a conversation about Gusman, whose name Rugaber had never even heard before reviewing the memorandum in 2015. Any reading of DeLoach's memoranda from his entire career must include a presumption that some of the messages they contained, often portraying himself as hero or martyr to Hoover's cause, may have been part of a self-promotional campaign, building himself up within the Bureau and in the eyes of the director.

Throughout his retirement, DeLoach remained a capable and credible defender of Hoover and the FBI. Just eight months before his death, a visibly slowed but still charming and eloquent DeLoach, then ninety-one years old, sat down for an interview with Carl Jensen from the University of Mississippi's Center for Intelligence and Security Studies. In the interview, DeLoach described Hoover's tenure in glowing terms. "[Hoover] was a well-disciplined leader," he said. "He changed the FBI from a loose-tongued, loose practice, little disciplined organization that practiced politics rather than being a disciplined law enforcement organization. [He] got rid of the rotten eggs and put in good people and good practices, not obeying the dictates of politics but putting into effect tough practices of discipline and education and good training."[206]

Chapter Seven

An Empire in Decline

Readers picking up the April 9, 1971, issue of *Life* magazine were confronted with a cover image featuring a marble bust of FBI director J. Edgar Hoover over the headline EMPEROR OF THE FBI: THE 47-YEAR REIGN OF J. EDGAR HOOVER. The themes implied by the image—that Hoover was a man from another time, a monolithic, unchanging figure who led a declining FBI empire with a battle for succession already under way—were highlighted in a series of stories inside. "The Director's growing intolerance of criticism has fed the talk inside the government about the need for a successor," wrote *Life* contributing editor William Lambert, whose byline did not appear on the story. "One longtime FBI agent speaks of his ex-boss sadly: 'The old man's getting childish,' he says. 'He's old and he should get out.'"[1] A sidebar story, again without a byline, aimed the spotlight at one of several public relations gaffes committed by Hoover in late 1970 and early 1971—gaffes that posed a significant challenge to the Bureau's PR staff, which was no longer guided by the savvy, charming, and authoritative Cartha DeLoach. Instead, Thomas Bishop, a capable administrator but nonetheless ill equipped for the monumental task of shaping Hoover's fading public image, led what had become the Crime Research Division; it included the former Crime Records Section, which churned out public relations materials bearing a message that, like Hoover, belonged in another time.

A Cincinnati native, Bishop joined the FBI in 1941 having never before held a full-time job. According to the performance reviews in his FBI file, he developed into a competent field agent serving in Baltimore and Cincinnati and then as the FBI's legal attaché in Caracas, Venezuela, and Montevideo, Uruguay. After a four-year stint in Crime Records with the Correspondence Unit, a routine assignment that primarily involved authoring responses to Hoover's mail, Bishop was returned to the field as special agent in charge of FBI offices in San Antonio; San Diego; San Juan, Puerto Rico; and Richmond,

Virginia. Thereafter, he rejoined the Crime Research Division as DeLoach's top deputy, in January 1966.[2] Like all SACs, he had limited public relations responsibilities in the field—monitoring the media and meeting with local opinion leaders, for example. He had no significant PR strategy or high-level media relations experience when he returned to Crime Research in 1966. Yet four years later, he found himself in a position formerly held by the sharp and affable DeLoach, who himself had replaced Assistant Director Louis Nichols, the sainted and well-liked networker. Given his extensive management experience, Bishop may have, in another time, developed into a towering figure like DeLoach or Nichols within the Bureau. In the late 1960s, though, he was tasked with promoting a significantly diminished director whose health was failing and whose formerly spotless reputation was under siege. Associate Director Clyde Tolson, who had always been a steady adviser for Hoover, had suffered multiple health setbacks and only sporadically went into work by the late 1960s. Unlike DeLoach or Nichols before him, Bishop oversaw public relations for an FBI that had been steadily losing its credibility with mainstream media for many years. Hoover's and Bishop's late 1960s and early 1970s FBI represented mainstream 1950s values in a counterculture America roiled by clashes over civil rights and the Vietnam War.

In addition to having only limited experience as a PR strategist, Bishop found his job—rebuilding Hoover's credibility in a culture that had, decades before, shifted out from under him as times and audiences changed—was complicated by the director's increasing stubbornness and unwillingness to adapt the Bureau's message. In the past, FBI icons such as Nichols and DeLoach had the authority within the Bureau and the insight to steer Hoover and Tolson clear of public relations disasters, and they had the credibility with the media to soften the impact of criticism when it did emerge. Bishop, by contrast, was an insider, a bright and capable administrator who simply lacked, on the one hand, DeLoach's gravitas inside the Bureau and government and, on the other hand, Nichols's contacts outside the Bureau—contacts he might have used to "fix" the out-of-control onslaught of PR problems that arose in 1970 and 1971.

The April 1971 *Life* cover story and sidebar landed on newsstands in the midst of a series of public relations challenges that, taken together, constituted a substantial threat to Hoover's continued leadership and to the Bureau's carefully tended but increasingly tarnished public image. The sidebar dealt specifically with one of those emerging—and largely self-inflicted—public relations crises. The story quoted a former FBI agent, Jack Shaw, who resigned earlier that year after daring to criticize the Bureau in a private letter he wrote in late 1970. He sent that letter to his professor, Abraham S. Blumberg, while studying for his master's degree at John Jay College in New York. In the letter, Shaw defended the FBI against the professor's charges, asserting the Bureau was no "Gestapo-like" agency. However, he did criticize the FBI as a rigid and overcautious bureaucracy that emphasized easy investigations into "dime-a-dozen" bank robbers while not placing enough emphasis on dealing with organized crime.[3]

Shaw made the mistake of having his fifteen-page, single-spaced private letter typed in the FBI's New York office typing pool, where its contents were brought to the attention of a supervisor. A copy of the letter was forwarded to Washington, where it was read by the director. Hoover was incensed both by its content and by the fact that all sixteen agents who were enrolled in the same course had failed to report Professor Blumberg's in-class criticism of the Bureau, however mild it had been. The director ordered all FBI personnel in the John Jay course to withdraw from the class, and he also issued orders suspending Shaw without pay for thirty days and transferring him from the Bureau's most glamorous office, in New York City, to one of its least attractive ones, in Butte, Montana.[4] In the letter to his professor, Shaw had noted that discipline in the Bureau was often harsh and swift, something he came to understand personally. "Unfortunately, too, it is often quite arbitrary," he wrote. "Punishment is usually meted out in direct proportion to the amount of bad publicity generated by a particular mistake or incident."[5] Although the FBI strongly denied the "doghouse" allegations at the time, the practice of punishing rogue agents by sending them to isolated, rural posts was later confirmed by a former FBI official. DeLoach, then a PepsiCo executive, told a reporter in 1972, after Hoover's death, that the director held "absolute dominion over his men and their families" and that he personally adjudicated disciplinary cases.[6]

Shaw, a father of four whose wife was ill and later died of cancer, opted to resign and file suit for back pay rather than agree to a transfer.[7] Hoover accepted Shaw's resignation "with prejudice" and included the black mark in his Civil Service Commission record in order to hinder his future employment prospects. The FBI later claimed, in response to a letter from Senator Mike Mansfield and Senator Lee Metcalf of Montana, that Butte was not a doghouse post.[8] Unsurprisingly, Hoover's tone-deaf, heavy-handed response to Shaw's relatively minor criticism soon drew the attention of the growing cadre of FBI critics. A powerful public relations manager like Nichols or De-

South Dakota Democratic senator George S. McGovern, shown here on June 30, 1972, was an outspoken critic of J. Edgar Hoover. (Library of Congress, U.S. News & World Report Magazine Photograph Collection, Call Number LC-U9-26137-21.)

Loach might have been able to contain the crisis by working with powerful friends in the media. Bishop, however, never developed that sort of influence outside the FBI. Instead of silencing a critic, then, Hoover's oafish response catalyzed additional criticism, which bubbled up not from fringe left-wing publications but from high-profile politicians and reporters.

South Dakota senator George S. McGovern, with easy access to media because of his place in the Democratic party leadership and because of his presidential ambitions, publicly intervened on Shaw's behalf: "The injustice which this man has suffered cannot be tolerated with respect to any citizen in a free society," McGovern said, adding that "the persecution of Shaw, despite excellent service, involves the integrity of our Government and the effective enforcement of our laws."[9] The American Civil Liberties Union eventually took up Shaw's cause, filing suit on his behalf and ultimately settling with the FBI, which withdrew the prejudicial finding and paid the former agent $13,000 in back pay.[10]

The director's handling of Shaw's criticism was merely the first incident in 1971 that prompted McGovern to attack Hoover and the FBI. Having escaped Hoover's orbit, Shaw was free to repeat his private sentiments in the pages of *Life*. "We've got to have an FBI, but let's meet our responsibilities to society and get away from the personality cult. It colors every investigation to suit the image of Mr. Hoover," he said. "I think he's trying to establish a legend as the greatest living American. He's a good bureaucrat, but he's not the savior of the country. Let him rest on his laurels."[11]

McGovern spent much of early 1971 publicly criticizing Hoover for his handling of various controversies. In March, the senator released a letter he had received from ten FBI agents alleging that they spent most of their time "polishing the image of J. Edgar Hoover."[12] The unsigned letter, provided to the press by McGovern and written on FBI letterhead, included charges that Hoover and the Bureau had inflated the agency's effectiveness by doctoring arrest and conviction statistics in its annual Uniform Crime Report. "We are not allowed to fight the real crime in this country which should be fought," the letter writers said. "It is long and hard work and does not produce the volume of convictions of which Mr. Hoover is so proud."[13] The authors of the letter claimed they were younger agents, between ages twenty-seven and thirty-one, and believed in the potential of the FBI—potential that could only be realized if "we could for only a few moments forget about the Director's image and the preservation thereof. At present that is all we exist for."[14] Hoover instructed his staff to review the charges: "The allegations by faceless informers should be analyzed particularly the matter relating to convictions."[15] Assistant to the Director Mark Felt (who later was revealed to be Watergate's Deep Throat) wrote a four-page memorandum refuting the former agents' claims and laying out a plan to identify the culprits.[16]

Deputy Attorney General Richard Kliendienst urged Hoover to respond, and on March 2, the director's most ardent defender, Tolson, sent a letter to McGovern and the news media. "I am appalled at the grossly irresponsible and opportunistic attack which you have launched on him," Tolson wrote. "You are not the first person I have encountered during almost 50 years in Washington whose ambition has far exceeded his ability, and I cannot help wondering how many other esteemed career public servants will be maligned and abused before your political balloon runs out of hot air."[17] Other headquarters officials followed with their own letters. Assistant Director John Mohr wrote to McGovern that he had "never witnessed any act so grossly irresponsible or so transparently self-serving as your reprehensible action."[18] Field agents joined in the defense. Special Agent William V. Cleveland wrote that McGovern's criticism "is a tested and proven sure fire public relations operation, and following P. T. Barnum's theory, there will doubtlessly be a few suckers who will go for it."[19] In addition to responses from FBI personnel, the public relations value of which was questionable, Crime Research staff wrote a Senate floor speech for Republican US senator Roman Hruska from Nebraska, obviously hoping to counter McGovern with a friendly heartland senator. "Anyone with a small degree of effort can obtain FBI stationery," Hruska said, in comments written by a Crime Research staffer. "And I have never in my long career of public service seen an anonymous letter—and I have seen many of them—in which the writer did not assert that he was genuine but that he could not reveal his identity for fear of reprisal."[20] The irony of citing his own authenticity to buttress a message decrying the anonymity of whistle-blowers while reading a speech ghostwritten for him by "genuine" but anonymous FBI agents was apparently lost on Hruska.

McGovern, buoyed by continued media attention, kept the pressure on Hoover, making numerous media appearances to discuss his critique of the FBI. Bishop's Crime Research agents attempted to engage media friends to defend the director. But the days when the giants of FBI public relations such as Nichols and DeLoach could prompt a deluge of defenses in response to a purported smear campaign were over. Bishop's efforts yielded a few regional newspaper and radio editorials and predictable denunciations of Mc-Govern from conservative voices, among them VFW commander Herbert R. Rainwater. But McGovern made front-page news, whereas stories on or by Hoover's friends and defenders occupied the corners of inside pages.[21] The failure of the director's defenses no doubt resulted from a number of factors, including the mounting effects of ongoing criticism of the FBI, Hoover's age and ill health, and Bishop's inexperience in PR and his inability to engage the kind of network of defenders that Nichols and DeLoach had readily at hand.

There is evidence that Bishop's public relations operation did not run with the same efficiency that prior Crime Records/Research leaders had developed. In March, Hoover asked Bishop why copies of favorable letters, stories, and editorials were not being forwarded to the attorney general, as was common in the past. "We have been endeavoring to meticulously follow the Director's instructions to see that favorable remarks concerning either the Director's administration of the FBI or the Bureau's work were sent to the Attorney General promptly," Agent Gordon Malmfeldt told Bishop. "We did not interpret this instruction to encompass correspondence relating to the charges made by Senator McGovern."[22] Surely, the Bureau's public relations office must have realized that to counter the most pressing PR problem facing the agency at that moment—McGovern's criticism—it was worth collecting and distributing favorable remarks to key stakeholders. The criticism of the FBI during the early 1970s clearly exceeded that at any other point in the Bureau's history. When what the agency saw as smear campaigns threatened the FBI in 1940 and 1958, the Crime Records Section's response was comprehensive and devastatingly effective in silencing critics. Yet in 1971, Bishop's staff failed to buttress Hoover's standing with the attorney general by simply forwarding letters defending the director down the hall in the Department of Justice building.

In April, McGovern charged that Hoover tried to get Trans World Airlines (TWA) to fire a pilot who criticized the Bureau's handling of a 1969 hijacking investigation.[23] McGovern demanded a Senate investigation into the FBI's conduct after the pilot, Donald J. Cook, Jr., faulted the Bureau's investigation into the hijacking of his plane by Raphael Minichiello on November 1, 1969. After the incident was resolved, Cook called the FBI's attempt to intervene in the hijacking while the plane was refueling in New York a "fiasco" and "damned near the prescription for getting the entire crew killed and the plane destroyed."[24] That was true, according to FBI files. When agents dressed as ground crew approached the plane at JFK Airport, the hijacker recognized the ruse and fired at them, causing them to retreat.[25] In the aftermath of the incident and Cook's statements, Hoover wrote to TWA president Forwood C. Wiser to complain about the pilot. In the letter, he disclosed derogatory information from Cook's private air force record.[26] McGovern's staff failed to obtain a copy of the letter from TWA, but a copy is included in the senator's voluminous FBI file, and it shows that the director stated, "I strongly resent the malicious, critical comments Captain Cook made to the press regarding this matter, especially since they come from an individual who experienced academic difficulties and was eliminated from pilot training while in the United States Air Force due to the fact he was found deficient in transition flying ability." Hoover also suggested that Cook was a coward for not picking up a rifle when it was placed on an airline seat by the hijacker.[27] In addition to Wiser, the letter was sent to all Bureau SACs and overseas legal attachés. Hoover also spoke to TWA chairman Charles Tillinghast, revealing the same information.[28] In a 1971 memorandum, an FBI public relations agent explained the Bureau's logic for releasing Cook's private information in the letter: "Although the information which resulted in Cook being eliminated from pilot training came from confidential Air Force records, it was not being credited specifically to such records in the outgoing letter and therefore no objection was seen to its inclusion in the letter."[29] The decision to include the private information in the letter, made by Tolson and approved by Hoover,[30] opened the Bureau up to criticism that fed directly into arguments about its excessive power and voluminous files. It also demonstrated how Tolson's and Hoover's judgment had deteriorated by 1969.

Even before the Shaw case prompted politicians and journalists to begin questioning and criticizing Hoover's leadership of the Bureau, *Los Angeles Times* reporters Jack Nelson and Ron Ostrow moved on from their inquiries into DeLoach's personal finances and began asking questions that could only lead to further embarrassment for the FBI and its director. On December 29, 1970, the reporters visited Tom Bishop. "Nelson is well known to the Bureau for his hatred of the FBI and for the critical articles concerning the Bureau which he has written in the past," Bishop reported to Sullivan. "In addition, he is one of the co-authors of a book entitled 'The Orangeburg Massacre' which was critical of the Bureau."[31] Nelson and Ostrow requested an interview with Hoover, a perk typically only allowed for friends of the FBI; they were immediately rebuffed. When Nelson asked Bishop about the FBI Recreation Association (FBIRA), he was told to submit his questions in writing. Nelson and Ostrow must have had inside information about alleged corruption in the association. Founded in 1931, the FBIRA was originally intended to "promote and encourage athletics as a means to better health, to stimulate fair play, and to create a better understanding of each other."[32] But by 1970, the FBIRA sometimes functioned like a money-laundering operation and slush fund for Hoover and Tolson. For example, it purchased thousands of copies of Hoover's books and other pro-FBI materials, assuring their commercial success.[33] Nelson's questions, like the DeLoach financial questions, carried the potential for causing serious embarrassment and provoking criticism. In addition to the FBIRA queries, Nelson asked to see copies of the *Investigator*, one of the Bureau's internal publications that was funded by the FBIRA. Before he could ask anything further, Bishop stopped him; Nelson "was told that this request should also be put in writing."[34]

Before visiting the Bureau to request an interview, Nelson and Ostrow spoke to an official at the General Services Administration (GSA), asking nine specific questions that related to perks Hoover might have received as director, among them: How often did Hoover's office get new carpeting? How much did Hoover's armored limousine cost? Did Hoover receive a new one each year? What make, Lincoln or Cadillac, did Hoover prefer? The specificity of Nelson's questions would again suggest he had a disgruntled FBI agent, perhaps Shaw, as a source. For instance, Nelson asked, "Is it true that the Director had a flat tire on the way to Philadelphia a number of years ago and has since demanded that a new set of tires be put on his car each time he leaves the city?"[35] Upon receiving word that Nelson and Ostrow had contacted the GSA, Tolson requested a check of FBI files for information on Ostrow.[36]

When the two reporters submitted their written questions, it was immediately clear to Bureau officials that they could have a serious public relations problem on their hands. In addition to asking about the FBIRA, the reporters asked again about DeLoach's finances and Hoover's limousine; about financial arrangements surrounding the FBI's prime-time television series starring Efrem Zimbalist, Jr.; about the FBI National Academy; and about information backing up Hoover's statements on whether agents were required to retire at sixty-five. "We feel the questions posed above deal with subjects that are clearly within the area of the public's right to know," Ostrow and Nelson wrote. "We hope you will give us an early reply."[37] Two days later, Bishop sent curt and sometimes nonresponsive answers to the reporters. He minimized the Bureau's role in producing *The F.B.I.* television series, suggesting the agency's participation involved merely providing story ideas. In fact, Crime Research officials under Bishop edited every script and even wrote dialogue. The Bureau also had two agents on the production set every day. Zimbalist and other recurring cast members were provided with tours of Bureau facilities and had meetings with Hoover and other FBI staff. The agency even vetted every cast and crew member, blackballing anyone with "subversive" connections. In reality, thousands of man-hours were expended by the Bureau to assist with the production of *The F.B.I.*[38] Bishop's response to the reporters' question about DeLoach possibly receiving payments for the television show was hardly an unequivocal no. "To the FBI's knowledge," he wrote, "Mr. DeLoach received no payments of any kind from the producer of the television series."

In response to a question about a statement Hoover made to *Time* magazine claiming the Bureau had numerous employees older than he was himself, Bishop was forced to reveal his boss's lie. "Only one employee is in his 80's," he wrote, referring to but not naming Albert D. Mehegan of the Chicago office. "He is an agent assigned to our field operations. There are no FBI [headquarters] officials in their 80's."[39] Hoover, of course, had been exempted from mandatory retirement in 1964 by President Johnson's executive order. The 1970 statement Hoover made to *Time* was intended to normalize what was in reality an extraordinary dispensation for an appointed federal official. The director was pleased with Bishop's "factual and straightforward" responses and shared them with Attorney General John Mitchell.[40] On a subsequent memorandum reporting on Nelson's appearance on a Los Angeles radio show, Hoover summarized his feelings about Nelson and Ostrow: "We don't wrestle with skunks."[41] Yet he was sufficiently concerned about the *Los Angeles Times* and the forthcoming *Life* profiles to write letters to Mitchell and to President Richard Nixon's assistant H. R. Haldeman, attempting to inoculate himself by explaining the circumstances of the stories. Hoover told Haldeman that Nelson's boss, managing editor of the *Los Angeles Times* Ed Guthman, was a former public information officer in the Department of Justice under Robert Kennedy. The *Life* article, Hoover stated to Haldeman, would be reported and written by Lambert, a friend of RFK. "While I have no reluctance to stand on my record and to let the facts of both my personal and official life speak for themselves," he wrote, "I nonetheless wanted you to have this background information regarding articles which should soon appear in these two publications."[42]

Bishop's evasive and incomplete answers to their first set of questions did not satisfy Ostrow and Nelson. On January 12, 1971, they wrote to him with a series of follow-up questions: Is there a written contract for *The F.B.I.* television series? Does any FBI official receive payment from the show's producers? How long does the Bureau keep Hoover's armored limousines? Who pays for Hoover's and Tolson's vacation hotel stays? Did Fern Stukenbroeker write *Masters of Deceit*? Who helped Tolson develop two "inventions" for which he received patents? Again, the questions were so specific that they could only have come from a current or former FBI official. To cite other examples, Ostrow and Nelson asked: "Does the FBI lab ever do any work for Mr. Hoover? Did the FBI lab construct a big mahogany 'Pirate's Chest' with brass hinges and latches and put a case of Jack Daniels Black Label in the chest and give it to him as a Christmas present some years ago?"[43] Bishop, on orders from Hoover, refused to answer the questions. "The FBI is much too busy an organization to engage in the apparently endless exchange of question-and-answer correspondence which you obviously have in mind," Bishop wrote to the reporters. "Furthermore, your demands upon us have strong overtones of harassment, and some of the questions you have posed are so tainted with false and malicious implications that they frankly do not deserve the dignity of an acknowledgment."[44]

When Ostrow and Nelson finally published a story based on Bishop's answers to the first round of questions on March 30, 1971, the story appeared on page 15 of the newspaper and debunked a longtime claim made by the Bureau that the majority of its agents had law or accounting degrees. "Actually fewer than one third of agents have such degrees," they wrote.[45] The story included an accounting of Hoover's annual limousine purchase, Bishop's incomplete response regarding the Bureau's assistance with its television series, and Hoover's lie about the number of agents aged eighty or older in the Bureau. Hoover's response to the article was muted. "It took them a long time to get around to it," he wrote.[46] When Nelson continued asking questions, turning to Congressman Alphonzo Bell of the powerful House Ways and Means Committee for more information about the director's limousine purchases, Hoover provided Bell with a blind memorandum, summarizing the "derogatory" information agents had compiled about Nelson, including a claim, based on a single report from a newspaper publisher, that the reporter had a drinking problem.[47] Bishop and Hoover no doubt believed that their chosen approach, providing no comment to *Los Angeles Times* reporters while simultaneously attempting to smear them with high-level sources, had minimized the embarrassment and public relations crisis to a single story that was buried deep in one day's newspaper. In a June 1971 memorandum, Bishop argued that the "policy of giving absolutely nothing" to the newspaper "is beginning to get to the 'Los Angeles Times.'"[48] He reported that he had a shouting match with a *Times* editor and told him, "When you get rid of that son-of-a-bitch with a vendetta against the FBI, we'll cooperate with you."[49] The FBI's no-comment policy was expanded by the Bureau's Executive Conference in 1971 to include the *New York Times*, CBS, and NBC. "The only answer to such inquiries is 'no comment,'" Tolson remarked.[50] *Washington Post* reporter Ken Clawson asked Bishop to confirm the policy in October 1971. Bishop lied and said no such memorandum existed.[51] "Obviously, someone has leaked to Clawson the general content of Mr. Tolson's Executive Conference memorandum of 8/16/71," Bishop wrote in a memo to Assistant Director Mark Felt. "Obviously," Hoover noted on the memorandum, "some 'rat' is leaking information to Clawson."[52] Former third-ranking FBI executive William Sullivan, who by then had been ousted by Hoover for disloyalty, was the most likely culprit. The Bureau had always maintained a "do not contact" list of reporters, editors, and publications, going back to Nichols's tenure. The names on that list shifted, and reporters or publications were added and subtracted frequently, depending on the day-to-day flow of news. Moreover, Nichols frequently maintained back-channel contact with reporters on the "do not contact" list, understanding as he did the long-term value of maintaining those contacts. Hoover and Bishop's blanket, unqualified no-comment policy was a major shift both from the approach of Nichols, who played the role of a "reporter" within the FBI in his efforts to network with journalists, and from the approach of DeLoach, who mixed charm and strong-arm tactics. As Hoover aged and as his public relations staff changed, the Bureau became increasingly insular and rigid in its dealings with the news media.

As a public relations strategist, Bishop received praise from Hoover most frequently for saying nothing. When Bishop reported that he had refused comment on a Nelson inquiry about a former FBI informant, the director wrote a note on the memorandum, "Excellently handled by Bishop."[53] When Bishop reported that he again offered no comment to another *Times* reporter's inquiry on September 11, 1970, Hoover wrote: "Right. Particularly as to any inquiry by L.A. Times."[54] And in December 1970, when Nelson and Ostrow were told Hoover would not meet with them and that Bishop would not speak to them, Hoover wrote that the inquiries were "properly handled."[55] A more capable public relations contact man like Nichols or DeLoach may have been able to finesse the Bureau's relationship even with a determined and uncompromising reporter like Nelson or Ostrow, but Bishop became combative and hostile. His anger and frustration reflected Hoover's own mentality, which was no doubt affected by his declining health. Bishop's contacts with Nelson and with reporters from Hoover's other nemeses, the *New York Times* and *Washington Post*, were always vituperative and often petty. His use, for instance, of the rumors about Nelson's drinking showed his basic lack of understanding of the news media. If one was fighting the perception of an out-of-control FBI, gathering dossiers of questionable information on a wide variety of Americans, why would a public relations person share some of that information widely with reporters, as Bishop did? At one point, he refused even to provide the official titles of five top FBI officials who wrote letters to the editor defending Hoover against criticism from McGovern and distributed them to several newspapers. When Nelson was told that he could not have the information, he said Bishop was not properly performing his duties as a public information officer. In response, "Bishop advised Nelson that he [was] not a 'Public Information Officer.'"[56] Hoover approved. "Right," he wrote on the memorandum detailing the exchange. "This jackal Nelson is to be given nothing."[57] Bishop and Crime Research Section chief Milton Jones believed that the strategy was "paying off," apparently overlooking the critical articles by Nelson that were appearing almost weekly.[58] After one of those broadsides, a story that identified an FBI informant in the peace movement, Hoover was apoplectic, writing that "Nelson, the lice covered ferret finally got his story!"[59]

It was not until late 1971 that Nelson learned why Hoover feared him and the *Times* so irrationally. On October 13, Hoover met with a *Times* executive to complain about Nelson's vendetta against him and the FBI. Agitated, the director told the executive that a "drunken" reporter with a "Jekyll and Hyde" personality was spreading a rumor about the director's alleged homosexuality, a charge Nelson always denied. After meeting with Hoover, *Times* executive David Kraslow reported in a memo that the director was clearly agitated. "He was intense," Kraslow wrote. "It was quite evident that he was upset, particularly on the question of the homosexual charge."[60] Prior to the meeting, Jones had provided Hoover with an eight-page, single-spaced memorandum on Nelson that the director read, word for word, to Kraslow.[61] After the meeting, Kraslow wrote a lengthy memo of his own recounting his recollections of Hoover's tirade, and then Nelson wrote a memorandum refuting all of the charges Hoover had read from Jones's memo. Nelson asked Hoover to include the document in his FBI file and to forward it to the attorney general for his files.[62] In the remarkable memorandum for inclusion in his secret FBI file, Nelson offered a detailed rebuttal of Hoover's complaints. He named the reporters who had been told about his alleged alcoholism by Bishop, and he also recounted the incident when Bishop lost his temper with a *Times* reporter and referred to Nelson as a "son of a bitch."[63]

Even as Nelson and Ostrow's increasingly combative approach to their dealings with the FBI persisted, the problem presented by *Life*'s "Emperor of the FBI" cover story could not be "solved" through any no-comment policy or personal smears. Unlike the regional *Los Angeles Times*, *Life* was a nationally circulated magazine that reached every drugstore and newsstand in the country. The *Life* story prompted further public relations crises for Hoover and the FBI in early 1971 as critics became more emboldened by the published criticism combined with the Bureau's relative silence. A few days after *Life*'s "emperor" issue appeared on newsstands, Senator Edmund Muskie of Maine disclosed documents showing that the Bureau had monitored Earth Day celebrations in 1970. "If there was widespread surveillance over Earth Day last year, is there any political activity in the country which the F.B.I. does not consider a legitimate subject for watching?" Muskie asked.[64] The

charge that the FBI believed a threat existed in a peaceful Earth Day com-
memoration fed perceptions that the Bureau was out of control. Such a
charge, directly addressing the Bureau's most pressing PR problem, required
a response. Interestingly, it was Assistant to the Director Sullivan, the FBI's
communism expert—instead of Bishop—who formulated the Bureau's public relations response to the criticism. Shortly after learning of Muskie's
charge, Sullivan called Hoover to read him the Bureau's public response. His
statement claimed the Bureau had information suggesting there was a potential for violence at the event: "The FBI's sole purpose in collecting and reporting information regarding this matter was to determine the extent of
efforts by extremist elements to exploit or disrupt these activities for their
own purposes."[65] But Sullivan's response was not released. Hoover chose,
over the objections of his staff and Attorney General Mitchell, to issue no
comment about the surveillance.[66] He may have opted to follow the no-
comment policy on the Earth Day controversy because the Bureau had
monitored four other such rallies that same day.[67]

One week after the Muskie Earth Day controversy, House Majority Leader
Hale Boggs of Louisiana accused the FBI of tapping the telephone lines of
members of Congress.[68] The accusation, coming as it did from the Democratic leader in the House of Representatives, attracted the full attention of
the news media. No doubt, Boggs's accusation also came as a surprise to
Hoover and his public relations staff, since the congressman had for decades
been considered friendly to the FBI. In 1950, for example, Boggs wrote to
thank Hoover and Inspector Mohr for an unspecified personal favor the FBI
had performed for him. Boggs did not mention the nature of the favor in his
letters, but in a memorandum prepared in regard this incident, Mohr stated,
"I feel sure that he [Boggs] is so non-committal in his letters so that his staff
will not be aware of the true situation affecting [redacted]."[69] On several occasions, Boggs had extended his remarks to add FBI materials such as
Hoover's speeches and published articles to the *Congressional Record*.[70] In
1962, when newspapers in New Orleans attacked a statement Boggs made
regarding vigilantism and communism, he asked Hoover to vouch publicly
for his anticommunist credentials. "In light of my long support of you and
the Bureau, I would appreciate a letter from you stating that I am now
and have been over the years one of the constant supporters of the Bureau
and that it goes without saying that I am fully aware of the Communist
threat from within and without," Boggs wrote to Hoover as he was facing a
serious primary challenger from the political Right.[71] DeLoach advised the

director to respond, and Boggs was sent a generally supportive letter: "I am certain you share my belief that if we are to effectively resist the eroding influence of subversion all of us must continually exhibit in positive ways the value and superiority of our form of government over any foreign ideology."[72] Ever the political opportunist, Boggs included a truncated quote from Hoover's letter—"My associates and I are particularly grateful to you"—in a political advertisement, thereby portraying Hoover as having endorsed his candidacy.[73] In his advertisement, Boggs left off the rest of Hoover's sentence, which read, "and your colleagues who have actively supported the work of the FBI in the field of internal security over the years."[74] After receiving a flurry of letters criticizing Hoover for "endorsing" a political candidate—and after a corresponding flurry of internal memoranda arguing about how to respond—the Bureau decided to stay silent and let Boggs's misrepresentation stand. However, in 1968 when Boggs, in a tough reelection campaign, again asked for Hoover's endorsement, the request was refused.[75] Undeterred, the congressman simply recycled the 1962 "My associates and I" quote from Hoover.[76] And when Boggs was elected majority leader in January 1971, just weeks before he would level his wiretapping charges against the Bureau, Hoover wrote to congratulate him.[77]

Given their cordial relationship going back more than twenty years, it must have been a surprise when Boggs criticized Hoover and the Bureau in a House floor speech on April 5, 1971. Alleging that the Bureau tapped congressional telephones and was spying on college students and faculty, he called for Hoover's resignation, saying the Bureau was using the "tactics of the Soviet Union and Hitler's Gestapo."[78] Boggs's charges came two weeks after New Mexico Democratic senator Joseph M. Montoya made similar charges. After news of Boggs's allegations was released in wire stories, Hoover called Attorney General Mitchell, who was vacationing in Key Biscane, Florida. Mitchell said he was as surprised as Hoover was about Boggs's outburst. The director replied by observing that, though he did not know Boggs well, "I never thought he was a jackal like Senator McGovern."[79] Hoover urged Mitchell to issue a statement of support.[80] He did so, and the statement was included in news stories the next day. Then, Hoover began marshaling his defense. Republican congressman William Dickinson of Alabama was asked by the SAC in Mobile to denounce Boggs on the House floor.[81] Hoover contacted other key congressional leaders, among them Democratic Speaker of the House Carl Albert of Oklahoma and Michigan Republican congressman Gerald R. Ford.[82] Hoover also made an unsuccessful attempt, working through the Washington FBI field office, to speak to Boggs directly.[83]

The private backstory to Boggs's charges was that he had been the subject of a bribery investigation in Baltimore in 1969 and 1970. He and other well-connected political figures, including Senator Russell B. Long of Louisiana and then-Speaker of the House John W. McCormack of Massachusetts, were suspected of doing favors for contractor Victor Frenkil and his Baltimore Contractors, Inc. In return for supporting the company's demand to be paid an extra $5 million over its bid to build a parking garage for the Rayburn House Office Building, Boggs allegedly received a half-price home renovation. The parking garage construction, begun in 1964, was not completed until fall 1967, about seventeen months late. Boggs and others were alleged to have pressured the office of the Architect of the Capitol to settle the Baltimore Contractors' claim for an extra $5 million in Frenkil's favor.[84] Though no criminal charges were ultimately filed, Maryland US attorney Stephen Sachs did produce a draft indictment that was rejected by the Nixon Justice Department.[85] In 1974, the federal government agreed to pay Frenkil $3.8 million for the cost overrun claim.[86] In the course of the US attorney's investigation of yet another scandal involving a building contract, the existence of tape recordings of a conversation between one of the defendants and a contractor became known to Boggs. Hoover speculated in a memorandum to Attorney General Mitchell that Boggs's knowledge of the tape-recorded conversations may have driven him to attack the FBI.[87]

To the public, however, the Boggs story was simply an indictment of the FBI as an out-of-control, politicized agency. As early as 1940, when the Bureau was charged with illegal wiretapping, Hoover had issued a vigorous response to any such charges. The Bureau's public relations program had, since the mid-1930s, sought to counter the image of the FBI as a reckless and politically motivated federal police force. Charges of wiretapping—particularly charges of wiretapping Congress—were a direct challenge to the Bureau's preferred public image. When Deputy Attorney General Richard Kleindienst, in an effort to counter Boggs's charges, told reporters that the Department of Justice would welcome an investigation into FBI surveillance practices, it was not viewed as helpful to the FBI. Kleindienst told the *Washington Post* that Boggs must have been "sick or . . . not in possession of his faculties" when he made the charges; he offered to provide a broad review of FBI surveillance and then narrowed that offer to a congressional review of Boggs's specific charges.[88] A Democratic congressman told a Crime Research agent that Kleindienst's comments were a mistake because they put the FBI "squarely in the middle of a purely political controversy." Hoover highlighted that statement in a memorandum with three hash marks, writing, "I certainly agree."[89] His direct involvement in liaison work to counter the Boggs charges demonstrated the importance he placed on batting down stories that focused attention on the Bureau's enormous power. His liaison also demonstrated that Bishop, ostensibly Hoover's new DeLoach or Nichols, did not have the kinds of established relationships with opinion leaders that his predecessors had developed. The FBI file covering the Boggs incident contains more than two dozen multipage memoranda from Hoover to Tolson and/or Bishop, detailing his efforts to counter the charges. The director personally called many members of Congress on April 6 and 7, telling them the FBI did not wiretap Congress and urging them to come out in defense of the Bureau.[90] Some responded. Republican congressman H. R. Gross of Iowa, for example, told Hoover that Boggs had been drunk before the floor speech and that he "almost got into a fist fight with [Missouri Republican congressman Durwood G.] Hall" after the speech.[91] During prior PR crises, Hoover had rarely involved himself in the daily management of the Bureau's relationships, instead ordering Nichols or DeLoach to handle the situation. It is remarkable that, so late in his career and at a time when he and Tolson were both in poor health, Hoover felt he could not rely on his Crime Records/Research team to manage an effective response after the FBI encountered its most severe criticism in years.

In his April 10, 1971, column, Jack Anderson charged that Hoover had "strained the truth" in claiming that no member of Congress had been under FBI surveillance.[92] The director requested a memorandum examining Anderson's charges. The resulting memo, from Crime Records agent R. D. Cotter, was a masterpiece of semantics, claiming that Anderson used his own semantic tricks. But Cotter admitted that "there are numerous instances where Congressmen have had conversations monitored when they happen to make telephone calls to individuals or establishments covered by electronic surveillances which had the approval of the Attorney General."[93] For instance, in 1945, an FBI agent reported to Hoover that a wiretap captured a conversation between former FDR adviser Thomas Corcoran and Idaho Democratic senator David Worth Clark involving a real estate deal they were considering.[94] The Bureau also listened in on several of Corcoran's conversations with South Carolina Democratic senator Burnet R. Maybank.[95] Just those two instances, in just one FBI file, suggest that catching the conversations of members of Congress on wiretaps and bugs was not an infrequent occurrence. In other words, Anderson's charge—that Hoover's unequivocal denial was itself a deception—was correct. To Hoover, the only "subject" of a wiretap was the individual upon whose phone the tap was issued, not anyone who happened to place or receive a call from the subject. Thus, Hoover was able to claim, as he did on April 7 in a phone call to House Speaker Carl Albert, that there "had never been any wiretapping performed on members of Congress."[96] For Anderson, surveillance was surveillance, no matter where bugs and wiretaps were placed.

Meanwhile, Boggs expanded on his charges, telling a CBS reporter not only that his phones had been bugged but also that the FBI had him under constant surveillance, again comparing the Bureau to the gestapo.[97] While the Bureau waited for Boggs to make good on his claims that he had evidence to support his charges against the FBI, the agency's efforts to undermine the story began to take a more personal turn. On April 12, Jack Anderson reported that FBI agents were peddling private information on Boggs. "A derogatory report on House Democratic leader Hale Boggs, including the allegation that he drinks heavily, has been traced to FBI sources," Anderson wrote, describing a document written on "plain paper without any FBI identifying marks."[98] The Bureau routinely provided information to its friends in the form of so-called blind memoranda, which bore no FBI identifiers. Hoover cautioned his agents to be careful about circulating the Boggs information. "This shows what comes from our dissemination of our memos & reports," he wrote on the Anderson article.[99] Anderson's column fed critics' claims that the FBI was an out-of-control political surveillance agency.

That caution about supplying derogatory information did not apply to Hoover's own conversations with friends in Congress. On April 21, he told Republican congressman Samuel DeVine of Ohio that Boggs was "an old drunk" who had begun unraveling under the pressure and that the charges against him in the Frenkil bribery case were true.[100] When Boggs finally addressed the House on April 22 to release his evidence, he mentioned eight senators and congressmen who, he said, had been the subjects of surveillance. He brought up the Dowdy case as well, and he even noted the Shaw controversy. In his analysis of Boggs's remarks for Hoover, Assistant Director Alex Rosen admitted that the charges were largely true, but he added that "any interceptions of members of Congress were through inadvertence [*sic*] on devices installed for National Security coverage."[101] Hoover confirmed that members of Congress had been subjects of electronic surveillance in a memorandum to Deputy Attorney General Kleindienst. Kleindienst had contacted the director to ask about electronic surveillance of Congress after he received a query from a *New York Times* reporter. Hoover explained the FBI's policy of denying any electronic surveillance of Congress to the press. "I told [Kleindienst] my feeling is that the less we expand on press inquiries, the better off we are," he wrote, recounting the conversation for Bishop and Tolson. "I said in other words I think the fact that we have stated that no phones at the Capitol compound have been tapped or any surveillance conducted of Congressmen is sufficient, because when you begin to answer these, particularly from a paper like the New York Times which is hostile you get other questions until you get into an expansion and I think the narrower you can keep the situation the better."[102]

Hoover's policy of narrow answers may have forestalled additional questions, but it did nothing to calm the media storm surrounding Boggs's charges. In the weeks following his April 22 speech, those charges became the subject of editorial commentary in newspapers around the country. The Shaw, Muskie, McGovern, and Boggs allegations added up to, as Tom Wicker put it in the *New York Times*, "the worst period of controversy Mr. Hoover has encountered in his 47-year career."[103] Veteran reporter William V. Shannon wrote that Hoover had begun "to look like the man who stayed too long. . . . Once virtually immune from public and Congressional criticism, the work of the F.B.I. has become a partisan issue and Mr. Hoover has become a symbol of an embattled Administration."[104]

With those public relations crises as context, Jones's Crime Research staff was forced in June to contend with a new complication in the form of a unique coast-to-coast collaboration involving a Los Angeles television star, a Chicago human rights attorney, and two Washington public relations and fund-raising entrepreneurs. Their collaboration in the creation of an advocacy organization—intended both to enrich some of the participants and to defend Hoover and the FBI against what they viewed as a smear campaign—quickly turned into a public relations fiasco that further damaged the director and the Bureau during a time when critics had become increasingly outspoken in their attacks.

On May 7, 1971, the president of the Society of Former Special Agents, Charles Noone—himself the leader of an organization Hoover distrusted—telephoned Jones at Bureau headquarters to inform him that a new FBI advocacy group had formed. According to Noone, a representative of Patrick J. Gorman Consultants, a Washington fund-raising organization, had contacted the society to request a mailing list of former special agents to use in soliciting donations for the group, which Noone incorrectly described as "Friends of Hoover."[105] In addition to Gorman, Noone reported, Washington, D.C., public relations man Lee Edwards and Chicago attorney Luis Kutner were involved in the effort to create a group of "friends" to advocate on behalf of the FBI.[106]

Kutner was well known by the Bureau's Chicago office and was generally viewed as a reliable supporter of the agency. A criminal defense attorney, he had been a so-called symbol number informant for the FBI, a documented intelligence source providing information on Chicago criminals and legal authorities from 1954 to 1955, when his services were terminated because he gave erroneous information. He was reinstated in 1958 to obtain information for the Bureau's Top Hoodlum program, but his informant services were again discontinued in 1961 because he provided "opinion and belief" rather than factual information.[107] Kutner's registered nonprofit organization, the Commission for the International Due Process of Law (CIDPL), was the umbrella under which the advocacy group Friends of the F.B.I. was ultimately formed. According to Bureau sources, Edwards, owner of Lee Edwards Associates, had been a member of Young Americans for Freedom, a national conservative youth organization during the early 1960s.[108] Gorman's firm was unknown to the FBI at the time. In his memorandum, Jones reported that Chicago SAC Charles Bates, instructed to provide no assistance to the organization, had interviewed Kutner, who said any money raised by a national appeal would be used to pay for direct-mail advocacy to counter criticism of the FBI. "Bates further noted that though Kutner is pro-FBI and sincere," Jones added, "he is overly ambitious and tends, at times, to go off half cocked."[109]

Bates's assessment of Kutner's tendencies may or may not have been accurate, but the presumption that the attorney was leading the Friends of the F.B.I. movement would prove false. The scheme was initially conceived by Edwards and Gorman in an April 1971 meeting with Kutner in Washington, D.C., that took place after the release of the *Life* "Emperor of the FBI" story. According to Kutner, Edwards and Gorman approached him during breakfast at the Washington Hilton Hotel. He later told the FBI that the idea to form an advocacy group for the Bureau appealed to him because he had noted the increasing criticism of Hoover and the FBI over time. He had also noticed the FBI's public relations team had failed to effectively counter the criticism. In a letterhead memorandum reporting on an interview with Kutner, an unnamed Chicago agent noted:

> [Kutner] was distressed, he said, that there was no spokesman for the FBI to publicly counter these attacks and he was confident that his viewpoint regarding this issue was well known to both Edwards and Gorman before this meeting and they approached him to undertake the plan as a project of the Commission for International Due Process of Law.[110]

Edwards similarly characterized the group's goals in a memorandum of understanding for his new partners. "It is obvious that a concerted unsavory campaign is underway to force the resignation of FBI Director J. Edgar Hoover and discredit the FBI," he wrote to Kutner and Gorman after their meeting. "As Luis [Kutner] pointed out to me, almost every individual or organization involved is either radical or leftist or communist."[111] Edwards outlined the creation of an organization under the auspices of Kutner's nonprofit. Funds raised through a direct-mail campaign would pay for a "scholarly, in-depth study" of the FBI. Kutner would lead a panel of "distinguished jurists, scholars and journalists" who would conduct the study, and Gorman's organization would coordinate the fund-raising campaign.[112]

About two months later, though, the FBI received word that one of its most important public allies, a man who had in some ways become the public face of the Bureau as Hoover grew older, Efrem Zimbalist, Jr., had become involved in the Friends of the F.B.I. as a celebrity endorser and honorary chairman. Zimbalist starred as Inspector Lew Erskine on the high-rated prime-time television series *The F.B.I.*, which aired every Sunday night on ABC television from 1965 to 1974.[113] Because of the show's highly successful, 241-episode run, Zimbalist became something of a quasi-FBI public relations official himself, standing in as a spokesman and defender of Hoover and the Bureau on talk shows and in other media appearances—a role he would continue to play until his death in 2014.[114] Zimbalist would report that Edwards had approached him during a thirty-minute break in production of *The F.B.I.* in May 1971, telling him that the FBI needed a public advocacy group to counter adverse publicity. Edwards had emphasized scholarly study of the Bureau in his pitch to Kutner, who fancied himself something of a scholar, but he sold Zimbalist with visions of news releases and video- and audiotapes promoting the Bureau.[115] Zimbalist quickly

Actor Efrem Zimbalist, Jr., with J. Edgar Hoover, May 13, 1966. (National Archives at College Park, Md., Record Group 65, Series H, Box 40, Folder 2049, #2.)

pledged his "all-out" support to make tapes in support of Hoover and the FBI and to serve as "honorary national chairman" once the advocacy group was operational.[116] Finally, he signed a statement outlining the goals of Friends of the F.B.I., although when interviewed by the Bureau later, he could not recall what those goals were.[117]

In early June 1971, the FBI began to receive reports that copies of a fund-raising letter addressed to "Dear Concerned American" and bearing Zimbalist's signature had begun appearing in mailboxes nationwide. The letter opened with the following words: "As the enclosed news reports reveal, the F.B.I. and J. Edgar Hoover are now being subjected to the degradation of a vicious partisan attack by self-serving politicians, their supporting media and certain radical elements that ultimately seek the destruction of all law and order in the United States." The letter then asserted, "This vicious smear campaign has grown to such shocking proportions that *Life* magazine cruelly parodied Mr. Hoover as 'The Emperor of the F.B.I.' on the cover of its

April 9, 1971, issue."[118] The enclosed flyer cited critical statements about the FBI from the *Washington Post* and House Majority Leader Hale Boggs as further evidence of a coordinated smear campaign from the Left. The letter went on to introduce the organization Friends of the F.B.I. and promised that any funds raised would be used to "counter the powerfully-backed campaign against the F.B.I. and J. Edgar Hoover."[119]

The involvement of Zimbalist, always a dutiful adherent to the FBI public relations program, caught the Bureau by surprise. "While there is no doubt whatsoever that the motives of Efrem Zimbalist and 'Friends of the F.B.I.' are of the highest order, nonetheless there exists a serious potential for embarrassment to the Bureau and the Director particularly in view of the solicitation of funds contained in the form letter over Zimbalist's signature," Jones wrote in a June 14 memo to Bishop. "Critical segments of the press are obviously going to try to infer that there is some connection between the Bureau and this organization and they will make every effort to impugn this group and its objectives."[120]

Embarrassment for the FBI was not long in coming. On June 15, the day after Jones's memo about Zimbalist's involvement in the group, Nelson published a critical article that, among other things, reported two of Kutner's board members had never heard of Friends of the F.B.I. Edwards told the reporters that board members of the Commission for International Due Process of Law supported the Friends of the F.B.I. project, but both ACLU founder Roger Baldwin and attorney Max M. Kampelman, who were listed as members of the board of the CIDPL, denied giving any support to the effort. "I have never heard of Friends of the FBI and I repudiate it," Baldwin declared. Kampelman not only denied any knowledge of Friends of the F.B.I. but also said he was not a member of the CIDPL board and had never heard of Kutner. Baldwin raised the question of whether the CIDPL's tax-exempt status could be lent to Friends of the F.B.I.: "I question whether it can now be used for another purpose and still be tax deductible."[121]

Complete control over the Bureau's PR messaging had been, before 1970, a pillar of the FBI's success ever since the mid-1930s. Just as Hoover refused to cede control over the Bureau's public image to other advocacy groups, such as the Society of Former Special Agents of the FBI, he would not allow the Friends of the F.B.I. to speak on his behalf. It was impossible, he well knew, to extend the mantra of "Don't embarrass the Bureau" to private entities. Whether or not any link between the two organizations existed, there would be a presumption in many circles that the advocacy group was doing

Hoover's bidding, and any embarrassing public relations mistakes the Friends of the F.B.I. made would tar the director and the FBI.

The Bureau immediately set out, via an inquiry led by Jones's Crime Research Section, to determine Zimbalist's actual involvement with the Friends of the F.B.I. Because Special Agent Richard G. Douce, as part of his liaison work for the Crime Records Division, was permanently assigned as a consultant to the production of *The F.B.I.*, Zimbalist was interviewed the very next day on location with the show's production group in June Lake, California. Douce reported that the actor said he had not granted the organization permission to use his name or signature to raise money. "Zimbalist indicated to Douce, however, that since this has already been done, he would not disavow the letter," Jones reported to Bishop. "When he accepted the position as honorary chairman of this organization he did so as a private citizen who feels very strongly about Mr. Hoover and the Bureau and as one who feels just as strongly that citizens so inclined must take a strong stand in support of the Bureau and against the malicious, vicious, and unwarranted attacks being made on the Director and the FBI."[122]

The fund-raising appeal was an enormous success, bringing in more than $400,000, but internal dissension among the three principals flared up within a few weeks of the first mailing.[123] On July 21, Edwards told the *New York Times*, without mentioning any totals, that the appeal had elicited an "excellent response." The *Times* story quoted Zimbalist from the fund-raising letter without clarifying the actor's actual role in the group or the authorship of the letter. In an indication of the internal fault lines within the organization, Kutner refused to comment for the story. Edwards asserted that gifts were tax-deductible because of the group's affiliation with Kutner's nonprofit organization, and he claimed the organization was "dedicated to research" to prove the FBI's value. "The one thing we'd like to emphasize is that our organization is called Friends of the F.B.I. as distinct from attempts being made by some to label us exclusively a pro-Hoover organization," Edwards pointed out. "What we're interested in getting at is the truth. We think the truth will best serve the F.B.I." Bishop acknowledged the FBI's connection to Zimbalist but emphasized that the agency had no involvement in Friends of the F.B.I.[124]

What Edwards failed to mention to the *Times* was that the three partners had never reached an official agreement on terms for their collaboration and actually had already begun the process of dissolving their partnership. According to Kutner, Edwards and Gorman originally agreed to give him an opportunity to edit the mailed solicitation and to provide a complete accounting of the funds raised. Neither of those conditions was met.[125] Early in the process, Kutner attempted to engage the J. Walter Thompson advertising agency as a consultant for the project, but Edwards and Gorman drove the Thompson officials away before any strategy could be produced.[126] Kutner further complained that Gorman "submitted a raft of bills" for his work; Gorman later admitted to the FBI that he received reimbursements in excess of $100,000 in addition to his $1,500 monthly fee for services.[127] Under the original agreement, signed on July 22, Kutner was to receive $7,500 monthly for the CIDPL involvement, and the fees paid to Edwards and Gormans would jump to $3,000 per month after the fourth month. A legal agreement to form the partnership was not signed and executed until July 22, and the termination agreement, effective September 1, was signed that same day.[128]

Four days later, Kutner wrote to Attorney General John Mitchell to explain the dissolution and the status of Friends of the F.B.I. going forward. He stated that the fund-raising letter was sent without his approval and that no audit of the donations had been done. The letter was clearly intended as both a protection against prosecution and as a threat to Edwards and Gorman. Regarding the legal requirement of an audit of donations, Kutner was clear: "As of this date PGC (Patrick Gorman Associates) and LEA (Lee Edwards and Associates) have failed completely in this obligation despite numerous promises and assurances of compliance."[129] FBI officials no doubt saw the potential for additional embarrassment in the increasingly acrimonious breakup of the original Friends of the F.B.I. partnership.

It was pressure from the political Left, a key constituency of the CIDPL—specifically, the involvement of a US congressman and sometimes FBI opponent, Democratic congressman Abner Mikva of Illinois—that forced Kutner's withdrawal from Friends of the F.B.I. and ultimately resulted in the public airing of the partners' feud. Mikva, a member of the CIDPL board, wrote to Kutner on June 23 expressing his concerns about providing support for the FBI and suggesting that Friends of the F.B.I. was merely a money-making scheme. "You can imagine my dismay when I read most recently that you had 'lent' the organization to Ephraim [*sic*] Zimbalist, Jr., for a promotion called Friends of the FBI," Mikva wrote. "I noted with further dismay that Mr. Zimbalist proceeded to attack everyone who has ever criticized the FBI or its director, as people desiring to undermine the whole structure of law and order in the United States."[130]

Mikva mentioned several of the ongoing themes taken up by FBI and

Hoover critics, including questions about the Bureau's illegal wiretapping activities, and he asserted that, having "prostituted" the CIDPL, Kutner might be endangering the group's tax exemption. "It grieves me to see such a worthy organization as you have established being used to enhance the money-making propensities of Mr. Zimbalist," Mikva said. "Were the cause he is using anything other than the FBI, I think the Internal Revenue Service might be looking askance at the idea that any of these activities are really entitled to the tax exempt status that Mr. Zimbalist claims."[131] Mikva's reference to the IRS and the fact that he copied other CIDPL board members—including Hubert Humphrey adviser Max Kampelman and ACLU founder Roger Baldwin—were clearly intended as threats. Mikva wanted the CIDPL to sever its ties to the pro-FBI group.

Kutner replied with a defense of both the concept and the motivations behind the group. "We, in this 'Project' of the COMMISSION are an independent, non-committed, and, obviously, not in predetermined preference to the FBI and Mr. Hoover," Kutner wrote. "Further, we are not anguished, duplicitous, traumatized partisans of the FBI."[132] One month later, Kutner wrote to Congressman Mikva to report on the CIDPL's withdrawal from the group.

Despite the CIDPL withdrawing its support for Friends of the F.B.I., Mikva went to the press. In early August, the *Chicago Sun-Times* and *Los Angeles Times* separately reported that Friends of the F.B.I. no longer enjoyed the CIDPL's sponsorship and tax-exempt status. *Los Angeles Times* reporter Bryce Nelson quoted from Mikva's June 23 letter asserting that the organization was merely a money-making scheme, and he noted that Kutner was unavailable for comment.[133] Kutner wrote Mikva a stinging letter complaining that the congressman had violated a right of "privacy of communication" by releasing the letter. "Your original letter to me was a petulant diatribe, full of tortured misreporting and mis-interpretation of our intended sober, penetrating, unbiased, constructive and unrestrictive study in-depth of the FBI and the stewardship of its distinguished director," Kutner wrote. "I answered your flavored letter with dignity and information you chose to ignore. I did not resort to polemics or pedantry."[134]

With the Friends of the F.B.I. feud made public, the Bureau set out to repair any damage that had occurred. On August 12, Hoover wrote a memorandum to Assistant Attorney General Will Wilson of the Criminal Division disavowing any Bureau connection to Friends of the F.B.I. and requesting authorization to investigate the group for a violation of 18 U.S.C 709, a public law that prohibited the use of "FBI" or the organization's symbols for commercial purposes.[135] On August 30, Wilson replied, saying a possible violation had occurred and authorizing the Bureau to interview the principals involved to ascertain how the group was formed, how much money had been raised, and what was being done with the money.[136]

Special agents interviewed Kutner, Gorman, and Zimbalist, but Edwards, acting on his attorney's recommendation, refused to be interviewed. The Bureau ultimately decided to forgo an interview with Edwards, and the matter was dropped. Hoover, however, continued to pursue the group through other channels, urging the IRS to consider whether contributions to the organization, which had lost its affiliation with the nonprofit CDIPL, were tax-deductible. On August 26, following an audit of the organization's finances, the IRS issued a news release stating that it could not assure contributors to Friends of the F.B.I. that their donations would be tax-deductible: "Since the Service cannot assure contributors of deductibility of contribution to the 'Friends of the F.B.I.' taxpayers making contributions to that organization must assume the risk that the service may deny deductions claimed for their contributions." The IRS news release included an editor's note unmasking Hoover's interest in the tax case, stating, "This Release is made with the full concurrence of the Federal Bureau of Investigation. Neither the Federal Bureau of Investigation nor its Director, Mr. J. Edgar Hoover, has any association with 'Friends of the F.B.I.'"[137] Walters had received Hoover's blessing for the news release two days earlier.[138]

One final ignominious moment in the Friends of the F.B.I. saga for Hoover and the FBI occurred a few months later, on February 15, 1972, when the group released the findings of its first national survey. The *New York Times* reported on the findings under the headline YOUTH FOUND COOL TO CAREER IN FBI: POLL SHOWS 'ONLY 21.5%' WOULD LIKE TO BE AGENTS. Almost 70 percent of the 2,500 young people surveyed, in fact, said they would not consider a career in the FBI, and only 17 percent of nonwhites surveyed said they would be interested in joining the Bureau. According to the *Times*, "The group said that this result, 'underscored the need for a major information program among young Americans from 14 through 25.'"[139]

Even as Hoover's public relations efforts faltered and gaffes uncovered cracks in his regime, another would-be successor and trusted adviser departed the scene, following DeLoach out the door. Assistant to the Director William Sullivan, whose rise in the Bureau mirrored DeLoach's and similarly involved a talent for currying Hoover's favor, was dispatched in 1971. By that time, with DeLoach gone and Tolson sidelined since the mid-1960s by serious health issues, Sullivan had become Hoover's closest adviser, the de facto number two official at the FBI. He was the Bureau's top expert on communism for nearly twenty years and developed his own contacts among the media. *Washington Post* reporter Ken Clawson called Sullivan the best FBI administrator he ever encountered. But Sullivan foundered when he attempted to alter Hoover's ossified worldview to fit the times.

Appointed as a special agent in 1941, Sullivan used a talent for research along with a flair for flattery to climb quickly up the FBI hierarchy. He served in the Bureau's Special Intelligence Service, a foreign espionage arm of the FBI, during World War II, supervising spying in Venezuela, British Guiana, Suriname, French Guiana, Aruba, Curaçao, and the Caribbean with the exception of Cuba.[140] He moved to the Atomic Energy Section and then to the Communist Research Desk of the Internal Security Division in 1947. There, he produced a series of monographs exploring different aspects of the communist threat, taking time out to write fawning letters to Hoover to curry favor with the boss. "Needless to say I am deeply grateful for this promotion," Sullivan wrote in 1948. "It is not, however, a transitory, materialistic gratitude based merely upon an increase in salary, helpful as that is in our badly inflated 'money economy.' On the contrary, my primary gratitude relates to the confidence which you appear to have in my efforts to reach and maintain the high standards wisely established by you for all Bureau employees."[141] Other Sullivan letters to Hoover were, similarly, masterpieces of flattery. "While I do not feel at all worthy of this recognition I am naturally very pleased and grateful to you," he wrote in 1949.[142] On his tenth anniversary with the Bureau in 1951, Sullivan stated, "The FBI seems to consist of a multiplicity of divergencies melded together into a fundamental unity under your strong leadership." Hoover bracketed the following sentences. "At the core of this unity is a stubborn fact," Sullivan wrote. "It is this: the FBI is our [Hoover underlined this word] family. It is a living, breathing, creative and organic entity with goals and with the means of reaching them. It is our family cemented together by durable bonds of loyalty, of good fellowship, of love of nation—all hammered out in the toil, heat and sweat of investigations, arrests, prosecutions, special assignments, deadlines and the like. It is our family, and as members of it we are conscious of a deep-rooted sense of common origin, purpose and objective."[143] On Hoover's orders, Sullivan's soliloquy was republished in the *Investigator* in September that year and sent out to every special agent in the FBI.[144] For ten years in the 1950s and 1960s,

Sullivan was the Bureau's top public speaker on the topic of communism, addressing more than 200 groups and prompting letters of praise to flood into FBI headquarters from hundreds who heard him speak. In 1957, he contributed as one of several ghostwriters on Hoover's book *Masters of Deceit.* And in 1961, he was named assistant director in charge of the Domestic Intelligence Division. There, he supervised the FBI's Counterintelligence Program, COINTELPRO, which, beginning with another 1971 PR crisis, ultimately became one of the darkest stains on Hoover's record.

The five-room, six-agent FBI Resident Agency in Media, Pennsylvania, was located on the second floor of a boxy apartment building across the street from the Delaware County Courthouse. Resident agencies were suboffices under the jurisdiction of a larger, regional FBI bureau located nearby. The Media Resident Agency was a satellite of the much larger Philadelphia FBI office. In areas with significant population centers, resident agencies allowed the Bureau to extend its presence by placing small offices, often with just a handful of special agents, in second-tier communities.

On March 8, 1971, eight ordinary people worked their normal day jobs and, when they got home, prepared to become burglars that evening. The members of the Citizens Commission to Investigate the FBI, as they called their group, had planned the break-in for months in secret. On the evening of March 8 and into the early morning of March 9, they broke into the small Media Resident Agency, emptied five unlocked file cabinets, pried open drawers in several desks, and hauled away thousands of secret FBI files in suitcases. They loaded the suitcases in their cars and drove them to a ramshackle former Quaker conference center on Fellowship Farm, 40 miles north of Philadelphia, where they sorted and photocopied documents. Then they called news organizations and sent out a press release declaring:

We have taken this action because:

- we believe that a law and order which depends on intimidation and repression to secure obedience can have but one name, and that name is tyranny;
- we believe that democracy can survive only in an order of justice, of an open society and public trust;
- we believe citizens have a right to scrutinize and control their own government and its agencies;
- and because we believe that the FBI has betrayed this democratic trust

and we wish to present evidence for this claim to the open and public judgment of our fellow citizens.[145]

The first packet of a dozen or so FBI documents was received by news reporters and sympathetic politicians, including Senator McGovern, a day or two after the burglary.[146] Given the ease with which it was carried off, the burglary raised embarrassing security concerns regarding FBI resident agencies. It was the content of the files, however, that posed the greatest threat to Hoover's carefully tended public image. The files taken from the unlocked cabinets in Media eventually unmasked the Bureau's COINTELPRO activities, primarily involving efforts to infiltrate and undermine lawful activist groups on the political Left. Widely viewed today, even by former FBI officials such as DeLoach, as an overzealous program (many others would term it illegal), COINTELPRO would confirm much of what critics had claimed about Hoover's FBI and its gestapo tactics and emphasis on political surveillance of Americans. But it was not until after Hoover's death in 1972 that the contents of the Media burglars' suitcases came to be widely understood as clear evidence of the overreach entailed in COINTELPRO. In addition to COINTELPRO information, the documents offered significant proof of the Bureau's political monitoring activities and its efforts, for example, to control dissent on college campuses and among civil rights groups. Informants were named in the documents, and techniques employed by the Bureau were highlighted, such as the ability to trace phone calls and check Selective Service and military records. A March 12 FBI memorandum prepared for Sullivan noted that "there is a potential of considerable embarrassment to the Bureau if these documents should be made available to the left-wing press or other individuals who could take them out of context and use them to attack the Bureau."[147] Hoover underlined that sentence when he read the memorandum.[148]

Much of the Bureau's initial response to the burglary involved an attempt by agents in the Special Investigations Division to catalog the documents that were stolen and determine whether their contents would become a significant PR embarrassment. For instance, on March 18, a memorandum addressed the contents of one of the documents likely among those stolen, SAC Letter 71-7 from February 16, 1971. The author of the memorandum, Special Agent A. B. Eddy, determined that even though the New Left was mentioned in the SAC letter, "no reference is made to sensitive techniques [FBI parlance for wiretapping, microphone surveillance, and other intrusive techniques] and there does not appear to be anything in the letter which could be particularly harmful if discovered."[149] A second review of a larger cache of identified documents produced on March 15 found that the "damage" to the FBI from documents covering New Left activities, civil rights, espionage, foreign intelligence, and other areas "could be considerable." Other documents revealed the continued maintenance of the Security Index, listing Americans to be incarcerated in a national emergency, and also revealed the existence of an "AI," or Agitator Index, although that was not specifically spelled out in the stolen documents.[150] The memorandum to Sullivan concluded that "revelation of these [campus surveillance] documents publicly could lead to distorted allegations of Bureau's interest in campus activities, could jeopardize our relationship with various private and Federal agencies, including Telephone Company, and could lessen public confidence in Bureau's ability to maintain confidential relationships."[151] Finally, the memo's author noted that disclosure of the documents could lead to allegations that the Bureau "engages in Gestapo-type investigations."[152] Yet another damage assessment on March 29 reviewed the documents released up to that date and described the damage as "serious," primarily based on public relations concerns.[153] On April 7, Assistant Director Charles D. Brennan of the Internal Security Division reported to Sullivan that additional documents identified as being among those stolen could pose "an additional source of possible embarrassment if the document containing information confidentially volunteered by [redacted] is publicized."[154] Many of the memoranda produced in the process of attempting to catalog and analyze the stolen material focused on potential embarrassment to the Bureau—a public relations concern—rather than on whether investigations or informants had been compromised.[155] One agent recommended that the Bureau contact news media and appeal to them to "exercise discretion," seeking their cooperation "in not disclosing information." Hoover overruled that recommendation. "This is futile," he wrote on the memorandum.[156]

Long before the full extent of the document contents became clear, the burglary nonetheless provided fuel for FBI critics such as Maryland Democratic congressman Parren Mitchell. Mitchell received a packet of Media documents from the Citizens Committee to Investigate the FBI shortly after the break-in. Within two weeks, the Media documents became part of his critique of government surveillance of citizens in a speech he delivered to a Pittsburgh law enforcement conference. "We are now in a climate of overreaction in this country," Mitchell said. "The attorney general's office boasts about the increase of wiretaps, and the military admits to its unwarranted invasion of privacy through surveillance and wiretapping." He added that he had turned the stolen Media documents he received over to the Department of Justice.[157] Another report on Mitchell's speech highlighted his concern, based on his reading of the first release of Media documents, that the Bureau was targeting African American groups for infiltration. "It appears if a group bears in its name 'freedom,' 'Afro' or 'Black,' it is suspect and therefore infiltrated," Mitchell claimed.[158] Two days after the speech, Hoover was forced to give the attorney general a "damage assessment" detailing the scope of files stolen from Media. The documents covered "racial extremist matters," "Communist and New Left extremist matters," and "espionage and foreign intelligence matters," Hoover reported. He added that he feared the documents "taken out of context could create the patently false impression that the FBI is conducting indiscriminate investigations of black groups and individuals."[159] The director did not mention that the documents also contained the first evidence that investigation had given way to the COINTELPRO infiltration of civil rights and other groups on the political Left.

As criticism mounted and news coverage turned from the burglary itself and the existence of the documents to the contents of the packets being mailed out by the Committee to Investigate the FBI, Hoover took personal control of the Bureau's response, declaring—perhaps unwisely—that all inquiries would be met with "no comment." For example, on March 31, 1971, reporter Morton Mintz of the *Washington Post* called Bishop with four specific questions related to documents republished by the *Harvard Crimson*. The questions were not about either COINTELPRO or other political surveillance but instead dealt with FBI policy regarding the identification of US citizens who had traveled to Russia. Mintz even seemed to misunderstand some of the language in the documents, suggesting it indicated the use of wiretaps or electronic surveillance. It is possible to imagine an FBI official with credibility among certain media groups, someone like Nichols or DeLoach, offering explanations for the language used and the unsurprising "news" that the FBI gathered names of individuals who traveled to Russia during the Cold War. But Nichols was long gone, and DeLoach had suddenly retired eight months before the Media burglary took place. Instead, Hoover had issued his blanket no-comment policy in an attempt to avoid confirming the kinds of information that were in his files. In effect, the blackout allowed the news media to report the contents as it wished, including misstatements and misunderstandings. In his memorandum to John Mohr, Bishop reported that Mintz was given no comment. In the margin, Hoover wrote, "Right."[160]

Bishop did handle another inquiry, this one from Clawson of the *Washington Post*, who contacted the FBI on March 30 armed with a rumor, from inside the Department of Justice, that the Bureau had failed to notify the attorney general about the burglary until after stolen documents had already been received by news media and politicians. In fact, Clawson's rumor was true. The FBI withheld its notification to the Department of Justice until March 18, ten days after the burglary, when a memorandum was sent to Assistant Attorney General Robert Mardian.[161] Attorney General Mitchell was not notified directly until March 24. Bishop denied the rumor and notified the attorney general, who then similarly denied it himself. "Clawson said, therefore, that the *Post* would not run a story," Bishop told Mohr.[162] Hoover criticized the failure to notify the attorney general on a March 24 memorandum, writing on the first page, "2 weeks elapsed & not a single memo to A.G. Atrocious handling by FBI." Then, on page 3, he added, "Your failure to advise A.G. is *inexcusable*. You dealt with underlings in the Dept."[163] Sullivan and Rosen were both censured for their failure to keep the attorney general, one of the most important audiences for FBI public relations, informed about the burglary.[164]

On March 29, the *New York Times* editorial board asked, "Who watches the watchman?" and it was critical of the emerging story of FBI political surveillance programs. "More disquieting than the bureau's internal security is the evidence, provided via the stolen files, of the F.B.I. incursions into political surveillance which far exceed legitimate efforts to protect the national interest."[165] The COINTELPRO routing slip that contained the only mention of that program was released with the third set of documents sent to the media, received at the beginning of April. The routing slip was attached to a *Barron's* magazine article entitled "Campus or Battleground," and it suggested distributing the article to educators and administrators who were "established sources." It also suggested mailing the article anonymously to educators "who have shown reluctance to take decisive action against the 'New Left.'" The "title" line of the August 9, 1968, routing slip read simply "COINTELPRO—New Left."[166] An April 8, 1971, article in the *New York Times* showed that although reporters understood the importance of revelations about FBI informants within civil rights and New Left organizations, they did not grasp the true nature of COINTELPRO, which was an effort to infiltrate and disrupt those organizations. In his April 8 story, Bill Kovack highlighted the "constant surveillance in black communities and New Left organizations." Kovack even made note of the *Barron's* article, but the word "COINTELPRO" from the routing slip attached to it was not mentioned.[167]

As the critical stories mounted, the FBI pressed its investigation into the burglary itself. Thousands of leads were developed and chased down. Agents tried for weeks to find all photocopiers of the model used to duplicate the documents in hopes that identifying marks on photocopier drums could lead them to the burglars. Agents attempted without success to identify the staples used to bind the packets of information. When photocopies made by the burglars could be obtained from news media and other sources, the FBI Crime Laboratory attempted to find fingerprints and other evidence, again without success.[168] The Bureau's file on the break-in, code-named MEDBUG, eventually ran to more than 10,000 pages. Yet the FBI never located a single one of the burglars, and the investigation was closed five years after the incident occurred. More than forty years later, four of the eight burglars broke their silence, admitting their part in the theft to author Betty Medsger. Another burglar died in 2013, and his identity was also revealed.

As Medsger noted in her masterful 2014 book *The Burglary*, even though the details of COINTELPRO would not have been evident right away to anyone reading the documents, the concern within the FBI was significant. For decades, Hoover had scrupulously protected the sanctity of his files, and he was largely successful in keeping them secret. The Media files included mention of both COINTELPRO and the Bureau's Security Index—the list of allegedly subversive individuals and groups to be monitored and possibly detained in case of a national emergency. The existence of the Security Index was revealed in a June 13, 1971, article in the *Washington Post*, and it prompted significant media coverage and public outcry.[169] "The possible exposure of the [COINTELPRO] program was regarded inside the bureau as the most dangerous bureau operation that could be exposed," Medsger wrote. "It was assumed by bureau officials that the public's reaction to it would be much more explosive than the reaction to the Security Index had been."[170] In fact, there was only one mention of "COINTELPRO–New Left" in the Media burglary files, on a routing slip encouraging agents to distribute an article on how campus protests should be handled. Nonetheless, Hoover, in a memorandum to Attorney General Mitchell, assured his supervisor that the code word COINTELPRO was unlikely to be decoded publicly, in effect highlighting the secrecy of the program. "The caption 'Cointelpro–

New Left,' is not readily comprehensible to the public," Hoover wrote. "Should this caption be deciphered, however, in the press as 'Counterintelligence Program–New Left,' it is still obviously innocuous within the context of information in the routing slip."[171]

Sullivan's departure came as the Media burglary and other controversies of 1971 were unraveling the FBI's public image. Like DeLoach, Sullivan had risen to the position of assistant to the director, officially third in command at the FBI, although Tolson's and Hoover's failing health effectively meant DeLoach and Sullivan served without any significant day-to-day supervision. The end of Sullivan's career began with a request from the Nixon White House, relayed by National Security Adviser Henry Kissinger, for wiretaps to identify the sources of press leaks about the Strategic Arms Limitation Treaty negotiations. The leaks (Kissinger termed them "egregious violations" of national security) prompted Nixon to order Kissinger to work through Attorney General Mitchell and Hoover for authorization of a "system of national security wiretaps."[172] Sullivan served as liaison to Kissinger and the White House on their leak investigation, and the FBI placed seventeen wiretaps, starting on May 12, 1969. Subjects of the wiretaps included National Security Council staff, broadcast reporter Marvin Kalb, and *New York Times* journalists William Beecher and Hedrick Smith.[173] The wiretaps were originally coordinated, and the resulting summaries were delivered to Kissinger, but at some point during the nearly two-year run of the secret program, White House chief of staff H. R. Haldeman issued the requests.[174] Among the FBI leadership, only Hoover and Sullivan were aware both of the wiretaps and of the White House origin of the leak investigation. The wiretaps were removed on June 9, 1971.

Sullivan, who was elevated to assistant to the director in June 1970, believed that Hoover had become overly cautious in his employment of break-ins, mail opening, wiretaps, and other electronic surveillance methods to combat extremists in the antiwar and New Left movements. In 1966, the director had restricted the use of those methods. Cracks in their relationship went public in October 1970 when Sullivan, speaking to a group of journalists, said the Communist Party was not involved in the campus unrest unfolding around the country. He told the editors and reporters that "the Communist party today is not nearly as extensive or effective as it was a number of years ago."[175] Upon learning of the speech, Hoover demanded an explanation, and Sullivan claimed he was misquoted. He had told a questioner that "the Communist Party was not the *sole* factor—and I repeat, the sole factor—in the unrest today," Sullivan told Tolson. "The word 'sole' was omitted in the press account."[176] In a lengthy handwritten note, Hoover re-stated FBI dogma. "We must be *most careful not to down grade* [*sic*] *the activities of the C.P.* for it is a *real contributing factor to our internal unrest*," Hoover wrote, adding that the Bureau's huge budget for monitoring the Communist Party might be questioned if the party's threat was minimized.[177] Despite his off-message speech, on August 4, 1971, Sullivan was congratulated by Hoover on his thirtieth anniversary of service to the FBI.[178]

Just before that anniversary, Sullivan realized that, due to his disdain for Hoover's management of the Bureau along with his own ambition to succeed Hoover, he would have to choose between the Nixon administration and loyalty to the director. The Bureau's records of the seventeen politically motivated wiretaps ordered by Nixon constituted a threat to the president's administration: release of that information would have been politically devastating. Sullivan saw an opportunity to consolidate his support in the White House and at the same time undermine Hoover, whom he hoped to succeed as FBI director. Sullivan had been designated by Hoover to maintain the wiretapping records, and in July 1971, he offered them to the assistant attorney general of the Internal Security Division at the Justice Department, Robert Mardian. Mardian accepted them on Nixon's orders and delivered them to the White House. According to a 1973 memorandum summarizing events of July to October 1971, "Sullivan told Mardian he was in trouble with Mr. Hoover and the possibility existed he would be fired . . . Sullivan's reason for doing this was to preclude Mr. Hoover's using the information to blackmail President Nixon, according to Mardian."[179] His relationship with the director deteriorating, Sullivan placed his future in Nixon's hands.

In mid-August, Hoover elevated Mark Felt to the third-ranking FBI post, effectively demoting Sullivan. And on August 28, Sullivan escalated his conflict with the director, sending him a letter summarizing many of their disagreements. Sullivan's letter specifically mentioned his disagreement with Hoover's public relations policies and the decision to bring in an outside agent to lead the Media burglary investigation.[180] Even before he learned of Sullivan's overt betrayal in turning over the wiretapping records to the White House, Hoover had ordered Tolson's assistant J. K. Ponder to begin compiling a catalog of the disagreements involving Sullivan.[181] Ponder's assessment no doubt matched Tolson's view of Sullivan: "A review of all these matters leaves the unbiased observer with the feeling that Mr. Sullivan has in recent months not displayed the kind of emotional stability which should be expected of a man in the important position which he holds."[182] On September 30, 1971, Hoover learned that the wiretapping records were no longer in possession of the FBI; after a brief investigation, he discovered that they had been given to the Nixon administration.[183] Hoover fired Sullivan that same day for "insolence and insubordination," and he told his Seat of Government executives that Sullivan had refused to retire voluntarily.[184] "Your recently demonstrated and continuing unwillingness to reconcile yourself to, and officially accept, final administrative decision on problems concerning which you and other Bureau officials so often present me with a variety of conflicting views has resulted in an incompatibility so fundamental that it is detrimental to the harmonious and efficient performance of our public duties," Hoover wrote to Sullivan.[185] He told his senior managers in a memo that "there has to be somebody at the top to make those decisions; that the President and the Attorney General have left me here; and that I intend to continue to make them."[186] When Sullivan, a thirty-year FBI employee, asked to keep his badge as a memento, Hoover said no and added that Sullivan should not be "shown any consideration."[187]

Sullivan responded to his firing with a letter he sent to the director's home. In it, he detailed twenty failings of Hoover's FBI, ranging from the director's enriching himself at taxpayer expense and taking credit for books written by his staff to the Bureau's "inbred situation" and the agency's spending on public relations. "It is only when work is mediocre that extensive public relations and propaganda are necessary," Sullivan wrote. "Why should taxpayers' money be spent answering letters as to how you like to have your steak done, or what is your favorite recipe for popovers, etc. Yet this has been done for years and years."[188] Sullivan closed with what could be seen now as a prophetic warning: "If you do not give reality to what to some degree has become a bubble[,] that bubble will burst and it will be bad for all."[189]

Thus, Hoover lost one of his closest advisers, and Sullivan's departure became yet another public relations fiasco for the Bureau. The story was front-page news in the *Washington Post* on October 2. Reporter Ken Clawson's article cast Hoover as the villain and Sullivan as a sympathetic, would-be progressive reformer who was forced out. The director's claim that Sullivan had voluntarily retired was, according to an anonymous FBI source, "a lie of the highest Hooverian order."[190] Similarly, a *Washington Evening Star* story headline declared that Sullivan had been EDGED DOWN EARLIER.[191] Longtime FBI foil James Wechsler of the *New York Post* suggested that the way Sullivan was dispatched—being locked out of his office after returning from sick leave, "declared a non-person"—cast doubt on Hoover's ability to continue at the FBI. "The mystery, of course, is why Hoover chose to make so large a production of Sullivan's ouster instead of allowing a few more weeks to elapse and then giving him a conventional farewell," Wechsler wrote. "To veteran Hoover-watchers in the capital the only explanation is the increasing irascibility and insecurity that the FBI chief has been manifesting in his latter years amid the growth of public criticism and the deterioration of morale within the Bureau."[192]

Even right-wing commentators were questioning Hoover's ability to continue at the FBI. "The director understandably will disdain the voices of the liberal left," conservative columnist James J. Kilpatrick stated. "But he should know of the increasing concern on the conservative right. We want him to go, when he goes, with trumpets and laurels. He is risking the loss of them now."[193] Syndicated columnists Rowland Evans and Robert Novak claimed the criticism of Hoover reached inside the FBI. They tied the Sullivan firing, the existence of internal FBI critics, a purge of critics, and the specter of Bureau surveillance into three loaded, critical sentences: "With the ruthless self-preservation born of 48 years as grand vizier of the FBI, Hoover has lashed back against in-house critics. The result, hidden from public view, has been a reign of terror. Some respected FBI officials have been demoted or summarily transferred, others reduced to nervous prostration in wholly realistic fear of surveillance by Hoover agents."[194]

In November, yet another damaging story broke when Clawson reported in the *Washington Post* that the FBI had, on orders from the White House, investigated CBS News reporter Daniel Schorr. On November 12, 1971, Hoover reported to his top managers that the White House would tell the press that Schorr was being considered for a federal position and was the subject of a "routine FBI investigation."[195] Whether the Schorr investigation was a legitimate one conducted for a potential appointment or whether the FBI was used by the Nixon White House to expedite an investigation of a member of the news media has never been fully established. Either way, the PR damage of a story seeming to confirm public concerns about FBI political surveillance was significant.

Hoover finally broke his media silence in late December 1971, agreeing to respond to written questions submitted by Isabelle Hall of United Press International. In the resulting story, the director blasted critics of the Sullivan firing, arguing that firm discipline was necessary to maintain the integrity of the FBI. "Yes, we have tight controls and firm discipline in the FBI," Hoover said. "Those that argue these organizational reins should be relaxed fail to understand the nature of FBI responsibilities and how little room they leave for error."[196] At the end of the story, the director's language resembled boiler-plate from the 1930s and the *Ten Thousand Public Enemies* theme that blamed passive citizens for the proliferation of crime. "Citizens must learn that being a passive ally to crime—that is, looking the other way when offenses are committed and patronizing criminal enterprises—will only continue to strengthen the lawless element," Hoover said in comments likely written by Bishop.[197] He was not pleased with the result of his attempt to set the record straight. "Henceforth," he stated, "we will answer no questions for this woman. She can't refrain from putting some 'sticky' things in."[198] In early 1972, perhaps spurred on by Hoover, Sullivan spoke to reporters for the first time since his firing. In a brief interview regarding his new job, he attempted to turn attention away from his firing to revelations about what he termed the "fossilized" FBI bureaucracy.[199] Ironically, Sullivan's first full-time job after leaving the Bureau was with the Insurance Crime Prevention Institute, where he joined a staff that included another former FBI agent forced out by Hoover, Jack Shaw.[200]

In a 1975 oral history interview, Clawson reiterated his view that Sullivan was the best administrator he had seen and certainly the most capable man left in the agency by the early 1970s. "[Sullivan] tried internally to the best of his ability to get the Old Man's opinions out of concrete, to make him a little more flexible, because it was a different time and a different set of circumstances," Clawson said. "But he made the major bureaucratic mistake in that he said [in the August 28, 1971, letter to Hoover] 'Either you accept some of my ideas or I'm getting out.' Well, before he could bat his eye, he was out."[201] The tenor of the coverage demonstrated that Sullivan had accrued more credibility with members of the news media than had Hoover or his top public relations official, Bishop. In just a few months, mired in a mounting series of PR crises that called his ability to manage the Bureau into question, Hoover had pushed out his longest-serving and perhaps most talented top adviser. Meanwhile, Tolson's health meant he was severely diminished in his ability to participate in crisis management. And Bishop clearly did not have the contacts outside or the credibility inside the Bureau to shape Hoover's public responses to events. In addition to the loss of sound advice, Sullivan's firing added yet another story to the emerging narrative of 1971 that an aging and temperamental Hoover was losing control of his agency.

The FBI's own files covering the public relations fiascos of 1970 and 1971 demonstrate Bishop's detachment from day-to-day messaging and liaison with members of the press, the type of hands-on work that made Nichols and DeLoach so successful in their efforts to control the Bureau's public image. Files of public relations crises in the 1940s, 1950s, and 1960s are replete with hundreds of pages of evidence demonstrating how Nichols and De-Loach and, to a lesser extent, Wick were part of the Bureau's highest-level decision-making processes. The files from the 1970 and 1971 controversies differ in that the Bureau's responses to those crises were managed by the director working through Milton Jones's Crime Research Section. Because of Tolson's ill health, his office was merely a transfer point for memoranda moving to Hoover. Tolson's own voice was almost entirely absent from the 1970 and 1971 controversies. Bishop was included in the discussions but appears to have acted most often as a go-between, passing messages back and forth between the director's office and Jones. Jones, meanwhile, operated as he always had—as a source of analysis and cautious recommendations but not as a contact man lobbying opinion shapers outside the FBI. Similar controversies arising in the 1940s, 1950s, or 1960s would have found Bishop's predecessors Nichols and DeLoach actively engaged on a daily basis in the decision-making processes inside the FBI and in shaping perceptions among the news media covering the Bureau. Nichols frequently lobbied reporters over lunch and gathered information via his vast network of telephone contacts. DeLoach wielded the telephone like a weapon, using his savvy combination of genteel chatter, polite arguments, and if needed naked threats to shape understandings of the Bureau. There is no documentation of any such day-to-day, active, and engaged messaging, networking, or contact work by Bishop in the record of the 1971 controversies.

It seems likely that the Bureau could have weathered the kinds of public relations challenges it faced in the late 1960s and early 1970s had its leadership team been at full strength. Clearly, though, age had taken its toll. By the early 1970s, Tolson, who had long been Hoover's most trusted and most strident defender inside and, less frequently, outside the FBI, was a shell of his former self. Several severe strokes had sapped his energy and severely limited his ability to manage the Bureau. The man who had formerly been chief enforcer of Hoover's declarations and mother-hen-style defender of the director himself appeared in his office only infrequently. His influence over the internal management of the Bureau and of events and public relations, formerly evidenced by his handwritten comments on memoranda, was all but entirely absent by 1970 and 1971. And though Hoover was not suffering from debilitating illnesses like Tolson was, his health, according to DeLoach's interactions with President Johnson, had already begun to fail by the late 1960s. Hoover turned seventy-seven in 1971, and even a particularly healthy septuagenarian would have struggled to maintain control of a vast and secretive bureaucracy like the FBI, not to mention its formerly pristine public image.

When Nichols was confronted with complex public relations challenges, he had the authority within the Bureau, based on the trust Hoover and Tolson placed in him, to engage his network of FBI defenders in the news media and other opinion-shaping positions inside and outside government. With a few phone calls, lunches, or letters, Nichols was able to activate the network he had painstakingly built through sustained personal outreach. DeLoach wielded power more directly, focusing most of his attention on members of Congress and LBJ. Whereas Nichols managed problems as an outsiders' representative inside the FBI, DeLoach pushed upward, using his charm to strengthen Bureau friendships in Washington's halls of power. Despite long and distinguished FBI careers, Nease, Wick, and Bishop had neither Nichols's network nor DeLoach's powerful friends. Bishop, in particular, worked within the altered reality created by a generational shift in the United States. The trusty Bureau messages of science, responsibility, and Hoover no longer carried the same kind of power in 1970 that they had in 1950s America. By the 1970s, the Bureau was an ossified entity, unable to shift its message to meet the times, and agents such as Wick and Bishop, whose entire careers were made by their abilities to internalize and parrot Hoover's xenophobic worldview, were completely unprepared to change and unable to conceptualize a new way to "sell" the Bureau as the culture shifted out from under them. As the controversies of the early 1970s mounted and as Hoover and Tolson continued to decline in health and authority, the diminished public relations staff in the FBI leaned on outdated strategies and messages, betraying the weakness of its leadership and emboldening critics.

Chapter Eight

The Fall

Throughout 1971 and into 1972, critics attacked Hoover and the FBI relentlessly. One Hoover nemesis, nationally syndicated columnist Jack Anderson, was particularly prolific, penning column after column attacking the director and the FBI. Anderson was also a particularly dangerous adversary. His "Washington Merry-Go-Round" column appeared in 1,000 newspapers nationally, with an estimated 40 million readers.[1] During prior smear campaigns, as the FBI termed them, the most innocuous anti-FBI comment could spark a comprehensive response from the Crime Records Section as the Bureau and the agency's defenders fought back, countering critical messages and sometimes smearing the critics themselves. That relentless defense reflected Nichols's and DeLoach's confidence and willingness to counterattack and parry critical messages. By 1971, though, those two men were gone and Crime Research was led by Bishop, a far less assertive public relations counselor than his predecessors. Not only was Bishop more cautious, he also lacked the internal cultural capital of Nichols and DeLoach, who were able to influence Hoover and Tolson, overcoming their reactionary tendencies or spurring them to oppose their critics when they would prefer to be more cautious.

As Anderson and other critics issued attack after attack in 1971 and 1972, the absence of an influential figure such as Nichols or DeLoach was manifest in the FBI's near-total silence. Only once, in September 1971, did Hoover directly respond to an Anderson broadside with a public statement: "There is not enough stationery at headquarters, nor are there enough hours in the workweek, to issue public denials of all the misinformation this purveyor of fiction has written regarding the FBI," Hoover wrote in a letter to the editor.[2] Privately, though, Hoover fumed. At one point during their decades of sparring, he declared that Anderson was "lower than the regurgitated filth of vultures."[3]

A protégé of famed muckraker Drew Pearson, Anderson was fond of be-ing characterized as the "Paul Revere of journalism," referring to his un-canny ability to uncover stories and set the agenda for their coverage. In his zeal to be the first to report stories, he often found himself embroiled in alle-gations that he illegally published government secrets, illegally eavesdropped on private conversations, used blackmail to get sources to talk, and many other effective if unethical journalistic practices. He was not above digging through garbage, as he did in 1971 when he put Hoover under the same kind of surveillance that the Bureau used on its critics. Reporter Charles Elliott, Anderson's assistant (just as Anderson had been Pearson's assistant before), was dispatched to interview Hoover's neighbors, stake out the director's house, follow his limousine, and trail Hoover and Tolson to lunch each day. Elliott's observations painted a picture of Hoover growing increasingly para-noid as he aged. He refused to leave or enter his car if there were strangers on his quiet street. He placed his hat on one side in the rear window of his lim-ousine and cowered on the other side. When they lunched together each day at the Rib Room restaurant, Hoover and Tolson sat side by side with their backs to the wall, facing the entrance.[4] One day in 1971, Elliott picked up Hoover's trash from a can on the north side of his house and returned it to Anderson for review. Anderson reported the "revelations" from the trash raid, noting that Elliott found small whiskey bottles, antacids, and handwrit-ten menus for Hoover's housekeeper to prepare.[5] Given the more serious revelations about the contents of FBI files that typically included similar trivial information gathered through far more intrusive means, Anderson must have enjoyed the irony of putting the FBI director under surveillance.

Anderson's muckraking skills were so effective that he drove leaders of government agencies to employ extreme and sometimes ridiculous methods to thwart him. "In one particularly madcap scene, CIA spooks bugged their own boss, Director Richard Helms, as he lunched with Anderson and asked the columnist not to publish details about U.S. eavesdropping on Kremlin telephones," journalist and professor Mark Feldstein reported in *Poisoning the Press: Richard Nixon, Jack Anderson, and the Rise of Washington's Scandal Culture*.[6] When CIA agents trailed him to his house, Anderson sent his nine children out to photograph the agents.[7] More chillingly, Watergate burglar G. Gordon Liddy, a former FBI agent, plotted to murder Anderson.[8]

In November 1971 alone, Anderson published three columns attacking the FBI, including one asserting that Hoover used extortion to remain in power. "All agree that Hoover has been able to awe Washington officialdom largely because he keeps files on the high and mighty," he wrote in November. "There is raw information on Presidents and peons alike that fills miles of cabinets."⁹ In a December broadcast, Anderson said the Bureau used electronic devices to spy on Americans, adding, "I predict a series of court cases will test the Government's right to use these all-seeing, all-knowing devices to invade the privacy of the individual."¹⁰ On a January 1972 broadcast, Anderson argued that the CIA had become the nation's preeminent domestic intelligence collector and was "taking advantage of J. Edgar Hoover's declining popularity to strip the FBI of one of its most celebrated functions."¹¹ On March 15, Anderson charged that crime conviction rates had slipped, prompting several lengthy FBI memoranda countering the charge to be created and sent to the attorney general.¹²

On Monday, May 1, 1972, Anderson's "Washington Merry-Go-Round" accused the FBI of conducting investigations into the sex lives of prominent Americans. "F.B.I. chief J. Edgar Hoover has demonstrated an intense interest in who is sleeping with whom in Washington," Anderson wrote, adding that he had seen "sex reports" that Hoover shared with LBJ. "President Johnson was one White House occupant who had a fine appreciation for stories about the extracurricular love affairs of public figures."¹³ The FBI, which had closely monitored the columnist for decades, issued a "no comment" in response to Anderson's claim.¹⁴ Hoover's busy morning calendar for Monday, May 1, included the presentation of a thirty-year service award to Special Agent George A. Zales; a posed photograph with Special Agent Thomas E. Burg of Chicago and his wife; a meeting with six students from the Clarke School for the Deaf in Northampton, Massachusetts; a posed photograph with Special Agent Charles E. Price; acceptance of a commemorative tiepin from the Knoxville, Tennessee, director of safety, Duane J. Ansetts; a retirement ceremony with former Crime Records assistant director Frank W. Waikart; and a meeting with FBI inspector Louis A. Giovanetti.¹⁵ Even as he was busy with mostly ceremonial duties, it seems likely that the Anderson column occupied a significant part of Hoover's final day as FBI director. Another ongoing concern was Tolson's poor health; in fact, Hoover cut his schedule short to leave early and eat dinner with Tolson.¹⁶

The next morning, May 2, 1972, at Hoover's genteel home in northwest Washington, a simple brick structure with a garish artificial turf yard, housekeeper Annie Fields prepared the director's normal breakfast of two soft-boiled eggs, white toast, and black coffee, to be served at 7:30 a.m. At precisely that time every workday, Hoover appeared at the bottom of the

The grave of J. Edgar Hoover, Congressional Cemetery, Washington, D.C. (Photo by the author.)

stairs for his first meal of the day. But on that Tuesday morning, Fields was alarmed when Hoover did not come downstairs for breakfast. A few minutes later, Hoover's driver, Tom Moton, arrived in the armored limousine to take his employer to work. (The fact that the director received a new, government-funded limousine each year had been cited by Anderson as an example of his megalomania.) A few minutes later, Hoover's former driver, James Crawford, then a general handyman around the house, arrived. Fields, Moton, and Crawford huddled in the kitchen and decided to check Hoover's bedroom. At about 8:30 a.m., Crawford, the only one with a key to the room, made his way up the stairs, unlocked the bedroom door, and found Hoover's lifeless body on the floor.[17] At some point during the night, J. Edgar Hoover, a seemingly indestructible giant in American society and the personification of the FBI he built in his own image, passed away from a heart attack. He was seventy-seven years old and had served as director for nearly forty-eight years at the time of his death.

In the hours and days after Hoover's death, FBI officials labored furiously to secure the secret files that held the potential to obliterate what was by then already a diminished legacy. His personal secretary for nearly his entire tenure as director, Helen Gandy, began sorting and moving files to his home, where she shredded thousands of "Personal and Confidential" files that were undoubtedly the most damning evidence of the FBI's thirty-plus years of domestic intelligence gathering. Gandy retired from the Bureau on the day Hoover died, but she continued to shred files at FBI headquarters for several days and then moved her records-destruction operation to Hoover's home; she shredded papers there for more than two months. Gandy later claimed in testimony to Congress that she removed just ten file cabinet drawers filled only with Hoover's personal papers. A truck driver who transported the files to Hoover's home, however, described moving a load containing twenty to twenty-five file cabinets.[18]

At the Bureau, meanwhile, Director Clyde Tolson resigned after serving just a few hours in Hoover's place, and President Richard Nixon appointed an FBI outsider, a former navy submarine commander who served for twenty years and in two wars, to as acting director of the FBI. A St. Louis native, L. Patrick Gray graduated from the US Naval Academy in 1940 and George Washington University's law school in 1949. He commanded a submarine during the Korean War and in 1958 served as an assistant to the chairman of the Joint Chiefs of Staff and special assistant to the secretary of defense. After retiring from the military in 1960, Gray briefly joined Nixon's vice presidential staff. From 1960 to 1969, he practiced law in Connecticut, and after Nixon's election as president, he accepted an appointment in the office of the secretary of health, education, and welfare before moving to the Department of Justice as assistant attorney general in charge of the department's civil division.[19] During his eleven-month tenure as acting director of the FBI, Gray hired the first female agents, relaxed the Bureau's straitlaced culture, and visited many field offices to boost morale.[20] In an apparent effort to assert control within Bureau headquarters, he disbanded the powerful Crime Research Section, leading to the retirement or transfer of stalwart Bureau loyalists such as Milton Jones and Fern Stukenbroeker. Bishop retired on February 5, 1973, after leading the Crime Research Section for seven years. The marginalization of Crime Research was demonstrated by the fact that Bishop's performance was not reviewed once in the sixteen months prior to his retirement.[21]

During the early months of Gray's tenure, the Crime Research Section was responsible for writing the acting director's speeches. Jones found that

Gray was difficult to please. "All he wanted was high-sounding rhetoric and a lot of guff," Jones wrote in his private memoirs. "Toward the end he seemed to give up on us completely and reportedly sought the services of a public relations man he knew in another agency for help on his speeches."[22] In late 1972, Gray disbanded the Crime Research Division. Bishop, who according to Jones had been outspoken in his advice to Gray, was exiled to the FBI training facility in Quantico, where "he had little to do . . . except read books and twiddle his thumbs."[23] A few days after Bishop was transferred, Jones resigned. Bishop had his revenge. When Gray was nominated by Nixon to have the "acting" qualifier removed from his title, Bishop contacted US Senate staffers to make sure "the most embarrassing questions were asked" during Gray's confirmation hearing.[24] Indeed, Gray's nomination was withdrawn after questions about his role in passing files from the FBI's Watergate investigation to White House counsel John W. Dean III were raised in the hearing.[25] The 1973 revelations about the role he played in assisting the Watergate cover-up comprised just one more public relations fiasco piled upon the disasters of 1971 and 1972. Gray later said that "the gravest mistake" of his life was getting involved with Nixon.[26]

Even after a new FBI director, Clarence M. Kelley, was nominated and confirmed, the excesses of the Hoover era lingered as an ongoing PR and perception problem for the Bureau. In 1975, following reports that the FBI had maintained files on members of Congress, the US Senate authorized a comprehensive investigation into the activities of the CIA and FBI. The Senate Select Committee to Study Governmental Operations with Respect to Intelligence Activities would become known as the Church Committee because it was chaired by Democratic senator Frank Church of Idaho. The *New York Times* reported that "the committee would be the most extensive public inquiry ever into the activities of the C.I.A., the F.B.I., [and] military intelligence agencies."[27] In late 1975 and into 1976, news from the Church Committee hearings made headlines across the country and prompted reflection on the Hoover era of the FBI.

Among the revelations from the hearings were details about the FBI's efforts to marginalize and even blackmail Martin Luther King, Jr., and the COINTELPRO efforts to disrupt dissident groups such as the antiwar and pro–civil rights New Left, along with black nationalists, communists, socialists, and white hate groups. In his testimony to the Church Committee, DeLoach frequently claimed he could not recall details of his FBI career, but he did confirm that COINTELPRO included a "mass media" or public relations program in which presumably derogatory information was provided to friendly news reporters and editors. "I do recall," he stated, "after my mind being refreshed by a memorandum you have shown me that part of the COINTELPRO, or Counterintelligence Program, the Domestic Intelligence Division did have a segment or phase of it called the mass media program, and from time to time the Domestic Intelligence Division would prepare memoranda and send to Mr. Hoover for his approval and then over to me information which was to be given to newspapers in connection with that program."[28] In his testimony, DeLoach repeatedly downplayed the involvement of Crime Records in COINTELPRO, the harassment of Dr. King, politically motivated investigations requested by the White House, and other activities that, when exposed in a public hearing, were unmasked as being well beyond the Bureau's legal mandate. Asked if he spoke to White House officials about the provision of political intelligence, DeLoach issued a blanket denial. "I have never talked with anyone at the White House, to the best of my knowledge, concerning the fact that the FBI should furnish political information, Senator," he said.[29] Subsequent releases of multiple tapes and transcripts of DeLoach's phone conversations with President Johnson, of course, revealed the misleading nature of that sworn testimony. Other FBI officials who testified similarly either claimed they could not recall or actively minimized their roles in the questionable activities of Hoover's FBI. Nevertheless, news stories on the subject matter of the inquiry—ranging from break-ins (called black bag jobs) to wiretaps to the disruptive and intrusive COINTELPRO—offered a devastating critique of the Hoover era.

In a *New York Times* column, Nicholas Horrock said the hearings painted a "sinister picture" of Hoover's FBI and marked the destruction of the director's carefully cultivated law-and-order legacy. "A lot of what is now labeled wrong about the bureau's methods was an outgrowth of the personality and attitude of J. Edgar Hoover," Horrock wrote, adding:

> To many in the United States Mr. Hoover was the symbol of law and order for nearly five decades, a cold, uncompromising foe of criminals and subversives. But in the last five years a more sinister picture has emerged. It was Mr. Hoover who urged his agents to discredit Dr. King and who authorized the tricks and turns of cointel. He wielded awesome power over his agents from an office lined with private files that contained personal secrets about Presidents, Congressmen and a host of

other officials. No man during Mr. Hoover's lifetime ever challenged his control of the F.B.I. and survived the experience unscathed."[30]

The committee's findings, released in April 1976, were highly critical of the domestic intelligence activities of Hoover's FBI. According to the committee report, the Bureau frequently used illegal and improper means to collect information, including surreptitious entries, illegal wiretaps, and other electronic surveillance, and it distorted the information it collected. Some of that information was released to the media or other parties. The report stated that "the most basic harm was to the values of privacy and freedom which our constitution seeks to protect and which intelligence activity infringed on a broad scale."[31] The report cited instances of "general efforts to discredit," and it specifically cited the Bureau's public relations efforts: "The FBI has attempted to covertly influence the public's perception of persons and organizations by disseminating derogatory information to the press, either anonymously or through 'friendly' news contacts. . . . The Bureau also attempted to influence media reporting which would have any impact on the public image of the FBI."[32] The Bureau, according to the committee's report, created a "chilling" effect on dissent and prevented the free exchange of ideas.[33] The 341-page document was an unequivocal rejection of J. Edgar Hoover's approach to law enforcement, and the appendixes included a blueprint for additional congressional oversight for the FBI and CIA. In a statement attached to the report, Democratic senator Robert Morgan of North Carolina specifically refuted Hoover's xenophobic and paranoid view of Americans. "FBI action was based, for example, on the assumption that all Americans opposed to this country's participation in the Vietnam War might one day take to the streets in violent protest, thereby threatening our national security," Morgan wrote. "It was assumed, for example, that every black student on every college campus in America would resort to violence, so procedures were undertaken to establish files on all of them. All of these actions deny American the right to decide for themselves what will not be tolerated in a free society."[34]

In the wake of the Church Committee report, the FBI was left with little credibility and no updated message to offer as a counternarrative. It was not that the FBI was ineffective in its core law enforcement duties. The problem was that as Hoover's true nature and the extent of the domestic intelligence operations he led were revealed, the shadow of corruption that the Bureau was born under in 1908 again came to the forefront, just as it had following the 1919 and 1920 Palmer Raids and in the later years of Hoover's tenure.

The unraveling of Hoover's legacy has been so complete that he has become the butt of late-night jokes, most often based on apocryphal claims that he was a cross-dresser. There has even been a movement to remove Hoover's name from the FBI building in Washington, D.C., which was completed after his death. Most recently, that campaign was driven by the release of a documentary film exploring the FBI's persecution of gays under Hoover. "I don't think his name should be on that building," Democratic congressman Steve Cohen of Tennessee told a reporter. "It was pretty disgusting to see some of the actions that were being engaged in."[35] Historian Douglas M. Charles, author of *Hoover's War on Gays: Exposing the FBI's "Sex Deviates" Program* (2015), called the dedication of the FBI building to Hoover "a tragedy of history."[36] There were prior calls to remove the late director's name from the building based on revelations of the excesses and outright crimes committed during the Hoover era.[37]

From the calls to remove his name to the name-calling from late-night comedians, Hoover's legacy has essentially been dismantled and replaced with a combination of truth and mythology. The good work he was able to do—including the creation of a remarkably effective FBI bureaucracy, the adoption of high educational and training standards for the Bureau, and the addition of fingerprint and other cutting-edge science to the American law enforcement tool kit—has been lost, ironically, in a torrent of negative publicity since the director's death in 1972. With DeLoach's passing in 2013 after decades defending Hoover's legacy, the "Boss" lost his last and most charming PR man.

DeLoach's voice was not nearly strong enough, however, to counter the frequent revelations about the excesses and illegalities perpetrated by Hoover's FBI. Clarence Kelley, who served as director from 1973 to 1978 and was one of the most respected and powerful of the post-Hoover FBI directors, found himself addressing the mistakes of his predecessor to the point where he made a speech in 1975 that essentially declared a new start for the FBI. "We know that integrity must be demonstrated," Kelley told the Pittsburgh Chapter of the Society of Former Special Agents of the FBI, noting specifically the criticism of the Hoover era Counterintelligence Program. "We can proclaim our integrity from the rooftops but unless we manifest integrity in our performance, we are as sounding brass or tinkling cymbal."[38]

Turning the Bureau's public image around has proceeded in fits and starts for decades, but the revelations of Hoover era excesses continue to trickle out. At the time of this book's publication, forty-four years have passed since Hoover's forty-eight-year tenure ended with his death in 1972, yet scholars and journalists continue to find "news" in document releases from the FBI under the Freedom of Information Act. That never-ending trickle of information begs the question, in fact, of whether the FBI's power to control the public conversation about itself has been lost for good. In February 2015, FBI director James Comey gave a speech at Georgetown University that columnist E. J. Dionne mused might have been viewed by Hoover as having subversive intent. "All of us in law enforcement must be honest enough to acknowledge that much of our history is not pretty," Comey said. "At many points in American history, law enforcement enforced the status quo, a status quo that was often brutally unfair to disfavored groups."[39]

The FBI was seen as America's indispensable agency in the 1930s, 1940s, and 1950s, but its reputation declined during the late 1960s and early 1970s as Hoover and Tolson, in ill health and ill prepared to deal with the churning of the insatiable scandal culture developing in Washington, lost control of the Bureau's public image. The departures of Nichols in 1957, DeLoach in 1970, and Sullivan in 1971 meant that there were no powerful figures left inside the FBI who could nudge Hoover and Tolson into changing their public relations messages or even mounting a meaningful defense against critics. In the 1930s, Nichols helped craft a compelling PR narrative emphasizing science, responsibility, and Hoover as protector of civil liberties. In addition, he shaped the policies and organization of the public relations–oriented Crime Records Section and trained its key contributors, such as the Bureau's "editor," Milton Jones, and its resident "professor," Fern Stukenbroeker. During the 1940s and 1950s, Nichols's vast network and his ability to maintain contact with critics allowed the engagement of defenders in the media and elsewhere and even the development of relationships with "liberal" moles such as the ACLU's Morris Ernst and Irving Ferman. Those defenders drowned out critics and, in the case of Ernst's "Why I No Longer Fear the F.B.I." article in *Reader's Digest*, inoculated the Bureau against criticism from the political Left. The public relations machinery and messages that Nichols built remained effective once Cartha DeLoach took over as assistant director of the renamed Crime Research Division. DeLoach's approach, however, was very different from his predecessor's, in that he managed upward, providing particularly effective liaison with potentially troublesome agencies such as the CIA and powerful FBI stakeholders including Congress and the Johnson

White House. His people-pleasing, smooth-talking nature and tough approach also masked a burning ambition to succeed Hoover as director. According to William Sullivan, DeLoach departed under a cloud of ambition run amok, a sin Hoover would never tolerate. Although he focused on domestic intelligence and was not part of the Bureau's public relations machinery, Sullivan nevertheless provided essential PR advice based on his reputation within the Bureau as an expert on communism and subversion.

The importance of the Bureau's public relations men is demonstrated by the arc of the FBI's public image. The Bureau of Investigation was founded despite the concerns of members of Congress who feared the potential for political influence and corruption within a federal law enforcement agency. When those predictions came true with the Palmer Raids of 1919 and 1920 and the Bureau's involvement in the Teapot Dome scandal in 1921 and 1922, Hoover's charge was to "clean up" the Bureau by removing political appointees and improving the quality of agents and the clarity of procedures. That question about the legitimacy of a federal law enforcement agency, however, remained an issue for the Bureau until the FDR administration vastly expanded the agency's jurisdiction in 1934. It was the public relations value of the high-profile outlaw cases of the 1930s, promoted first by Hoover and Tolson and then by Nichols, that brought the FBI into public view. And as the Bureau's "enemies" shifted from outlaws to spies and then to communists in the late 1930s and 1940s, it was public relations that maintained the FBI's respected public image and marginalized critics who questioned the agency's legitimacy. With Nichols gone, DeLoach stepped in and kept the public relations momentum going in the 1960s, relying on stalwarts such as Jones and Stukenbroeker to craft and help deliver the Bureau's PR messages.

The steepest downward arc of the Bureau's public image may be traced to the early 1970s when the failing health of Tolson and then Hoover, combined with the absence of DeLoach and Sullivan and an emerging Washington scandal culture, led to a steady stream of critical revelations about the excesses and illegalities of Bureau domestic intelligence and about Hoover's own isolation and xenophobia. When Hoover needed talented PR men most, they were gone—retired or pushed out of the Bureau by the director himself when they became too powerful. For many reasons, including his own relative inexperience in public relations and his inability to manipulate Hoover as Nichols and DeLoach did, Bishop simply was unable to marshal the sort of public defense that his predecessors might have offered. Hoover's sudden death and Tolson's resignation led to Gray's ill-advised elimination of the seasoned and capable Crime Records/Research team, which had served the Bureau so well for nearly forty years. Thus, Hoover's PR men—larger-than-life characters such as Nichols and DeLoach, capable and loyal insiders such as Jones and Stukenbroeker, and outsiders such as Ernst and the myriad journalists and entertainment figures who helped craft and amplify the Bureau's message—were essential actors in the forty-eight-year arc of the Hoover era.

In a letter to Kelley in 1973, Jones summarized the importance of Hoover's PR men and recommended that the Crime Records Section that was disbanded by Gray be reconstituted. "Soon, I hope, former Agents like me will again be proud to say, 'I once was with the FBI,'" Jones wrote. "Under such Bureau greats as L. B. Nichols, Deke DeLoach, Bob Wick and Tom Bishop, this [Crime Records] Division perhaps more than any other, made the Bureau what it was in the Hoover days."

NOTES

Introduction: Defining a "Hoover Era"

1. Mary Russell, "House Votes to Override Two Ford Vetoes," *Washington Post*, November 21, 1974, A1, A5.

2. See, for example, Matthew Cecil, *Hoover's FBI and the Fourth Estate* (Lawrence: University Press of Kansas, 2014), 77–86, for an examination of the shooting of bank robber Benjamin Dickson.

3. Tim Wiener, *Enemies: A History of the FBI* (New York: Random House, 2012), 88.

4. Athan Theoharis and John Stuart Cox, *The Boss: J. Edgar Hoover and the Great American Inquisition* (Philadelphia: Temple University Press, 1988), 9–11.

5. Ibid., 312–314.

6. Clarence M. Kelley, transcript of speech to the Pittsburgh Chapter of the Former Special Agents of the Federal Bureau of Investigation, "The FBI—It Still Stands for Fidelity, Bravery and Integrity," June 10, 1975, FBI 67-338721-556.

7. Kenneth Ackerman, "Five Myths about J. Edgar Hoover," *Washington Post*, November 9, 2011, accessed at http://www.washingtonpost.com/opinions/five-myths -about-j-edgar-hoover/2011/11/07/gIQASLlo5M_story.html.

8. Cecil, *Hoover's FBI*, 287.

9. Ibid., 55–57.

10. Richard Gid Powers, *G-Men: The FBI in American Popular Culture* (Carbondale: Southern Illinois University Press, 1983), 127.

11. Theoharis and Cox, *Boss*, 86–94.

12. Athan G. Theoharis, Tony G. Poveda, Susan Rosenfeld, and Richard Gid Powers, eds., *The FBI: A Comprehensive Reference Guide* (New York: Oryx Press, 2000), 346.

13. Powers, *G-Men*, 51–64; for a review of the development of *The F.B.I.*, see Cecil, *Hoover's FBI*, 265–281.

14. Morris Ernst, "Why I No Longer Fear the F.B.I.," *Reader's Digest*, December 21, 1950, 27–30.

15. For example, Mark Felt and John O'Connor, *A G-Man's Life: The FBI, Being "Deep Throat," and the Struggle for Honor in Washington* (New York: Public Affairs, 2006), 90.

16. Theoharis and Cox, *Boss*, 416–417.

17. Athan G. Theoharis, *J. Edgar Hoover, Sex and Crime: An Historical Antidote* (Chicago: Ivan R. Dee, 1995).

Chapter One: From Corrupt to Indispensable

1. Caroline P. Chambers, letter to J. Edgar Hoover, January 2, 1951, FBI 67-109183-196X.

2. Louis B. Nichols, memorandum to Clyde Tolson, January 15, 1943, FBI 67-109183-107.

3. J. Edgar Hoover, letter to Mrs. James (Caroline P.) Chambers, St. Cloud, Fla., January 12, 1951, FBI 67-109183-196X.

4. Caroline P. Chambers, letter to the Department of Justice, January 2, 1951, FBI 67-109183-196X.

5. Louis B. Nichols, memorandum to Clyde Tolson, April 9, 1951, FBI 66-1855-L-487.

6. Milton A. Jones, memorandum to Louis B. Nichols, April 13, 1951, FBI 67-109183-197, 3.

7. Ibid., 2.

8. Ibid.

9. Ibid., 2–3.

10. Louis B. Nichols, memorandum to J. Edgar Hoover, April 19, 1951, FBI 67-109183-unserialized.

11. Founded in 1934, the Crime Records Section was for decades housed within the FBI's Administrative Division. In the early 1960s, the division was reorganized and the Crime Records Division created, with the Crime Research Section taking on the duties of the former Crime Records Section. For clarity, this manuscript will employ the Crime Records Section nomenclature throughout.

12. Clyde Tolson, memorandum to J. Edgar Hoover, February 14, 1934, FBI 80-67-1.

13. Henry Suydam, "How Kidnapers Are Caught," *Forum*, April 1934, 208.

14. Ibid., 213.

15. J. Edgar Hoover, memorandum to Clyde Tolson, March 24, 1934, FBI 80-67-3.

16. Matthew Cecil, *Hoover's FBI and the Fourth Estate: The Campaign to Control the Press and the Bureau's Image* (Lawrence: University Press of Kansas, 2014), 45–47.

17. Assignment History of Clyde A. Tolson, FBI 67-9524-unserialized; Athan Theoharis, Tony G. Poveda, Susan Rosenfeld, and Richard Gid Powers, eds., *The FBI: A Comprehensive Reference Guide* (New York: Oryx Press, 2000), 358.

18. Douglas M. Charles, *Hoover's War on Gays: Exposing the FBI's "Sex Deviates" Program* (Lawrence: University Press of Kansas, 2015), 1.

19. Theoharis et al., *FBI*, 7.

20. Ibid., 12.

21. J. Edgar Hoover, memorandum to Clyde Tolson, September 19, 1930, FBI 67-9524-118.

22. Clyde Tolson, memorandum to J. Edgar Hoover, September 30, 1930, FBI 67-9524-119.

23. Kenneth O'Reilly, "A New Deal for the FBI: The Roosevelt Administration, Crime Control, and National Security," *Journal of American History* 69, no. 3 (December 1982): 639.

24. "Crime War Real, Asserts Cummings," *New York Times*, September 12, 1933, 3.

25. O'Reilly, "New Deal," 643.

26. Stephen Early, letter to FDR, July 12, 1940, President's Personal File 2993, Franklin D. Roosevelt Papers, Roosevelt Library, Hyde Park, N.Y., cited in O'Reilly, "New Deal," 644.

27. Robert Cromie and Joseph Pinkston, *Dillinger: A Short and Violent Life* (New York: McGraw, 1962), 169.

28. "Gibe at Raid on Dillinger," *New York Times*, April 25, 1934, 3.

29. Richard Gid Powers, *G-Men: Hoover's FBI in American Popular Culture* (Carbondale: Southern Illinois University Press, 1983), 121.

30. Ibid.

31. Melvin Purvis and Samuel Cowley, Affidavit of Special Agent in Charge M. H. Purvis and S. P. Cowley, July 28, 1934, FBI 62-29777-1-24.

32. "Dillinger Slain in Chicago; Shot Dead by Federal Men in Front of Movie Theatre," *New York Times*, July 23, 1934, 1.

33. "Cummings Says Slaying of Dillinger Is 'Gratifying as Well as Reassuring,'" *New York Times*, July 23, 1934, 1.

34. Ibid.

35. Alton Purvis, *The Vendetta: Special Agents Melvin Purvis, John Dillinger, and Hoover's FBI in the Age of Gangsters* (New York: Public Affairs, 2009), 270.

36. Powers, *G-Men*, 128.

37. "Purvis Hides Name of the Informer," *New York Times*, July 24, 1934, 3.

38. "Hoover and Purvis Confer," *New York Times*, July 26, 1934, 1.

39. Hal H. Smith, "Agents of Justice Who 'Got' Dillinger," *New York Times*, July 29, 1934, 130.

40. Richard Gid Powers, *Broken: The Troubled Past and Uncertain Future of the FBI* (New York: Free Press, 2004), 155.

41. Rex Collier, "Why Uncle Sam's Agents Get Their Men: Hoover, Their Chief, Says There Is No Mystery in Crime Detection, Merely Painstaking Work and Common Sense," *New York Times Magazine*, August 19, 1934, 4.

42. Powers, *G-Men*, 129.

Chapter Two: The Networker

1. Louis B. Nichols, memorandum to Clyde Tolson, November 29, 1944, FBI 94-1-31913-33X4.

2. Louis B. Nichols, memorandum to Robert E. Joseph, March 25, 1936, FBI 67-39021-71.

3. Louis B. Nichols, memorandum to Robert E. Joseph, February 4, 1936, FBI 67039021-70.

4. J. Edgar Hoover, memorandum to Robert E. Joseph, January 16, 1937, FBI 67-80004-83.

5. J. Edgar Hoover, handwritten note on Hugh Clegg, memorandum to J. Edgar Hoover, December 22, 1936, unserialized (Nichols Personnel File).

6. Clyde Tolson and J. Edgar Hoover, handwritten notes on Louis B. Nichols, memorandum to Clyde Tolson, May 18, 1951, FBI 67-39021-406.

7. Unsigned memorandum to J. Edgar Hoover, April 13, 1936, FBI 67-0-4584.

8. Athan Theoharis, Tony G. Poveda, Susan Rosenfeld, and Richard Gid Powers, eds., *The FBI: A Comprehensive Reference Guide* (New York: Oryx Press, 2000), 346.

9. Matthew Cecil, *Hoover's FBI and the Fourth Estate: The Campaign to Control the Press and the Bureau's Image* (Lawrence: University Press of Kansas, 2014), 43–75.

10. Theoharis et al., *FBI*, 346.

11. Ibid.

12. Frederick L. Collins to [redacted, probably Milton Biow], September 18, 1944, FBI 94-1-31913-29X.

13. Nichols to Tolson, November 29, 1944.

14. For a comprehensive exploration of the development of the FBI's entertainment narrative formula, see Richard Gid Powers, *G-Men: The FBI in American Popular Culture* (Carbondale: Southern Illinois University Press, 1983).

15. Athan Theoharis and John Stuart Cox, *The Boss: J. Edgar Hoover and the Great American Inquisition* (Philadelphia: Temple University Press, 1988), 157. For a review of the cultural growth of the FBI during Hoover's tenure, see Powers, *G-Men*.

16. For a thorough review of the legitimacy questions surrounding the FBI, see Cecil, *Hoover's FBI*.

17. Robert D. McFadden, "Phillips H. Lord Is Dead at 73; Created 'Gangbusters' on Radio," *New York Times*, October 20, 1975, 36.

18. Theoharis et al., *FBI*, 275–276.

19. Ibid.

20. Phillips H. Lord, letter to J. Edgar Hoover, January 3, 1936, FBI 62-39708-1X.

21. Maurice F. Hanson, letter to J. Edgar Hoover, January 7, 1936, FBI 62-39708-1.

22. See Cecil, *Hoover's FBI*.

23. Carl Behrens, "Henry Suydam, 64, Dead; State Dept. Press Officer," *Washington Post and Times-Herald*, December 12, 1955, 16.

24. J. Edgar Hoover, memorandum to Henry Suydam, January 20, 1936, FBI 62-39708-6.

25. J. Edgar Hoover, memorandum to Clyde Tolson, January 23, 1936, FBI 62-39708-7.

26. Phillips H. Lord, letter to Clyde Tolson, January 27, 1936, FBI 62-39708-11.

27. SAC Rhea E. Whitley, New York, personal and confidential letter to J. Edgar Hoover, February 5, 1936, FBI 62-39708-12.

28. Rhea E. Whitley, memorandum to Clyde Tolson, February 6, 1936, FBI 62-39708-14, 1, 3.

29. J. Edgar Hoover, memorandum to Henry Suydam, March 3, 1936, FBI 62-39708-23.

30. Edward A. Tamm, memorandum to J. Edgar Hoover, February 29, 1936, FBI 62-39708-28.

31. Hoover to Suydam, March 3, 1936.

32. J. Edgar Hoover, memorandum to Clyde Tolson, March 4, 1936, FBI 97-39708-26.

33. Phillips H. Lord, letter to J. Edgar Hoover, August 6, 1936, FBI 62-39708-49.

34. J. Edgar Hoover, letter to Phillips H. Lord, August 11, 1936, FBI 62-39708-49.

35. Phillips H. Lord, letter to J. Edgar Hoover, September 8, 1936, FBI 62-39708-52.

36. J. Edgar Hoover, letter to Phillips H. Lord, September 15, 1936, FBI 62-39708-52.

37. Phillips H. Lord, letter to J. Edgar Hoover, May 18, 1937, FBI 62-39708-64.

38. J. Edgar Hoover, letter to Phillips H. Lord, May 21, 1937, FBI 62-39708-64.

39. "The Brady Gang," FBI website, accessed at https://www.fbi.gov/about-us/history/famous-cases/the-brady-gang/.

40. J. Edgar Hoover, handwritten note on Gwen Jones, letter to J. Edgar Hoover, October 29, 1937, FBI 62-39708-71.

41. Mrs. J. P. Adams, letter to J. Edgar Hoover, March 18, 1937, FBI 62-39708-58.

42. William Connery, letter to J. Edgar Hoover, December 16, 1937, FBI 62-39708-74.

43. Leona Hosford, letter to J. Edgar Hoover, December 9, 1937, FBI 62-39708-72.

44. T. L. Bath, letter to J. Edgar Hoover, January 24, 1938, FBI 62-39708-75.

45. W. R. Glavin, memorandum to Clyde Tolson, September 7, 1938, FBI 62-39708-85.

46. J. Edgar Hoover, letter to Frank R. McNinch, January 29, 1938, FBI 62-39708-75.

47. Louis B. Nichols, memorandum to Clyde Tolson, November 17, 1943, FBI 62-39708-140.

48. Leonard L. Bass, letter to John J. McGuire, November 17, 1943, FBI 62-39708-141.

49. J. Edgar Hoover, letter to Leonard L. Bass, November 20, 1943, FBI 62-39708-141.

50. O. H. Patterson, memorandum for Louis B. Nichols, February 15, 1944, FBI 62-39708-147.

51. Louis B. Nichols, memorandum to Clyde Tolson, April 11, 1945, FBI 94-1-31913-49.

52. Ibid.

53. Frederick L. Collins, letter to J. Edgar Hoover, September 28, 1944, FBI 94-1-31913-28X3. Though Hoover's disapproval is not mentioned in FBI memoranda, it was clearly communicated to Collins, who began the letter with "I am sorry that the first draft of the radio program did not please you."

54. Frederick L. Collins, letter to Louis B. Nichols, September 18, 1944, FBI 94-1-31913-28X.

55. Frederick L. Collins, letter to Clyde Tolson, September 21, 1944, FBI 94-1-31913-28X1.

56. Louis B. Nichols, memorandum to Clyde Tolson, September 25, 1944, FBI 94-1-31913-28X2.

57. Frederick L. Collins, memorandum to J. Edgar Hoover, September 28, 1944, FBI 94-1-31913-28X3.

58. Louis B. Nichols, memorandum to Clyde Tolson, October 2, 1944, FBI 94-1-31913-28X7.

59. Ibid.

60. Louis B. Nichols, memorandum to Clyde Tolson, October 31, 1944, FBI 94-1-31913-29X, 2.

61. Ibid., 3.

62. Frederick L. Collins, letter to Louis B. Nichols, December 28, 1944, FBI 94-1-31913-29X.

63. Frederick L. Collins, undated letter to Louis B. Nichols (ca. December 1944), FBI 94-1-31913-29X.

64. Ibid.

65. Louis B. Nichols, memorandum to Clyde Tolson, January 10, 1945, FBI 94-1-31913-35X.

66. Louis B. Nichols, letter to Frederick L. Collins, January 9, 1945, FBI 94-1-31913-unserialized.

67. Frederick L. Collins, letter to Louis B. Nichols, January 12, 1945, FBI 94-1-31913-39.

68. Ibid.

69. [Redacted], letter to Louis B. Nichols, January 16, 1945, FBI 94-1-31913-39X; [Redacted], letter to Louis B. Nichols, January 17, 1945, FBI 94-1-31913-40.

70. J. Edgar Hoover, handwritten note on office routing slip, January 18, 1945, FBI 94-1-31913-unserialized.

71. For a review of the FBI's granular control of its authorized television program in the 1960s and 1970s, see Cecil, *Hoover's FBI*, 265–281.

72. Louis B. Nichols, memorandum to Clyde Tolson, January 30, 1945, FBI 94-1-31913-41, 1–3.

73. Louis B. Nichols, memorandum to Clyde Tolson, February 2, 1945, FBI 94-1-31913-42, 1.

74. J. Edgar Hoover, handwritten note on [Redacted], letter to J. Edgar Hoover, February 11, 1945, FBI 94-1-31913-43.

75. Louis B. Nichols, memorandum to Clyde Tolson, February 2, 1945, FBI 94-1-31913-38.

76. J. Edgar Hoover, letter to [Redacted], April 3, 1945, FBI 94-1-31913-47.

77. Louis B. Nichols, memorandum to Clyde Tolson, February 19, 1945, FBI 94-1-31913-44X.

78. Ibid.

79. "This Is Your FBI," memorandum, undated [probably early March 1945], FBI 94-1-31913-unserialized, 1.

80. Ibid.

81. Ibid., 2.

82. SAC, San Francisco, telegram to J. Edgar Hoover, March 17, 1948, FBI 94-1-31913-89.

83. J. Edgar Hoover, memorandum to Thomas C. Clark, March 18, 1947, FBI 94-1-31913-unserialized, 2.

84. Freund recounted the 1947 committee findings in Arthur J. Freund, "The Mass Media before the Bar," *Hollywood Quarterly* 4, no. 1 (Autumn 1949): 90.

85. Ibid., 92.

86. Jack Gould, "NBC to Ban Its Crime Shows Except after 9:30 at Night," *New York Times*, September 14, 1947, 1.

87. Jack Gould, "Networks Deride 'Crime Ban' of NBC," *New York Times*, September 15, 1947, 1.

88. Mark Woods, letter to J. Edgar Hoover, September 23, 1947, FBI 94-1-31913-unserialized.

89. J. Edgar Hoover, letter to Mark Woods, September 27, 1947, FBI 94-1-31913-unserialized.

90. "FBI Head Urges Maximum Audience for Crime Prevention Broadcasts," ABC news release, October 7, 1947, FBI 94-1-31913-unserialized.

91. J. Edgar Hoover, memorandum to Leo M. Cadison, November 5, 1947, FBI 94-1-31913-unserialized, 1.

92. "Merits of FBI Radio Show Debated at Bar Meeting," *St. Louis Post-Dispatch*, September 8, 1949, 1.

93. Ibid.

94. J. Edgar Hoover, telegram to SAC, Los Angeles, November 19, 1947, FBI 94-1-31913-83.

95. "Georgia Mob of 20 Men Massacres 2 Negroes, Wives; One Was Ex-GI," *New York Times*, July 27, 1946, 1, 32.

96. "FBI Investigated Politics in '46 Lynching of 2 Georgia Couples," *New York Times*, June 16, 2007, accessed at http://www.nytimes.com/2007/06/16/us/16lynching.html.

97. Ibid.

98. John D. Morris, "Truman Creates Civil Rights Board," *New York Times*, December 6, 1946, 1.

99. J. C. Strickland, memorandum to D. M. "Mickey" Ladd, April 9, 1947, FBI 12-82915-3.

100. Robert K. Carr, letter to J. Edgar Hoover, March 7, 1947, FBI 62-82915-1.

101. The President's Committee on Civil Rights, transcript of Thursday, March 20, 1947, FBI 62-82915-unserialized, 80.

102. Ibid., 94.

103. Ibid., 106.

104. Ibid.

105. J. C. Strickland, memorandum to D. M. "Mickey" Ladd, April 9, 1947, FBI 62-82915-3.

106. Theoharis et al., *FBI*, 338.

107. D. M. "Mickey" Ladd, memorandum to J. Edgar Hoover, September 10, 1947, FBI 62-82915-33, 1, 2.

108. J. Edgar Hoover, letter to Charles E. Wilson, September 9, 1947, FBI 62-82915-21, 1, 2.

109. Louis B. Nichols, memorandum to Clyde Tolson, September 10, 1947, FBI 62-82915-8, 1.

110. Ibid.

111. J. Edgar Hoover, handwritten note on Nichols to Tolson, September 10, 1947, 2.

112. Louis B. Nichols, memorandum to Clyde Tolson, September 10, 1947, FBI 62-82915-13, 1, 2.

113. Louis B. Nichols, memorandum to Clyde Tolson, September 13, 1947, FBI 62-82915-18.

114. Report attached to Louis B. Nichols, memorandum to Clyde Tolson, September 12, 1947, FBI 62-82915-19, 6.

115. Ibid., 1.

116. Report attached to Louis B. Nichols, memorandum to Clyde Tolson, September 12, 1947, FBI 62-82915-19, 7.

117. Ibid., 8.

118. J. Edgar Hoover, handwritten note on Nichols to Tolson, September 12, 1947, 2.

119. Clyde Tolson, handwritten note on Nichols to Tolson, September 12, 1947, 2.

120. Louis B. Nichols, memorandum to Clyde Tolson, September 13, 1947, FBI 62-82915-23, 1.

121. Louis B. Nichols, memorandum to Clyde Tolson, October 3, 1947, FBI 62-82915-25, 1.

122. Ibid.

123. Ibid., 2.

124. Ibid.

125. J. Edgar Hoover, memorandum to T. Vincent Quinn, August 25, 1947, FBI 62-82915-29.

126. J. Edgar Hoover, letter to Charles E. Wilson, September 29, 1947, FBI 62-82915-unserialized.

127. Nichols to Tolson, October 3, 1947, 3.

128. Ibid.

129. Ibid.

130. Louis B. Nichols, memorandum to Clyde Tolson, October 11, 1947, FBI 62-82915-30.

131. Louis B. Nichols, memorandum to Clyde Tolson, October 14, 1947, FBI 62-82915-31.

132. Louis B. Nichols, memorandum to Clyde Tolson, November 3, 1947, FBI 62-82915-36.

133. J. Edgar Hoover, handwritten note on Nichols to Tolson, November 3, 1947.

134. J. Edgar Hoover, handwritten note on Emanuel Celler, letter to J. Edgar Hoover, November 13, 1947, FBI 62-82915-40.

135. Edward A. Tamm, memorandum to D. M. "Mickey" Ladd, December 23, 1947, FBI 62-82915-44.

136. Louis B. Nichols, memorandum to Clyde Tolson, August 5, 1949, FBI 62-82915-49.

137. "Commie Report on Williams Came from FBI, Disclosed," *Cincinnati Times*, October 10, 1953, 1.

138. Louis B. Nichols, memorandum to Clyde Tolson, October 12, 1953, FBI 62-98619-unserialized.

139. Ibid., 3.

140. J. Edgar Hoover, handwritten note on Nichols to Tolson, October 12, 1953, 4.

141. Nichols to Tolson, October 12, 1953.

142. Ibid., 3.

143. Louis B. Nichols, memorandum to Clyde Tolson, October 23, 1953, FBI 62-98619-unserialized, 2.

144. Speech text attached to Gordon A. Nease, memorandum to Clyde Tolson, May 12, 1958, FBI 62-98519-16, 3, 5.

145. Louis B. Nichols, memorandum to Clyde Tolson, May 28, 1953, FBI 100-114575-1.

146. "Professor Harry A. Overstreet Dies; Author and Lecturer Was 94," *New York Times*, August 18, 1970, 35.

147. "Bonaro W. Overstreet, Author, Is Dead at 82," *New York Times*, September 11, 1985, accessed at http://www.nytimes.com/1985/09/11/arts/bonaro-w-overstreet -author-is-dead-at-82.html.

148. Harry Overstreet obituary, *New York Times*.

149. Harry A. Overstreet, "Information for the Committee on Un-American Activities," July 22, 1953, FBI 100-114575-unserialized, 2.

150. Ibid., 7–12.

151. Harold H. Velde, letter to Harry A. Overstreet, October 7, 1953, FBI 100-114575-unserialized.

152. Richard B. Evans, "An Open Letter," *Tucson Daily Citizen*, December 7, 1953, 2.

153. Bonaro Overstreet, letter to Louis B. Nichols, November 21, 1954, FBI 100-114575-28.

154. Louis B. Nichols, memorandum to Clyde Tolson, November 22, 1954, FBI 100-114575-28, 2.

155. Cartha DeLoach, memorandum to Louis B. Nichols, December 6, 1954, FBI 100-114575-29.

156. Louis B. Nichols, memorandum to Clyde Tolson, April 12, 1955, FBI 100-114575-32, 2.

157. Louis B. Nichols, memorandum to Clyde Tolson, May 16, 1955, FBI 100-114575-33, 2.

158. Bonaro Overstreet, letter to Louis B. Nichols, May 14, 1955, FBI 100-114575-33, 2.

159. Louis B. Nichols, memorandum to Clyde Tolson, October 19, 1955, FBI 100-114575-43.

160. Mrs. V. M. Haldiman, letter to the editor, *Phoenix Republic*, December 4, 1955, FBI 100-114575-44.

161. Lottie Holman O'Neill, letter to J. Edgar Hoover, December 10, 1955, FBI 100-114575-46.

162. Clyde Tolson, handwritten note on Milton A. Jones, memorandum to Louis B. Nichols, December 9, 1955, FBI 100-114575-47, 2.

163. Louis B. Nichols, memorandum to Clyde Tolson, December 13, 1955, FBI 100-114575-48, 1.

164. J. Edgar Hoover, handwritten note on Nichols to Tolson, December 13, 1955, FBI 100-114575-48, 2.

165. Verland M. Haldiman, letter to J. Edgar Hoover, December 7, 1955, FBI 100-114575-51, 2.

166. Louis B. Nichols, handwritten note on Louis B. Nichols, memorandum to Clyde Tolson, February 20, 1956, FBI 100-114575-57.

167. Louis B. Nichols, memorandum to Clyde Tolson, July 10, 1956, FBI 100-114575-unserialized.

168. Ibid.

169. Louis B. Nichols, letter to Harry A. Overstreet, July 10, 1956, FBI 100-114575-109.

170. Harry and Bonaro Overstreet, "Crime's Face Looks Like Your Own," *Detroit Free Press*, December 2, 1956, C6.

171. Louis B. Nichols, memorandum to Clyde Tolson, July 8, 1957, FBI 100-114575-80.

172. Ibid.

173. Clyde Tolson, handwritten note on William C. Sullivan, memorandum to Alan H. Belmont, April 8, 1959, FBI 100-114575-108, 2.

174. R. W. Smith, memorandum to William C. Sullivan, January 22, 1963, FBI 100-114575-unserialized.

175. Dr. C. P. King, letter to J. Edgar Hoover, July 15, 1936, FBI 67-39021-89.

176. Louis B. Nichols, letter to J. Edgar Hoover, July 17, 1935, FBI 67-39021-86.

177. Press release, "Louis B. Nichols," October 17, 1957, FBI 67-39021-unserialized, 1.

178. Louis B. Nichols, letter to J. Edgar Hoover, October 15, 1957, FBI 67-39021-572.

179. Frederick C. Belen, letter to Louis B. Nichols, October 23, 1957, FBI 67-39021-583.

180. Leslie C. Stratton, letter to Louis B. Nichols, October 23, 1957, FBI 67-39021-584.

181. Charles S. Rhyne, letter to Louis B. Nichols, October 21, 1957, FBI 67-39021-585.

182. For example, Michael A. Gorman (*Flint [Mich.] Journal*), letter to Louis B. Nichols, October 21, 1957, FBI 67-39021-587; Barry Feris (International News Service), letter to Louis B. Nichols, October 23, 1957, FBI 67-39021-588.

183. Sen. James Eastland, letter to Louis B. Nichols, October 21, 1957, FBI 67-39021-590.

184. Sen. Estes Kefauver, letter to Louis B. Nichols, October 21, 1957, FBI 67-39021-593.

185. Sen. Lyndon B. Johnson, letter to Louis B. Nichols, October 31, 1957, FBI 67-39021-608.

186. Rex Collier, "Loss to Government," *Washington Star*, November 4, 1957, A12.

187. Hank Messick, "The Schenley Chapter," *Nation*, April 5, 1971, 428–431.

188. Ovid Demaris, *The Director: An Oral Biography of J. Edgar Hoover* (New York: Harper's Magazine Press, 1975), 67–68.

189. Nicholas Gage, "Rosenstiel Link to Crime Denied," *New York Times*, March 12, 1971, 33.

190. Ibid.

191. Messick, 430, 431.

192. Gage, "Rosenstiel Link to Crime Denied."

193. Demaris, *Director*, 92.

194. "Watchers," UPI story, November 6, 1968, FBI 67-39021-2147.

195. J. Edgar Hoover, handwritten note on "Watchers," November 6, 1968.

196. Marvin Smilon, "J. Edgar Hoover Fund Pledged $1,000,000," *New York Post*, June 1, 1968, 1.

197. Maxine Cheshire, "The Director and the Foundation," *Washington Post*, June 1, 1969, E1, E2.

198. Demaris, *Director*, 99–100.

199. The FBI maintained a series of files on Cohn, including investigations of alleged impropriety, a series of threats against him, and a lengthy file of "miscellaneous/nonsubversive" information primarily focused on his dealings with the FBI.

200. Louis B. Nichols, memorandum to Clyde Tolson, January 21, 1954, FBI 62-97564-26, 1, 2.

201. Louis B. Nichols, memorandum to Clyde Tolson, January 5, 1953, FBI 62-97564-13, 1.

202. Ibid., 2.

203. Louis B. Nichols, memorandum to Clyde Tolson, December 10, 1956, FBI 62-97564-67.

204. Alan H. Belmont, memorandum to D. M. "Mickey" Ladd, January 18, 1954, FBI 62-97564-27.

205. J. Edgar Hoover, handwritten note on Belmont to Ladd, January 18, 1954, 2.

206. Albin Krebs, "Roy Cohn, Aide to McCarthy and Fiery Lawyer, Dies at 59," *New York Times*, August 3, 1986, accessed at http://www.nytimes.com/1986/08/03/obituaries/roy-cohn-aide-to-mccarthy-and-fiery-lawyer-dies-at-59.html.

207. SAC, New York, memorandum to J. Edgar Hoover, May 9, 1969, FBI 67-39021-unserialized, 1–2.

208. William Lambert, "The Hotshot One-Man Roy," *Life*, September 5, 1969, 30.

209. J. Edgar Hoover, handwritten note on SAC, New York, to J. Edgar Hoover, May 7, 1969, FBI 67-39021-unserialized.

210. J. Edgar Hoover, handwritten note on SAC, New York, to J. Edgar Hoover, May 9, 1969, FBI 67-39021-unserialized, 4.

211. Louis B. Nichols, letter to L. Patrick Gray, April 24, 1973, FBI 67-39021-779.

Chapter Three: Speaking with One Voice

1. David Nasaw, *The Patriarch: The Remarkable Life and Turbulent Times of Joseph P. Kennedy* (New York: Penguin Books, 2013), 539.

2. Ibid.

3. Edward A. Soucy, letter to J. Edgar Hoover, September 7, 1943, FBI 94-37808-1X.

4. J. Edgar Hoover, letter to Edward A. Soucy, October 18, 1943, FBI 94-37808-unserialized.

5. J. Edgar Hoover, SAC Letter No. 50, series 1950, July 31, 1950, FBI 66-04-1162, 2.

6. Edward A. Soucy, letter to J. Edgar Hoover, December 27, 1943, FBI 94-37808-unserialized, 2.

7. SAC Boston, memorandum to J. Edgar Hoover, August 4, 1950, FBI 94-37808-5X.

8. SAC Boston, memorandum to J. Edgar Hoover, January 11, 1955, FBI 94-37808-unserialized.

9. Alan H. Belmont, memorandum to D. M. "Mickey" Ladd, October 16, 1953, FBI 67-045-1732.

10. J. Edgar Hoover, memorandum to Edward A. Tamm, Hugh Clegg, November 18, 1940, FBI 66-9330-2, 2.

11. Alan H. Belmont, memorandum to D. Milton "Mickey" Ladd, July 31, 1950, FBI 66-9330-204, 1.

12. J. Edgar Hoover, speech to the 22nd Annual Convention, American Legion, Boston, Mass., September 23, 1940, 1, Athan Theoharis, FBI Investigation and Surveillance Records, Raynor Library Special Collections, Marquette University.

13. Ibid., 6.

14. Athan Theoharis and John Stuart Cox, *The Boss: J. Edgar Hoover and the Great American Inquisition* (Philadelphia: Temple University Press, 1988), 181.

15. Hoover to Tamm, Clegg, November 18, 1940, 1.

16. Ibid.

17. J. Edgar Hoover, memorandum to Attorney General Robert H. Jackson, November 18, 1940, FBI 66-9330-1, 1.

18. Ibid.

19. Hoover to Tamm, Clegg, November 18, 1940, 3.

20. J. Edgar Hoover, memorandum to Seat of Government administrators, February 4, 1941, FBI 66-9330-27.

21. Theoharis and Cox, *Boss*, 195.

22. *Bureau Bulletin*, no. 34158, December 2, 1940, FBI 66-9330-5, 2–3.

23. R. J. Brandt, memorandum to Edward A. Tamm, February 8, 1941, FBI 66-9330-30, 2; J. Edgar Hoover, letter to SACs, April 29, 1941, FBI 66-9330-44.

24. Percy E. Foxworth, memorandum to J. Edgar Hoover, April 29, 1941, FBI 66-9330-49, 7; J. Edgar Hoover, handwritten note on Foxworth to Hoover, April 29, 1941, 1.

25. Marquis James, "The Voice of the New Day," *American Legion Weekly* 1, no. 4 (November 28, 1919): 8.

26. B. Edwin Sackett, letter to J. Edgar Hoover, May 6, 1941, FBI 66-9330-50, 2.

27. J. Edgar Hoover, memorandum to Clyde Tolson, Edward A. Tamm, and Percy E. Foxworth, May 1, 1941, FBI 66-9330-46, 2.

28. Sackett, letter to Hoover, May 6, 1941, 4.

29. Ibid.

30. Percy. E Foxworth, memorandum to J. Edgar Hoover, July 26, 1941, FBI 66-9330-67, 5.

31. J. Edgar Hoover, letter to SACs, October 7, 1941, FBI 66-9330-70, 1.

32. B. Edwin Sackett, letter to J. Edgar Hoover, September 27, 1941, FBI 66-9330-75, 2.

33. Hoover to SACs, October 7, 1941, 1.

34. Edward A. Tamm, memorandum to J. Edgar Hoover, November 4, 1941, FBI 66-9330-77, with attached form letters.

35. J. Edgar Hoover, *Bureau Bulletin*, no. 63, second series 1941, FBI 66-9330-unserialized, 1.

36. Ibid., 9.

37. J. Edgar Hoover, *Bureau Bulletin*, no. 27, first series 1942, FBI 66-9330-99, 1.

38. Birmingham SAC, memorandum to J. Edgar Hoover, June 2, 1930, FBI 67-322-15.

39. L. M. Olney, letter to R. E. Vetterli, July 2, 1930, FBI 67-322-unserialized.

40. J. S. Egan, memorandum to J. Edgar Hoover, October 3, 1933, FBI 67-11938-99.

41. Assignment History of Lee R. Pennington, undated, FBI 67-11938-unserialized.

42. Edward A. Tamm, Efficiency Rating Sheet for Lee R. Pennington, May 1, 1938, FBI 67-11938-230, 2.

43. J. Edgar Hoover, letter to Lee R. Pennington, September 24, 1940, FBI 67-11938-256.

44. B. Edwin Sackett, letter to J. Edgar Hoover, November 6, 1941, FBI 67-11938-268.

45. Lee R. Pennington, memorandum to Alex Rosen, January 29, 1942, FBI 67-11938-273.

46. Lee R. Pennington, memorandum to J. Edgar Hoover, July 21, 1943, FBI 67-11938-286.

47. J. Edgar Hoover, letter to Lee R. Pennington, July 31, 1944, FBI 67-11938-298.

48. Lee R. Pennington, memorandum to Edward A. Tamm, April 30, 1942, FBI 66-9330-114, 1, 4.

49. J. Edgar Hoover, handwritten note on Pennington to Tamm, April 30, 1942, 4.

50. D. M. "Mickey" Ladd, memorandum to J. Edgar Hoover, FBI 66-9330-130.

51. J. Edgar Hoover, SAC Letter No. 243, series 1943, June 11, 1943, FBI 66-9330-126.

52. G. C. Callan, memorandum to D. M. "Mickey" Ladd, July 12, 1943, FBI 66-9330-127, 1.

53. J. Edgar Hoover, SAC Letter No. 440, series 1943, November 18, 1943, FBI 66-9330-132, 1.

54. Ibid., 2.

55. Executive Conference, memorandum to J. Edgar Hoover, November 1, 1945, FBI 66-9330-171.

56. *Bureau Bulletin*, page attached to Clyde Tolson and Edward A. Tamm, memorandum to J. Edgar Hoover, November 1, 1945, FBI 66-9330-171.

57. Executive Conference, memorandum to J. Edgar Hoover, July 17, 1950, FBI 66-9330-205, 1.

58. Ibid., 1–2.

59. Ibid., 2.

60. Lee R. Pennington, memorandum to D. Milton "Mickey" Ladd, July 26, 1950, FBI 94-1-17998-922.

61. J. Edgar Hoover, *Bureau Bulletin*, no. 42, series 1950, August 14, 1950, FBI 66-9330-204, 3–4.

62. D. Milton "Mickey" Ladd, memorandum to J. Edgar Hoover, July 18, 1951, FBI 66-933-242.

63. Clyde Tolson for the Executive Conference, memorandum to J. Edgar Hoover, September 6, 1951, FBI 66-9330-252, 1–2.

64. Ibid., 2.

65. Ibid.

66. Ibid., 3.

67. J. Edgar Hoover, handwritten note on routing slip, September 6, 1951, FBI 66-9330-252.

68. J. Edgar Hoover, handwritten note on Lee R. Pennington, memorandum to D. Milton "Mickey" Ladd, October 31, 1951, FBI 94-1-17998-969.

69. D. Milton "Mickey" Ladd, memorandum to J. Edgar Hoover, October 29, 1951, FBI 66-9330-256.

70. D. Milton "Mickey" Ladd, memorandum to J. Edgar Hoover, January 25, 1952, FBI 66-9330-258.

71. SAC Letter No. 27, series 1952, March 15, 1952, FBI 66-9330-270, 7.

72. D. Milton "Mickey" Ladd, memorandum to J. Edgar Hoover, April 28, 1952, FBI 66-9330-271.

73. Clyde Tolson for the Executive Conference, memorandum to J. Edgar Hoover, April 24, 1952, FBI 66-9330-278, 1–2.

74. For example, SAC Letter No. 58, series 1952, June 19, 1952, FBI 66-9330-285, simplified tracking of contacts by local offices.

75. Alan H. Belmont, memorandum to D. Milton "Mickey" Ladd, October 2, 1952, FBI 66-9330-297, 4.

76. Ibid., 3.

77. D. Milton "Mickey" Ladd, memorandum to J. Edgar Hoover, January 21, 1953, FBI 66-9330-308.

78. C. W. Stein, memorandum to J. Edgar Hoover, July 27, 1954, FBI 66-9330-354, 1.

79. Ibid., 2.

80. Athan Theoharis, "The FBI and the American Legion Contact Program, 1940–1966," *Political Science Quarterly* 100, no. 2 (Summer 1985): 280.

81. J. Edgar Hoover, memorandum to Clyde Tolson, October 27, 1953, FBI 67-11938-384; "F.B.I. Man in Legion Post: Pennington to Head National Americanism Commission," *New York Times*, November 19, 1953, 12.

82. Lee R. Pennington, letter to J. Edgar Hoover, November 2, 1953, FBI 67-11938-383.

83. See, for example, Lee R. Pennington, letter to J. Edgar Hoover, November 24, 1953, FBI 97-1-17998-1040.

84. Lee R. Pennington, letter to D. Milton "Mickey" Ladd, January 14, 1954, FBI 94-1-17998-1046.

85. Lee R. Pennington, letter to D. Milton "Mickey" Ladd, January 15, 1954, FBI 94-1-17998-1049.

86. Joseph A. Sizoo, memorandum to Alan H. Belmont, February 1, 1954, FBI 94-1-17998-1098.

87. Louis B. Nichols, memorandum to Clyde Tolson, February 24, 1954, FBI 94-1-17998-1050x.

88. Milton A. Jones, memorandum to Louis B. Nichols, March 25, 1954, FBI 94-1-17998-1054.

89. Louis B. Nichols, memorandum to Clyde Tolson, May 15, 1954, FBI 67-338728-unserialized.

90. Lee R. Pennington, letter to J. Edgar Hoover, July 1, 1954, FBI 94-1-17998-1074.

91. Louis B. Nichols, memorandum to Clyde Tolson, August 10, 1954, FBI 94-1-17998-1102.

92. Alan H. Belmont, memorandum to Leland V. Boardman, August 3, 1954, FBI 66-9330-357, 2.

93. SAC Letter No. 54-42, August 17, 1954, FBI 66-9330-357, 4.

94. Fred J. Baumgardner, memorandum to Alan H. Belmont, December 22, 1958, FBI 66-9330-379, 2.

95. Theoharis, "FBI and the American Legion," 281.

96. Fred J. Baumgardner, memorandum to William C. Sullivan, September 17, 1964, FBI 66-9330-406, 2.

97. Fred J. Baumgardner, memorandum to William C. Sullivan, February 16, 1965, FBI 66-9330-409, 1.

98. Fred J. Baumgardner, memorandum to William C. Sullivan, March 7, 1966, FBI 66-9330-417, 1.

99. Cathleen Thom and Patrick Jung, "The Responsibilities Program of the FBI, 1951–1955," *Historian* 59, no. 2 (December 1997): 348.

100. Theoharis, "FBI and the American Legion," 273.

101. Ibid., 286.

Chapter Four: The Editor and the Professor

1. "Luncheon Guests at the White House," *Washington Post*, January 19, 1968, E2.

2. Transcript, Elizabeth Carpenter Oral History Interview, April 4, 1969, by Joe B. Frantz, p. 33, Lyndon Johnson Presidential Library, accessed at http://www.lbjlibrary.net/assets/documents/archives/oral_histories/carpenter_e/carpenter_2_web.pdf.

3. Marie Smith, "Eartha Kitt Confronts the Johnsons: Startled First Lady Responds to Singer's Attack on War," *Washington Post*, January 19, 1968, A1.

4. Ibid.

5. Transcript, Carpenter Oral History Interview, 34.

6. Ibid.

7. UPI, "Eartha Kit Denounces War Policy to Mrs. Johnson," *New York Times*, January 20, 1968, 1.

8. Smith, "Earth Kitt Confronts the Johnsons," 1.

9. Ibid.

10. Remarks at First Lady's Luncheon for Women Doers, January 18, 1968, Social Files, Elizabeth Carpenter, Subject Files, Box 45, reprinted in Janet Mezzack, "Without Manners You Are Nothing: Lady Bird Johnson, Eartha Kitt, and the Women Doers' Luncheon of January 18, 1968," *Presidential Studies Quarterly* 20, no. 4 (Fall 1990): 750.

11. Ibid.

12. Ibid.

13. Ibid.

14. Milton A. Jones, memorandum to Thomas E. Bishop, January 19, 1968, FBI 67-204108-415, 1.

15. Damon Runyon, Jr., "'Sour Notes' and 'Mawkish Indignation,'" *Washington Examiner*, January 26–28, 1968, 6.

16. "From the Heart of Eartha Kitt," *New York Times*, January 20, 1968, 28.

17. Nancy H. Dickerson, letter to Lyndon Baines Johnson, January 24, 1968, White House Social Files, Alphabetical Files, "Dickerson, Mrs. C. Wyatt (Nancy H.)," Box 665, emphasis in original, reprinted in Mezzack, "Without Manners," 753.

18. "Miss Kitt Defends Remarks on War; Denies Rudeness," *New York Times*, January 23, 1968, 21.

19. Transcript, Carpenter Oral History Interview, 35.

20. "Mrs. Johnson Sorry Furor Obscured Other Ideas," *New York Times*, January 20, 1968, 5.

21. Mezzack, "Without Manners," 750.

22. Bernard F. Conners, *Don't Embarrass the Bureau* (New York: Bobbs Merrill, 1972), 30.

23. M. Wesley Swearingen, *FBI Secrets: An Agent's Exposé* (Boston: South End Press, 1999), 5.

24. Ibid., 6.

25. Nicholas deB. Katzenbach, testimony, Senate Select Committee to Study Governmental Operations with Respect to Intelligence Agencies, 94th Cong., December 3, 1975, vol. 6, 209.

26. Transcript, Oral History Interview with Former Special Agent James R. Healy (1948–1980), May 3, 2007, by Sandra Robinette, Society of Former Special Agents of the FBI, Inc., 31, accessed at http://www.nleomf.org/assets/pdfs/nlem/oral-histories/FBI_Healy_interview.pdf.

27. Athan Theoharis and John Stuart Cox, *The Boss: J. Edgar Hoover and the Great American Inquisition* (Philadelphia: Temple University Press, 1988), 353.

28. Richard Daley, telephone conversation with Lyndon Baines Johnson and Lady Bird Johnson, January 20, 1968, 10:05 a.m., Tape WH6801.01, Citation No. 12606, digital version accessed via the University of Virginia Miller Center at http://millercenter.org/presidentialrecordings/lbj-wh6801.01-12606.

29. Joseph A. Sizoo, memorandum to William C. Sullivan, January 19, 1968, FBI 62-1120092-unserialized, 1–2.

30. Milton A. Jones, memorandum to Louis B. Nichols, December 22, 1953, FBI 62-52444-unserialized, 2.

31. Milton A. Jones, memorandum to Robert E. Wick, December 28, 1966, FBI 62-107060-4371, 2.

32. Jones to Bishop, January 19, 1967, 1.

33. J. Edgar Hoover, handwritten note on Jones to Bishop, January 19, 1967, 1.

34. Jones to Bishop, January 19, 1967, 2.

35. Ibid.

36. Ibid., 3.

37. J. Edgar Hoover, Clyde Tolson, and Cartha DeLoach, handwritten notes on Jones to Bishop, January 19, 1967, 3.

38. J. Edgar Hoover, letter to Milton A. Jones, January 22, 1968, FBI 67-109106-416 (emphasis added).

39. Milton A. Jones, "The Story of My Life," unpublished memoir, August 7, 1979, 32; a copy of the memoir was provided to the author by Jones's daughter, Dr. Muriel Jones Cashdollar.

40. Ibid., 34.

41. Ibid., 40.

42. Ibid., 44.

43. Alan H. Belmont, memorandum to Clyde Tolson, December 23, 1938, FBI 67-109106-4.

44. Jones, "Story of My Life," 47.

45. Ibid., 61.

46. Edward Scheidt, SAC, Charlotte, N.C., memorandum to J. Edgar Hoover, January 15, 1939, FBI 67-109106-10, 2.

47. Edward Scheidt, teletype to J. Edgar Hoover, January 19, 1939, FBI 67-109106-16.

48. J. E. Clegg, Memphis, Tenn., investigative report, January 28, 1939, FBI 67-109106-29, 2.

49. A. H. Crowl, Boston, investigative brief, January 25, 1939, FBI 67-109106-32, 1.

50. Jones, "Story of My Life," 62.

51. J. Edgar Hoover, telegram to Milton A. Jones, January 28, 1939, FBI 67-109106-35.

52. Jones, "Story of My Life," 64.

53. Milton A. Jones, telegram to J. Edgar Hoover, January 31, 1939, FBI 67-109106-37.

54. Milton A. Jones, letter to J. Edgar Hoover, January 31, 1939, FBI 67-109106-39.

55. Jones, "Story of My Life," 64.

56. Clyde Tolson, handwritten note on Jones to Hoover, January 31, 1939.

57. Milton A. Jones, telegram to J. Edgar Hoover, February 1, 1939, FBI 67-109106-42.

58. J. Edgar Hoover, memorandum to Hugh Clegg, February 3, 1939, FBI 67-109106-unserialized, 2.

59. Tony Poveda, "Controversies and Issues," in Athan Theoharis, Tony Poveda, Susan Rosenfeld, and Richard Gid Powers, eds., *The FBI: A Comprehensive Reference Guide* (New York: Oryx Press, 2000), 113.

60. Tony Poveda, "The Traditions and Culture of the FBI," in Theoharis et al., *FBI*, 175.

61. Theoharis et al., *FBI*, 4.

62. Harold Nathan, memorandum to J. Edgar Hoover, January 10, 1940, FBI 67-109106-59.

63. Louis B. Nichols, typewritten note on Nathan to Hoover, January 10, 1940.

64. Ibid.

65. Robert C. Hendon, memorandum to Clyde Tolson, April 9, 1940, FBI 67-109106-77.

66. Robert C. Hendon, memorandum to Clyde Tolson, April 9, 1940, FBI 67-109106-unserialized, 1.

67. Robert C. Hendon, memorandum to Louis B. Nichols, May 1, 1940, FBI 67-109106-78, 1.

68. Robert C. Hendon, "Remarks," Efficiency Rating Sheet, June 4, 1940, FBI 67-109106-unserialized, 2.

69. "Painter Confesses Plane Sabotage," *New York Times*, October 30, 1941, 13.

70. For useful descriptions of Hoover and Tolson, including discussion of Hoover's forgiving nature, see Ovid Demaris, *The Director: An Oral Biography of J. Edgar Hoover* (New York: Harper's Magazine Press, 1975), 3–53.

71. Milton A. Jones, memorandum to Louis B. Nichols, May 14, 1942, FBI 67-109106-103.

72. Ibid.

73. J. Edgar Hoover, letter to Milton A. Jones, May 28, 1942, FBI 67-109106-105.

74. J. Edgar Hoover, letter to Milton A. Jones, February 10, 1944, FBI 67-109106-117.

75. Hugh H. Clegg and W. R. Glavin, memorandum to the Director, June 13, 1944, FBI 67-109106-unserialized.

76. Ibid.

77. Louis B. Nichols, "General Comments," annual review of Milton A. Jones, March 31, 1945, FBI 67-109106-unserialized.

78. For example, on September 3, 1947, Jones was censured after one of his agents failed to identify the subject of a memorandum as a member of the American Legion. The next day, he was censured when reporter Hedda Hopper reported she was unhappy with the information she received from Crime Records. One month later, on October 11, he was censured for initialing as acceptable a letter, prepared by a member of his staff, that contained a typographic error. Jones's personnel file, FBI 67-109106, contains hundreds of censure letters.

79. John P. Mohr, memorandum to Clyde Tolson, January 25, 1949, FBI 67-109106-66, 2.

80. J. Edgar Hoover, handwritten note on Louis B. Nichols, memorandum to Clyde Tolson, October 17, 1949, FBI 67-80004-492.

81. J. Edgar Hoover, letter to Louis B. Nichols, February 16, 1950, FBI 67-109106-177.

82. J. Edgar Hoover, letter to Milton A. Jones, October 25, 1950, FBI 67-109106-186.

83. Louis B. Nichols, memorandum to Clyde Tolson, October 18, 1950, FBI 67-109106-unserialized.

84. Louis B. Nichols, memorandum to Clyde Tolson, October 18, 1950, FBI 67-80004-528.

85. Clyde Tolson, handwritten note on Nichols to Tolson, October 18, 1950, FBI 67-80004-528.

86. H. L. Edwards, memorandum to Mr. Glavin, February 5, 1951, FBI 67-109106-193.

87. Louis B. Nichols, memorandum to Clyde Tolson, November 20, 1950, FBI 62-25733-178, 1.

88. Ibid.

89. Louis B. Nichols, memorandum to Clyde Tolson, December 2, 1950, FBI 62-25733-179.

90. J. Edgar Hoover, letter to Milton A. Jones, February 10, 1951, FBI 67-109106-195.

91. Louis B. Nichols, memorandum to Clyde Tolson, September 7, 1955, FBI 67-109106-unserialized.

92. J. Edgar Hoover, handwritten note on Nichols to Tolson, September 7, 1955.

93. J. Edgar Hoover, letter to Milton A. Jones, November 15, 1956, FBI 67-109106-274.

94. Milton A. Jones, handwritten note on routing slip, ca. November 19, 1956, FBI 67-109106-284.

95. Louis B. Nichols, memorandum with no recipient listed, ca. November 19, 1956, FBI 67-109106-284, 1.

96. Clyde Tolson, memorandum to J. Edgar Hoover, November 19, 1956, FBI 67-109106-284.

97. J. Edgar Hoover, handwritten note on Tolson to Hoover, November 19, 1956.

98. J. Edgar Hoover, handwritten note on Louis B. Nichols, memorandum to Clyde Tolson, November 21, 1956, FBI 67-109106-275, 2.

99. Louis B. Nichols, memorandum to Clyde Tolson, November 21, 1956, FBI 67-109106-275, 1.

100. Jones, "Story of My Life," 90.

101. J. Edgar Hoover, memorandum to Clyde Tolson and John P. Mohr, November 23, 1956, FBI 67-109106-277, 2–3.

102. J. Edgar Hoover, letter to Milton A. Jones, June 6, 1957, FBI 67-109106-297.

103. J. Edgar Hoover, letter to Milton A. Jones, September 11, 1957, FBI 67-109106-299.

104. Jones, "Story of My Life," 88.

105. Milton A. Jones, memorandum to Louis B. Nichols, September 18, 1957, FBI 67-80004-765.

106. Clyde Tolson, handwritten note on Jones to Nichols, September 18, 1957.

107. Milton A. Jones, letter to Gordon A. Nease, August 18, 1958, FBI 67-308185-unserialized.

108. J. Edgar Hoover, handwritten note on Jones to Nease, August 18, 1958.

109. Gordon A. Nease, memorandum to Clyde Tolson, September 8, 1958, FBI 67-109106-320, 1.

110. Ibid., 2.

111. Ibid.

112. Ibid.

113. Jones, "Story of My Life," 90.

114. For a thorough review of the Cook smear campaign of 1958, see Matthew Cecil, "Press Every Angle: FBI Public Relations and the 'Smear Campaign' of 1958," *American Journalism* 19, no. 1 (Winter 2002): 39–58.

115. J. Edgar Hoover, handwritten note on Milton A. Jones to Gordon A. Nease, October 15, 1958, FBI 62-104779-25, 5.

116. Milton A. Jones, memorandum to Gordon A. Nease, October 14, 1958, FBI 61-901-unserialized.

117. William C. Sullivan, memorandum to Alan H. Belmont, December 24, 1958, FBI 61-901-176; Quinn Tamm, memorandum to Clyde Tolson, January 16, 1959, FBI 67-50942-328, 3.

118. J. Edgar Hoover, letter to Gordon A. Nease, January 19, 1959, FBI 67-50942-unserialized.

119. Clyde Tolson and J. Edgar Hoover, handwritten notes on Gordon A. Nease, memorandum to Clyde Tolson, December 9, 1958, FBI 67-94639-unserialized, 2.

120. "The Smear Campaign against the FBI," April 1939, FBI monograph 59D175.

121. Quinn Tamm, memorandum to Clyde Tolson, January 16, 1959, FBI 67-7400-C-84X5, 4.

122. Ibid., 5.

123. Ibid., 6.

124. Quinn Tamm, memorandum to Clyde Tolson, January 15, 1958, FBI 67-7400-C-84X2, 4.

125. Ibid., 12.

126. Clyde Tolson, handwritten note on Tamm to Tolson, January 15, 1958, FBI 67-7400-C-84X2, 4.

127. Gordon A. Nease, letter to J. Edgar Hoover, January 27, 1959, FBI 67-50942-325.

128. Jones, "Story of My Life," 91.

129. Cartha DeLoach, "General Comments," annual review of Milton A. Jones, February 19, 1959, FBI 67-109106-unserialized.

130. Cartha DeLoach, "General Comments," annual review of Milton A. Jones, March 31, 1960, FBI 67-109106-unserialized.

131. Muriel Jones Cashdollar, telephone interview with the author, October 9, 2014.

132. Gerald B. Norris, letter to J. Edgar Hoover, May 7, 1942, FBI 67-308185-6.

133. Gerald B. Norris, teletype message to J. Edgar Hoover, April 10, 1942, FBI 67-308185-unserialized.

134. Gerald B. Norris, memorandum to J. Edgar Hoover, April 21, 1942, FBI 67-308185-4.

135. W. R. Glavin, memorandum to J. Edgar Hoover, May 14, 1942, FBI 67-308185-9.

136. J. Edgar Hoover, letter to Fern C. Stukenbroeker, October 12, 1942, FBI 67-308185-unserialized.

137. Gerald B. Norris, teletype message to J. Edgar Hoover, October 8, 1942, FBI 67-308185-16.

138. Service Record of Fern C. Stukenbroeker, last updated January 3, 1975, FBI 67-308185-unserialized.

139. J. Edgar Hoover, handwritten note on Louis B. Nichols, performance review of Fern C. Stukenbroeker, November 13, 1949, FBI 67-308185-86.

140. Louis B. Nichols, performance review of Fern C. Stukenbroeker, April 19, 1950, FBI 67-308185-89.

141. Milton A. Jones, memorandum to Louis B. Nichols, April 12, 1950, FBI 67-308185-90, 2.

142. Ibid.

143. Ibid.

144. Louis B. Nichols, memorandum to Clyde Tolson, June 21, 1950, FBI 67-308185-92.

145. J. Edgar Hoover (ghostwritten for Hoover by Fern Stukenbroeker), "Civil Liberties and Law Enforcement: The Role of the FBI," *Iowa Law Review* 37 (1951–1952): 176.

146. Ibid.

147. Ibid., 177.

148. Ibid., 180–182.

149. Ibid., 182–183.

150. Ibid., 186.

151. Ibid.

152. Ibid., 194.

153. Clyde Tolson, handwritten note on Milton A. Jones, memorandum to Louis B. Nichols, October 27, 1951, FBI 67-308185-100; J. Edgar Hoover, letter to Fern C. Stukenbroeker, November 14, 1951, FBI 67-308185-99.

154. Milton A. Jones, memorandum to Louis B. Nichols, March 31, 1954, FBI 67-308185-123.

155. Milton A. Jones, memorandum to Louis B. Nichols, November 30, 1955, FBI 67-308185-131; J. Edgar Hoover, letter to Fern C. Stukenbroeker, December 5, 1955, FBI 67-308185-130.

156. Louis B. Nichols, memorandum to Clyde Tolson, November 6, 1956, FBI 67-

109106-272; for a review of the production of *The FBI Story: A Report to the People*, see Matthew Cecil, *Hoover's FBI and the Fourth Estate: The Campaign to Control the Press and the Bureau's Image* (Lawrence: University Press of Kansas, 2014), 241–243.

157. Milton A. Jones, memorandum to Louis B. Nichols, November 6, 1956, FBI 67-308185-136.

158. Louis B. Nichols, memorandum to Clyde Tolson, November 6, 1956, FBI 67-308185-139.

159. Louis B. Nichols, memorandum to J. Edgar Hoover, March 21, 1956, FBI 62-104277-1.

160. Louis B. Nichols, memorandum to Clyde Tolson, October 23, 1957, FBI 67-308185-145.

161. William C. Sullivan, quoted in Ovid Demaris, *The Director: An Oral Biography of J. Edgar Hoover* (New York: Harper's Magazine Press, 1975), 90.

162. Ibid.

163. Ibid., 91.

164. H. L. Edwards, memorandum to John P. Mohr, June 9, 1958, FBI 67-308185-150, 2.

165. Ibid., 4.

166. J. Edgar Hoover, letter to Cartha DeLoach, March 29, 1961, FBI 67-338728-unserialized.

167. W. Mark Felt, memorandum to Clyde Tolson, December 21, 1964, FBI 67-338728-unserialized, 7.

168. T. M. Cordell, letter to J. Edgar Hoover, November 20, 1959, FBI 67-308185-167.

169. Pauline Stephens, "Noted Speakers Give Talks on Communism at ABAC," *Albany (Ga.) Herald*, November 18, 1959, 1.

170. Milton A. Jones, "General Comments," annual review of Fern C. Stukenbroeker, March 31, 1960, FBI 67-308185-170.

171. J. Edgar Hoover, letter to Fern C. Stukenbroeker, August 18, 1960, FBI 67-308185-171.

172. [Redacted], letter to J. Edgar Hoover, September 20, 1960, FBI 67-308185-173.

173. Various letters and memoranda, October to December 1960, FBI 67-308185.

174. Milton A. Jones, memorandum to Cartha DeLoach, March 3, 1961, FBI 94-3443-1610.

175. Milton A. Jones, "General Comments," annual review of Fern C. Stukenbroeker, March 31, 1961, FBI 67-308185-189.

176. E. D. Mason, letter to J. Edgar Hoover, undated, ca. June 1961, FBI 67-308185-unserialized.

177. Milton A. Jones, memorandum to Cartha DeLoach, May 22, 1961, FBI 67-308185-188, 2.

178. Milton A. Jones, memorandum to Cartha DeLoach, November 9, 1961, FBI 67-308185-196.

179. SAC, San Antonio, memorandum to J. Edgar Hoover, January 12, 1963, FBI 67-308185-215.

180. Willard J. Gambold, letter to J. Edgar Hoover, December 18, 1962, FBI 67-308185-unserialized.

181. Col. Homer Garrison, Jr., quoted in Milton Jones, "General Comments," annual review of Fern C. Stukenbroeker, March 31, 1963, FBI 67-308185-216.

182. For example, "Russia Spies on Business, F.B.I. Specialist Cautions," *New York Times*, October 27, 1962, 36; Anita Brewer, "Reds Topic in Schools," *Austin (Tex.) Statesman*, January 8, 1963, 15; "Fight Reds Wisely, FBI Aide Says," *Deseret News and Telegram* (Salt Lake City, Utah), May 6, 1963, C11; "FBI Speaker Points Out Freedom Takes Work," *Salt Lake Tribune*, May 7, 1963, B23; "Positive Approach on Reds Urged," *Flint (Mich.) Journal*, February 25, 1964, 2; Barbara Thornhill, "FBI Agent Stresses Need to Be Better Informed about Communism," *Macon (Ga.) News*, October 14, 1965, 2; "Communists Grow Bold," *Illinois State Journal* (Springfield), March 3, 1966, 4.

183. Milton A. Jones, memorandum to Cartha DeLoach, October 14, 1963, FBI 67-02-1014.

184. Milton A. Jones, memorandum to Cartha DeLoach, April 27, 1965, FBI 67-308185-233.

185. Attendance at Stukenbroeker's speeches in Indianapolis drew 16,000 high school students in 1967 and 15,000 in 1968; Milton A. Jones, memorandum to Thomas E. Bishop, November 27, 1967, FBI 67-308185-266; Norman R. Booher, letter to J. Edgar Hoover, November 8, 1968, FBI 67-308185-unserialized. Another 15,000 attended in 1969; Milton A. Jones, memorandum to Thomas E. Bishop, November 13, 1969, FBI 67-308185-285.

186. Norman R. Booher, letter to J. Edgar Hoover, November 20, 1965, FBI 67-308185-unserialized.

187. Milton A. Jones, "General Comments," annual review of Fern C. Stukenbroeker, March 31, 1968, FBI 67-308185-271.

188. T. J. Feeney, Jones service record summary, October 4, 1972, FBI 67-109106-unserialized, 36.

189. Milton A. Jones, memorandum to Thomas E. Bishop, March 13, 1970, FBI 67-308185-287.

190. J. Edgar Hoover, "A Study in Marxist Revolutionary Violence: Students for a Democratic Society, 1962–1969," *Fordham Law Review* 38, no. 2 (December 1969): 289–290.

191. Ibid., 306.

192. J. Edgar Hoover, "The SDS and the High Schools: A Study in Student Extremism," *PTA Magazine* 64 (January–February 1970): 3.

193. J. Edgar Hoover, "An Open Letter to College Students," news release for United Press International, September 21, 1970, FBI 67-308185-291, 1.

194. Ibid., 6.

195. Jones, "Story of My Life," 92.

196. Ibid., 93.

197. Ibid., 94.

198. Nichols P. Callahan, memorandum to Mr. Marshall, December 26, 1972, FBI 67-308105-unserialized.

199. Lawrence J. Heim, "General Comments," annual review of Fern C. Stukenbroeker, April 2, 1973, FBI 67-308105-317.

200. Nicholas P. Callahan, memorandum to Mr. Marshall, May 7, 1973, FBI 67-308105-unserialized; E. W. Walsh, memorandum to Mr. Marshall, October 12, 1973, FBI 67-308105-unserialized.

201. Fern C. Stukenbroeker, letter to Clarence M. Kelley, December 19, 1974, FBI 67-308105-322.

202. Jones, "Story of My Life," 96.

Chapter Five: Taming the Octopus

1. "How Earnest Is Ernst?," *New York Daily Mirror*, July 31, 1957, 11.

2. Athan Theoharis and John Stuart Cox, *The Boss: J. Edgar Hoover and the Great American Inquisition* (Philadelphia: Temple University Press, 1988), 206.

3. Fred Rodell, "Morris Ernst: The Censor's Enemy, the President's Friend," *Life*, February 21, 1944, 102.

4. Alan H. Belmont, memorandum to L. V. Boardman, August 14, 1957, FBI 94-4-5366-136, 3.

5. Rodell, "Morris Ernst," 102.

6. Harrison E. Salisbury, "The Strange Correspondence of Morris Ernst and J. Edgar Hoover," *Nation*, December 1, 1984, accessed at http://www.thenation.com/article/strange-correspondence-morris-ernst-and-j-edgar-hoover.

7. Ibid.

8. Biographical Sketch, Morris Leopold Ernst Papers, Harry Ransom Center, University of Texas at Austin, accessed at http://norman.hrc.utexas.edu/fasearch/findingAid.cfm?eadid=00602p1.

9. Rodell, "Morris Ernst," 97.

10. Ibid.

11. Ibid., 105.

12. Brett Gary, "Morris Ernst's Troubled Legacy," *Reconstruction: Studies in Contemporary Culture* 8, no. 1 (2008), accessed at http://reconstruction.eserver.org/Issues/081/gary.shtml#5.

13. Ernst quoted in Rodell, "Morris Ernst," 97.

14. "Court Undecided on 'Ulysses' Ban," *New York Times*, November 26, 1933, accessed at http://www.nytimes.com/books/00/01/09/specials/joyce-courtban.html.

15. Rodger Streitmatter, *Voices of a Revolution: The Dissident Press in America* (New York: Columbia University Press, 2001), 73.

16. Emma Goldman, *Living My Life* (New York: Alfred A. Knopf, 1931), 142.

17. Ibid., 73, 162.

18. "Court Lifts Ban on 'Ulysses' Here," *New York Times*, December 7, 1933, 21.

19. Ibid.

20. "Morris Watson, Newsman, Dies; Won Key Labor Law Test Case," *New York Times*, February 13, 1972, 62.

21. "News Guild Wins Point in Labor Suit," *New York Times*, March 18, 1936, 18; "Texts of Majority and Minority Opinions in the Case of the Associated Press," *New York Times*, April 13, 1937, 19.

22. Alden Whitman, "Morris Ernst, 'Ulysses' Case Lawyer, Dies," *New York Times*, May 23, 1976, 40.

23. Watson obituary, *New York Times*.

24. C. F. Lanman, Investigative Summary, New York City, February 4, 1935, FBI 94-4-5366-X5, 2.

25. Ibid., 3.

26. Christopher H. Johnson, *Maurice Sugar: Law, Labor and the Left in Detroit, 1912–1950* (Detroit, Mich.: Wayne State University Press, 1988), 221.

27. Ibid.

28. "Rift in Law Guild on Red Row Widens," *New York Times*, February 24, 1939, 1.

29. Ibid., 20.

30. Guenter Lewy, *The Cause That Failed: Communism in American Political Life* (New York: Oxford University Press, 1990), 283.

31. Morris Ernst, letter to J. Edgar Hoover, October 14, 1941, FBI 94-4-5366-unserialized.

32. J. Edgar Hoover, letter to Morris Ernst, October 17, 1941, FBI 94-4-5366-unserialized.

33. T. R. B., "What Has the FBI Been Doing?," *New Republic*, January 5, 1942, 21. Note that T. R. B was an alias created by editors to disguise the identity of the author of their "Washington Notes" column.

34. Morris Ernst, letter to J. Edgar Hoover, December 2, 1941, FBI 94-4-5366-9.

35. D. M. "Mickey" Ladd, memorandum to J. Edgar Hoover, December 4, 1941, FBI 94-4-5366-unserialized, 1.

36. For a full discussion of the Detroit raids, see Matthew Cecil, *Hoover's FBI and the Fourth Estate: The Campaign to Control the Press and the Bureau's Image* (Lawrence: University Press of Kansas, 2014), 86–100.

37. Ladd to Hoover, December 4, 1941, 2.

38. For further discussion of the CDI, see Cecil, *Hoover's FBI*, 118–120.

39. Ladd to Hoover, December 4, 1941, 3.

40. Morris Ernst, policy statement attached to Morris Ernst to J. Edgar Hoover, December 11, 1941, FBI 94-4-5366-2.

41. J. Edgar Hoover, letter to Morris Ernst, December 12, 1941, FBI 94-4-5366-2.

42. Morris Ernst, letter to Marvin McIntyre, March 23, 1942, FBI 94-4-5366-4.

43. J. Edgar Hoover, letter to Morris Ernst, April 13, 1942, FBI 94-4-5366-4.

44. For a more complete account of the FBI's dealings with the *Nation* and the *New Republic*, see Cecil, *Hoover's FBI*, 124–155.

45. Morris Ernst, letter to J. Edgar Hoover, August 2, 1943, Louis B. Nichols Official and Confidential File, unserialized.

46. J. Edgar Hoover, letter to Morris Ernst, August 3, 1943, Louis B. Nichols Official and Confidential File, unserialized.

47. Office of the Director, typewritten note, August 4, 1943, Louis B. Nichols Official and Confidential File, unserialized.

48. Morris Ernst, letter to Freda Kirchwey, August 26, 1943, Louis B. Nichols Official and Confidential File, unserialized.

49. Morris Ernst, letter to the editors, *Nation*, September 25, 1943, 362.

50. Ibid.

51. J. Edgar Hoover, letter to Morris Ernst, August 30, 1943, Louis B. Nichols Official and Confidential File, unserialized.

52. I. F. Stone, "XXX and the FBI," *Nation*, September 25, 1943, 343.

53. Morris Ernst, letter to the editors, *Nation*, October 23, 1943, 482; I. F. Stone, response to Morris Ernst, *Nation*, October 23, 1943, 482.

54. J. Edgar Hoover, letter to Morris Ernst, October 8, 1942, FBI 94-4-5366-12.

55. Milton A. Jones, memorandum to Louis B. Nichols, October 9, 1943, FBI 94-4-5366-12X1.

56. Morris Ernst, letter to J. Edgar Hoover, October 6, 1943, FBI 94-4-5366-12X. The FBI typically did name checks on individuals and publications cited in letters to the Bureau, and its extensive indexing system resulted in copies of those letters being added to files for those individuals and publications, in addition to the files of the letters' author or authors.

57. Milton A. Jones, memorandum to Louis B. Nichols, December 31, 1943, FBI 94-4-5366-12X4.

58. George E. Lipe, memorandum to F. L. Welch, March 6, 1943, FBI 94-4-5366-6, 2–6.

59. Morris Ernst, letter to the editor, *New York Times*, January 18, 1944, 19.

60. J. Edgar Hoover, letter to Morris Ernst, January 22, 1944, FBI 94-4-5366-13.

61. Morris Ernst, draft chapter, attached to Morris Ernst, letter to J. Edgar Hoover, August 30, 1944, FBI 94-4-5366-14.

62. Ernst to Hoover, August 30, 1944.

63. J. Edgar Hoover, letter to Morris Ernst, September 15, 1944, FBI 94-4-5366-14.

64. J. Edgar Hoover, letter to Mary S. Griffith, May 7, 1945, FBI 94-4-5366-15.

65. Fred Rodell, review of *The Best Is Yet* by Morris Ernst, *Harvard Law Review* 58, no. 7 (September 1945): 1104.

66. "Book review: Morris Ernst—The Best Is Yet . . . ," *New York Guild Lawyer*, July 1945, 6.

67. Morris Ernst, letter to Harry S. Truman, November 8, 1945, Louis B. Nichols Official and Confidential File, unserialized.

68. J. Edgar Hoover, letter to Morris Ernst, October 5, 1945, FBI 94-4-5366-18.

69. Paul E. Ertzinger, letter to D. M. Mickey Ladd, June 10, 1946, FBI 94-4-5366-20.

70. Morris Ernst, letter to J. Edgar Hoover, January 11, 1947, FBI 94-4-5366-22.

71. Morris Ernst, letter to J. Edgar Hoover, June 15, 1947, FBI 94-4-5366-27.

72. J. Edgar Hoover, letter to Morris Ernst, June 18, 1947, FBI 94-4-5366-27.

73. President's Committee on Civil Rights, "To Secure These Rights: The Report of the President's Committee on Civil Rights," chap, 3, p. 123, accessed at http://www .trumanlibrary.org/civilrights/srights3.htm.

74. Anthony Leviero, "Guardians for Civil Rights Proposed by Truman Board; Report Asks End of Biases," *New York Times*, October 30, 1947, 1.

75. "Recommendations Made in the Report on Civil Rights," *New York Times*, October 30, 1947, 14.

76. Edward A. Tamm, memorandum to J. Edgar Hoover, November 10, 1947, FBI 94-4-5366-28.

77. Ibid.

78. Ibid.

79. Walter H. Waggoner, "FBI Will Aid Study," *New York Times*, March 23, 1947, 1, 48.

80. Michael J. Hogan, *A Cross of Iron: Harry S. Truman and the Origins of the National Security State, 1945–1954* (New York: Cambridge University Press, 2000), 255.

81. J. Edgar Hoover, handwritten note, ca. January 1948, Louis B. Nichols Official and Confidential File, unserialized.

82. Morris Ernst, letter to Louis B. Nichols, undated but filed on February 3, 1948, Louis B. Nichols Official and Confidential File, unserialized, 3.

83. William S. White, "To Shield Accusers and Sources of FBI," *New York Times*, December 28, 1947, 1.

84. Jay Walz, "Loyalty to Be Tested in Chain of Hearings," *New York Times*, January 4, 1948, 93.

85. J. Edgar Hoover, handwritten note on draft of J. Edgar Hoover, letter to Morris Ernst, January 30, 1948, Louis B. Nichols Official and Confidential File, unserialized.

86. J. Edgar Hoover, letter to Morris Ernst, January 30, 1948, Louis B. Nichols Official and Confidential File, unserialized, with handwritten notes.

87. Morris Ernst, letter to J. Edgar Hoover, February 2, 1948, FBI 94-4-5366-31.

88. Edward A. Tamm, handwritten note on Ernst to Hoover, February 2, 1948.

89. J. Edgar Hoover, letter to Morris Ernst, February 5, 1948, FBI 94-4-5366-31.

90. Morris Ernst, letter to J. Edgar Hoover, February 13, 1948, FBI 94-4-5366-32.

91. J. Edgar Hoover, handwritten note on Louis B. Nichols, memorandum to Clyde Tolson, December 20, 1948, Louis B. Nichols Official and Confidential File, unserialized, 2.

92. Morris Ernst, "Miasma of Suspicion," *Saturday Review*, December 24, 1949, 18.

93. Ibid.

94. Morris Ernst, memorandum attached to Morris Ernst to Louis B. Nichols, November 1, 1949, Louis B. Nichols Official and Confidential File, unserialized, 1–2.

95. Ibid.

96. For a full review of Oursler's relationship with Hoover, see Cecil, *Hoover's FBI*, 199–202.

97. Louis B. Nichols, memorandum to Clyde Tolson, October 18, 1949, Louis B. Nichols Official and Confidential File, unserialized.

98. Louis B. Nichols, memorandum to Clyde Tolson, November 2, 1949, Louis B. Nichols Official and Confidential File, unserialized.

99. J. Edgar Hoover, handwritten comment on Nichols to Tolson, November 2, 1949.

100. "Film 'Communists' Listed in FBI File in Coplon Spy Case," *New York Times*, June 9, 1949, 1.

101. Louis B. Nichols, memorandum to Clyde Tolson, November 3, 1949, Louis B. Nichols Official and Confidential File, unserialized.

102. J. Edgar Hoover, handwritten comment on Nichols to Tolson, November 3, 1949.

103. Morris Ernst, letter to Fulton Oursler, November 22, 1949, Louis B. Nichols Official and Confidential File, unserialized, 1–3.

104. "James L. Fly Dies; Ex-Head of F.C.C.," *New York Times*, January 7, 1966, 29.

105. Ibid.

106. James L. Fly, letter to Tom Clark, June 14, 1949, FBI 62-73756-4, 1.

107. Ibid.

108. J. Edgar Hoover, handwritten comment on routing slip attached to Fly to Clark, June 14, 1949.

109. "Justice Department Bans Wire Tapping: Jackson Acts on Hoover Recommendations," *New York Times*, March 17, 1940.

110. Tim Wiener, *Enemies: A History of the FBI* (New York: Random House, 2012), 77.

111. James Lawrence Fly, "The Case against Wire Tapping," *Look*, September 27, 1949, 35.

112. James L. Fly, letter to Morris Ernst, November 10, 1949, Louis B. Nichols Official and Confidential File, unserialized, 1.

113. Ibid., 2.

114. Ibid.

115. Ibid.

116. J. Edgar Hoover, handwritten note on routing slip attached to Fly to Ernst, November 10, 1949.

117. James L. Fly, letter to Morris Ernst, November 15, 1949, Louis B. Nichols Official and Confidential File, unserialized.

118. J. Edgar Hoover, handwritten note on routing slip attached to Fly to Ernst, November 15, 1949.

119. Louis B. Nichols, memorandum to Clyde Tolson, December 30, 1949, Louis B. Nichols Official and Confidential File, unserialized, 1.

120. Louis B. Nichols, memorandum to Clyde Tolson, December 13, 1949, Louis B. Nichols Official and Confidential File, unserialized, 2.

121. J. Edgar Hoover, handwritten note on Nichols to Tolson, December 13, 1949, 2.

122. Bernard DeVoto, "Due Notice to the F.B.I.," *Harper's*, October 19, 1949, 67.

123. Ibid.

124. Louis B. Nichols, memorandum to Clyde Tolson, November 15, 1949, Louis B. Nichols Official and Confidential File, unserialized.

125. J. Edgar Hoover, memorandum to Special Agents in Charge, November 25, 1941, Louis B. Nichols Official and Confidential File, unserialized.

126. J. Edgar Hoover, *Bureau Bulletin*, no. 71, November 19, 1947, Louis B. Nichols Official and Confidential File, unserialized, 2.

127. J. Edgar Hoover, letter to Morris Ernst, November 17, 1949, Louis B. Nichols Official and Confidential File, unserialized, 1.

128. J. Edgar Hoover, draft letter to Daniel Mebane, undated, Louis B. Nichols Official and Confidential File, unserialized, 1.

129. Louis B. Nichols, memorandum to Clyde Tolson, November 17, 1949, Louis B. Nichols Official and Confidential File, unserialized.

130. Louis B. Nichols, memorandum to Clyde Tolson, November 28, 1949, Louis B. Nichols Official and Confidential File, unserialized.

131. Ibid.

132. Ibid.

133. Edward Ranzal, "Coplon Conviction Voided on Appeal," *New York Times*, December 6, 1950, 1, 23.

134. James L. Fly, letter to Morris Ernst, January 17, 1950, Louis B. Nichols Official and Confidential File, unserialized.

135. J. Edgar Hoover, handwritten note on routing slip attached to Morris Ernst to

James L. Fly, January 18, 1950, Louis B. Nichols Official and Confidential File, unserialized.

136. "Text of the Report of the Roberts Commission on the Facts of the Japanese Attack on Pearl Harbor," *New York Times*, January 25, 1942, 30.

137. Susan L. Brinson, *The Red Scare, Politics, and the Federal Communications Commission* (Westport, Conn.: Greenwood Publishing, 2004), 83.

138. J. Edgar Hoover, handwritten note on Louis B. Nichols, memorandum to Clyde Tolson, January 11, 1950, Louis B. Nichols Official and Confidential File, unserialized, 2.

139. Morris Ernst, letter to Phillip Graham, January 16, 1950, Louis B. Nichols Official and Confidential File, unserialized.

140. Louis B. Nichols, memorandum to Clyde Tolson, January 17, 1950, Louis B. Nichols Official and Confidential File, unserialized.

141. Morris Ernst, letter to J. Edgar Hoover, February 3, 1950, Louis B. Nichols Official and Confidential File, unserialized.

142. Louis B. Nichols, memorandum to Clyde Tolson, February 8, 1950, Louis B. Nichols Official and Confidential File, unserialized.

143. J. Edgar Hoover, handwritten note on James L. Fly, letter to Morris Ernst, February 8, 1950, Louis B. Nichols Official and Confidential File, unserialized.

144. Louis B. Nichols, memorandum to Clyde Tolson, February 16, 1950, Louis B. Nichols Official and Confidential File, unserialized.

145. Milton A. Jones, memorandum to Louis B. Nichols, March 9, 1950, Louis B. Nichols Official and Confidential File, unserialized.

146. Fulton Oursler, letter to Morris Ernst, March 24, 1950, Louis B. Nichols Official and Confidential File, unserialized.

147. Louis B. Nichols, memorandum to Clyde Tolson, April 4, 1950, Louis B. Nichols Official and Confidential File, unserialized.

148. J. Edgar Hoover, letter to Morris Ernst, August 17, 1950, Louis B. Nichols Official and Confidential File, unserialized.

149. Morris Ernst, letter to Louis B. Nichols, May 3, 1950, Louis B. Nichols Official and Confidential File, Ernst folder, unserialized.

150. Louis B. Nichols, memorandum to Clyde Tolson, May 23, 1950, Louis B. Nichols Official and Confidential File, Ernst folder, unserialized.

151. Theoharis and Cox, *Boss*, 275–277.

152. Louis B. Nichols, memorandum to Clyde Tolson, August 24, 1950, FBI 62-25733-62.

153. Ibid.

154. Louis B. Nichols, memorandum to Clyde Tolson, September 18, 1950, FBI 62-25733-unserialized.

155. Morris Ernst, letter to Louis B. Nichols, September 22, 1950, Louis B. Nichols Official and Confidential File, Ernst folder, unserialized.

156. J. Edgar Hoover, handwritten note on Louis B. Nichols, memorandum to Clyde Tolson, September 20, 1950, FBI 62-25733-88.

157. Morris Ernst, "Why I No Longer Fear the F.B.I.," *Reader's Digest*, December 21, 1950, 27.

158. Louis B. Nichols, memorandum to Clyde Tolson, December 28, 1950, Louis B. Nichols Official and Confidential File, Ernst folder, unserialized.

159. William C. Sullivan, *The Bureau: My Thirty Years in Hoover's FBI* (New York: W. W. Norton, 1979), 94.

160. Mark Felt and John O'Connor, *A G-Man's Life: The FBI, Being "Deep Throat" and the Struggle for Honor in Washington* (New York: Public Affairs, 2006), 90.

161. "F.B.I. Head Denies a Charge by Hiss," *New York Times*, May 9, 1957, 14.

162. Ralph de Toledano, letter to Morris Ernst, May 13, 1957, FBI 100-418978-5, 1.

163. Morris Ernst, quoted in advertisement for Alger Hiss, *In the Court of Public Opinion*, in *New York Times*, May 13, 1957, 29.

164. Ralph de Toledano, letter to J. Edgar Hoover, May 13, 1957, FBI 94-4-5366-130.

165. J. Edgar Hoover, letter to Ralph de Toledano, May 16, 1957, FBI 94-4-5366-130.

166. "Political Murder and Terror Marked Trujillo Dictatorship," *New York Times*, June 1, 1961, 14.

167. "Galindez Search by F.B.I. Is Urged," *New York Times*, May 21, 1956, 29.

168. Milton Bracker, "Trujillo's Rule Denounced in Missing Scholar's Book," *New York Times*, May 29, 1956, 1.

169. Louis B. Nichols, memorandum to Clyde Tolson, July 11, 1957, FBI 94-4-5366-132, 1.

170. J. Edgar Hoover, handwritten notes on Nichols to Tolson, July 11, 1957, 2, 3.

171. Louis B. Nichols, memorandum to Clyde Tolson, August 7, 1957, FBI 94-4-5366-unseralized.

172. Morris Ernst, letter to Louis B. Nichols, August 7, 1957, FBI 94-4-5366-135.

173. J. Edgar Hoover, handwritten note on Nichols to Tolson, August 7, 1957, 3.

174. Alan H. Belmont, memorandum to Leland V. Boardman, ca. July 1958, FBI 100-375346-unserialized.

175. Louis B. Nichols, handwritten note on Morris Ernst to Louis B. Nichols, October 9, 1957, FBI 94-4-5366-140.

176. Anthony Marro, "F.B.I.'s Files Disclose A.C.L.U. Gave Data on Activities and Members to Bureau in 1950s, *New York Times*, August 4, 1977, A1, B5.

177. Louis B. Nichols, letter to Morris Ernst, October 16, 1957, FBI 94-4-5366-140.

178. J. Edgar Hoover, handwritten note on routing slip attached to Nichols to Ernst, October 16, 1957.

179. Samuel Walker, *In Defense of American Liberties: A History of the ACLU* (New York: Oxford University Press, 1997), 210–211.

180. Morris Ernst, letter to J. Edgar Hoover, February 6, 1958, FBI 94-4-5366-142.

181. Morris Ernst, letter to Edward Powers, February 4, 1958, FBI 94-4-5366-142.

182. Helen W. Gandy, letter to Morris Ernst, April 9, 1958, FBI 94-4-5366-148.

183. Peter Kihss, "Ernst Report on Galindez Clears Dominican Dictator," *New York Times*, June 2, 1958, 1, 14.

184. S. B. Donahoe, memorandum to Alan H. Belmont, December 3, 1958, FBI 94-4-5366-unserialized.

185. Anthony Lewis, "$500,000 Is Spent in Galindez Case," *New York Times*, October 1, 1958, 1.

186. Gordon A. Nease, memorandum to Clyde Tolson, December 1, 1958, FBI 94-4-5366-158.

187. J. J. McGuire, memorandum to Clyde Tolson, November 21, 1958, FBI 94-4-5366-unserialized.

188. Clyde Tolson, memorandum to J. Edgar Hoover, May 4, 1959, FBI 94-4-5366-unserialized.

189. Rodell, "Morris Ernst," 97.

190. For a full discussion of Cooper's work with Hoover, see Cecil, *Hoover's FBI*, 43–75.

Chapter Six: The Heir Apparent

1. Randy Kennedy, "Andrew Tully, 78, Author, Columnist, and War Reporter," *New York Times*, September 29, 1993, accessed at http://www.nytimes.com/1993/09/29/obituaries/andrew-tully-78-author-columnist-and-war-reporter.html.

2. Andrew Tully, "National Whirligig," release by Bell-McClure Syndicate included in FBI file, May 22, 1963, FBI 94-51742-6, 1.

3. Ibid.

4. Ibid., 2.

5. Cartha DeLoach, memorandum to John P. Mohr, May 27, 1963, FBI 94-51742-5, 3.

6. Cartha DeLoach, letter to Andrew Tully, May 27, 1963, FBI 94-51742-unserialized, 3.

7. DeLoach to Mohr, May 27, 1963, 3.

8. Washington Capital News Service, March 2, 1967, FBI 69-10960-4662.

9. Cartha DeLoach, memorandum to Clyde Tolson, May 15, 1967, FBI 62-109070-5251, 3.

10. J. Edgar Hoover, handwritten note on Washington Capital News Service, March 2, 1967.

11. Ken W. Clawson, "FBI's Hoover Scores Ramsey Clark, RFK," *Washington Post*, November 17, 1970, 1.

12. Curt Gentry, *J. Edgar Hoover: The Man and the Secrets* (New York: W. W. Norton, 1991), 323.

13. Cartha DeLoach, memorandum to Clyde Tolson, March 3, 1967, FBI 62-109070-4691, 1–2.

14. Cartha DeLoach, memorandum to Clyde Tolson, March 3, 1967, FBI 62-109070-4744, 1.

15. J. Edgar Hoover, handwritten note on DeLoach to Tolson, March 3, 1967, 2.

16. Robert E. Wick, memorandum to Cartha DeLoach, March 9, 1967, FBI 62-109070-4772, 1–2.

17. J. Edgar Hoover, handwritten note on Wick to DeLoach, March 9, 1967, 2.

18. DeLoach to Tolson, May 15, 1967, 2.

19. Ibid., 3.

20. Ibid., 4.

21. Ibid., 5.

22. J. Edgar Hoover, handwritten note on DeLoach to Tolson, May 15, 1967, 5.

23. Cartha DeLoach, memorandum to Clyde Tolson, March 31, 1967, FBI 62-109070-5403, 1–3.

24. J. Edgar Hoover, handwritten notes on DeLoach to Tolson, March 31, 1967, 4, 5.

25. J. Saxton Daniel, letter to J. Edgar Hoover, December 12, 1942, FBI 67-338728-30.

26. SAC, Savannah, Ga., teletype to J. Edgar Hoover, August 7, 1942, FBI 67-338728-unseralized.

27. SAC, Miami, Fla., teletype to J. Edgar Hoover, July 25, 1942, FBI 67-338728-9.

28. J. Edgar Hoover, letter to Cartha Dekle DeLoach, August 20, 1942, FBI 67-338728-unserialized.

29. Everett J. Adolf, memorandum to Mr. Tracy, September 8, 1942, FBI 67-338728-16.

30. Quinn Tamm, memorandum to Mr. Tracy, September 24, 1942, FBI 67-338728-18.

31. M. G. O'Melia, memorandum to Mr. Tracy, November 5, 1942, FBI 67-338728-21; J. W. Mackle, memorandum to J. Edgar Hoover, November 23, 1942, FBI 67-338728-26; Cartha DeLoach, letter to J. Edgar Hoover, May 16, 1944, FBI 67-338728-52.

32. J. Edgar Hoover, letter to Local Board Number 1, Selective Service System, Claxton, Ga., November 9, 1942, FBI 67-338728-22.

33. J. Edgar Hoover, letter to J. Sexton Daniel, December 10, 1942, FBI 67-338728-unseralized; J. Edgar Hoover, letter to Cartha DeLoach, December 10, 1942, FBI 67-338728-29.

34. Daniel to Hoover, December 12, 1942.

35. J. Edgar Hoover, letter to Local Board Number 1, Selective Service System, Claxton, Ga., December 30, 1942, FBI 67-338728-33.

36. Cartha DeLoach, memorandum to Hugh H. Clegg, January 19, 1943, FBI 67-338728-36.

37. SAC, Norfolk, Va., Cartha DeLoach Efficiency Rating, July 17, 1943, FBI 67-338728-41.

38. J. Edgar Hoover, letter to Cartha DeLoach, February 7, 1944, FBI 67-338728-48.

39. J. Edgar Hoover, teletype to SAC Cleveland, April 13, 1944, FBI 67-338728-50.

40. DeLoach to Hoover, May 16, 1944.

41. Mr. Callahan, memorandum to Mr. Glavin, July 24, 1944, FBI 67-338728-59.

42. Robert C. Hendon, memorandum to Clyde Tolson, August 21, 1944, FBI 67-338728-61.

43. H. B. Fletcher, memorandum to J. Edgar Hoover, September 26, 1944, FBI 67-338728-63.

44. Notice of Separation from the U.S. Naval Service for Specialist Second Class Cartha Dekle DeLoach, March 25, 1946, FBI 67-338728-unserialized; Guy Hottel, teletype to J. Edgar Hoover, April 8, 1946, FBI 67-338728-78.

45. Cartha DeLoach, letter to J. Edgar Hoover, February 20, 1946, FBI 67-338728-unserialized.

46. J. Edgar Hoover, letter to Cartha DeLoach, September 24, 1945, FBI 67-338728-69; J. Edgar Hoover, letter to SAC, Cleveland, March 11, 1946, FBI 67-338728-70; SAC, Cleveland, letter to J. Edgar Hoover, April 30, 1946, FBI 67-338728-82.

47. E. C. Richardson, Special Efficiency Rating, Cartha DeLoach, January 24, 1947, FBI 67-338728-89.

48. John P. Mohr, memorandum to Clyde Tolson, May 21, 1947, FBI 67-338728-94.

49. Ibid.

50. Victor P. Keay, Annual Efficiency Report for Cartha DeLoach, March 31, 1948, FBI 67-338728-104.

51. John P. Mohr, memorandum to Clyde Tolson, September 25, 1951, FBI 14-9000-1369, 1–3.

52. Victor P. Keay, memorandum to D. M. "Mickey" Ladd, March 23, 1948, FBI 67-338728-unserialized.

53. Victor P. Keay, memorandum to D. M. "Mickey" Ladd, December 21, 1948, FBI 67-338728-110.

54. Ibid.; H. L. Edwards, memorandum to Mr. Glavin, December 28, 1948, FBI 67-338728-111.

55. J. Edgar Hoover, letter to Roscoe H. Hillenkoetter, December 6, 1948, FBI 67-338728-unserialized.

56. Victor P. Keay, Annual Efficiency Report, Cartha DeLoach, March 31, 1949, FBI 67-338728-unserialized.

57. Inspector Gurnea, Inspection Report, Security Division, ca. October 1949, FBI 67-338728-unserialized.

58. Ibid.

59. Victor P. Keay, memorandum to H. B. Fletcher, July 14, 1949, FBI 67-338728-unserialized, 1.

60. Ibid., 2.

61. Ibid., 3.

62. J. Edgar Hoover, handwritten note on Keay to Fletcher, July 14, 1949, 3.

63. J. Edgar Hoover, memorandum to Clyde Tolson and D. M. "Mickey" Ladd, October 18, 1950, FBI 67-338728-130.

64. J. Edgar Hoover, handwritten note on John P. Mohr, memorandum to Clyde Tolson, July 14, 1951, FBI 67-338728-145.

65. J. Edgar Hoover, handwritten note on Hugh H. Clegg, memorandum to Clyde Tolson, October 26, 1951, FBI 67-338728-unserialized; Hugh H. Clegg, memorandum to Mr. Glavin, December 10, 1951, FBI 67-338728-153.

66. Hugh H. Clegg, memorandum to Clyde Tolson, April 4, 1952, FBI 67-338728-158.

67. J. Edgar Hoover, memorandum to Clyde Tolson, September 1, 1953, FBI 67-338728-187.

68. John P. Mohr, memorandum to Clyde Tolson, October 22, 1953, FBI 67-338728-191; John P. Mohr, memorandum to Clyde Tolson, March 4, 1954, FBI 67-338728-197.

69. J. Edgar Hoover, letter to Cartha DeLoach, March 8, 1954, FBI 67-338728-196.

70. Cartha DeLoach Personnel File, FBI 67-338728; for a detailed examination of DeLoach's liaison work with the American Legion, see chapter 3.

71. Louis B. Nichols, memorandum to Clyde Tolson, October 17, 1955, FBI 67-338728-unserialized.

72. Cartha DeLoach, memorandum to Louis B. Nichols, March 6, 1956, FBI 67-338728-unserialized.

73. Ibid.

74. Ibid., 2.

75. J. Edgar Hoover, handwritten note on DeLoach to Nichols, March 6, 1956.

76. Gordon A. Nease, memorandum to Clyde Tolson, November 15, 1957, FBI 67-338728-261.

77. J. Edgar Hoover, letter to Cartha DeLoach, January 28, 1959, FBI 67-338728-299.

78. John F. Malone, memorandum to John P. Mohr, February 15, 1960, FBI 67-7400-M-33X1, 4.

79. Ibid., 5.

80. Cartha DeLoach, memorandum to John P. Mohr, April 1, 1969, FBI 67-338728-347, 1.

81. Ibid.

82. Ibid.

83. Ibid., 1–6.

84. Ibid., 2.

85. Ibid., 3.

86. Ibid., 4.

87. Ibid., 3.

88. Ibid., 6.

89. J. Edgar Hoover, handwritten note on DeLoach to Mohr, April 1, 1969, 6.

90. Cartha DeLoach, letter to the editor, *Denver Post*, April 29, 1960, 23.

91. Jack Guinn, "Anyone for Tennis," *Denver Post*, April 29, 1960, 24.

92. James A. Wechsler, "Optical Illusion," *New York Post*, May 5, 1960, 34.

93. UPI story, August 31, 1960, FBI 62-43763-148.

94. J. Edgar Hoover, handwritten note on UPI story, August 31, 1960.

95. Cartha DeLoach, memorandum to John P. Mohr, August 31, 1960, FBI 62-43763-149, 1.

96. Ibid.

97. Ibid., 3.

98. J. Edgar Hoover, handwritten note on DeLoach to Mohr, August 31, 1960, 2.

99. Ibid., 3.

100. Cartha DeLoach, memorandum to John P. Mohr, February 28, 1961, FBI 94-1-21523-15.

101. Ibid.

102. Ibid.

103. Ibid.

104. J. Edgar Hoover, handwritten note on DeLoach to Mohr, February 28, 1961, 2.

105. Dennis Hart, *Monitor: The Last Great Radio Show* (self-published, iUniverse, 2003), xiii.

106. Sally Bedell, "Dave Garroway, 69, Found Dead; First Host of 'Today' on NBC-TV," *New York Times*, July 22, 1982, accessed at http://www.nytimes.com/1982/07/22/obituaries/dave-garroway-69-found-dead-first-host-of-today-on-nbc-tv.html.

107. Milton A. Jones, memorandum to Cartha DeLoach, November 13, 1964, FBI 67-338728-451.

108. J. Edgar Hoover, letter to Cartha DeLoach, August 15, 1962, FBI 67-338728-unserialized.

109. Clyde Tolson, memorandum to J. Edgar Hoover, November 29, 1963, FBI 67-338728-unserialized.

110. Michael L. Gilette, oral history transcript, Cartha D. "Deke" DeLoach, January 11, 1992, Accession Number 96-12, 1, Lyndon Baines Johnson Presidential Library and Museum, Austin, Tex.

111. Athan Theoharis, Tony G. Poveda, Susan Rosenfeld, and Richard Gid Powers, eds,. *The FBI: A Comprehensive Reference Guide* (New York: Oryx Press, 2000), 324; John F. Malone, memorandum to Clyde Tolson, October 4, 1962, FBI 67-163462-unserialized, 2.

112. Ken W. Clawson, oral history interview, in Ovid Demaris, *The Director: An Oral Biography of J. Edgar Hoover* (New York: Harper's Magazine Press, 1975), 217–218.

113. Ibid., 7.

114. Lyndon Johnson, telephone conversation with Hubert Humphrey, August 14, 1964, accessed at the Miller Center, University of Virginia, at http://web2.millercenter.org/lbj/audiovisual/whrecordings/telephone/conversations/1964/lbj_wh6408_19_4917.mp3.

115. Cartha DeLoach, memorandum to John P. Mohr, August 29, 1964, FBI 67-338728-450, 1.

116. Ibid.

117. Ibid.

118. Ibid.

119. Ibid., 2.

120. Ibid.

121. The organizations named by DeLoach included: the MFDP, COFO, CORE, SNCC, the Independent Citizens Committee, the American Nazi Party, the White Party of America, W.E.B. DuBois Clubs, Communist Party USA, the Women's International League for Peace and Freedom, and the Progressive Labor Movement. See ibid., 6.

122. Ibid., 7–8.

123. Ibid., 8.

124. Cartha DeLoach, *Hoover's FBI: The Inside Story by Hoover's Trusted Lieutenant* (New York: Regnery, 1995), 5.

125. Ibid.

126. Lyndon B. Johnson, Executive Order 11154, May 8, 1964.

127. DeLoach, *Hoover's FBI*, 203.

128. Ibid., 204.

129. Ben A. Franklin, "Hoover Assails Warren Findings; Says F.B.I. Was Criticized Unfairly on Oswald Check—Calls Dr. King a 'Liar,'" *New York Times*, November 19, 1964, 1.

130. Cartha DeLoach, "Booknotes," C-SPAN2, August 20, 1995, accessed at http://www.booknotes.org/Watch/66346-1/Cartha+Deke+DeLoach.aspx.

131. DeLoach, *Hoover's FBI*, 211.

132. Ibid., 212.

133. Athan Theoharis and John Stuart Cox, *The Boss: J. Edgar Hoover and the Great American Inquisition* (Philadelphia: Temple University Press, 1988), 357.

134. Ben Bradlee, *A Good Life: Newspapering and Other Adventures* (New York: Touchstone, 1995), 272.

135. Nicholas deB. Katzenbach, *Some of It Was Fun: Working with RFK and LBJ* (New York: W. W. Norton, 2008), 154.

136. Ibid.

137. DeLoach, *Hoover's FBI*, 212.

138. Ibid., 405.

139. All quotes from this telephone conversation are from Telephone Conversation, Ref. #13730, Cartha "Deke" DeLoach, 11/12/1968, 8:30P, Recordings and Transcripts of Telephone Conversations, LBJ Presidential Library, accessed March 30, 2015, at http://digital.lbjlibrary.org/record/TEL-13730.

140. DeMaris, *Director*, 220.

141. Ibid., 221.

142. W. Mark Felt, memorandum to Clyde Tolson, January 5, 1966, FBI 67-338728-unserialized, 4–6.

143. Ibid., 8.

144. Ibid., 3.

145. Ronald Kessler, *The FBI: Inside the World's Most Powerful Law Enforcement Agency* (New York: Pocket Books, 1993), 241–242.

146. Cartha DeLoach, memorandum to Clyde Tolson, December 29, 1969, FBI file 94-8-150-229, 1.

147. Ibid., 2.

148. Ibid.

149. Cartha DeLoach, memorandum to Clyde Tolson, March 12, 1970, FBI 67-338728-513, 1–2.

150. Cartha DeLoach, memorandum to Clyde Tolson, September 13, 1968, FBI 67-153-4497.

151. Ibid.

152. Ibid., 3.

153. Cartha DeLoach, memorandum to Clyde Tolson, February 27, 1970, FBI 94-8-150-232; Clark R. Mollenhoff, memorandum to J. Edgar Hoover, February 23, 1970, FBI 94-8-150-unserialized.

154. J. Edgar Hoover, handwritten note on DeLoach to Tolson, March 12, 1970, 3.

155. Milton A. Jones, handwritten note on DeLoach to Tolson, March 12, 1970, 3.

156. Cartha DeLoach, letter to J. Edgar Hoover, April 8, 1966, FBI 67-338728-478.

157. Cartha DeLoach, letter to J. Edgar Hoover, April 11, 1967, FBI 67-338728-486.

158. Cartha DeLoach, letter to J. Edgar Hoover, April 3, 1968, FBI 67-338728-493.

159. Cartha DeLoach, letter to J. Edgar Hoover, April 10, 1969, FBI 67-338728-506.

160. Cartha DeLoach, letter to J. Edgar Hoover, April 3, 1970, FBI 67-338728-516.

161. Cartha DeLoach, letter to J. Edgar Hoover, April 18, 1953, FBI 67-338728-unserialized.

162. Cartha DeLoach, letter to J. Edgar Hoover, February 23, 1953, FBI 67-338728-176.

163. Cartha DeLoach, letter to J. Edgar Hoover, January 29, 1957, FBI 67-338728-243.

164. Cartha DeLoach, letter to J. Edgar Hoover, February 2, 1960 FBI 67-338728-333.

165. Cartha DeLoach, letter to J. Edgar Hoover, April 25, 1960, FBI 67-338728-349.

166. Cartha DeLoach, letter to J. Edgar Hoover, September 25, 1961, FBI 67-338728-392.

167. Gentry, *J. Edgar Hoover*, 449.

168. Jack Nelson, *Scoop: The Evolution of a Southern Reporter* (Jackson: University Press of Mississippi, 2013), 162.

169. "Maurice Gusman, 91, of Miami; Ukrainian Emigré Built a Fortune," *New York Times*, April 4, 1980, 24.

170. Secretary of Commerce Luther H. Hodges, telegram to Maurice Gusman, October 16, 1964, Maurice Gusman Papers, 1944–1976, accession SC-4410, American Jewish Archives, Hebrew Union College/Jewish Institute of Religion, Cincinnati, Ohio.

171. Maurice Gusman, letter to President Lyndon B. Johnson, December 14, 1964, Maurice Gusman Papers, 1944–1976, accession SC-4410, American Jewish Archives, Hebrew Union College/Jewish Institute of Religion, Cincinnati, Ohio.

172. Lillian Erlich, *Money Isn't Important: The Life of Maurice Gusman* (Miami, Fla.: E. A. Seemann Publishing, 1976), 119.

173. Efrem Zimbalist, Jr., *My Dinner of Herbs* (New York: Proscenium, 2003), 160.

174. Maurice Gusman, letter to J. Edgar Hoover, September 26, 1944, FBI 67-338728-62.

175. Erlich, *Money Isn't Important*, 93–96.

176. Walter Rugaber, telephone interview with the author, January 15, 2015.

177. Ibid.

178. Cartha DeLoach, memorandum to Clyde Tolson, July 2, 1970, FBI 67-338728-531, 1.

179. Ibid.

180. Rugaber interview, January 15, 2015.

181. DeLoach to Tolson, July 2, 1970, 1.

182. Rugaber interview, January 15, 2015.

183. Ibid.

184. DeLoach to Tolson, July 2, 1970, 2.

185. Frederick N. Rasmussen, "Philanthropist Frenkil, 90, Dies," *Baltimore Sun*, June 4, 1999, accessed at http://articles.baltimoresun.com/1999-06-04/news/990604 0021_1_baltimore-contractors-local-landmarks-maryland.

186. DeLoach to Tolson, July 2, 1970, 2.

187. Jacques Kelly and Anthony Weir, *"Get Me the White House": The Untold Story of Victor Frenkil's Rise from Immigrant Obscurity to Prominence in the Turbulent Worlds of Business and Politics* (Baltimore, Md.: Gateway Press, 2006), 101. Their source on the Jenkins matter was, according to a note on p. 249, an interview with Cartha DeLoach.

188. Ibid., 2–3.

189. Rugaber interview, January 15, 2015.

190. Ibid.

191. Ibid.

192. Ibid., 3.

193. Ibid.

194. Ibid.

195. J. Edgar Hoover, memorandum to Clyde Tolson, Alan H. Belmont, Cartha DeLoach, John P. Mohr, Mr. Casper, Mr. Callahan, Mr. Conrad, Mark Felt, Mr. Gale, Alex Rosen, William C. Sullivan, Mr. Trotter, Robert E. Wick, December 1, 1965, unserialized, Clyde Tolson Personal File.

196. J. Edgar Hoover, memorandum to Clyde Tolson, John P. Mohr, Cartha De-Loach, Mr. Casper, September 27, 1965, unserialized, Clyde Tolson Personal File.

197. Demaris, *Director*, 221.

198. W. R. Wannall, memorandum to C. D. Brennan, September 30, 1970, FBI 94-8-150-unserialized, 1.

199. Ibid., 2.

200. Legal Counsel, letter to Clarence Kelley, June 10, 1977, FBI 67-338728-561, 1.

201. Legal Counsel, memorandum to J. B. Adams, November 12, 1975, FBI 67-338728-unserialized.

202. Ramsey Clark, oral history interview, in Demaris, *Director*, 230.

203. Gentry, *J. Edgar Hoover*.

204. Cartha DeLoach, letter to J. Edgar Hoover, April 8, 1965, FBI 67-338728-2.

205. Cartha DeLoach, telephone interview with the author, April 12, 2001.

206. Carl J. Jensen, interview with Cartha D. DeLoach, June 18, 2013, accessed at https://vimeo.com/58377015.

Chapter Seven: An Empire in Decline

1. "The Many Faces That Made the Hoover Image," *Life*, April 9, 1971, 40.

2. Service Record for Thomas Bishop, FBI 67E-204108-unserialized, 2.

3. "Unwanted: Any Criticism from within the Ranks," *Life*, April 9, 1971, 42.

4. Athan Theoharis, Tony Poveda, Susan Rosenfeld, and Richard Gid Powers, eds., *The FBI: A Comprehensive Reference Guide* (New York: Oryx Press, 2000), 188.

5. David Burnham, "Agent Who Quit F.B.I. Scores Bureau Investigations, Discipline and Leadership," *New York Times*, January 23, 1971, 27.

6. "Hoover's Doghouse," *Washington Evening Star*, July 6, 1972, A3.

7. Jack Nelson, *Scoop: The Evolution of a Southern Reporter* (Jackson: University Press of Mississippi, 2012), 161.

8. "Hoover Denies Charge of 'Doghouse' in Butte," *New York Times*, February 14, 1971, 73.

9. "Inquiry on Hoover Asked by McGovern," *New York Times*, February 1, 1971, 13.

10. Gilbert Geis and Colin Goff, "Lifting the Cover from Undercover Operations: J. Edgar Hoover and Some of the Other Criminologists," *Crime, Law and Social Change* 18 (1992): 99.

11. "Unwanted," 42.

12. "Criticism of Hoover by Agents Alleged," *New York Times*, March 1, 1971, 15.

13. Anonymous letter to Sen. George S. McGovern on FBI letterhead, February 2, 1971, FBI unserialized (George S. McGovern FBI file), 2.

14. Ibid.

15. W. Mark Felt, memorandum to Clyde Tolson, March 3, 1971, FBI unserialized (George S. McGovern FBI file), 1.

16. Ibid., 1–4.

17. Clyde Tolson, letter to George McGovern, March 2, 1971, FBI 67-9524-457.

18. "FBI Letters Rap McGovern for Criticism of Hoover," *Idaho* (Boise) *Daily Statesman*, March 10, 1971, 8A.

19. Ibid.

20. Text of Senate floor speech, undated and FBI unserialized (George S. McGovern FBI file), 2.

21. For example, "McGovern Hit by VFW Head," *Washington Post*, February 22, 1971, A14.

22. Gordon E. Malmfeldt, memorandum to Thomas E. Bishop, March 8, 1971, FBI 66-36653-4523.

23. Robert D. McFadden, "McGovern Says Hoover Tried to Get Pilot Dismissed," *New York Times*, April 20, 1971, 34.

24. Joseph Lelyveld, "Pilot Criticizes F.B.I.'s Action Here," *New York Times*, Novem-

ber 2, 1969, 1; Alex Rosen, memorandum to William C. Sullivan, April 19, 1971, FBI 164-978-158, 1.

25. Gordon E. Malmfeldt, memorandum to Thomas E. Bishop, May 19, 1971, FBI 94-54066-unserialized, 2a.

26. "McGovern Renews Attack against Hoover over Pilot," *New York Times*, May 10, 1971, 8.

27. J. Edgar Hoover, letter to Forwood C. Wiser, November 10, 1969, FBI 94-50466-76, 1.

28. Nick Kotz, "TWA Says FBI Sent It AF Data on Pilot-Critic," *Washington Post*, May 11, 1971, A1.

29. Gordon E. Malmfeldt, memorandum to Thomas E. Bishop, May 10, 1971, FBI 95-54066-unserialized, 2.

30. Thomas E. Bishop, memorandum to Cartha DeLoach, November 10, 1969, FBI 164-991-5.

31. Thomas Bishop, memorandum to William C. Sullivan, December 29, 1970, FBI 62-113355-6, 1.

32. Theoharis et al., *FBI*, 243.

33. See, for example, Matthew Cecil, *Hoover's FBI and the Fourth Estate: The Campaign to Control the Press and the Bureau's Image* (Lawrence: University Press of Kansas, 2014), 239–264.

34. Bishop to Sullivan, December 29, 1970, 1–2.

35. Thomas Bishop, memorandum to William C. Sullivan, December 22, 1970, FBI 62-113355-5, 1.

36. Milton A. Jones, memorandum to Thomas Bishop, January 14, 1971, FBI 94-8-150-248, 1.

37. Ron Ostrow and Jack Nelson, letter to Thomas Bishop, January 5, 1971, FBI 94-8-150-249, 1–2.

38. See Cecil, *Hoover's FBI*, 265–281.

39. Thomas Bishop, letter to Jack Nelson, January 7, 1971, FBI 94-7-150-250, 9.

40. J. Edgar Hoover, memorandum to John Mitchell, January 7, 1971, FBI 94-8-150-251.

41. J. Edgar Hoover, handwritten note on Milton A. Jones, memorandum to Thomas Bishop, January 30, 1971, FBI 62-113355-13.

42. J. Edgar Hoover, memorandum to H. R. Haldeman, January 26, 1971, FBI 94-3-4-205-398, 1.

43. Ron Ostrow and Jack Nelson, letter to Thomas Bishop, January 12, 1971, FBI 94-8-150-257, 1–2.

44. Thomas Bishop, letter to Jack Nelson, January 14, 1971, FBI 94-8-150-unserialized.

45. Jack Nelson and Ron Ostrow, "FBI Clarifies Its Degree Requirements," *Los Angeles Times*, March 30, 1971, 15.

46. J. Edgar Hoover, handwritten note on cover sheet attached to Nelson and Ostrow, "FBI Clarifies Its Degree Requirements," March 30, 1971.

47. Nichols P. Callahan, memorandum to John Mohr, April 5, 1971, FBI 94-8-150-259.

48. Thomas Bishop, memorandum to John Mohr, June 18, 1971, FBI 94-8-150-265, 2.

49. Ibid., 1.

50. Clyde Tolson, memorandum to J. Edgar Hoover, August 26, 1971, FBI 94-8-6-607.

51. Thomas Bishop, memorandum to Mark Felt, October 4, 1971, FBI 94-8-6-617.

52. J. Edgar Hoover, handwritten note on Bishop to Felt, October 4, 1971.

53. Thomas E. Bishop, memorandum to William C. Sullivan, September 15, 1970, FBI 94-8-150-unserialized.

54. Thomas E. Bishop, memorandum to William C. Sullivan, September 11, 1970, FBI 88-51548-309.

55. J. Edgar Hoover, handwritten note on Bishop to Sullivan, December 29, 1970, 2.

56. Thomas E. Bishop, memorandum to Clyde Tolson, March 8, 1971, FBI 62-113355-15.

57. J. Edgar Hoover, handwritten note on Bishop to Tolson, March 8, 1971.

58. Milton A. Jones, memorandum to Thomas E. Bishop, September 28, 1971, FBI 62-113355-25.

59. J. Edgar Hoover, handwritten note on news clipping, Jack Nelson, "Peace Activist May Be Star FBI Spy," *Los Angeles Times*, August 26, 1971, A3, FBI 62-113355-unserialized.

60. Jack Nelson, "My FBI File: (Censored)," *Nieman Report* 34, no. 4 (Winter 1980): 5.

61. Jones to Bishop, September 28, 1971.

62. Jack Nelson, memorandum to J. Edgar Hoover, October 19, 1971, FBI 62-113355-26.

63. Ibid.

64. John W. Finney, "Muskie Says F.B.I. Spied at Rallies on '70 Earth Day," *New York Times*, April 15, 1971, 1.

65. J. Edgar Hoover, memorandum to Clyde Tolson and Thomas Bishop, April 14, 1971, unserialized, Clyde Tolson Personal File.

66. J. Edgar Hoover, memorandum to Clyde Tolson, William C. Sullivan, Thomas Bishop, and Charles Brennan, April 15, 1971, unserialized, Clyde Tolson Personal File.

67. Ibid.

68. John W. Finney, "Boggs Tells House of Tap on Phone," *New York Times*, April 23, 1971.

69. John P. Mohr, note on J. Edgar Hoover, letter to Hale Boggs, January 17, 1950, FBI 94-37804-2.

70. For example, John P. Mohr, memorandum to J. Edgar Hoover, January 19, 1959, FBI 94-37804-unserialized; Nicholas P. Callahan, memorandum to J. Edgar Hoover, June 1, 1962, FBI 94-37804-unserialized; J. Edgar Hoover, letter to Hale Boggs, December 10, 1963, FBI 94-37804-31; Nicholas P. Callahan, memorandum to J. Edgar Hoover, May 18, 1967, FBI 94-37804-unserialized.

71. Hale Boggs, letter to J. Edgar Hoover, January 27, 1962, FBI 94-37804-19.

72. J. Edgar Hoover, letter to Hale Boggs, February 12, 1962, FBI 94-37804-19.

73. Milton A. Jones, memorandum to Cartha DeLoach, July 11, 1962, FBI 94-37804-unserialized.

74. Milton A. Jones, memorandum to Cartha DeLoach, July 20, 1962, FBI 94-37804-unserialized.

75. Milton A. Jones, memorandum to Thomas E. Bishop, October 22, 1968, FBI 94-37804-41.

76. SAC, New Orleans, memorandum to J. Edgar Hoover, October 24, 1968, FBI-94-37804-43.

77. J. Edgar Hoover, letter to Hale Boggs, January 20, 1971, FBI 94-37804-50.

78. Majorie Hunter, "Boggs Demands That Hoover Quit: Accuses F.B.I. of Tapping Congressmen's Phones—Mitchell Denies Charge," *New York Times*, April 6, 1971, 1.

79. J. Edgar Hoover, memorandum to Clyde Tolson, April 5, 1971, FBI 94-37808-65, 2.

80. Ibid.

81. SAC, Mobile, Ala., teletype to J. Edgar Hoover, April 6, 1971, 94-37808-52.

82. J. Edgar Hoover, memorandum to Clyde Tolson and Thomas Bishop, April 6, 1971, FBI 94-37804-54.

83. J. Edgar Hoover, memorandum to Clyde Tolson and Thomas Bishop, April 7, 1971, FBI 94-37808-53.

84. SAC, Baltimore, memorandum to J. Edgar Hoover, September 4, 1959, FBI 58-6996-202.

85. "New Details Told in Bribe Probe," *Chicago Tribune*, June 22, 1970, 2.

86. Jacques Kelly and Anthony Weir, *"Get Me the White House!": The Untold Story of Victor Frenkil's Rise from Immigrant Obscurity to Prominence in the Turbulent Worlds of Business and Politics* (Baltimore, Md.: Gateway Press, 2006), 142.

87. J. Edgar Hoover, memorandum to John N. Mitchell, April 8, 1971, FBI 94-37804-unserialized; J. Edgar Hoover, memorandum to Clyde Tolson and Thomas Bishop, April 7, 1971, FBI 94-37804-55.

88. Ken W. Clawson and Spencer Rich, "Justice Dept. Asks Hill Inquiry on FBI," *Washington Post*, April 8, 1971, A1.

89. Milton A. Jones, memorandum to Thomas Bishop, April 8, 1971, FBI 94-37804-60; J. Edgar Hoover, handwritten comments on Jones to Bishop, April 8, 1971.

90. For example, Hoover recounted his conversation with Republican US senator Hugh Scott of Pennsylvania in J. Edgar Hoover, memorandum to Clyde Tolson and

Thomas Bishop, April 6, 1971, FBI 94-37804-unserialized; Hoover recounted his discussion with Republican congressman H. R. Gross of Iowa in J. Edgar Hoover, memorandum to Clyde Tolson and Thomas Bishop, April 7, 1971, FBI 94-40480-39; Hoover recounted his phone call with House Speaker Carl Albert in J. Edgar Hoover, memorandum to Clyde Tolson and Thomas Bishop, April 8, 1971, FBI 94-37804-140.

91. Hoover to Tolson and Bishop, April 7, 1971.

92. Jack Anderson, "Truth Strained on Hill Shadowing," *Washington Post*, April 10, 1971, C35.

93. R. D. Cotter, memorandum to C. D. Brennan, April 13, 1971, FBI 94-50053-68, 2.

94. M. E. Gurnea, memorandum to J. Edgar Hoover, September 17, 1945, FBI 62-63007-1X1.

95. J. Edgar Hoover, memorandum to Francis Biddle, December 3, 1945, FBI 62-63007-unserialized; J. Edgar Hoover, memorandum to Francis Biddle, January 3, 1946, FBI 62-63007-10.

96. Director's Office, telephone message, 12:41 p.m., April 7, 1971, FBI 94-37804-89.

97. Thomas E. Bishop, memorandum to John P. Mohr, April 6, 1971, FBI 94-37804-101.

98. Jack Anderson, "Boggs Drinking Data Traced to FBI," *Washington Post*, April 12, 1971, B1.

99. J. Edgar Hoover, handwritten note on Anderson, "Boggs Drinking Data," FBI 94-37804-157.

100. J. Edgar Hoover, memorandum to Clyde Tolson, William C. Sullivan, Thomas Bishop, and Alex Rosen, April 21, 1971, FBI 94-37804-unserialized.

101. Alex Rosen, memorandum to William C. Sullivan, April 23, 1971, FBI 67-37804-unserialized.

102. J. Edgar Hoover, memorandum to Clyde Tolson and Thomas Bishop, date obscured, ca. April 15, 1971, FBI 94-8-573591, 1.

103. Tom Wicker, "The Heat on the F.B.I.," *New York Times*, April 15, 1971, 43.

104. William V. Shannon, "Hoover: He May Be the Man Who Stayed Too Long," *New York Times*, April 18, 1971, E5.

105. Milton A. Jones, memorandum to Thomas E. Bishop, May 10, 1971, FBI 62-78248-unserialized, 1.

106. Ibid.

107. Ibid.

108. Ibid.

109. Ibid., 2.

110. "Friends of the F.B.I.," letterhead memorandum (LHM), September 8, 1971, FBI 62-114406-100.

111. Lee Edwards, memorandum to Luis Kutner and Patrick J. Gorman, April 30, 1971, FBI 62-114406-80.

112. Ibid.

113. Cecil, *Hoover's FBI*, 265–281.

114. Susan Stewart, "Efrem Zimbalist, Jr., Star of '77 Sunset Strip' and 'The F.B.I.,' Is Dead at 95," *New York Times*, May 3, 2014, accessed at http://www.nytimes.com /2014/05/04/arts/television/efrem-zimbalist-jr-star-of-77-sunset-strip-and-the-fbi -is-dead-at-95.html.

115. Letterhead Memorandum, "'Friends of the FBI': Research (Crime Records)," September 9, 1971, FBI 62-114406-102, 1.

116. Ibid., 1–2.

117. Ibid., 2.

118. Lee Edwards and Patrick J. Gorman, fund-raising letter signed "Efrem Zimbalist, Jr.," FBI 62-114406-3, 1.

119. Ibid., 2.

120. Milton A. Jones, memorandum to Thomas E. Bishop, June 14, 1971, FBI 62-114406-3, 3.

121. Jack Nelson and Bryce Nelson, "Zimbalist, Two Others Open Drive to Back FBI," *Los Angeles Times*, June 15, 1971, 17.

122. Milton A. Jones, memorandum to Thomas E. Bishop, June 15, 1971, FBI 94-61410-68.

123. Daniel C. Mahan, investigative report, September 9, 1971, FBI 62-114406-103, 2.

124. Robert M. Smith, "Friends of FBI in a Fund Appeal," *New York Times*, July 21, 1971, 20.

125. "Friends of the F.B.I." LHM, 2.

126. Ibid., 2–3.

127. Ibid., 3; Mahan investigative report, 3.

128. Luis Kutner, Patrick Gorman, and Lee Edwards, agreement to form "Friends of the F.B.I.," July 22, 1971, attached to FBI 62-114406-103; Luis Kutner, Patrick Gorman, and Lee Edwards, termination of "Friends of the F.B.I." agreement, July 22, 1971, attached to FBI 62-11406-103.

129. Luis Kutner, letter to Attorney General John N. Mitchell and Secretary of State William P. Rogers, July 26, 1971, FBI 62-114406-unserialized, 3.

130. Rep. Abner Mikva, letter to Luis Kutner, June 23, 1971, FBI 62-114406-unserialized.

131. Ibid.

132. Luis Kutner, letter to Rep. Abner Mikva, June 28, 1971, FBI 62-114406-unserialized.

133. Bryce Nelson, "Law Group Ends Ties with Friends of the FBI," *Los Angeles Times*, August 10, 1971, 18.

134. Luis Kutner, letter to Rep. Abner Mikva, August 9, 1971, FBI 62-114406-unserialized.

135. J. Edgar Hoover, memorandum to Will Wilson, Assistant Attorney General, Criminal Division, August 12, 1971, FBI 62-114406-79.

136. Will Wilson, memorandum to J. Edgar Hoover, August 30, 1971, FBI 62-11406-83.

137. Internal Revenue Service, news release, August 26, 1971, IR-1162, included in FBI 62-114406-103.

138. J. Edgar Hoover, memorandum to Clyde Tolson, Mark Felt, and John P. Mohr, August 24, 1971, unserialized, Clyde Tolson Personal File.

139. Robert M. Smith, "Youth Found Cool to Career in F.B.I.: Poll Shows 'Only 21.5%' Would Like to Be Agents," *New York Times*, February 15, 1972, 11.

140. William C. Sullivan, letter to J. Edgar Hoover, September 30, 1944, FBI 67-205182-109.

141. William C. Sullivan, letter to J. Edgar Hoover, April 19, 1948, FBI 67-205182-155.

142. William C. Sullivan, letter to J. Edgar Hoover, December 19, 1949, FBI 67-205182-183.

143. William C. Sullivan, letter to J. Edgar Hoover, August 11, 1951, FBI 67-205182-215, 1, 2.

144. Milton A. Jones, memorandum to Louis B. Nichols, August 25, 1951, FBI 67-205182-216.

145. Committee to Investigate the FBI, press release, March 9, 1971, FBI 52-94527-93.

146. For a full account of the burglars' lives, the burglary itself, and the aftermath of the crime, see Betty Medsger, *The Burglary: The Discovery of J. Edgar Hoover's Secret FBI* (New York: Vintage Books, 2014).

147. Charles D. Brennan, memorandum to William C. Sullivan, March 12, 1971, FBI 52-94527-99, 2.

148. Hoover, handwritten marks on Brennan to Sullivan, March 12, 1971, 2.

149. A. B. Eddy, memorandum to Mr. Gale, March 18, 1971, FBI 52-94527-120.

150. Charles D. Brennan, memorandum to William C. Sullivan, March 15, 1971, FBI 52-94527-215, 1.

151. Ibid., 8.

152. Ibid., 10.

153. Charles D. Brennan, memorandum to William C. Sullivan, March 29, 1971, FBI 52-94527-573, 2.

154. Charles D. Brennan, memorandum to William C. Sullivan, April 7, 1971, FBI 52-94527-736, 3.

155. In addition to Eddy to Gale, March 18, 1971, and Brennan to Sullivan, March 15, 1971, see A. Rosen, memorandum to William C. Sullivan, March 23, 1971, FBI 52-94527-251.

156. J. Edgar Hoover, handwritten note on A. Rosen, memorandum to William C. Sullivan, March 24, 1971, FBI 52-94527-264.

157. Ron Paglia, "Lawmaker Hits Federal Wiretapping," *Pittsburgh Post-Gazette*, March 23, 1971, 4.

158. Joseph Barsotti, "Black Lawmaker Raps FBI 'Spies,'" *Pittsburgh Press*, March 23, 1971, 7.

159. J. Edgar Hoover, memorandum to John Mitchell, March 25, 1971, FBI 52-94527-9, 2.

160. Thomas E. Bishop, memorandum to John P. Mohr, March 31, 1971, FBI 52-94527-942; Hoover, handwritten note on Bishop to Mohr, March 31, 1971.

161. J. Edgar Hoover, memorandum to Robert Mardian, March 18, 1971, FBI 52-94527-54.

162. Thomas Bishop, memorandum to John P. Mohr, March 29, 1971, FBI 52-94527-459; Thomas Bishop, memorandum to John P. Mohr, March 30, 1971, FBI 52-94527-430.

163. J. Edgar Hoover, handwritten note on A. Rosen to William C. Sullivan, March 24, 1971, FBI 67-253-4456, 1, 3.

164. Rosen to Sullivan, March 24, 1971, 3.

165. "Policies of Paranoia," *New York Times*, March 29, 1971, 30.

166. Routing slip dated August 9, 1968, attached to "Campus or Battleground: Columbia Is a Warning to All American Universities," *Barron's*, undated, FBI 52-94527-unserialized.

167. Bill Kovack, "Stolen Files Show F.B.I. Seeks Black Informers," *New York Times*, April 8, 1971, 22.

168. For an overview of the first month of the FBI's investigation, see Investigative Summary, April 27, 1971, FBI 52-94527-1518, 1–108.

169. William Greider, "10,000 'Potential Subversives,'" *Washington Post*, June 13, 1971, A1.

170. Medsger, *Burglary*, 270.

171. J. Edgar Hoover, memorandum to John Mitchell, April 8, 1971, FBI 52-94527-475, 5.

172. "Transcript of Kissinger Statement and Answers to Questions at News Conference," *New York Times*, June 12, 1974, 34.

173. E. S. Miller, memorandum to Alex Rosen, October 20, 1971, FBI 67-75085-unserialized., 2.

174. O. T. Jacobson, memorandum to Mr. Walters, May 12, 1973, FBI 65-75085-14.

175. "F.B.I. Aide Doubts That Reds Cause Unrest in U.S.," *New York Times*, October 13, 1970, 27.

176. William C. Sullivan, memorandum to Clyde Tolson, October 13, 1970, FBI 67-205182-unserialized, 2.

177. J. Edgar Hoover, handwritten note on Sullivan to Tolson, October 13, 1970, 2.

178. J. Edgar Hoover, letter to William C. Sullivan, August 4, 1971, FBI 67-205182-629.

179. Jacobson to Walters, May 12, 1973, 2.

180. J. K. Ponder, memorandum to Clyde Tolson, September 9, 1941, FBI 67-205182-unserialized, 4.

181. Ibid., 1.

182. Ibid., 5.

183. Jacobson to Walters, May 12, 1973, 3.

184. J. Edgar Hoover, memorandum for Clyde Tolson, Mark Felt, Alex Rosen, John P. Mohr, and Thomas Bishop, October 1, 1971, FBI 67-205187-637, 1.

185. J. Edgar Hoover, letter to William Sullivan, September 30, 1971, reproduced in William C. Sullivan, *The Bureau: My Thirty Years in Hoover's FBI* (New York: W. W. Norton, 1979), 264.

186. Ibid., 2.

187. J. Edgar Hoover, handwritten note on H. N. Bassett, memorandum to Mr. Callahan, October 6, 1971, FBI 67-205182-643.

188. William Sullivan, letter to J. Edgar Hoover, reproduced in Sullivan, *Bureau*, 265–277.

189. Ibid.

190. Ken W. Clawson, "Top FBI Official Forced Out in Policy Feud with Hoover," *Washington Post*, October 2, 1971, A1.

191. "Edged Down Earlier: Key FBI Official Leaving," *Washington Evening Star*, October 2, 1971, A1.

192. James A. Wechsler, "Hoover's Twilight," *New York Post*, October 6, 1971, 53.

193. James J. Kilpatrick, "Exit Open for Hoover?," *Atlanta Constitution*, undated, ca. late October 1971, FBI 94-66048-3.

194. Rowland Evans and Robert Novack, "Hoover's FBI Crisis," Publishers Hall Syndicate copy attached to Senator Gordon Allott, letter to Deputy Attorney General Wallace H. Johnson, November 9, 1971, FBI 67-205182-670.

195. J. Edgar Hoover, memorandum to Clyde Tolson, Mark Felt, Alex Rosen, and Mr. Cleveland, November 12, 1971, unserialized, Clyde Tolson Personal File.

196. Isabelle Hall, Hoover interview wire story, United Press International, December 20, 1971, FBI 94-8-95-663.

197. Ibid.

198. J. Edgar Hoover, handwritten note on Hall, Hoover interview wire story.

199. Jack Nelson, "Ex-FBI Man Hits 'Fossil' Bureaucracy," *Los Angeles Times*, January 10, 1972, 9.

200. Ibid.

201. Ovid Demaris, *The Director: An Oral Biography of J. Edgar Hoover* (New York: Harper's Magazine Press, 1975), 217.

Chapter Eight: The Fall

1. Douglas Martin, "Jack Anderson, Investigative Journalist Who Angered the Powerful, Dies at 83," *New York Times*, December 18, 2005, accessed at http://www .nytimes.com/2005/12/18/us/jack-anderson-investigative-journalist-who-angered -the-powerful-dies-at-83.html.

2. J. Edgar Hoover, "FBI Director on Two Anderson Columns," *Washington Post*, September 17, 1971, accessed at http://jfk.hood.edu/Collection/Weisberg%20Sub ject%20Index%20Files/F%20Disk/FBI/FBI%20Miscellaneous/Item%20096.pdf.

3. Martin, Anderson obituary, *New York Times*.

4. Charles Elliott, "A Unique Perspective on 'J. Edgar,'" *Clarity Research* (blog), November 16, 2011, accessed at https://clarityresearch.wordpress.com/2011/11/16/a -unique-perspective-on-j-edgar/.

5. Ibid.

6. Mark Feldstein, *Poisoning the Press: Richard Nixon, Jack Anderson and the Rise of Washington's Scandal Culture* (New York: Farrar, Straus and Giroux, 2010), 208.

7. Ibid., 210.

8. Martin, Anderson obituary, *New York Times*.

9. Jack Anderson, "A Close Friend of Presidents," *Everett (Wash.) Herald*, November 12, 1971, FBI 94-50053-126.

10. Milton A. Jones, memorandum to Thomas Bishop, December 23, 1971, FBI 94-50053-131.

11. Milton A. Jones, memorandum to Thomas Bishop, January 19, 1972, FBI 94-50053-133.

12. R. J. Gallagher, memorandum to Mr. Bates, March 15, 1971, FBI 94-50053-141.

13. "Columnist Urges Secret-Data Curb," *New York Times*, May 2, 1972, 29.

14. Ibid.

15. J. Edgar Hoover Appointment Calendar, May 1, 1972; J. Edgar Hoover Telephone Logs, May 1, 1972.

16. Richard Hack, *Puppetmaster: The Secret Life of J. Edgar Hoover* (Beverly Hills, Calif.: New Millennium Press, 2004), 6.

17. Ibid., 1–4.

18. Michael Newton, *The FBI Encyclopedia* (Jefferson, N.C.: McFarland, 2003), 129.

19. Patricia Sullivan, "Watergate-Era FBI Chief L. Patrick Gray III Dies at 88," *Washington Post*, July 7, 2005, accessed at http://www.washingtonpost.com/politics /watergate-era-fbi-chief-l-patrick-gray-iii-dies-at-88/2012/05/31/gJQA9fX2FV_story .html.

20. Todd S. Purdum, "L. Patrick Gray III, Who Led the F.B.I. during Watergate, Dies

at 88," *New York Times*, July 7, 2005, accessed at http://www.nytimes.com/2005/07/07/politics/l-patrick-gray-iii-who-led-the-fbi-during-watergate-dies-at-88.html.

21. H. N. Bassett and Thomas E. Bishop, "Permanent Brief," June 29, 1971, FBI 67-518854-unserialized, 44.

22. Milton A. Jones, "The Story of My Life," unpublished memoir, 91.

23. Ibid., 92.

24. Ibid., 94.

25. Sullivan, Gray obituary.

26. Ibid.

27. David E. Rosenbaum, "C.I.A.-F.B.I. Inquiry Voted by Senate," *New York Times*, January 28, 1975, 1, 12.

28. Testimony of Cartha D. DeLoach, Hearings Before the Select Committee to Study Governmental Operations with Respect to Intelligence Activities of the United States Senate, 94th Cong., 1st sess., vol. 6, 171.

29. Ibid., 176.

30. Nicholas M. Horrock, "Polishing Up the F.B.I.'s Reputation," *New York Times*, November 23, 1975, 2E.

31. *Final Report of the Select Committee to Study Governmental Operations with Respect to Intelligence Activities of the United States Senate* (Washington, DC: US Government Printing Office, April 26, 1976), 15.

32. Ibid., 15–16.

33. Ibid., 18.

34. Ibid., 364.

35. Michael Isikoff, "New Film about US Persecution of Gays Spurs Calls to Remove Hoover's Name from FBI Building," *Yahoo News*, June 26, 2015, accessed at https://www.yahoo.com/politics/new-film-about-us-persecution-of-gays-spurs-calls-122438340656.html.

36. "Historian Featured in Documentary about FBI Persecution of Gays and Lesbians," *Penn State News*, July 22, 2015, accessed at http://news.psu.edu/story/363625/2015/07/22/research/historian-featured-documentary-about-fbi-persecution-gays-and.

37. See, for example, Richard Cohen, "Memo to Rand Paul: Take Down J. Edgar Hoover's Name from the FBI Building," *Washington Post*, March 20, 2014, accessed at http://www.washingtonpost.com/blogs/post-partisan/wp/2014/03/20/memo-to-rand-paul-take-down-j-edgar-hoovers-name-from-the-fbi-building/; Ray Jenkins, "Take J. Edgar Hoover's Name off the FBI Building," *Seattle Times*, November 26, 1990, accessed at http://community.seattletimes.nwsource.com/archive/?date =1990 1126&slug=1106218; Jeff Johnson, "Congressmen Want Hoover's Name off FBI Building," *Capitol News Service*, July 7, 2008, accessed at http://cnsnews.com/news/article/congressmen-want-hoovers-name-fbi-building.

38. Clarence Kelley, "The FBI—It Still Stands for Fidelity, Bravery and Integrity" (speech), June 10, 1975, FBI 67-338721-556, 8.

39. E. J. Dionne, "The Subversive James Comey," *St. Louis Post-Dispatch*, February 16, 2015, accessed at http://m.stltoday.com/news/opinion/columns/ej-dionne/e-j -dionne-the-subversive-james-comey/article_857b2b33-0ee2-5f57-b651-f088830e 2097.html.

SELECTED BIBLIOGRAPHY

FBI Files

ACLU
American Business Consultants
American Legion National Americanism Commission
Anderson, Jack
Bishop, Thomas
Boardman, Leland V.
Carusi, Ugo
Cochran, Edward Louis
COINTELPRO
Collier, Neil (Rex)
Connelly, Earl J.
Cook, Fred J.
Cooper, Courtney Ryley
Coplon, Judith
Crosby, Francis E.
Cummings, Homer S.
Custodial Detention Index
de Galindez, Jesus
DeLoach, Cartha D.
de Toledano, Ralph
Dodd, Thomas J.
Ernst, Morris
FBI Book Reviews
FBI Executive Conference
FBI In Peace and War (Radio Program)
FBI Media, Penn., Burglary
FBI Monograph (Smear Campaign 1958)
FBI Responsibilities in Internal Security
FBI SAC Letters
Felt, W. Mark
Firing Line (American Legion)

Wechsler, James A.
Weschsler, Nancy S.
Wick, Robert E.
Zimbalist, Efrem, Jr.

Interviews

Cashdollar, Muriel Jones (daughter of FBI Crime Records Section chief Milton A. Jones). October 9, 2015.
DeLoach, Cartha D. April 12, 2001.
Pellegrom, Sally (Stukenbroeker) (daughter of Crime Records agent Fern C. Stukenbroeker). September 21, 2015.
Rugaber, Walter (retired *New York Times* reporter and newspaper publisher). January 15, 2015.

Manuscript Collections

FBI Investigation and Surveillance Records. Raynor Library Special Collections, Marquette University, Milwaukee, Wis.
Gusman, Maurice. Papers. American Jewish Archives, Cincinnati, Ohio.
Johnson, Lyndon Baines. Telephone Conversation Tapes. Miller Center, University of Virginia (accessed online).
Nichols, Louis B. FBI File. National Archives and Records Administration, College Park, Md.
Oral History Collection. Lyndon Johnson Presidential Library, Austin, Tex.

Newspapers and Magazines

Albany (Ga.) Herald
American Legion Firing Line
American Legion Weekly
Atlanta Constitution
Austin (Tex.) Statesman
Baltimore Sun
Chicago Tribune
Cincinnati Times
Denver Post
Deseret News and Telegram (Salt Lake City, Utah)
Detroit Free Press
Everett (Wash.) Herald
Flint (Mich.) Journal

Idaho (Boise) *Daily Statesman*
Illinois State Journal (Springfield)
Life
Los Angeles Times
Macon (Ga.) News
Nation
New Republic
New York Daily Mirror
New York Post
New York Times
Phoenix Republic
Pittsburgh Post-Gazette
Pittsburgh Press
Salt Lake (Utah) Tribune
St. Louis Post-Dispatch
Tucson (Ariz.) Daily Citizen
Washington Examiner
Washington Post
Washington Star

Books and Articles

Bradlee, Ben. *A Good Life: Newspapering and Other Adventures.* New York: Touchstone, 1995.

Brinson, Susan L. *The Red Scare, Politics, and the Federal Communications Commission.* Westport, Conn.: Greenwood Publishing, 2004.

Cecil, Matthew. "Press Every Angle: FBI Public Relations and the 'Smear Campaign' of 1958." *American Journalism* 19, no. 1 (Winter 2002): 39–58.

———. *Hoover's FBI and the Fourth Estate: The Campaign to Control the Press and the Bureau's Image.* Lawrence: University Press of Kansas, 2014.

Charles, Douglas M. *Hoover's War on Gays: Exposing the FBI's "Sex Deviates" Program.* Lawrence: University Press of Kansas, 2015.

Conners, Bernard F. *Don't Embarrass the Bureau.* New York: Bobbs Merrill, 1972.

Cromie, Robert, and Joseph Pinkston. *Dillinger: A Short and Violent Life.* New York: McGraw, 1962.

DeLoach, Cartha. *Hoover's FBI: The Inside Story by Hoover's Trusted Lieutenant.* New York: Regnery, 1995.

Demaris, Ovid. *The Director: An Oral Biography of J. Edgar Hoover.* New York: Harper's Magazine Press, 1975.

DeVoto, Bernard. "Due Notice to the F.B.I." *Harper's*, October 19, 1949. Accessed at http://harpers.org/archive.

Erlich, Lillian. *Money Isn't Important: The Life of Maurice Gusman*. Miami, Fla.: E. A. Seemann Publishing, 1976.

Ernst, Morris. "Miasma of Suspicion." *Saturday Review*, December 24, 1949, 18–19.

———. "Why I No Longer Fear the F.B.I." *Reader's Digest*, December 21, 1950.

Feldstein, Mark. *Poisoning the Press: Richard Nixon, Jack Anderson and the Rise of Washington's Scandal Culture*. New York: Farrar, Straus and Giroux, 2010.

Felt, Mark, and John O'Connor. *A G-Man's Life: The FBI, Being "Deep Throat" and the Struggle for Honor in Washington*. New York: Public Affairs, 2006.

Final Report of the Select Committee to Study Governmental Operations with Respect to Intelligence Activities of the United States Senate. Washington, D.C.: US Government Printing Office, April 26, 1976.

Fly, James Lawrence. "The Case against Wire Tapping." *Look*, September 27, 1949.

Gary, Brett. "Morris Ernst's Troubled Legacy." *Reconstruction: Studies in Contemporary Culture* 8, no. 1 (2008). Accessed at http://reconstruction.eserver.org/Issues/081/gary.shtml#5.

Geis, Gilbert, and Colin Goff. "Lifting the Cover from Undercover Operations: J. Edgar Hoover and Some of the Other Criminologists." *Crime, Law and Social Change* 18 (1992): 91–104.

Gentry, Curt. *J. Edgar Hoover: The Man and the Secrets*. New York: W. W. Norton, 1991.

Goldman, Emma. *Living My Life*. New York: Alfred A. Knopf, 1931.

Hack, Richard. *Puppetmaster: The Secret Life of J. Edgar Hoover*. Beverly Hills, Calif.: New Millennium Press, 2004.

Hart, Dennis. *Monitor: The Last Great Radio Show*. Self-published, iUniverse, 2003.

Hogan, Michael J. *A Cross of Iron: Harry S. Truman and the Origins of the National Security State, 1945–1954*. New York: Cambridge University Press, 2000.

Hoover, J. Edgar. "Civil Liberties and Law Enforcement: The Role of the FBI." *Iowa Law Review* 37 (1951–1952): 175–195.

———. "A Study in Marxist Revolutionary Violence: Students for a Democratic Society, 1962–1969." *Fordham Law Review* 38, no. 2 (December 1969): 289–306.

———. "The SDS and the High Schools: A Study in Student Extremism." *PTA Magazine* 64 (January–February 1970): 3.

Johnson, Christopher H. *Maurice Sugar: Law, Labor and the Left in Detroit, 1912–1950*. Detroit, Mich.: Wayne State University Press, 1988.

Jones, Milton A. "My Life" (manuscript). Courtesy of Muriel Jones Cashdollar.

Katzenbach, Nicholas deB. *Some of It Was Fun: Working with RFK and LBJ*. New York: W. W. Norton, 2008.

Kelly, Jacques, and Anthony Weir. *"Get Me the White House": The Untold Story of Victor Frenkil's Rise from Immigrant Obscurity to Prominence in the Turbulent Worlds of Business and Politics*. Baltimore, Md.: Gateway Press, 2006.

Kessler, Ronald. *The FBI: Inside the World's Most Powerful Law Enforcement Agency.* New York: Pocket Books, 1993.

Lewy, Guenter. *The Cause That Failed: Communism in American Political Life.* New York: Oxford University Press, 1990.

Medsger, Betty. *The Burglary: The Discovery of J. Edgar Hoover's Secret FBI.* New York: Vintage Books, 2014.

Mezzack, Janet. "Without Manners You Are Nothing: Lady Bird Johnson, Eartha Kitt, and the Women Doers' Luncheon of January 18, 1968." *Presidential Studies Quarterly* 20, no. 4 (Fall 1990): 745–760.

Nasaw, David. *The Patriarch: The Remarkable Life and Turbulent Times of Joseph P. Kennedy.* New York: Penguin Books, 2013.

Nelson, Jack. "My FBI File: (Censored)." *Nieman Report* 34, no. 4 (Winter 1980): 4–6.

———. *Scoop: The Evolution of a Southern Reporter.* Jackson: University Press of Mississippi, 2013.

Newton, Michael. *The FBI Encyclopedia.* Jefferson, N.C.: McFarland, 2003.

O'Reilly, Kenneth. "A New Deal for the FBI: The Roosevelt Administration, Crime Control, and National Security." *Journal of American History* 69, no. 3 (December 1982): 638–658.

Powers, Richard Gid. *G-Men: Hoover's FBI in American Popular Culture.* Carbondale: Southern Illinois University Press, 1983.

Purvis, Alton. *The Vendetta: Special Agents Melvin Purvis, John Dillinger, and Hoover's FBI in the Age of Gangsters.* New York: Public Affairs, 2009.

Rodell, Fred. "Morris Ernst: The Censor's Enemy, the President's Friend." *Life*, February 21, 1944, 97–100.

Salisbury, Harrison E. "The Strange Correspondence of Morris Ernst and J. Edgar Hoover." *Nation*, December 1, 1984. Accessed at http://www.thenation.com/article /strange-correspondence-morris-ernst-and-j-edgar-hoover.

Streitmatter, Rodger. *Voices of a Revolution: The Dissident Press in America.* New York: Columbia University Press, 2001.

Sullivan, William C. *The Bureau: My Thirty Years in Hoover's FBI.* New York: W. W. Norton, 1979.

Suydam, Henry. "How Kidnapers Are Caught." *Forum*, April 1934, 208–213.

Swearingen, M. Wesley. *FBI Secrets: An Agent's Exposé.* Boston: South End Press, 1999.

Theoharis, Athan. "The FBI and the American Legion Contact Program, 1940–1966." *Political Science Quarterly* 100, no. 2 (Summer 1985): 271–286.

Theoharis, Athan, and John Stuart Cox. *The Boss: J. Edgar Hoover and the Great American Inquisition.* Philadelphia: Temple University Press, 1988.

Theoharis, Athan, Tony G. Poveda, Susan Rosenfeld, and Richard Gid Powers, eds. *The FBI: A Comprehensive Reference Guide.* New York: Oryx Press, 2000.

Thom, Cathleen, and Patrick Jung. "The Responsibilities Program of the FBI, 1951–1955." *Historian* 59, no. 2 (December 1997): 347–370.

Walker, Samuel. *In Defense of American Liberties: A History of the ACLU.* New York: Oxford University Press, 1997.

Wiener, Tim. *Enemies: A History of the FBI.* New York: Random House, 2012.

Zimbalist, Jr., Efrem. *My Dinner of Herbs.* New York: Proscenium, 2003.

INDEX